We finally made it to volume 10!
Back in volume 1, I wrote that my top priority
was creating a manga that I could enjoy. But with
the anime starting and so many people involved
in the enterprise now, it'd be a little irresponsible
to keep prioritizing my own enjoyment. That said,
all the new stuff is fun too. Maybe even more
fun than when the series was starting out.

KOHEI HORIKOSHI

MY HERO ACADEMIA

10

SHONEN JUMP Manga Edition

STORY & ART KOHEI HORIKOSHI

TRANSLATION & ENGLISH ADAPTATION **Caleb Cook**
TOUCH-UP ART & LETTERING **John Hunt**
DESIGNER **Shawn Carrico**
SHONEN JUMP SERIES EDITOR **John Bae**
GRAPHIC NOVEL EDITOR **Mike Montesa**

BOKU NO HERO ACADEMIA © 2014 by Kohei Horikoshi
All rights reserved.
First published in Japan in 2014 by SHUEISHA Inc., Tokyo.
English translation rights arranged by SHUEISHA Inc.

The stories, characters and incidents mentioned in this publication are entirely fictional.

Printed in the U.S.A.

Published by VIZ Media, LLC
P.O. Box 77010
San Francisco, CA 94107

10 9 8 7 6 5 4 3 2
First printing, November 2017
Second printing, September 2018

PARENTAL ADVISORY
MY HERO ACADEMIA is rated T for Teen
and is recommended for ages 13 and up.
This volume contains fantasy violence.

shonenjump.com

MY HERO ACADEMIA

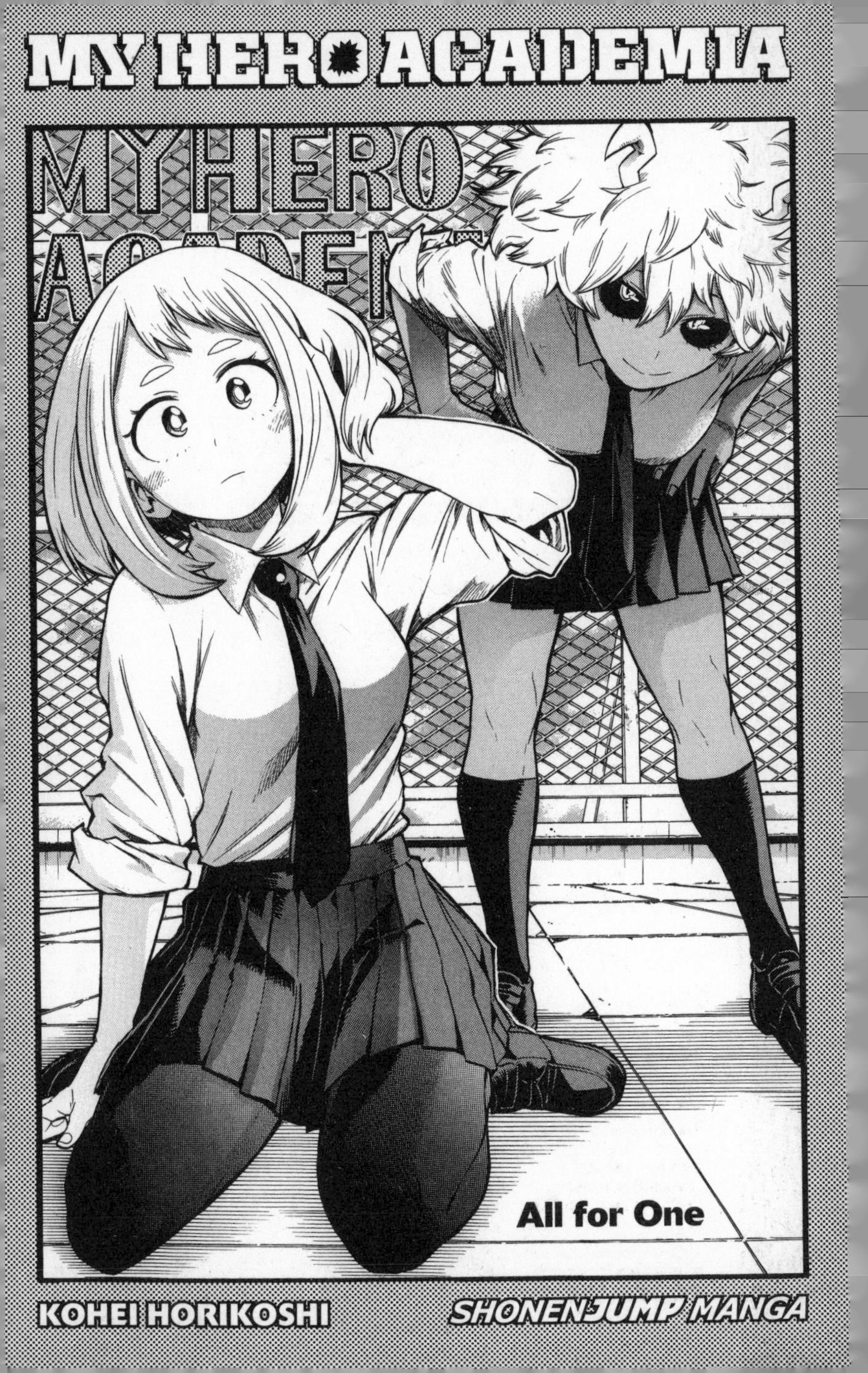
All for One

KOHEI HORIKOSHI

SHONEN JUMP MANGA

Vol.10

MY HERO ACADEMIA

CONTENTS

All for One

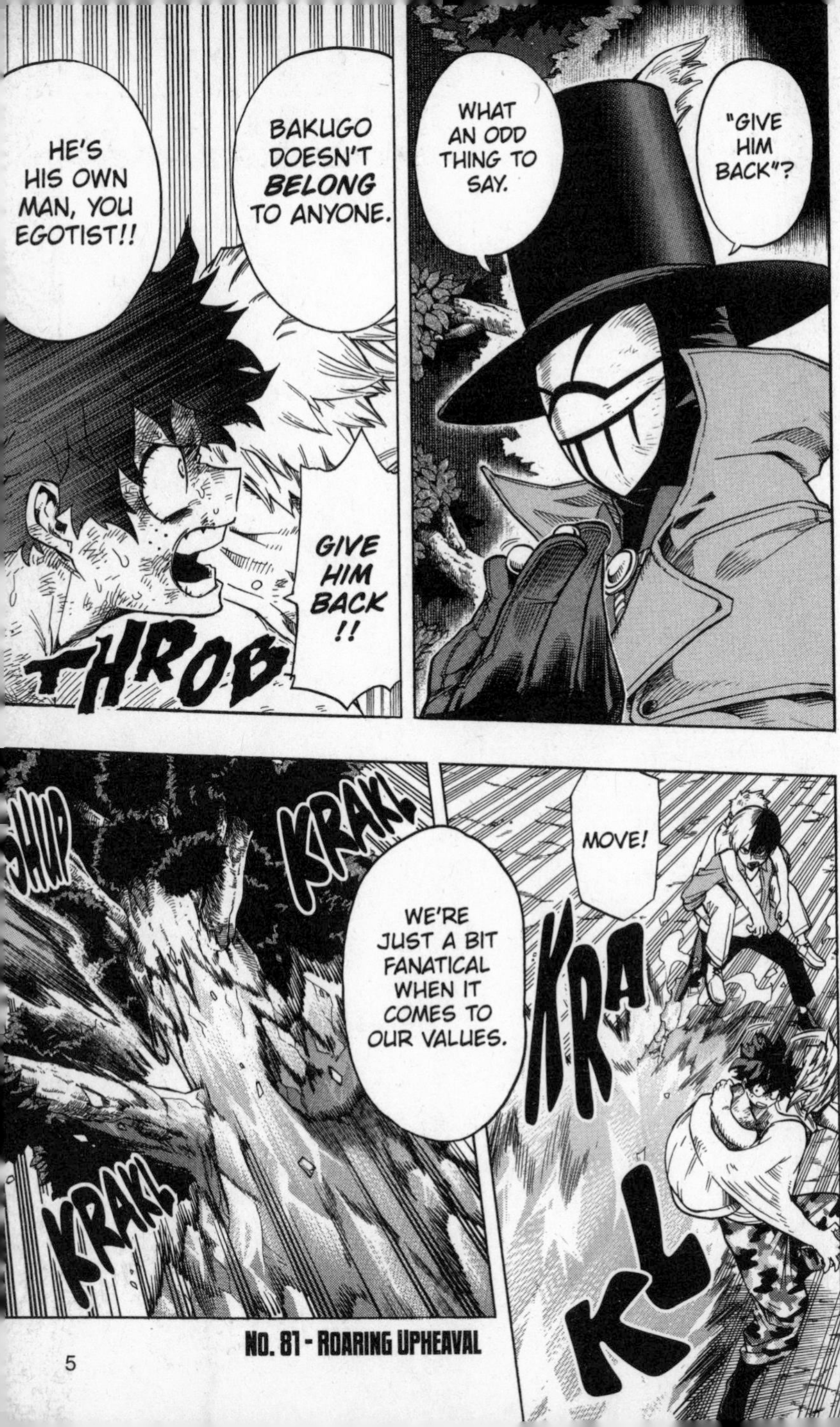
"GIVE HIM BACK"?
WHAT AN ODD THING TO SAY.
BAKUGO DOESN'T *BELONG* TO ANYONE.
HE'S HIS OWN MAN, YOU EGOTIST!!
GIVE HIM BACK !!
THROB
MOVE!
WE'RE JUST A BIT FANATICAL WHEN IT COMES TO OUR VALUES.
KRA
KL
KRAK
SHUP
KRAK

No. 81 - Roaring Upheaval

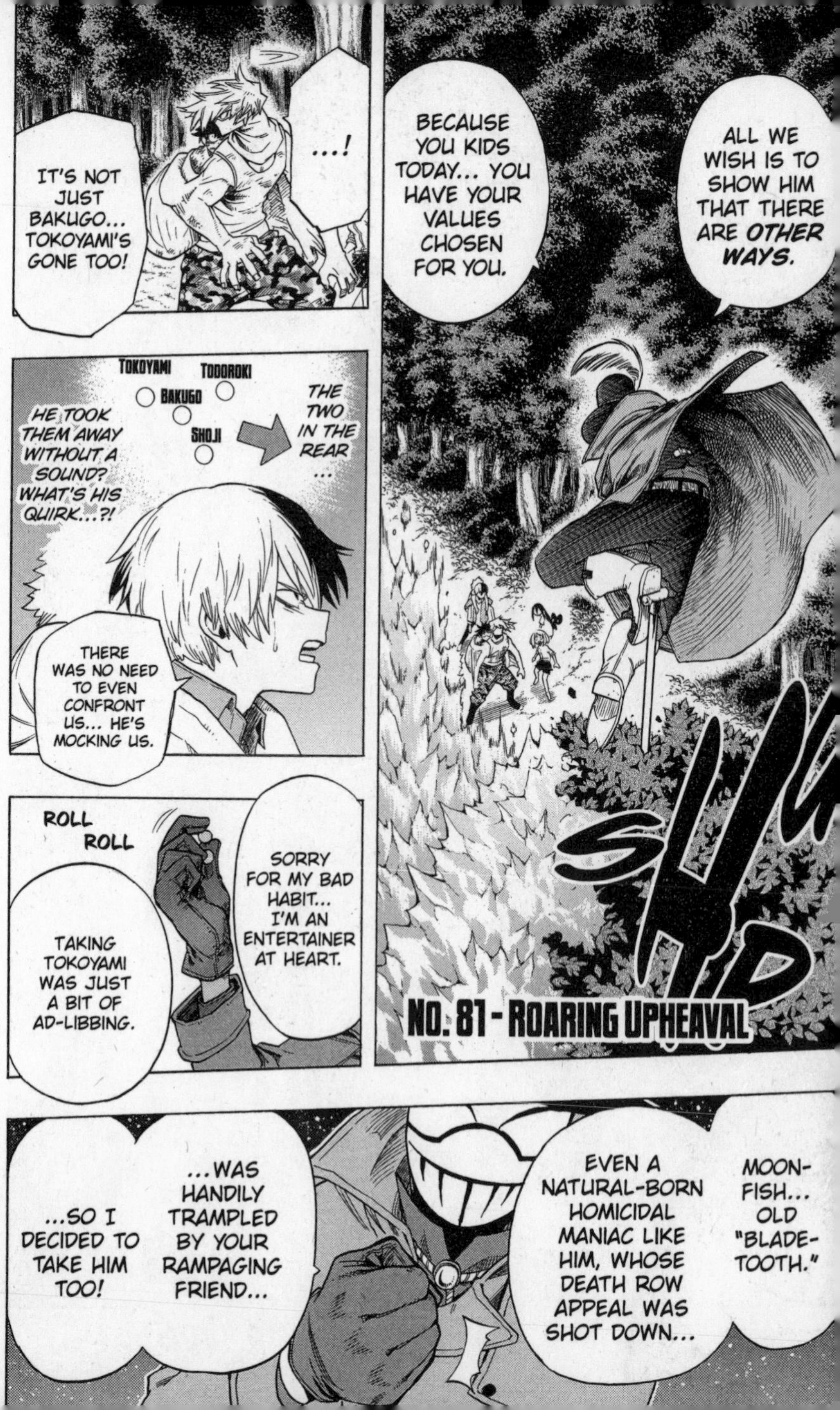
ALL WE WISH IS TO SHOW HIM THAT THERE ARE *OTHER WAYS.*
BECAUSE YOU KIDS TODAY... YOU HAVE YOUR VALUES CHOSEN FOR YOU.
SHUP
NO. 81 - ROARING UPHEAVAL
...!
IT'S NOT JUST BAKUGO... TOKOYAMI'S GONE TOO!
THE TWO IN THE REAR...
TOKOYAMI
TODOROKI
BAKUGO
SHOJI
HE TOOK THEM AWAY WITHOUT A SOUND? WHAT'S HIS QUIRK...?!
THERE WAS NO NEED TO EVEN CONFRONT US... HE'S MOCKING US.
SORRY FOR MY BAD HABIT... I'M AN ENTERTAINER AT HEART.
ROLL
ROLL
TAKING TOKOYAMI WAS JUST A BIT OF AD-LIBBING.
MOON-FISH... OLD "BLADE-TOOTH."
EVEN A NATURAL-BORN HOMICIDAL MANIAC LIKE HIM, WHOSE DEATH ROW APPEAL WAS SHOT DOWN...
...WAS HANDILY TRAMPLED BY YOUR RAMPAGING FRIEND...
...SO I DECIDED TO TAKE HIM TOO!

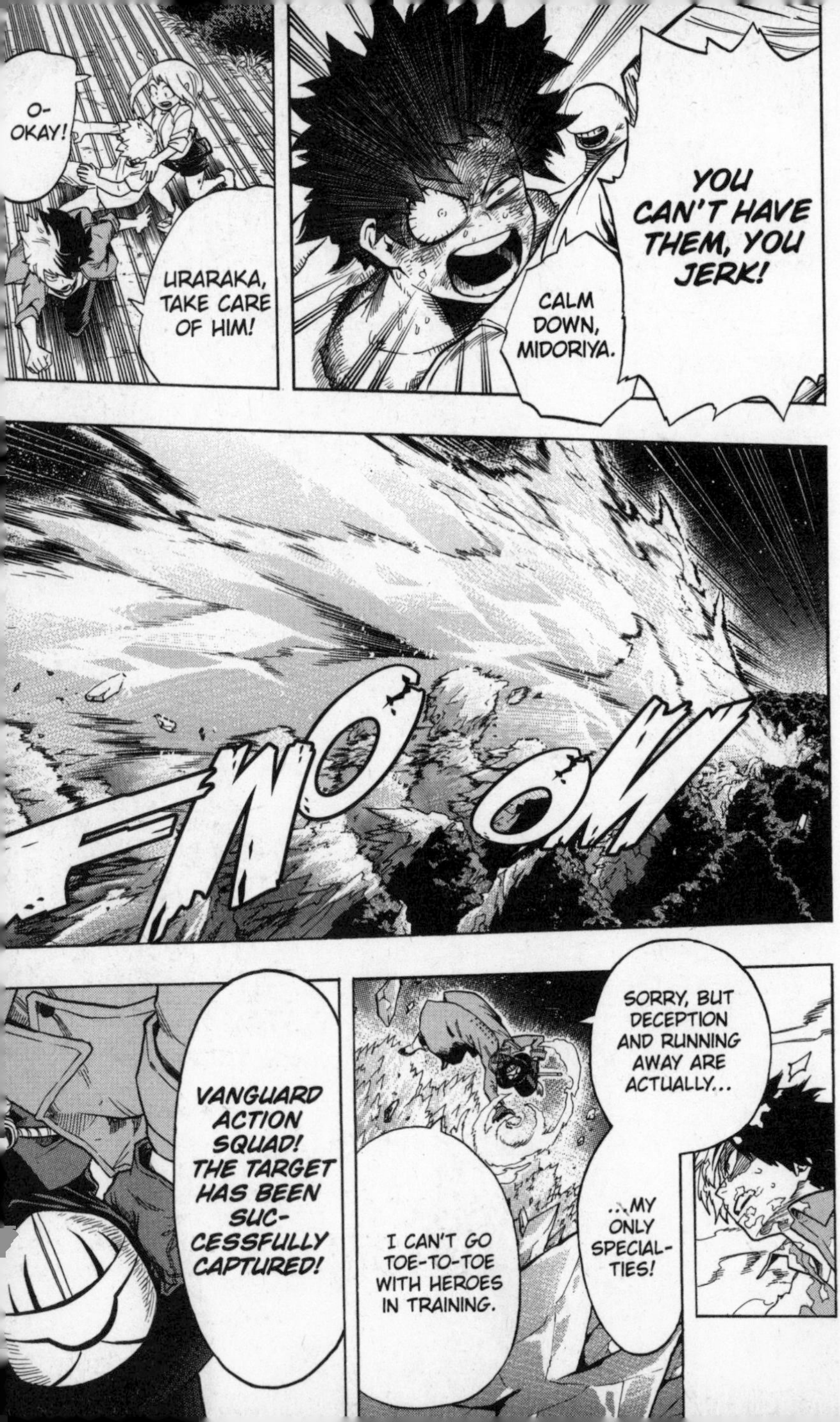
YOU CAN'T HAVE THEM, YOU JERK!
CALM DOWN, MIDORIYA.
URARAKA, TAKE CARE OF HIM!
O-OKAY!
SORRY, BUT DECEPTION AND RUNNING AWAY ARE ACTUALLY...
...MY ONLY SPECIAL-TIES!
I CAN'T GO TOE-TO-TOE WITH HEROES IN TRAINING.
VANGUARD ACTION SQUAD! THE TARGET HAS BEEN SUC-CESSFULLY CAPTURED!

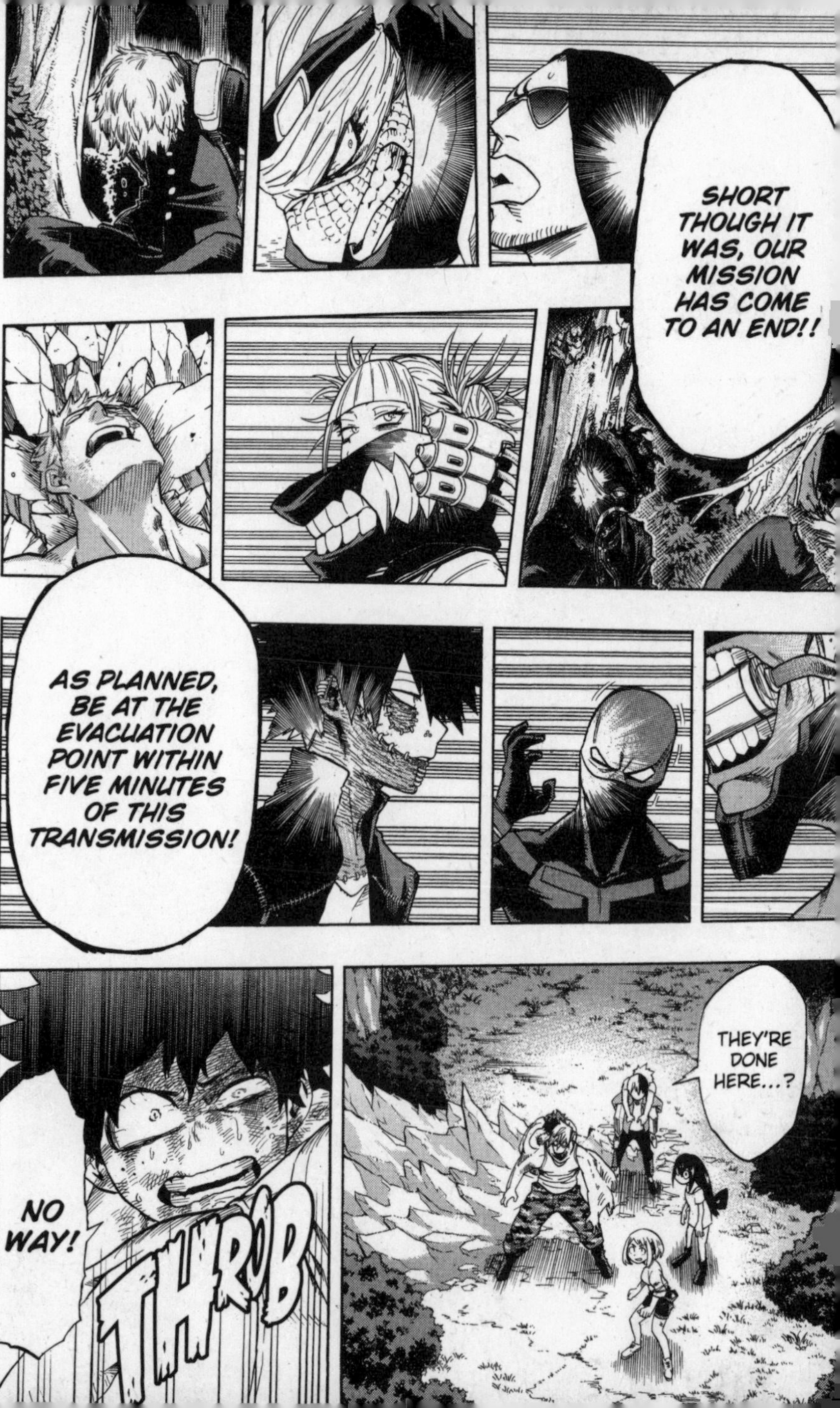
SHORT THOUGH IT WAS, OUR MISSION HAS COME TO AN END!!
AS PLANNED, BE AT THE EVACUATION POINT WITHIN FIVE MINUTES OF THIS TRANSMISSION!
THEY'RE DONE HERE...?
NO WAY!
THROB

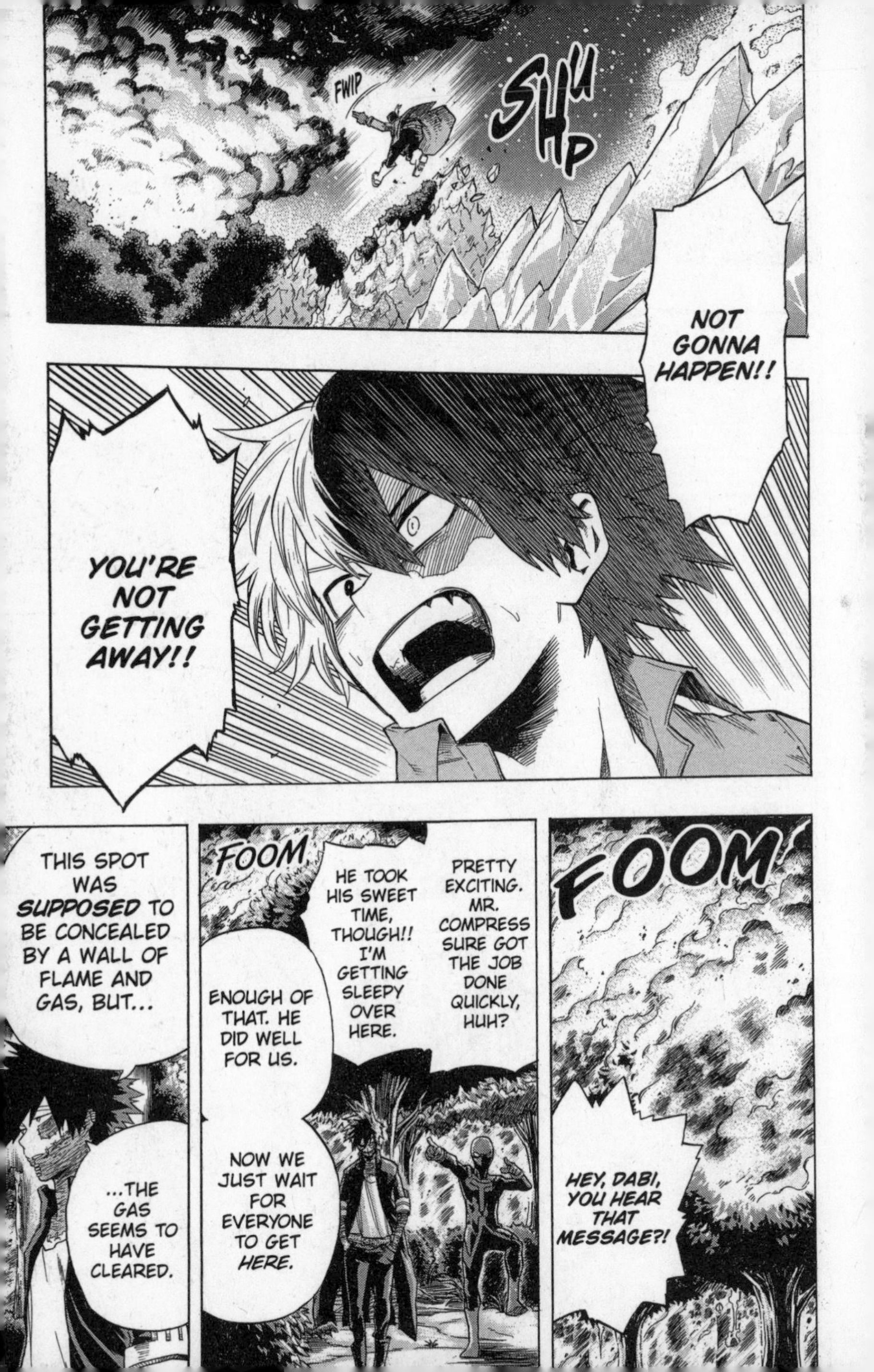
SHUP
FWIP
NOT GONNA HAPPEN!!
YOU'RE NOT GETTING AWAY!!
FOOM
HEY, DABI, YOU HEAR THAT MESSAGE?!
FOOM
PRETTY EXCITING. MR. COMPRESS SURE GOT THE JOB DONE QUICKLY, HUH?
HE TOOK HIS SWEET TIME, THOUGH!! I'M GETTING SLEEPY OVER HERE.
ENOUGH OF THAT. HE DID WELL FOR US.
NOW WE JUST WAIT FOR EVERYONE TO GET HERE.
THIS SPOT WAS *SUPPOSED* TO BE CONCEALED BY A WALL OF FLAME AND GAS, BUT...
...THE GAS SEEMS TO HAVE CLEARED.

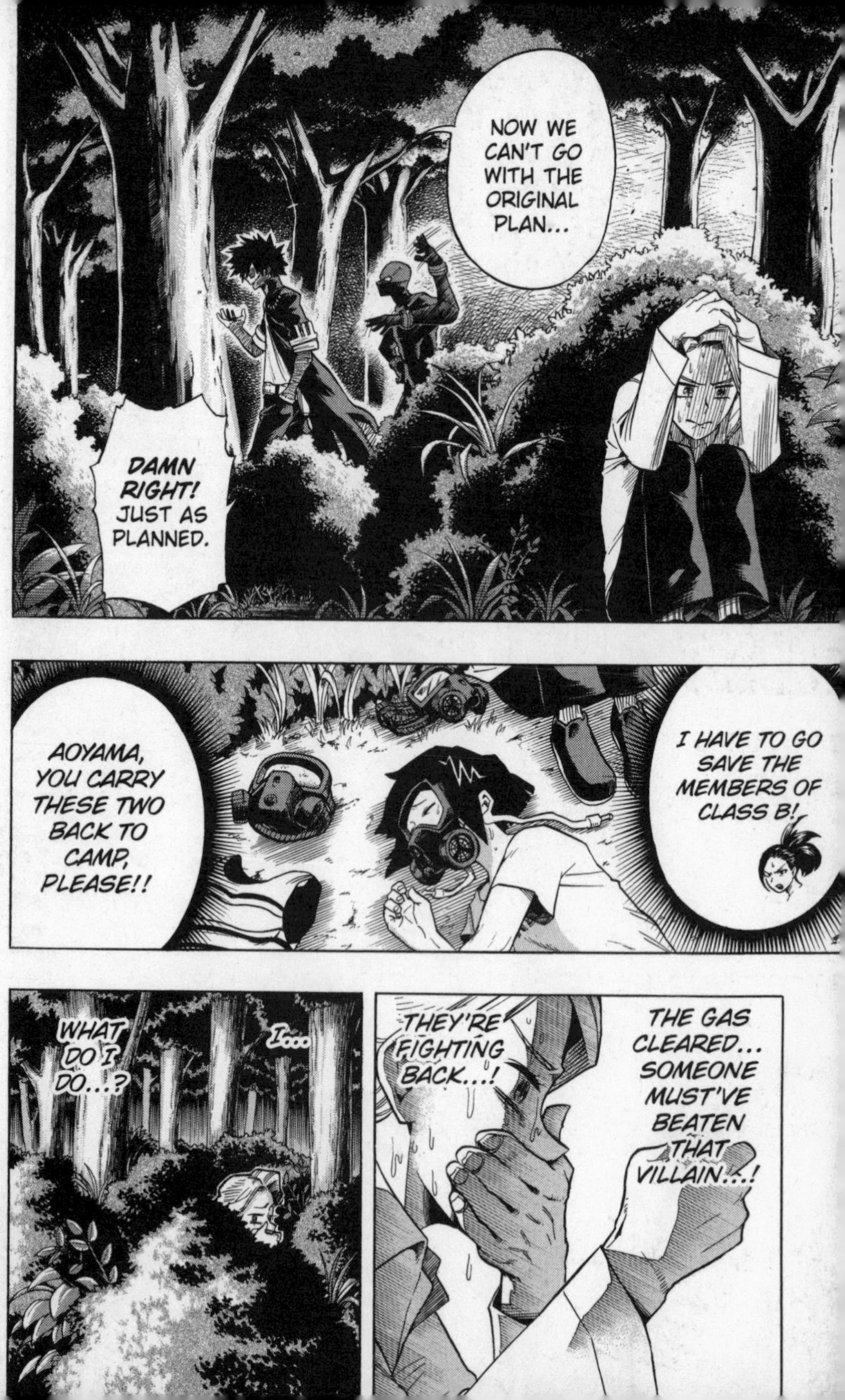

NOW WE CAN'T GO WITH THE ORIGINAL PLAN...
DAMN RIGHT! JUST AS PLANNED.
I HAVE TO GO SAVE THE MEMBERS OF CLASS B!
AOYAMA, YOU CARRY THESE TWO BACK TO CAMP, PLEASE!!
THE GAS CLEARED... SOMEONE MUST'VE BEATEN THAT VILLAIN...!
THEY'RE FIGHTING BACK...!
I...
WHAT DO I DO...?

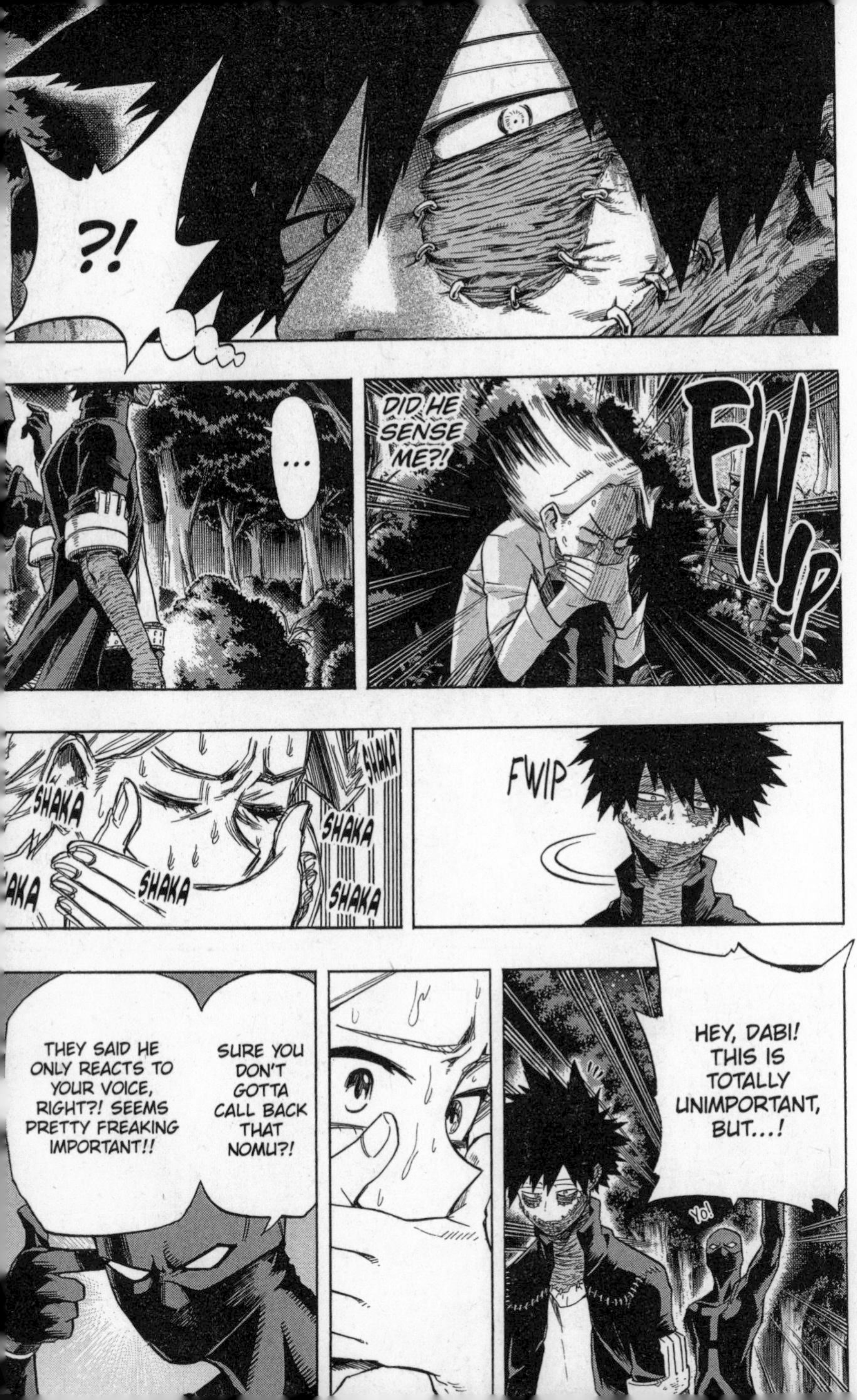
?!
DID HE SENSE ME?!
FWIP
...
FWIP
SHAKA
SHAKA
SHAKA
SHAKA
SHAKA
AKA
HEY, DABI! THIS IS TOTALLY UNIMPORTANT, BUT...!
YO!
SURE YOU DON'T GOTTA CALL BACK THAT NOMU?!
THEY SAID HE ONLY REACTS TO YOUR VOICE, RIGHT?! SEEMS PRETTY FREAKING IMPORTANT!!

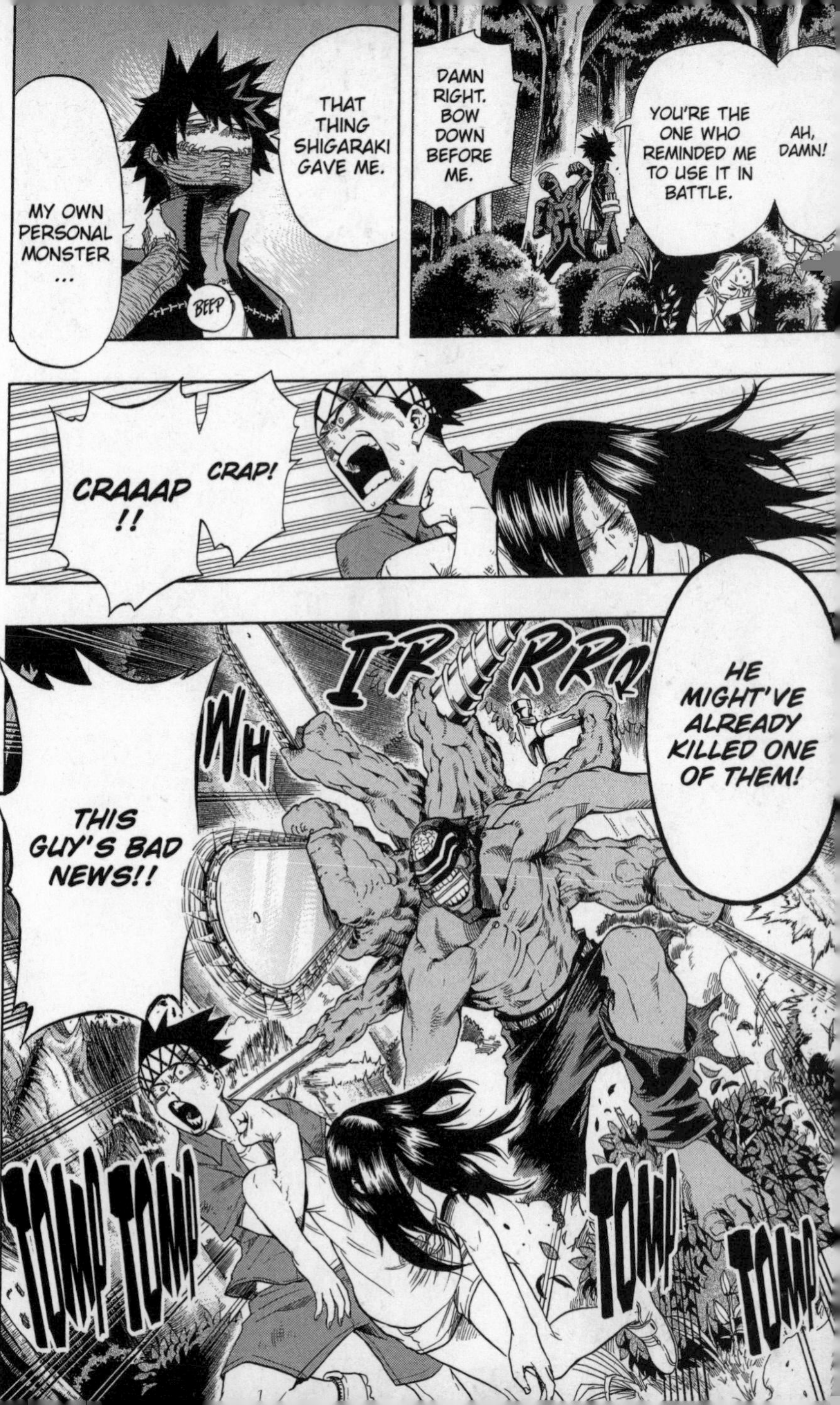
AH, DAMN!
YOU'RE THE ONE WHO REMINDED ME TO USE IT IN BATTLE.
DAMN RIGHT. BOW DOWN BEFORE ME.
THAT THING SHIGARAKI GAVE ME.
MY OWN PERSONAL MONSTER ...
BEEP
CRAP!
CRAAAP !!
HE MIGHT'VE ALREADY KILLED ONE OF THEM!
THIS GUY'S BAD NEWS!!
TOMP TOMP
TOMP TOMP
TOMP TOMP

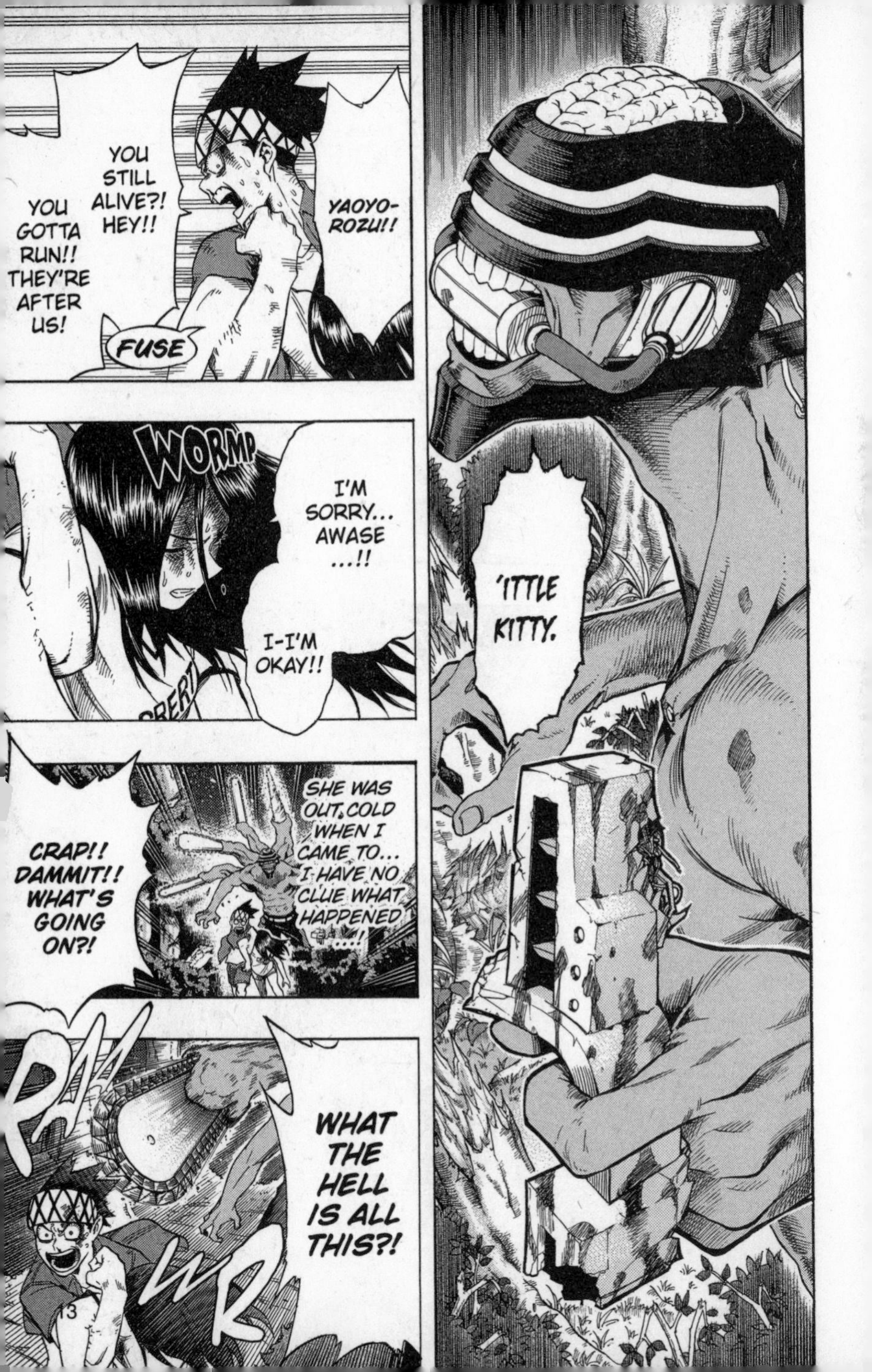
'ITTLE KITTY.
YAOYO-ROZU!!
YOU STILL ALIVE?! HEY!!
YOU GOTTA RUN!! THEY'RE AFTER US!
FUSE
WORMP
I'M SORRY... AWASE ...!!
I-I'M OKAY!!
SHE WAS OUT COLD WHEN I CAME TO... I HAVE NO CLUE WHAT HAPPENED ...!!
CRAP!! DAMMIT!! WHAT'S GOING ON?!
WHAT THE HELL IS ALL THIS?!

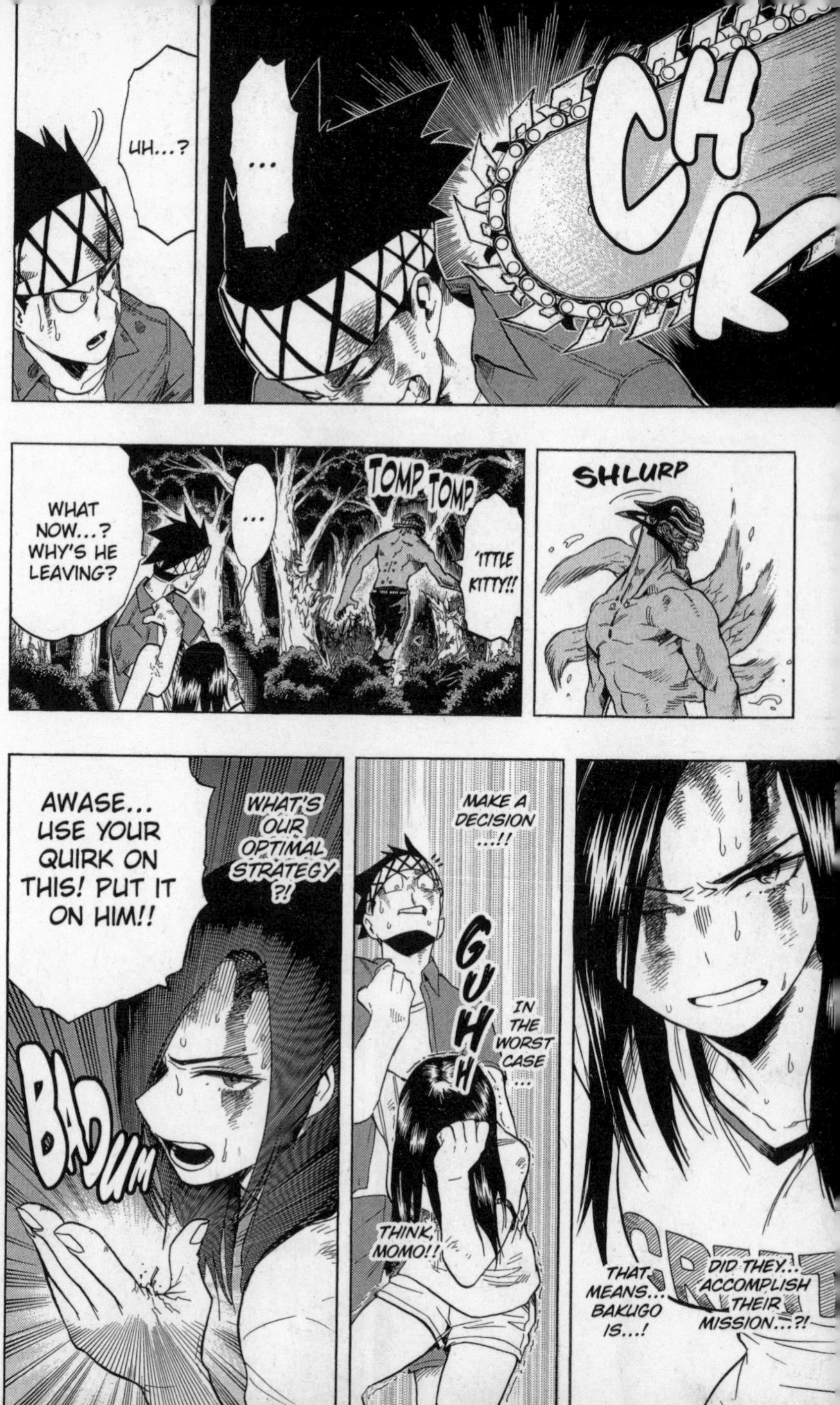
CHK
...
UH...?
SHLURP
TOMP TOMP
'ITTLE KITTY!!
...
WHAT NOW...? WHY'S HE LEAVING?
DID THEY... ACCOMPLISH THEIR MISSION...?!
THAT MEANS... BAKUGO IS...!
MAKE A DECISION...!!
GUHH
IN THE WORST CASE...
THINK, MOMO!!
WHAT'S OUR OPTIMAL STRATEGY?!
AWASE... USE YOUR QUIRK ON THIS! PUT IT ON HIM!!
BADUM

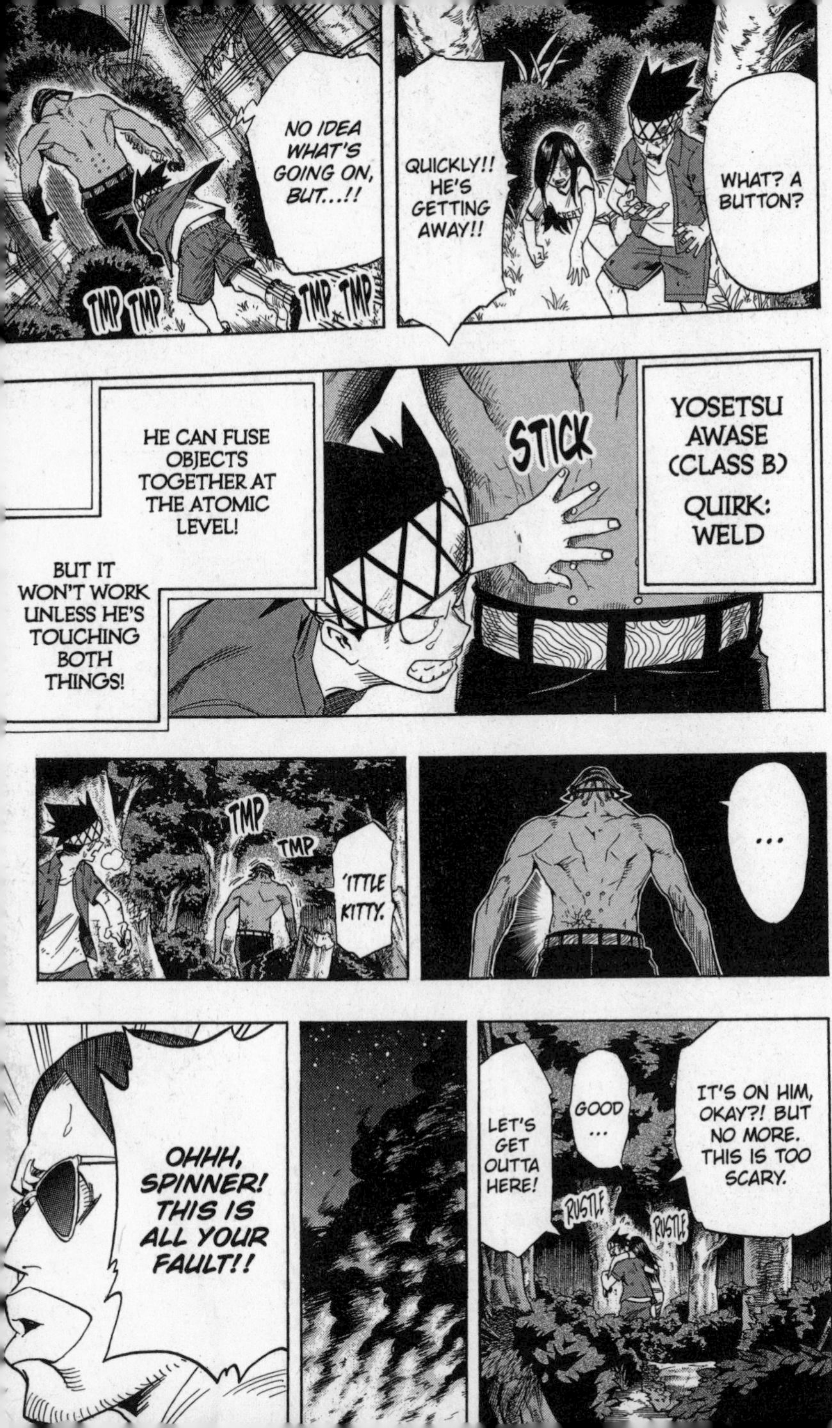
WHAT? A BUTTON?
QUICKLY!! HE'S GETTING AWAY!!
NO IDEA WHAT'S GOING ON, BUT...!!
TMP TMP
TMP TMP
YOSETSU AWASE (CLASS B)
QUIRK: WELD
STICK
HE CAN FUSE OBJECTS TOGETHER AT THE ATOMIC LEVEL!
BUT IT WON'T WORK UNLESS HE'S TOUCHING BOTH THINGS!
...
TMP
TMP
'ITTLE KITTY.
IT'S ON HIM, OKAY?! BUT NO MORE. THIS IS TOO SCARY.
GOOD...
LET'S GET OUTTA HERE!
RUSTLE
RUSTLE
OHHH, SPINNER! THIS IS ALL YOUR FAULT!!

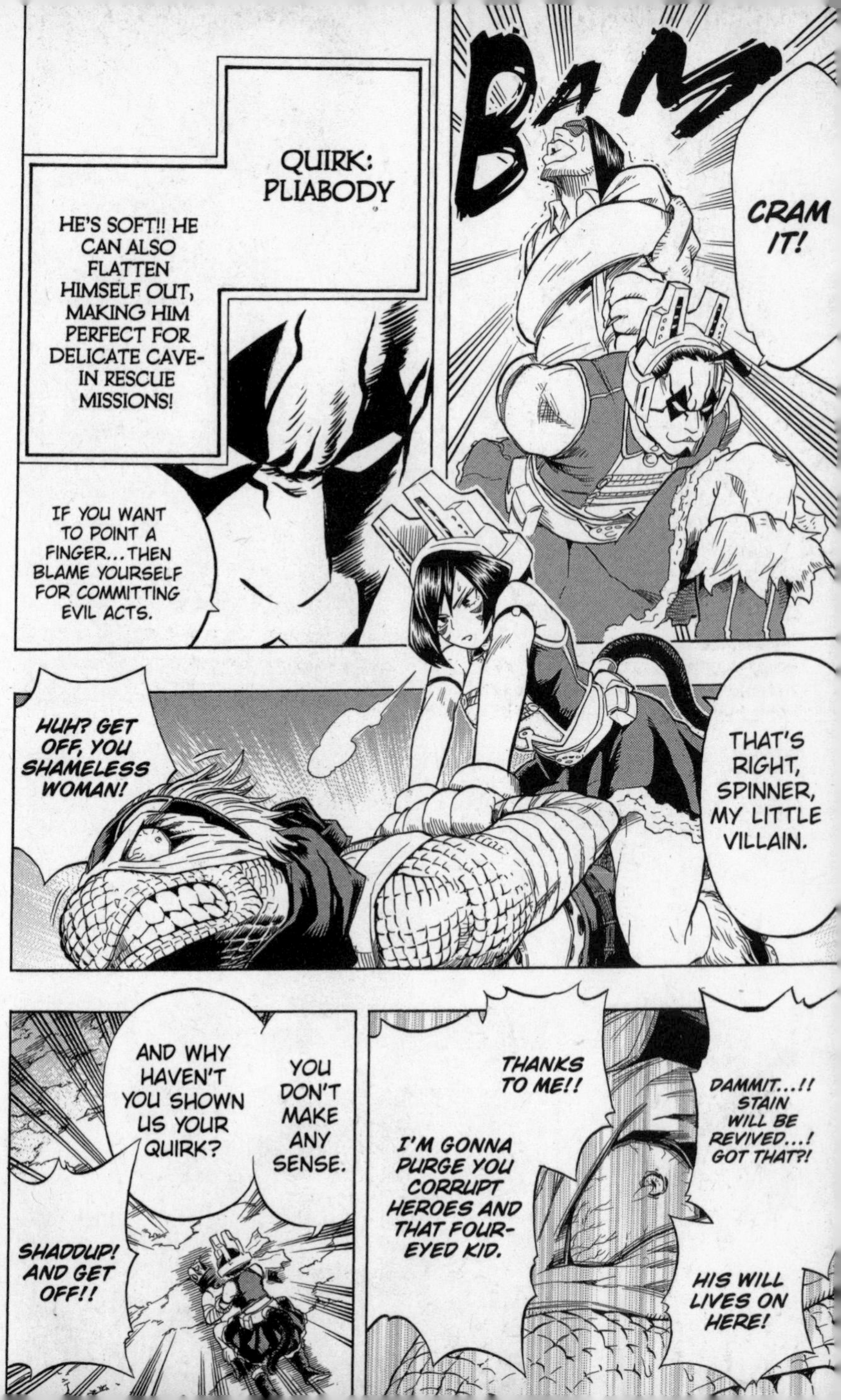
BAM
CRAM IT!
QUIRK: PLIABODY
HE'S SOFT!! HE CAN ALSO FLATTEN HIMSELF OUT, MAKING HIM PERFECT FOR DELICATE CAVE-IN RESCUE MISSIONS!
IF YOU WANT TO POINT A FINGER...THEN BLAME YOURSELF FOR COMMITTING EVIL ACTS.
THAT'S RIGHT, SPINNER, MY LITTLE VILLAIN.
HUH? GET OFF, YOU SHAMELESS WOMAN!
DAMMIT...!! STAIN WILL BE REVIVED...! GOT THAT?!
THANKS TO ME!!
I'M GONNA PURGE YOU CORRUPT HEROES AND THAT FOUR-EYED KID.
HIS WILL LIVES ON HERE!
YOU DON'T MAKE ANY SENSE.
AND WHY HAVEN'T YOU SHOWN US YOUR QUIRK?
SHADDUP! AND GET OFF!!

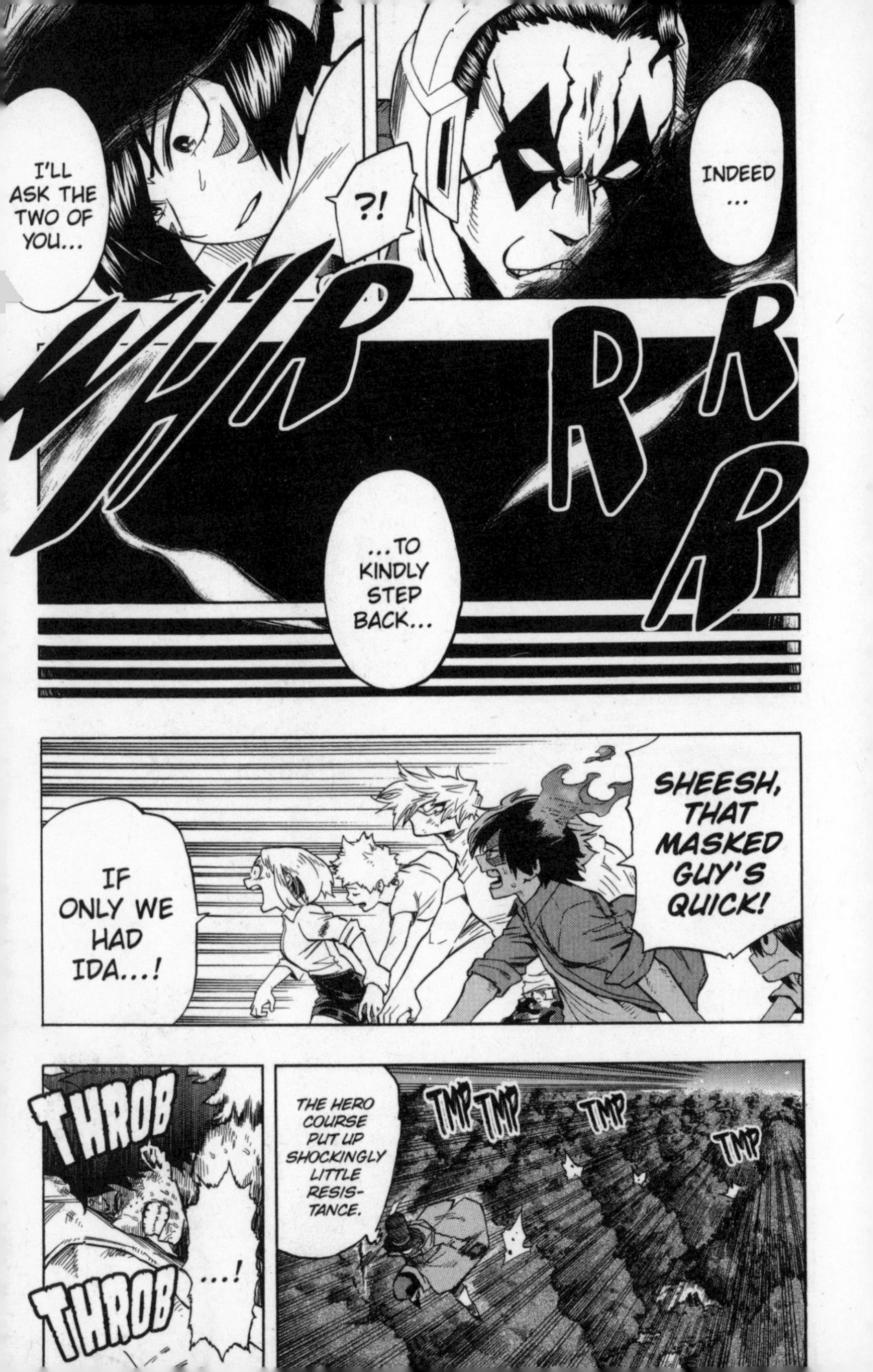
INDEED ...
?!
I'LL ASK THE TWO OF YOU...
WHRRRR
...TO KINDLY STEP BACK...
SHEESH, THAT MASKED GUY'S QUICK!
IF ONLY WE HAD IDA...!
THE HERO COURSE PUT UP SHOCKINGLY LITTLE RESIS-TANCE.
TMP TMP
TMP
TMP
THROB
THROB
...!

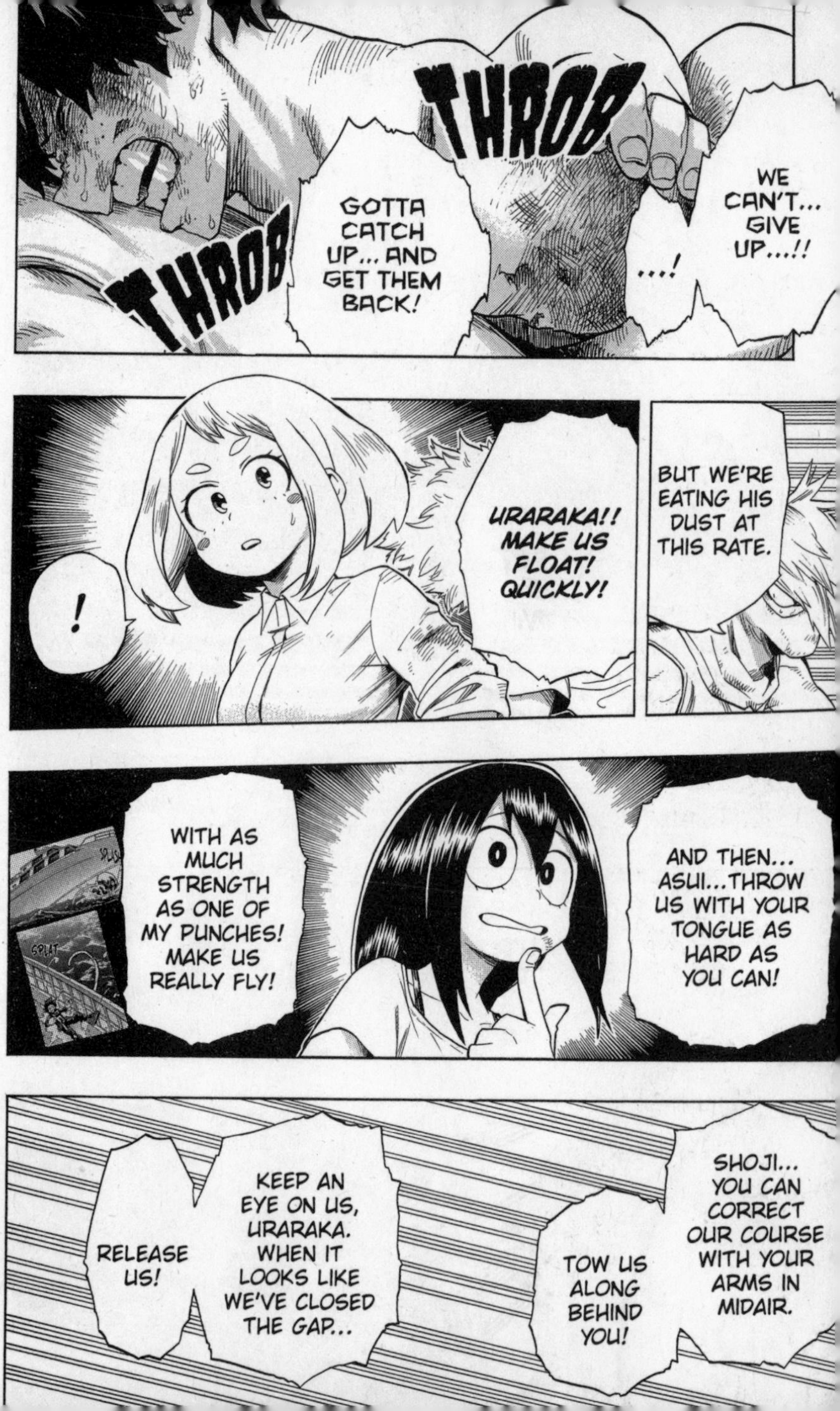
WE CAN'T... GIVE UP...!!
...!
THROB
GOTTA CATCH UP... AND GET THEM BACK!
THROB
BUT WE'RE EATING HIS DUST AT THIS RATE.
URARAKA!! MAKE US FLOAT! QUICKLY!
!
AND THEN... ASUI...THROW US WITH YOUR TONGUE AS HARD AS YOU CAN!
WITH AS MUCH STRENGTH AS ONE OF MY PUNCHES! MAKE US REALLY FLY!
SPLAT
SHOJI... YOU CAN CORRECT OUR COURSE WITH YOUR ARMS IN MIDAIR.
TOW US ALONG BEHIND YOU!
KEEP AN EYE ON US, URARAKA. WHEN IT LOOKS LIKE WE'VE CLOSED THE GAP...
RELEASE US!

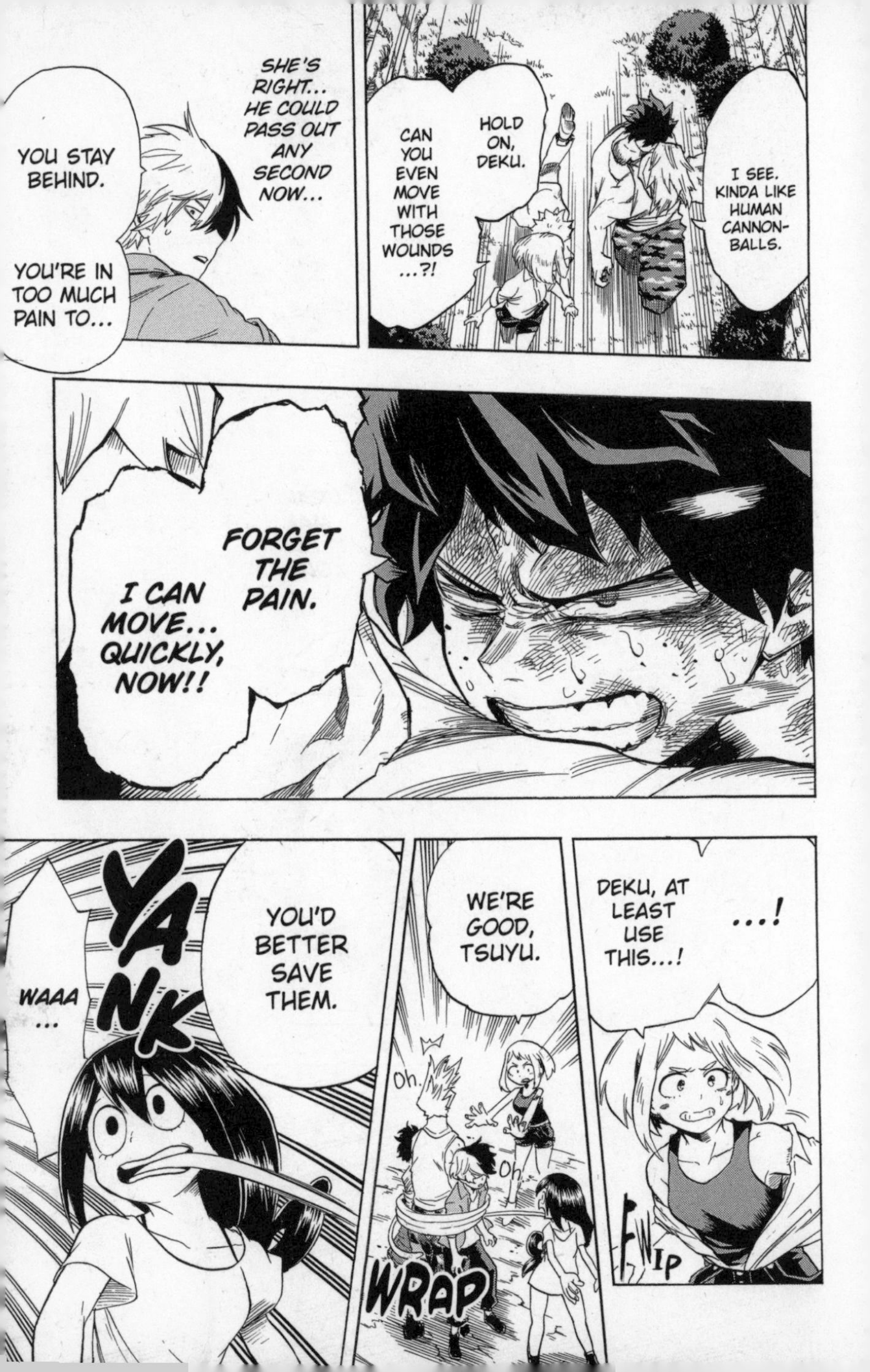
I SEE. KINDA LIKE HUMAN CANNON-BALLS.
HOLD ON, DEKU.
CAN YOU EVEN MOVE WITH THOSE WOUNDS ...?!
SHE'S RIGHT... HE COULD PASS OUT ANY SECOND NOW...
YOU STAY BEHIND.
YOU'RE IN TOO MUCH PAIN TO...
FORGET THE PAIN.
I CAN MOVE... QUICKLY, NOW!!
...!
DEKU, AT LEAST USE THIS...!
FWIP
WE'RE GOOD, TSUYU.
Oh.
Oh.
WRAP
YOU'D BETTER SAVE THEM.
YANK
WAAA ...

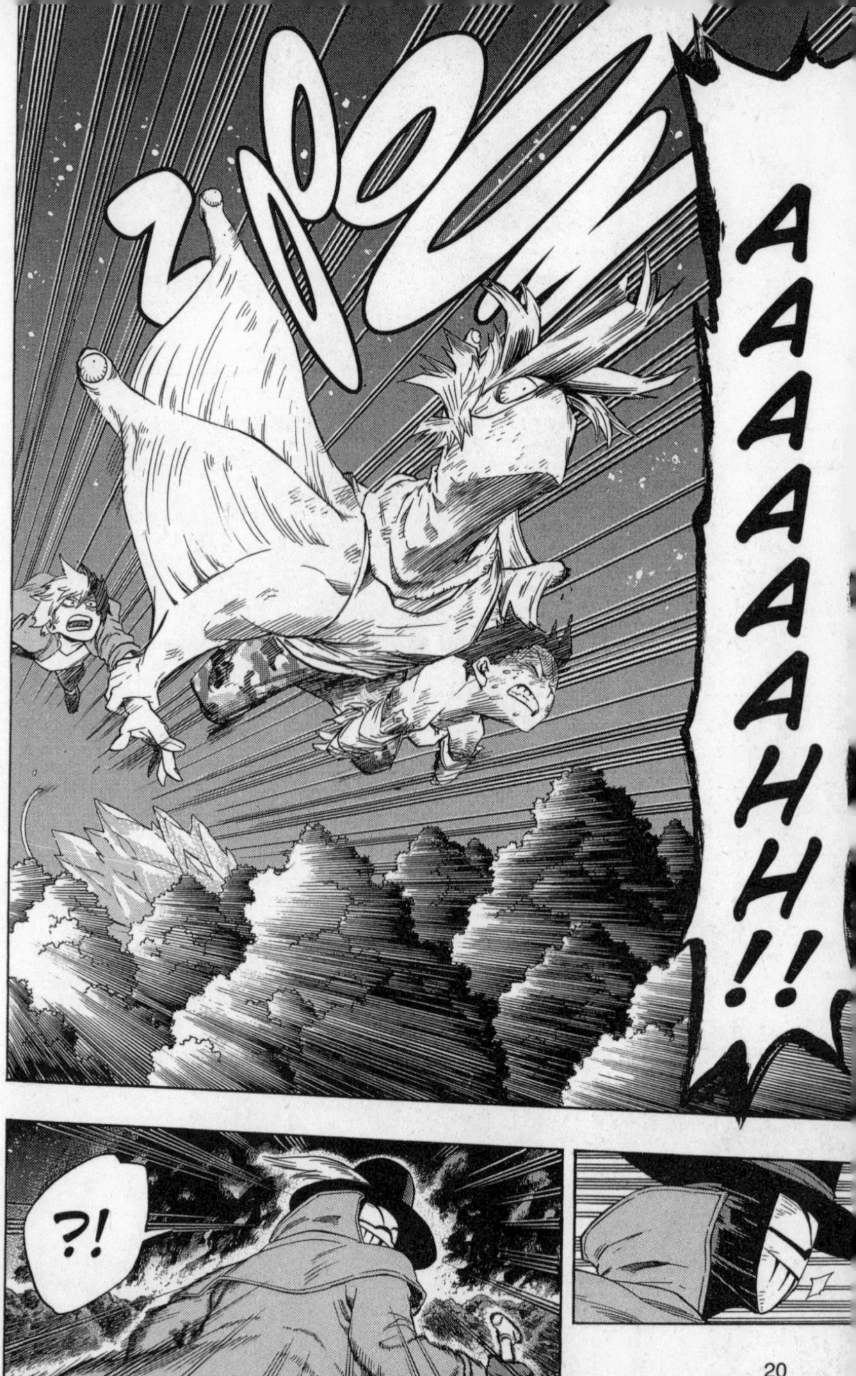
ZOOOM
AAAAAAHH!!
?!

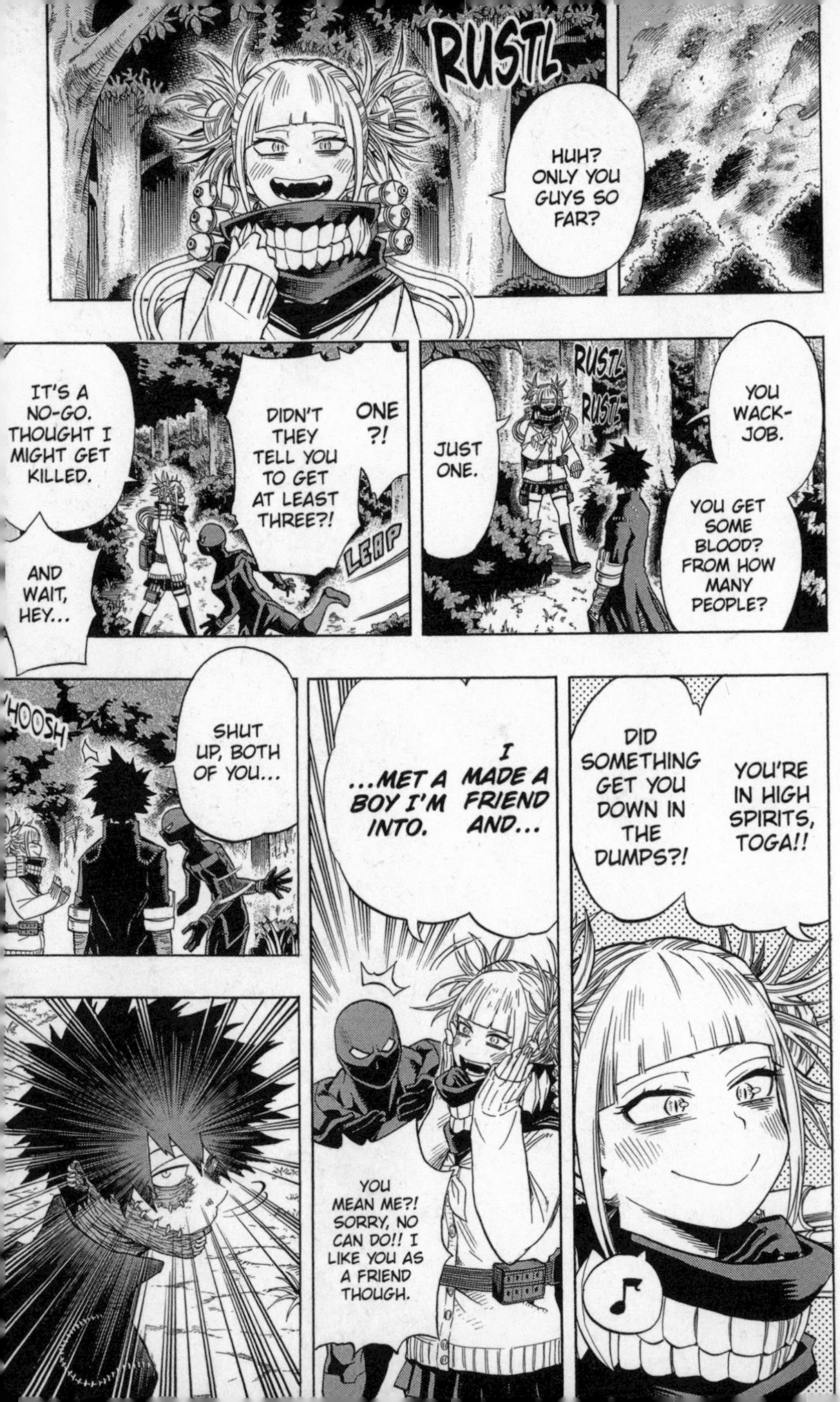
RUSTL
HUH? ONLY YOU GUYS SO FAR?
RUSTL RUSTL
YOU WACK-JOB.
YOU GET SOME BLOOD? FROM HOW MANY PEOPLE?
JUST ONE.
ONE ?!
DIDN'T THEY TELL YOU TO GET AT LEAST THREE?!
LEAP
IT'S A NO-GO. THOUGHT I MIGHT GET KILLED.
AND WAIT, HEY...
YOU'RE IN HIGH SPIRITS, TOGA!!
DID SOMETHING GET YOU DOWN IN THE DUMPS?!
I MADE A FRIEND AND...
...MET A BOY I'M INTO.
YOU MEAN ME?! SORRY, NO CAN DO!! I LIKE YOU AS A FRIEND THOUGH.
WHOOSH
SHUT UP, BOTH OF YOU...

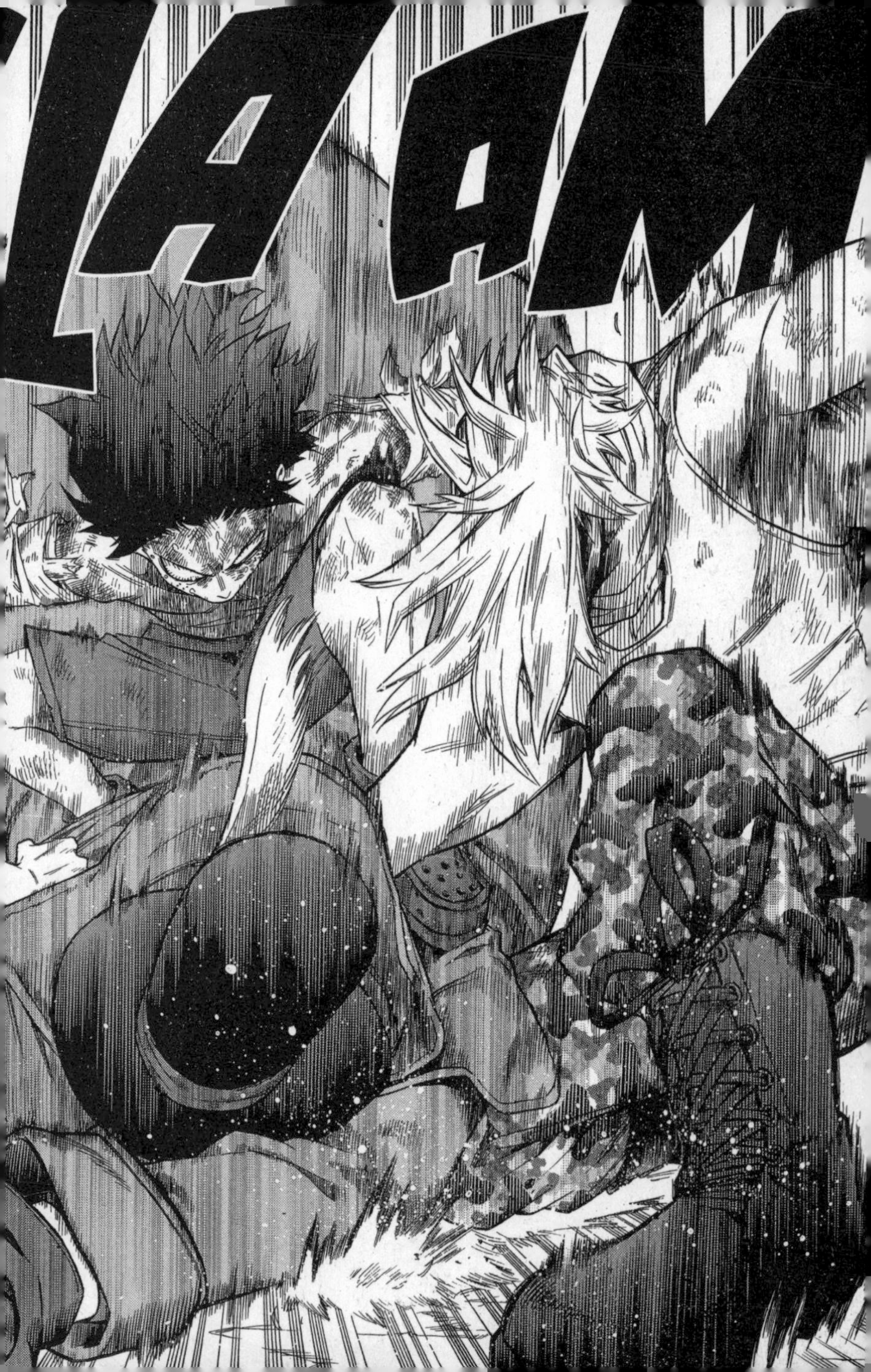
LAAM

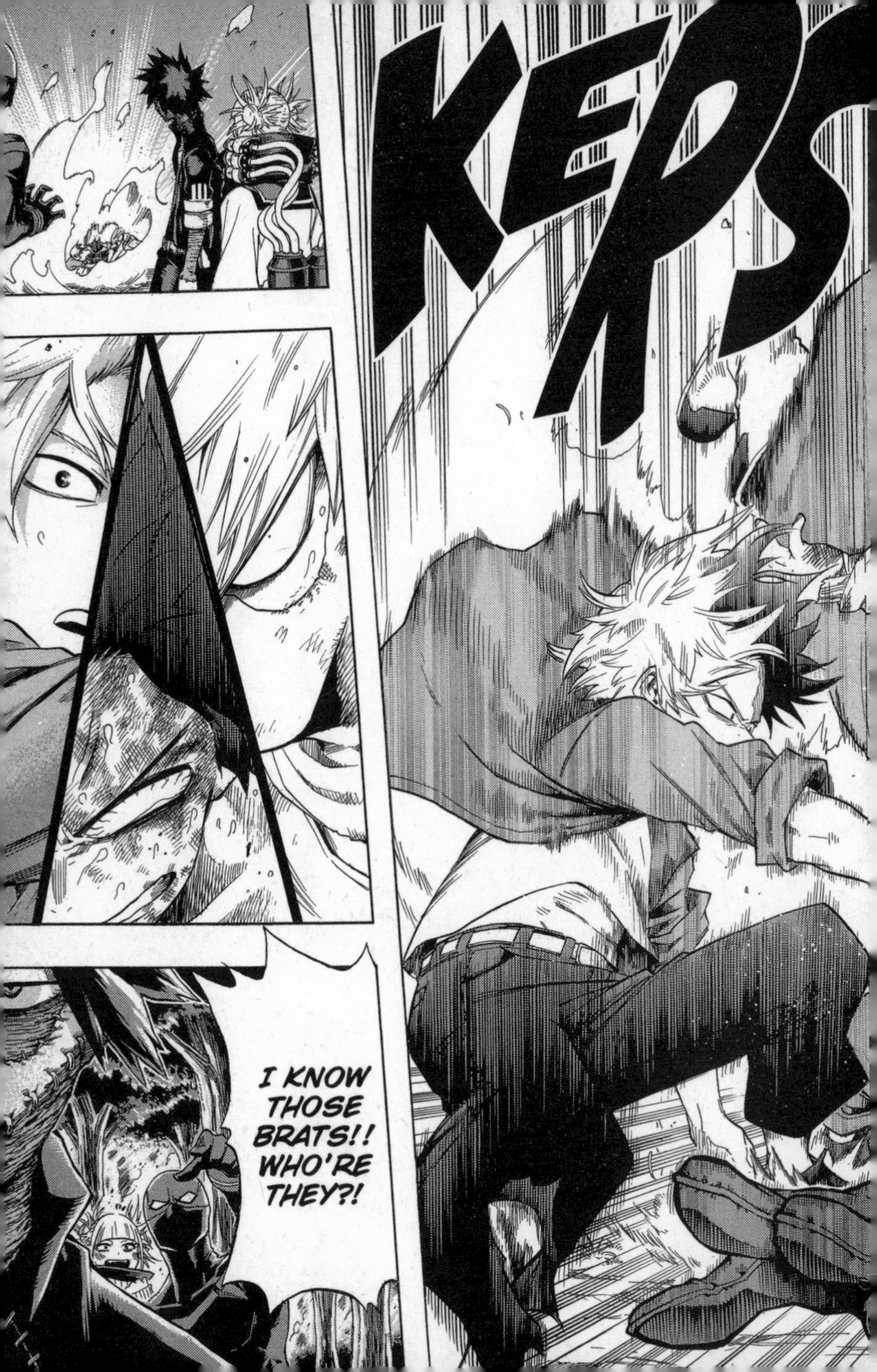
I KNOW THOSE BRATS!! WHO'RE THEY?!

HERO

YOSETSU AWASE (15)

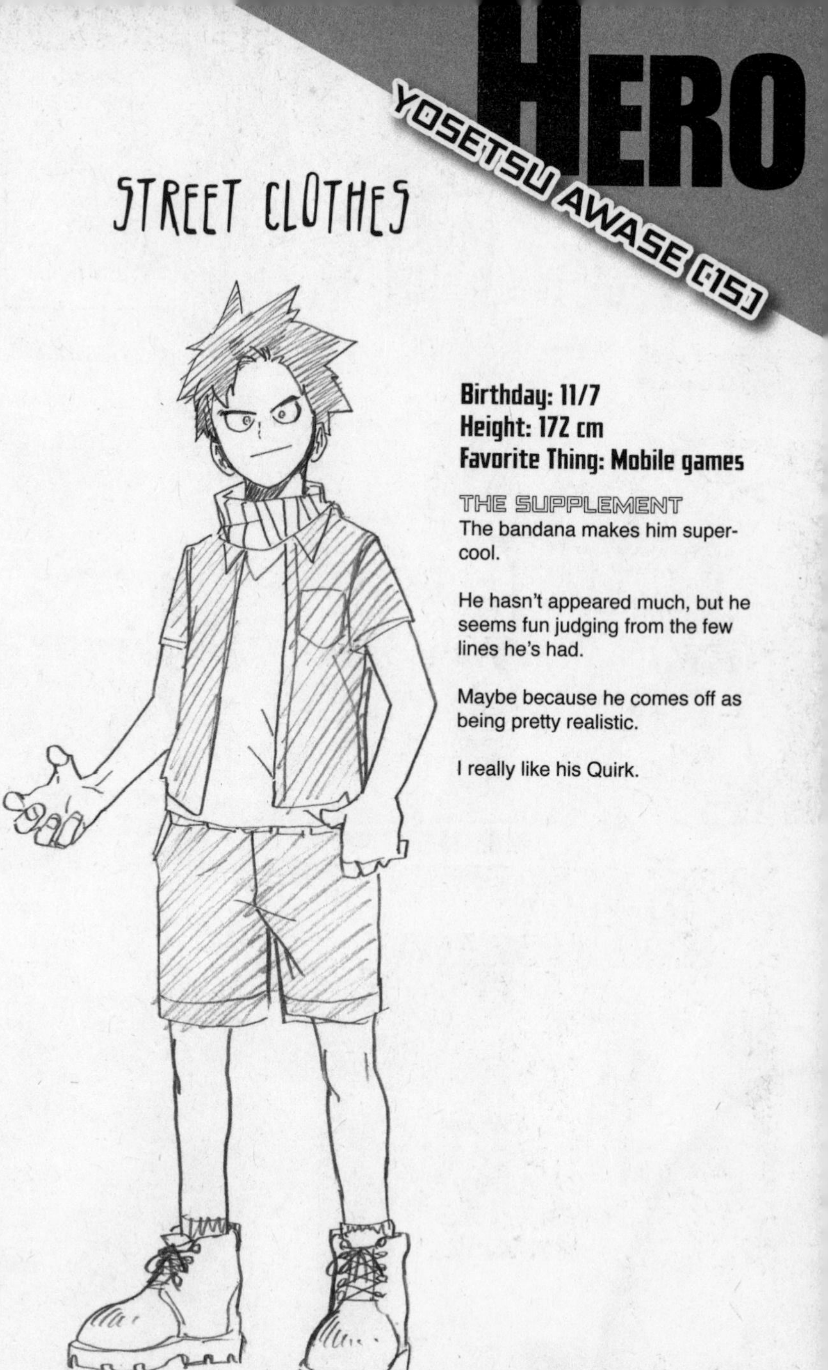
STREET CLOTHES

Birthday: 11/7
Height: 172 cm
Favorite Thing: Mobile games

THE SUPPLEMENT

The bandana makes him super-cool.

He hasn't appeared much, but he seems fun judging from the few lines he's had.

Maybe because he comes off as being pretty realistic.

I really like his Quirk.

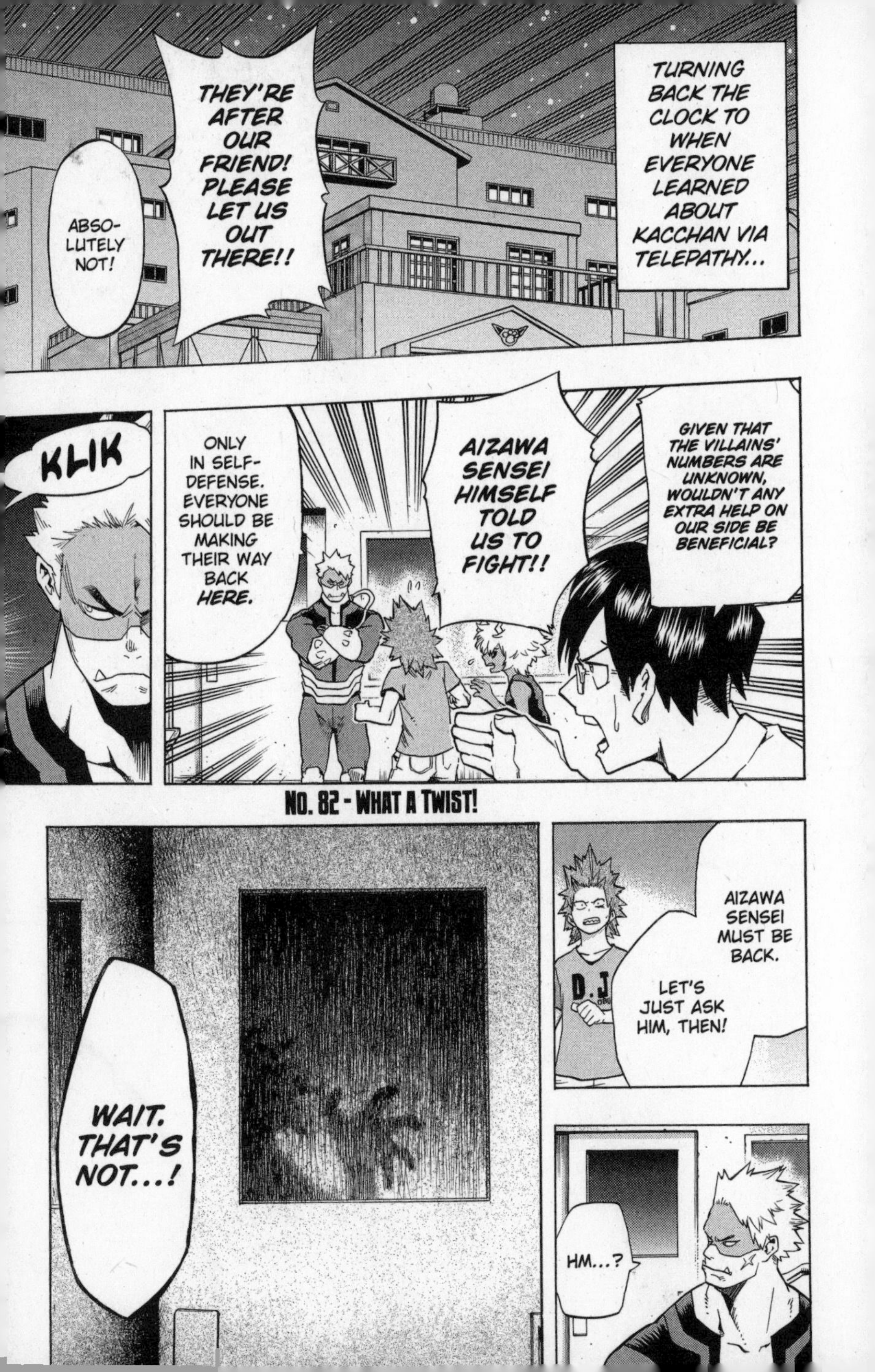
TURNING BACK THE CLOCK TO WHEN EVERYONE LEARNED ABOUT KACCHAN VIA TELEPATHY...
THEY'RE AFTER OUR FRIEND! PLEASE LET US OUT THERE!!
ABSOLUTELY NOT!
GIVEN THAT THE VILLAINS' NUMBERS ARE UNKNOWN, WOULDN'T ANY EXTRA HELP ON OUR SIDE BE BENEFICIAL?
AIZAWA SENSEI HIMSELF TOLD US TO FIGHT!!
ONLY IN SELF-DEFENSE. EVERYONE SHOULD BE MAKING THEIR WAY BACK HERE.
KLIK
NO. 82 - WHAT A TWIST!
AIZAWA SENSEI MUST BE BACK.
LET'S JUST ASK HIM, THEN!
HM...?
WAIT. THAT'S NOT...!

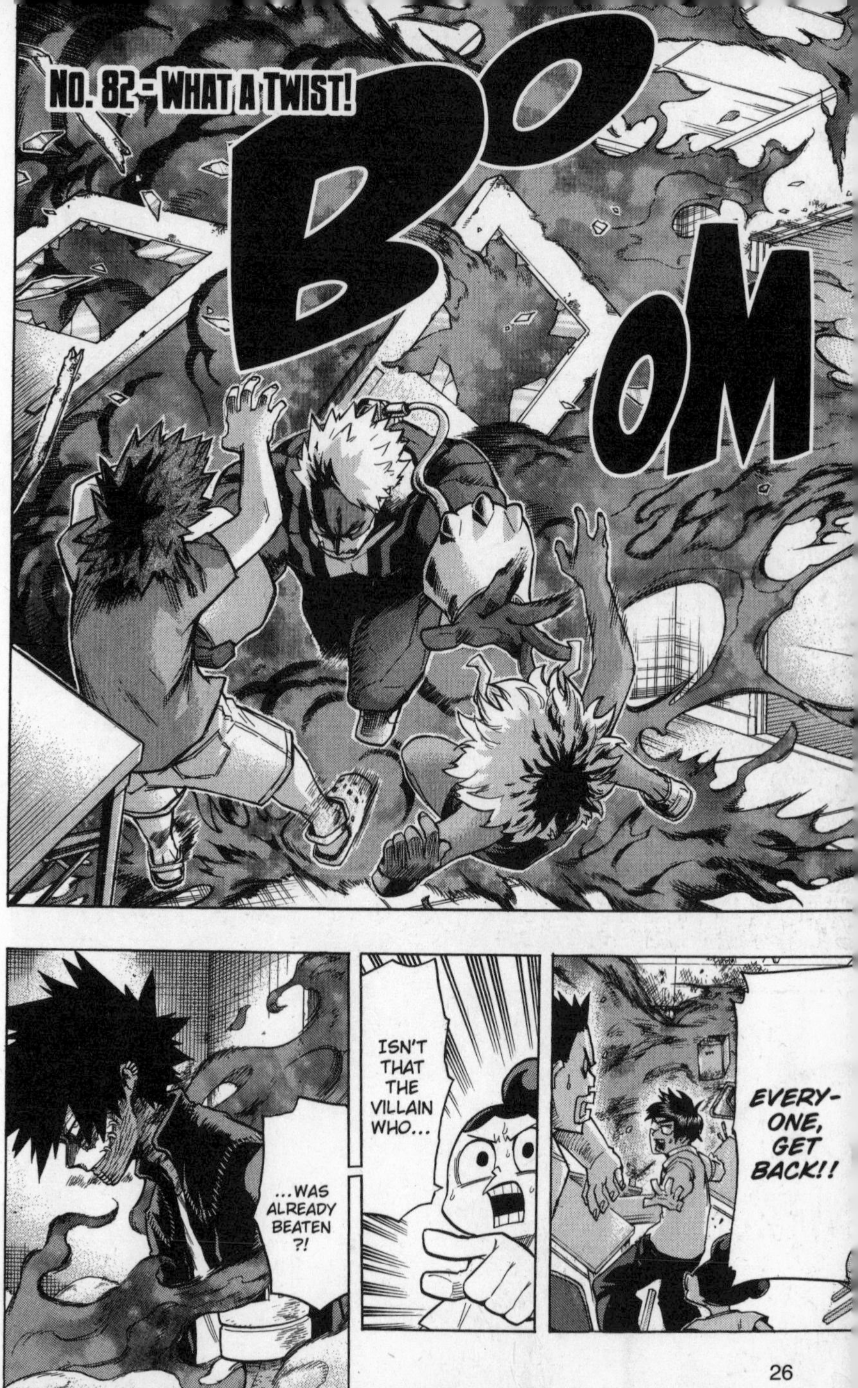
No. 82 - What a Twist!
BOOM
EVERY-ONE, GET BACK!!
ISN'T THAT THE VILLAIN WHO...
...WAS ALREADY BEATEN ?!

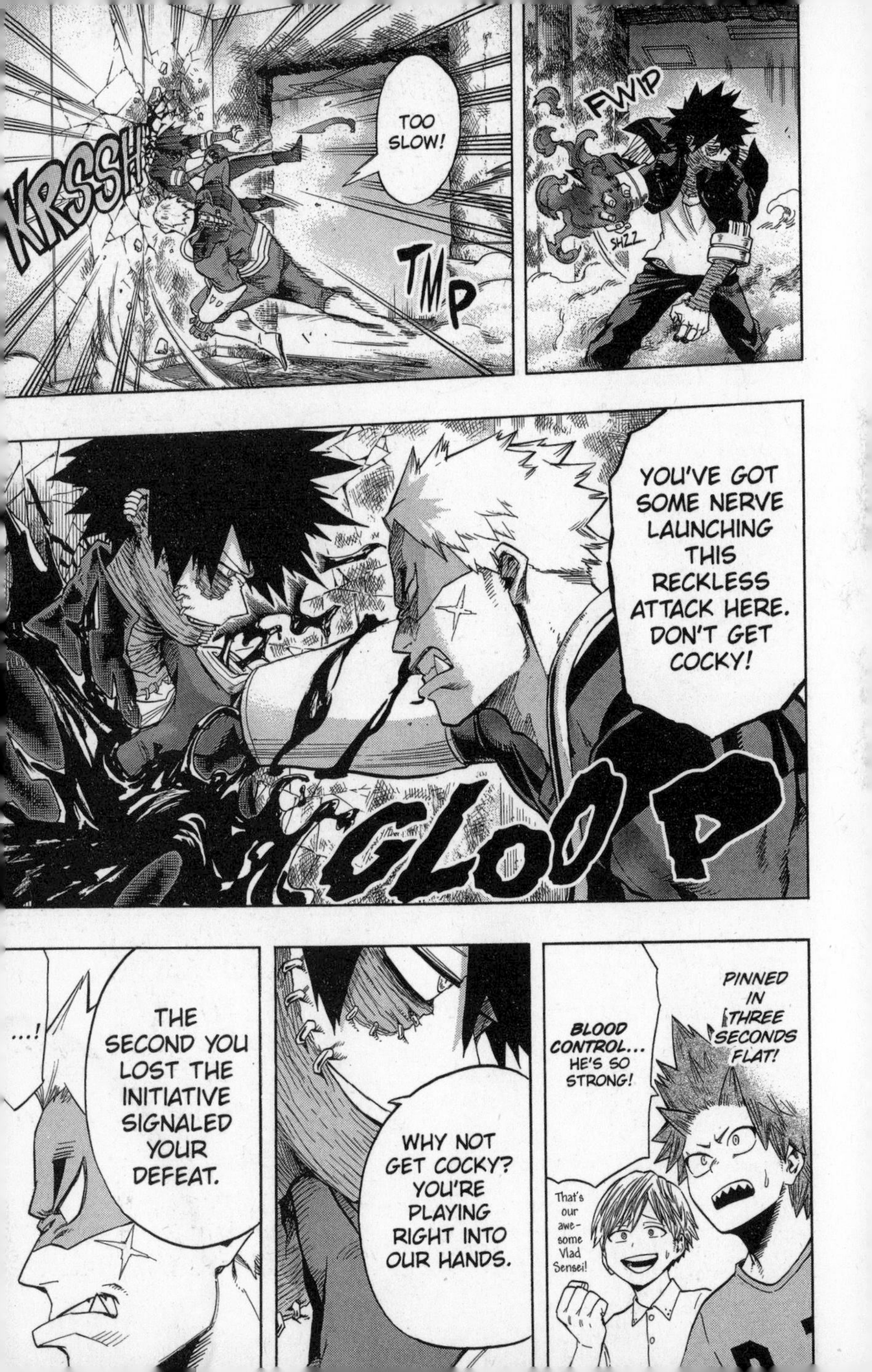
FWIP
SHZZ
TOO SLOW!
KRSSH
TMP
YOU'VE GOT SOME NERVE LAUNCHING THIS RECKLESS ATTACK HERE. DON'T GET COCKY!
GLOOP
PINNED IN THREE SECONDS FLAT!
BLOOD CONTROL... HE'S SO STRONG!
That's our awe-some Vlad Sensei!
WHY NOT GET COCKY? YOU'RE PLAYING RIGHT INTO OUR HANDS.
THE SECOND YOU LOST THE INITIATIVE SIGNALED YOUR DEFEAT.
...!

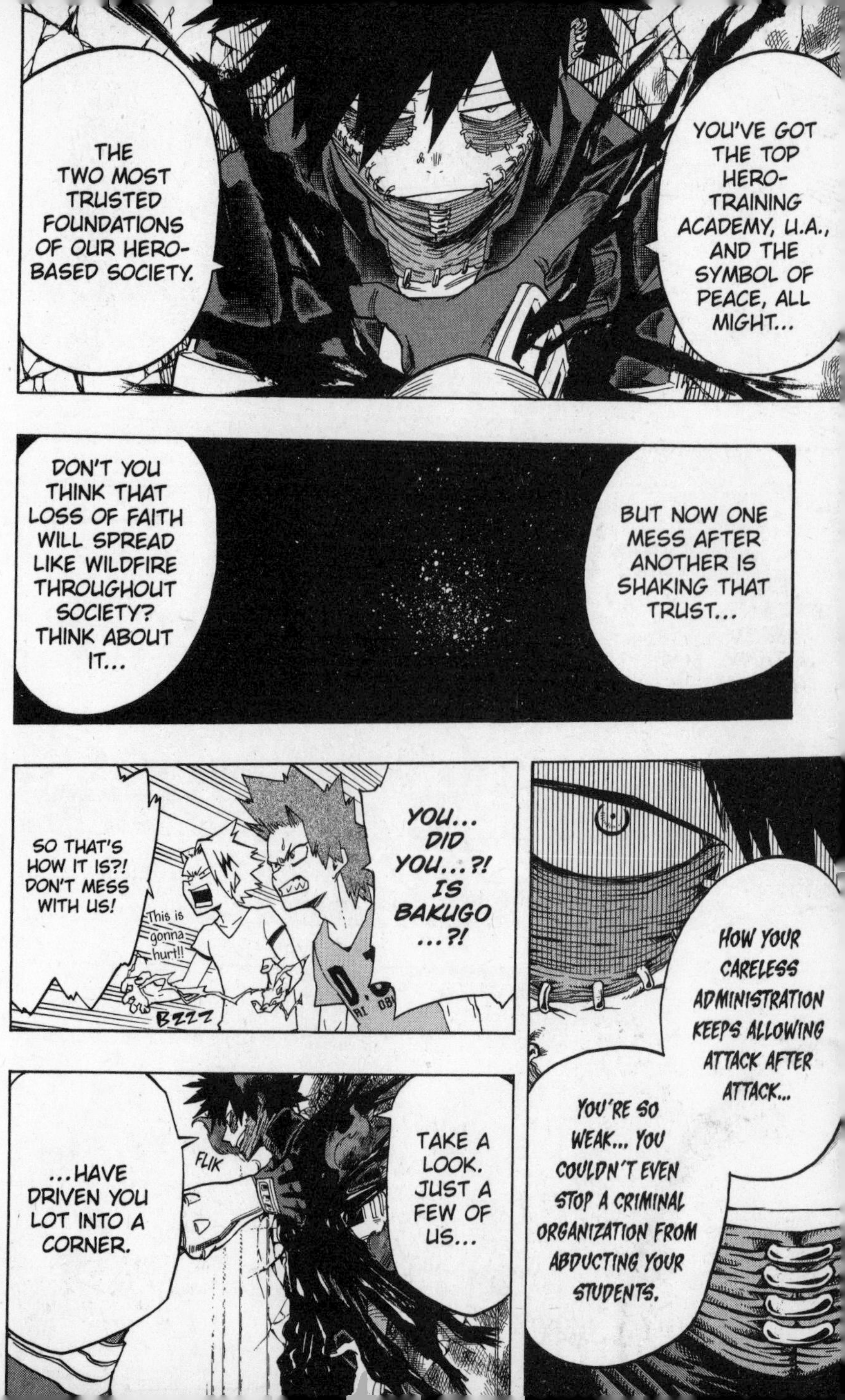
YOU'VE GOT THE TOP HERO-TRAINING ACADEMY, U.A., AND THE SYMBOL OF PEACE, ALL MIGHT...
THE TWO MOST TRUSTED FOUNDATIONS OF OUR HERO-BASED SOCIETY.
BUT NOW ONE MESS AFTER ANOTHER IS SHAKING THAT TRUST...
DON'T YOU THINK THAT LOSS OF FAITH WILL SPREAD LIKE WILDFIRE THROUGHOUT SOCIETY? THINK ABOUT IT...
HOW YOUR CARELESS ADMINISTRATION KEEPS ALLOWING ATTACK AFTER ATTACK...
YOU'RE SO WEAK... YOU COULDN'T EVEN STOP A CRIMINAL ORGANIZATION FROM ABDUCTING YOUR STUDENTS.
YOU... DID YOU...?! IS BAKUGO...?!
SO THAT'S HOW IT IS?! DON'T MESS WITH US!
This is gonna hurt!!
BZZZ
TAKE A LOOK. JUST A FEW OF US...
FLIK
...HAVE DRIVEN YOU LOT INTO A CORNER.

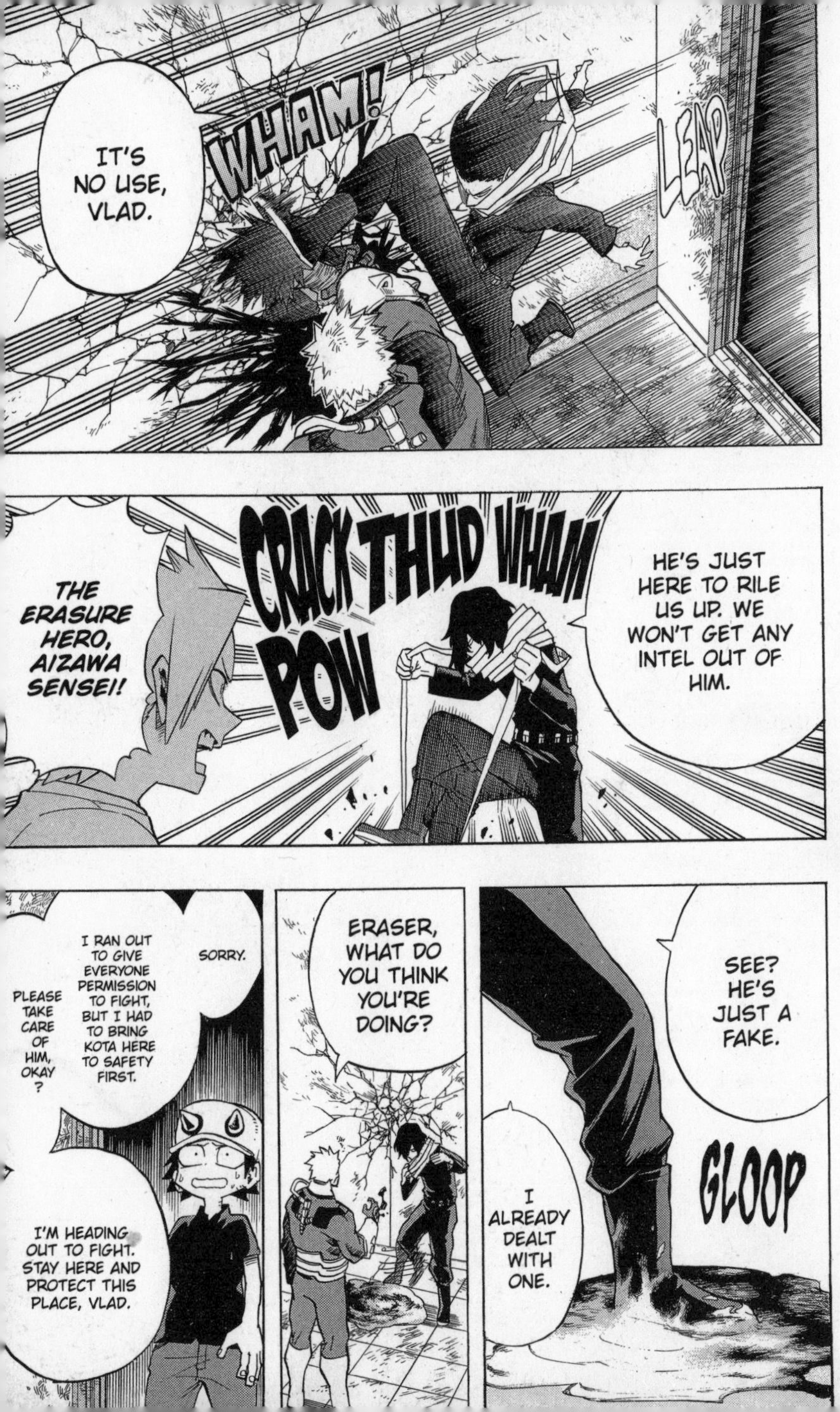
LEAP
WHAM!
IT'S NO USE, VLAD.
HE'S JUST HERE TO RILE US UP. WE WON'T GET ANY INTEL OUT OF HIM.
CRACK THUD WHAM POW
THE ERASURE HERO, AIZAWA SENSEI!
SEE? HE'S JUST A FAKE.
GLOOP
I ALREADY DEALT WITH ONE.
ERASER, WHAT DO YOU THINK YOU'RE DOING?
SORRY.
I RAN OUT TO GIVE EVERYONE PERMISSION TO FIGHT, BUT I HAD TO BRING KOTA HERE TO SAFETY FIRST.
PLEASE TAKE CARE OF HIM, OKAY?
I'M HEADING OUT TO FIGHT. STAY HERE AND PROTECT THIS PLACE, VLAD.

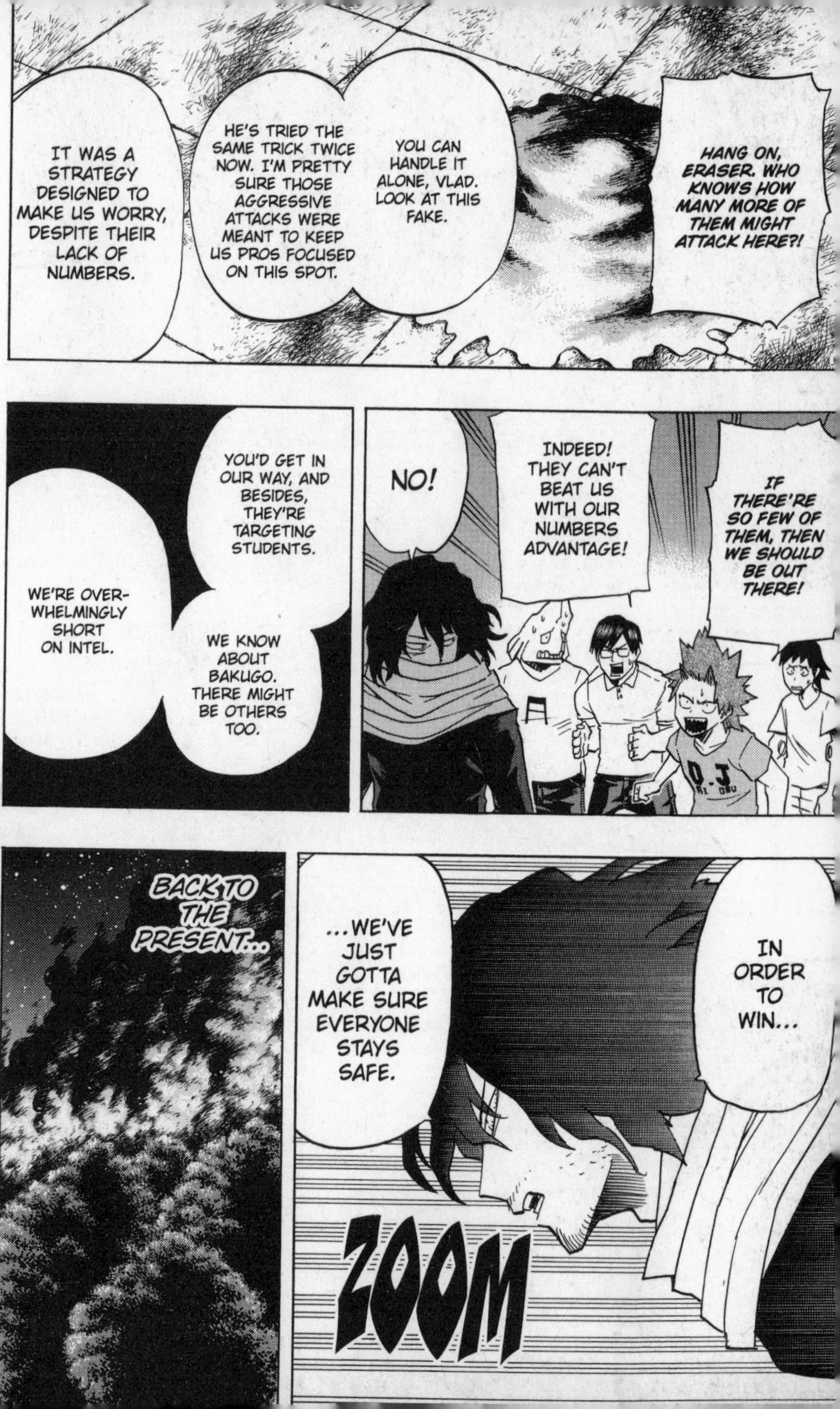
HANG ON, ERASER. WHO KNOWS HOW MANY MORE OF THEM MIGHT ATTACK HERE?!
YOU CAN HANDLE IT ALONE, VLAD. LOOK AT THIS FAKE.
HE'S TRIED THE SAME TRICK TWICE NOW. I'M PRETTY SURE THOSE AGGRESSIVE ATTACKS WERE MEANT TO KEEP US PROS FOCUSED ON THIS SPOT.
IT WAS A STRATEGY DESIGNED TO MAKE US WORRY, DESPITE THEIR LACK OF NUMBERS.
IF THERE'RE SO FEW OF THEM, THEN WE SHOULD BE OUT THERE!
INDEED! THEY CAN'T BEAT US WITH OUR NUMBERS ADVANTAGE!
NO!
YOU'D GET IN OUR WAY, AND BESIDES, THEY'RE TARGETING STUDENTS.
WE KNOW ABOUT BAKUGO. THERE MIGHT BE OTHERS TOO.
WE'RE OVER-WHELMINGLY SHORT ON INTEL.
IN ORDER TO WIN...
...WE'VE JUST GOTTA MAKE SURE EVERYONE STAYS SAFE.
ZOOM
BACK TO THE PRESENT...

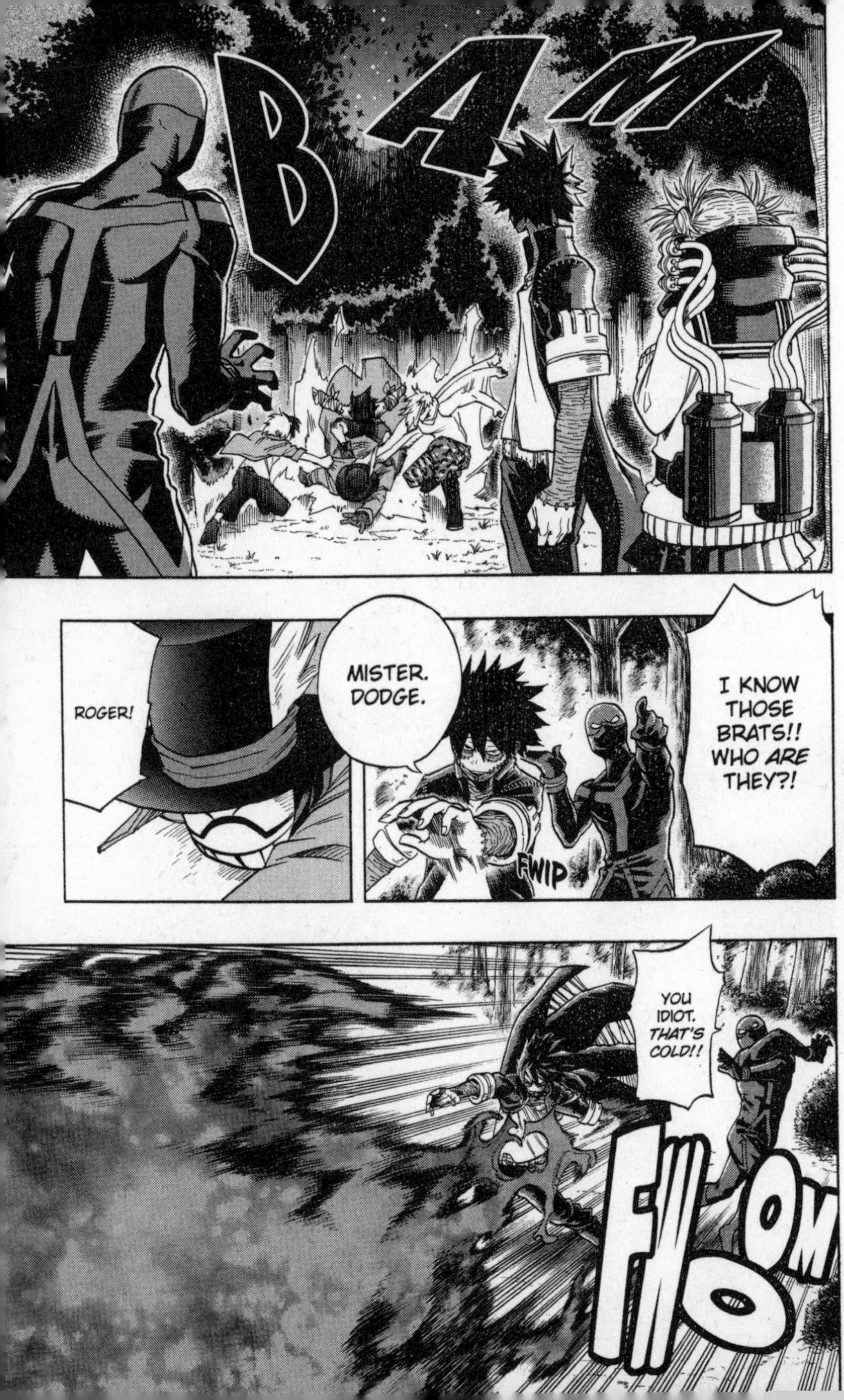
BAM
I KNOW THOSE BRATS!! WHO ARE THEY?!
MISTER. DODGE.
FWIP
ROGER!
YOU IDIOT. THAT'S COLD!!
FWOOM

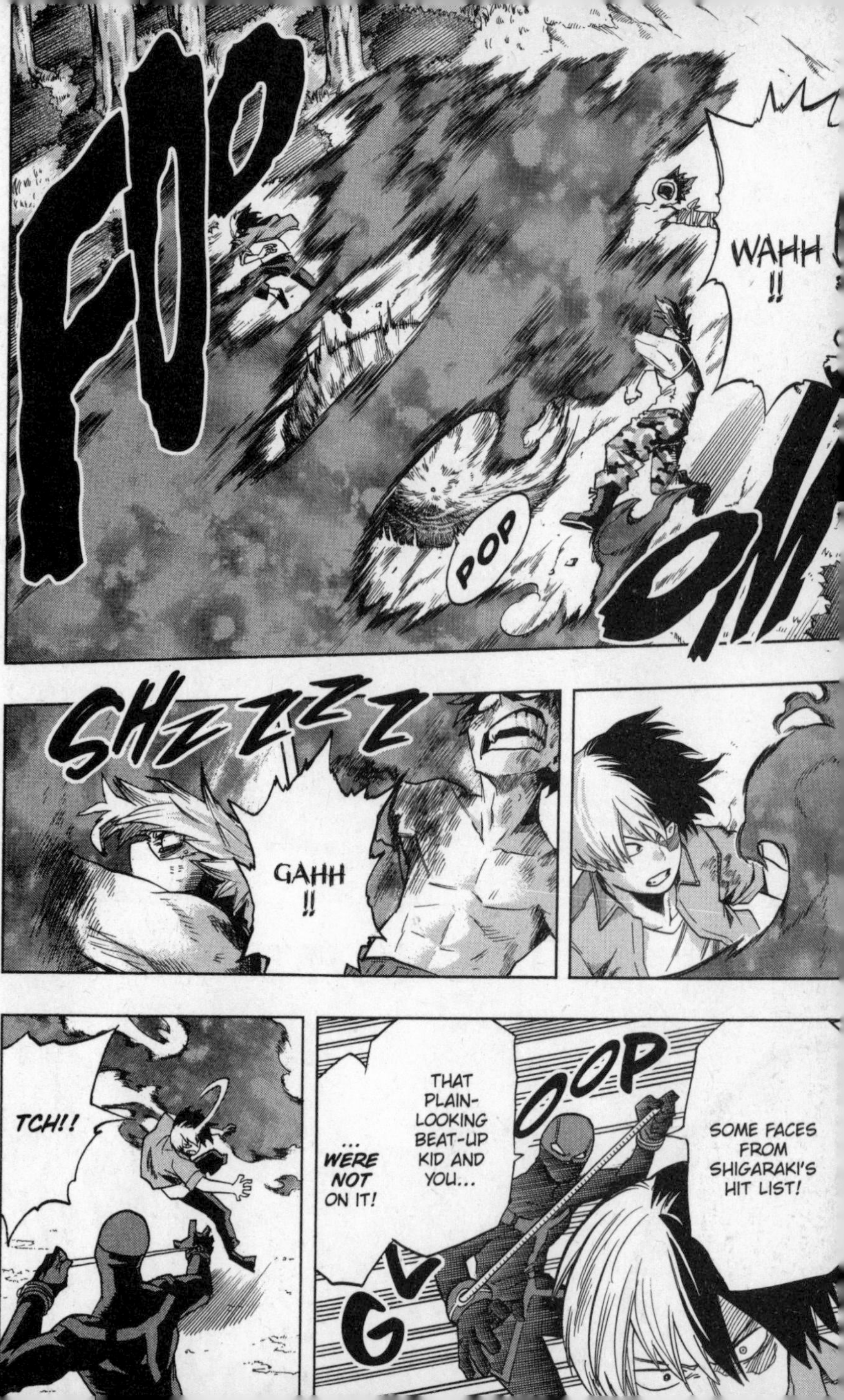
WAHH !!
POP
SHZZZZ
GAHH !!
SOME FACES FROM SHIGARAKI'S HIT LIST!
THAT PLAIN-LOOKING BEAT-UP KID AND YOU...
... WERE NOT ON IT!
TCH!!

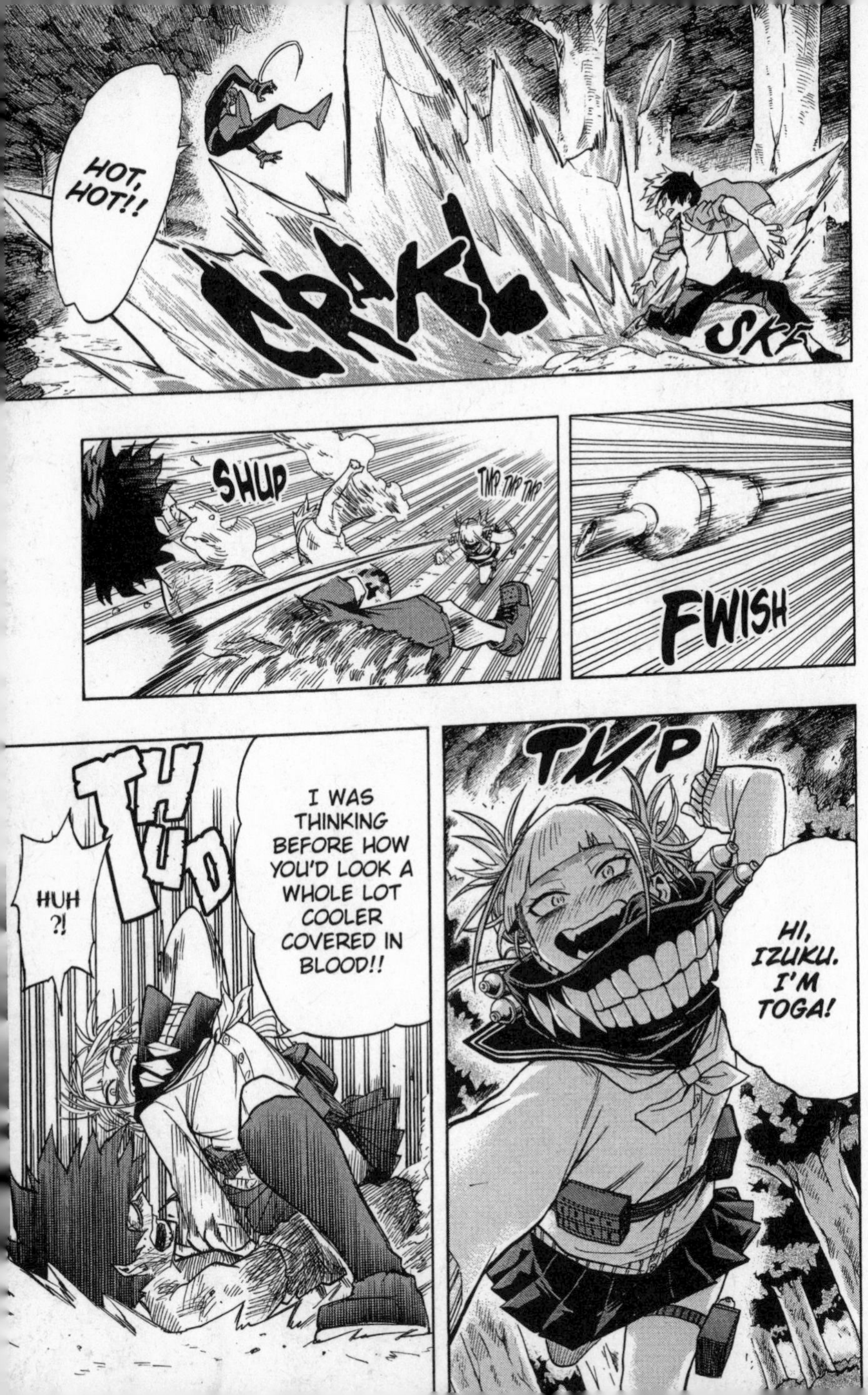
HOT, HOT!!
CRKL
SKF
FWISH
TMP TMP TMP
SHUP
TMP
HI, IZUKU. I'M TOGA!
I WAS THINKING BEFORE HOW YOU'D LOOK A WHOLE LOT COOLER COVERED IN BLOOD!!
THUD
HUH?!

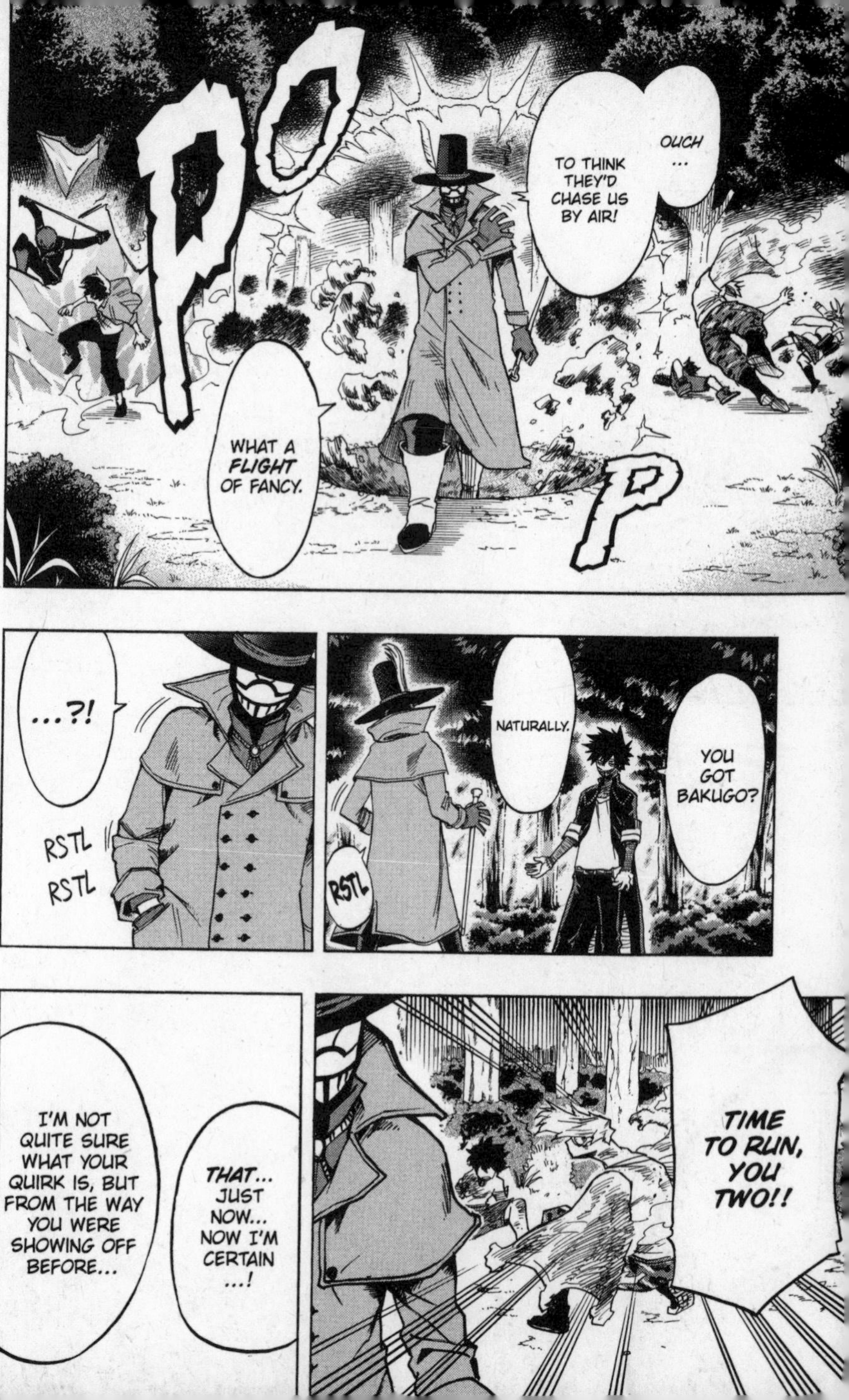
OUCH ...
TO THINK THEY'D CHASE US BY AIR!
POP
WHAT A *FLIGHT* OF FANCY.
YOU GOT BAKUGO?
NATURALLY.
RSTL
...?!
RSTL RSTL
TIME TO RUN, YOU TWO!!
I'M NOT QUITE SURE WHAT YOUR QUIRK IS, BUT FROM THE WAY YOU WERE SHOWING OFF BEFORE...
THAT... JUST NOW... NOW I'M CERTAIN ...!

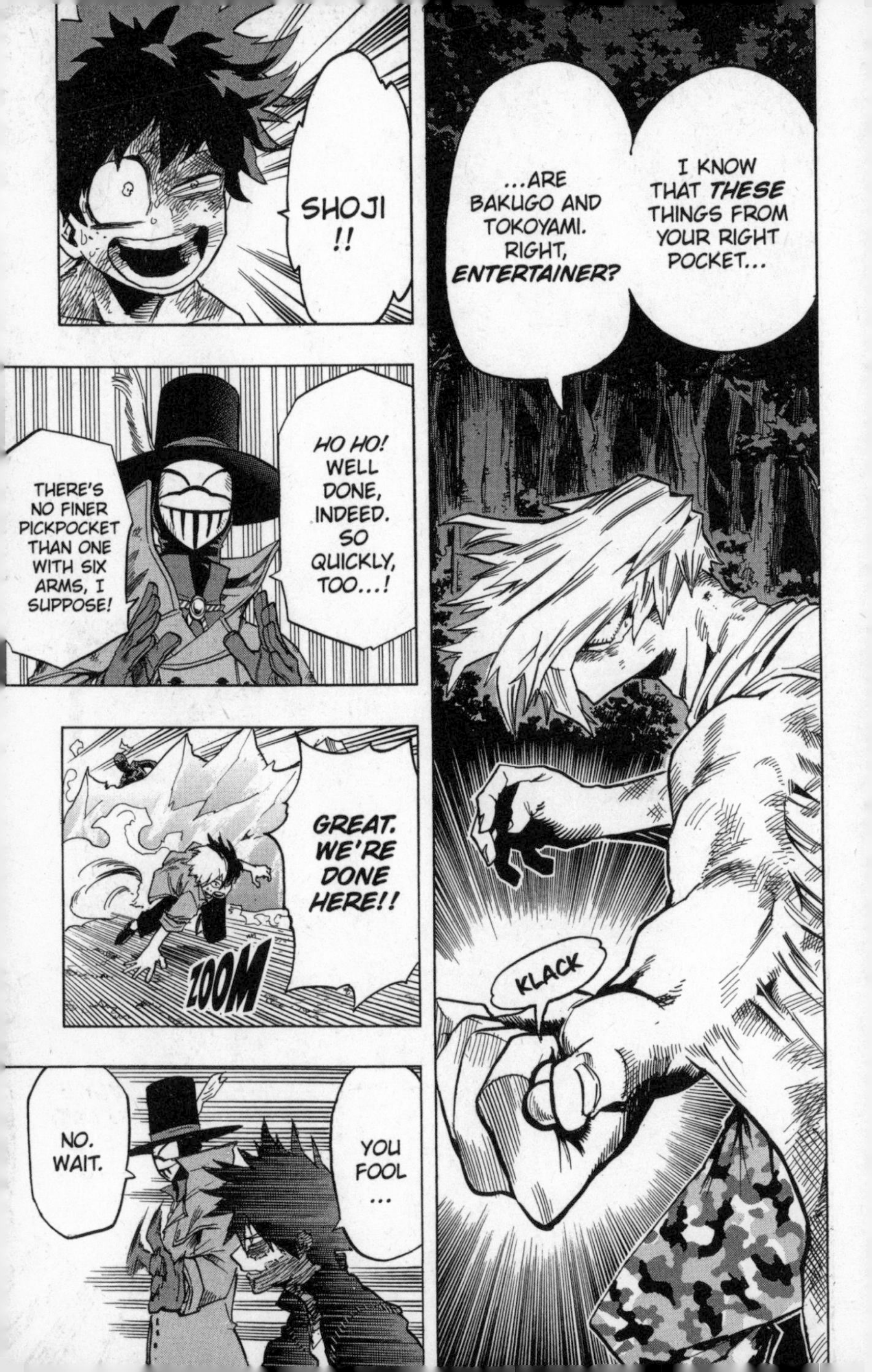
I KNOW THAT THESE THINGS FROM YOUR RIGHT POCKET...
...ARE BAKUGO AND TOKOYAMI. RIGHT, ENTERTAINER?
KLACK
SHOJI!!
HO HO! WELL DONE, INDEED. SO QUICKLY, TOO...!
THERE'S NO FINER PICKPOCKET THAN ONE WITH SIX ARMS, I SUPPOSE!
GREAT. WE'RE DONE HERE!!
ZOOM
YOU FOOL...
NO. WAIT.

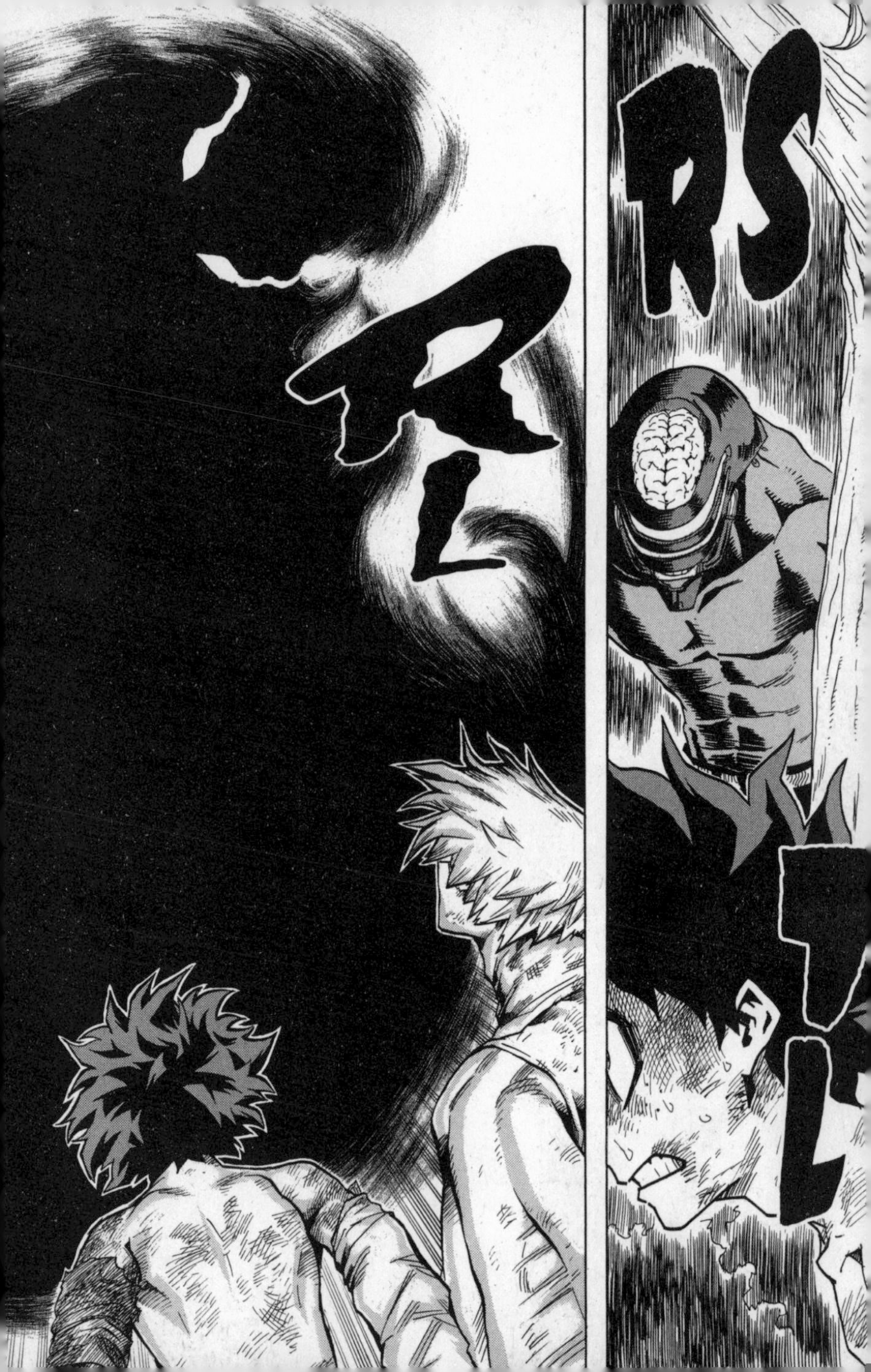

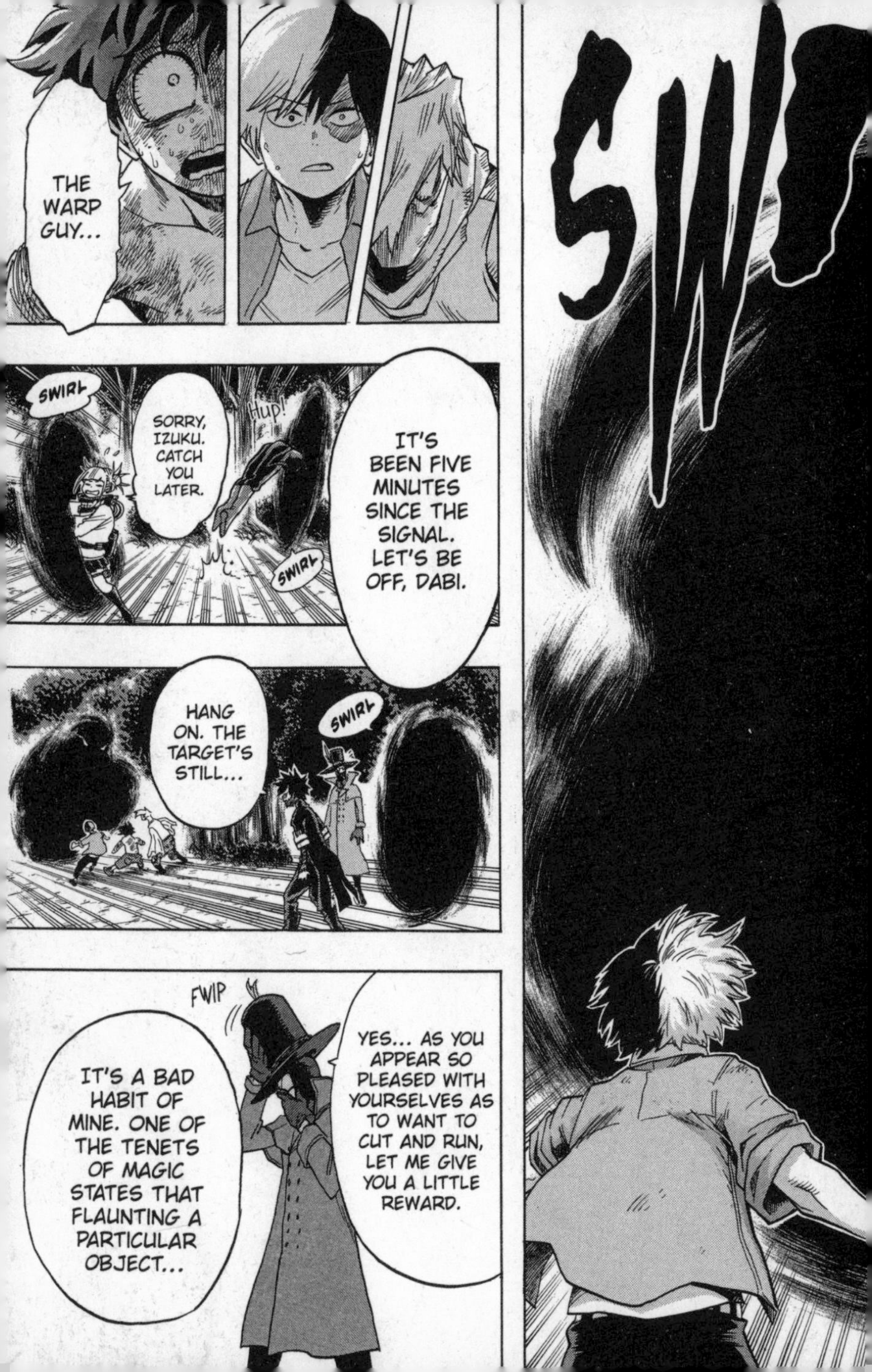
THE WARP GUY...
IT'S BEEN FIVE MINUTES SINCE THE SIGNAL. LET'S BE OFF, DABI.
Hup!
SORRY, IZUKU. CATCH YOU LATER.
SWIRL
SWIRL
SWIRL
HANG ON. THE TARGET'S STILL...
YES... AS YOU APPEAR SO PLEASED WITH YOURSELVES AS TO WANT TO CUT AND RUN, LET ME GIVE YOU A LITTLE REWARD.
FWIP
IT'S A BAD HABIT OF MINE. ONE OF THE TENETS OF MAGIC STATES THAT FLAUNTING A PARTICULAR OBJECT...

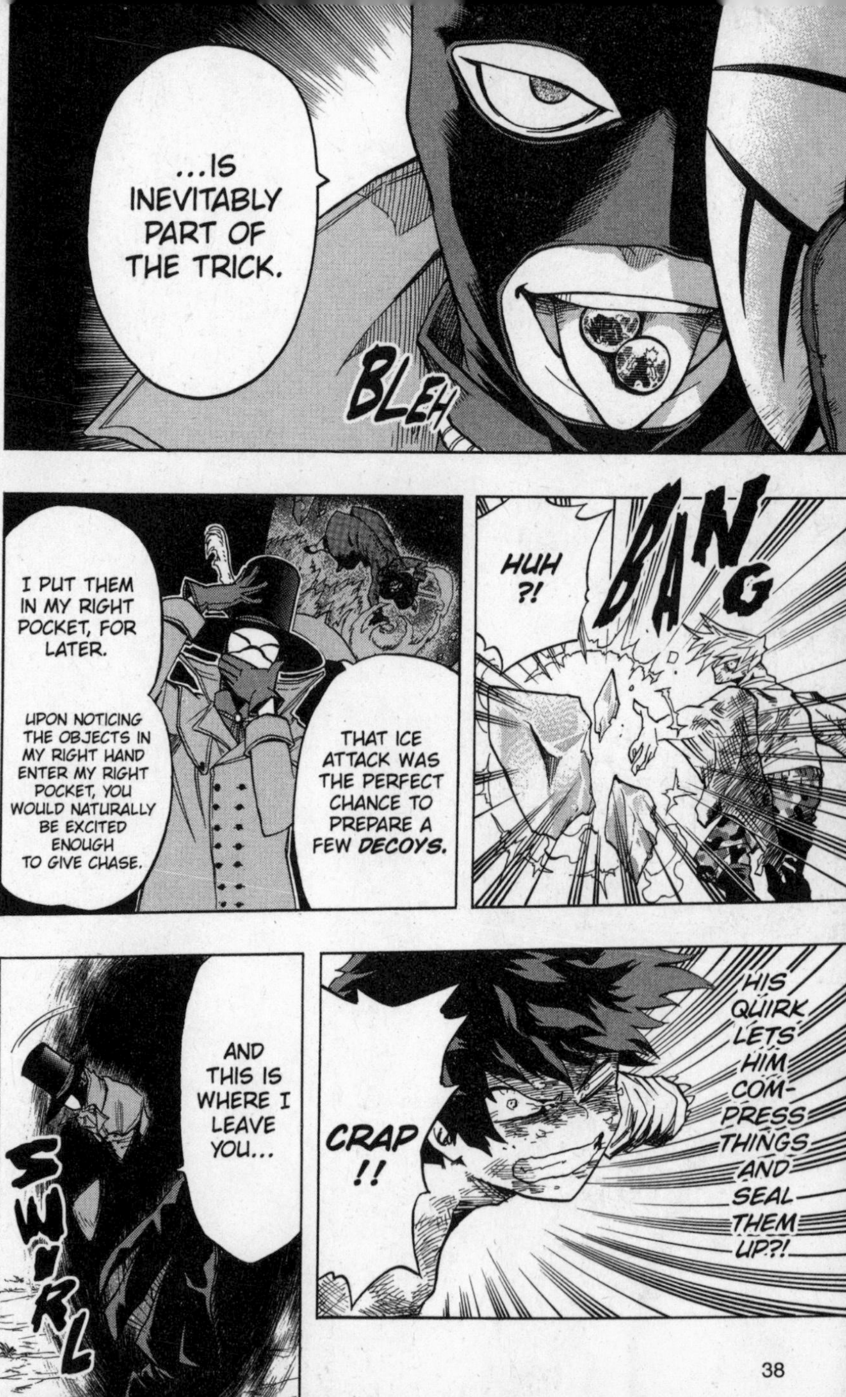
...IS INEVITABLY PART OF THE TRICK.
BLEH
HUH?!
BANG
THAT ICE ATTACK WAS THE PERFECT CHANCE TO PREPARE A FEW *DECOYS*.
I PUT THEM IN MY RIGHT POCKET, FOR LATER.
UPON NOTICING THE OBJECTS IN MY RIGHT HAND ENTER MY RIGHT POCKET, YOU WOULD NATURALLY BE EXCITED ENOUGH TO GIVE CHASE.
HIS QUIRK LETS HIM COM-PRESS THINGS AND SEAL THEM UP?!
CRAP!!
AND THIS IS WHERE I LEAVE YOU...
SWIRL

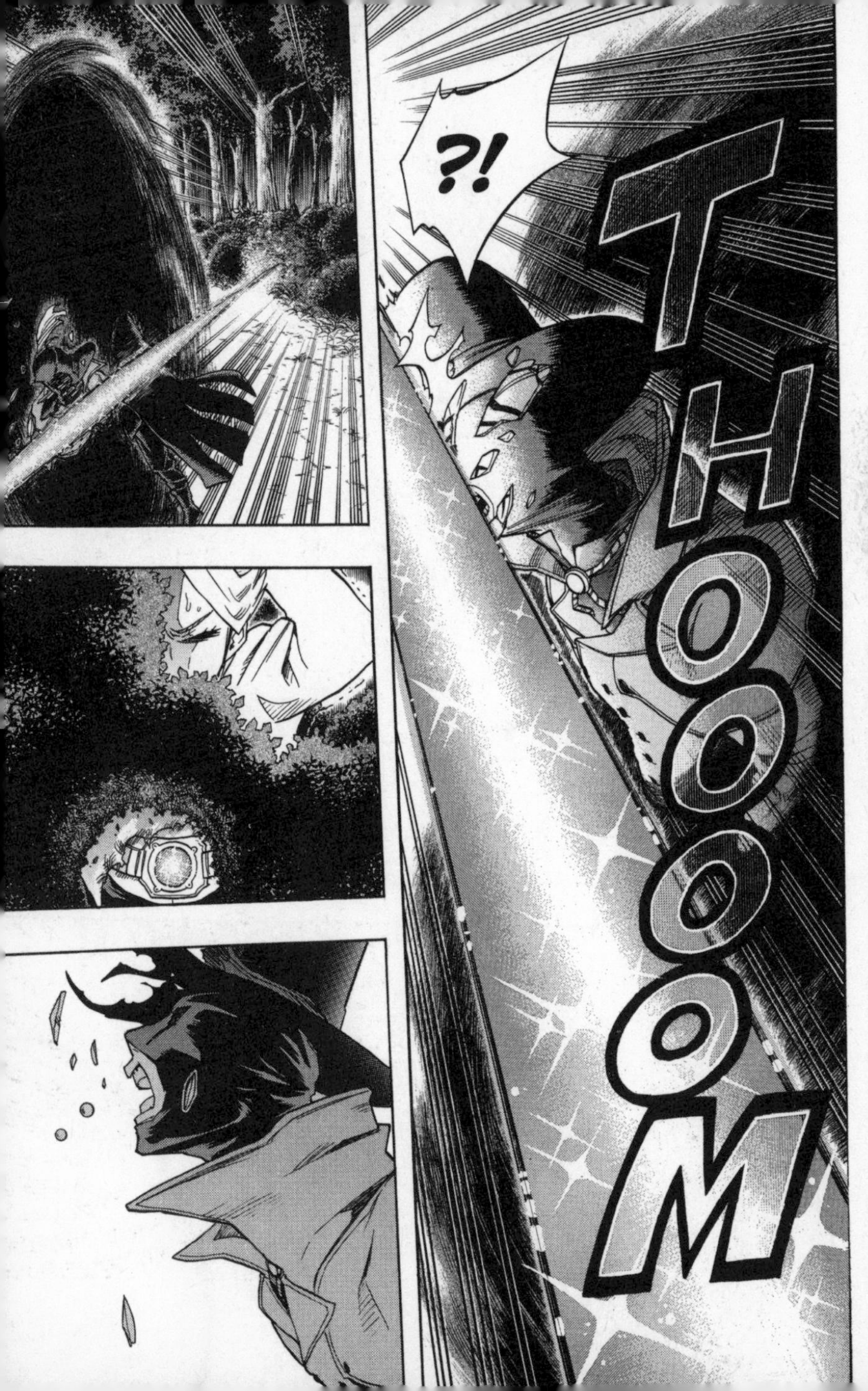
?!
THOOOOM

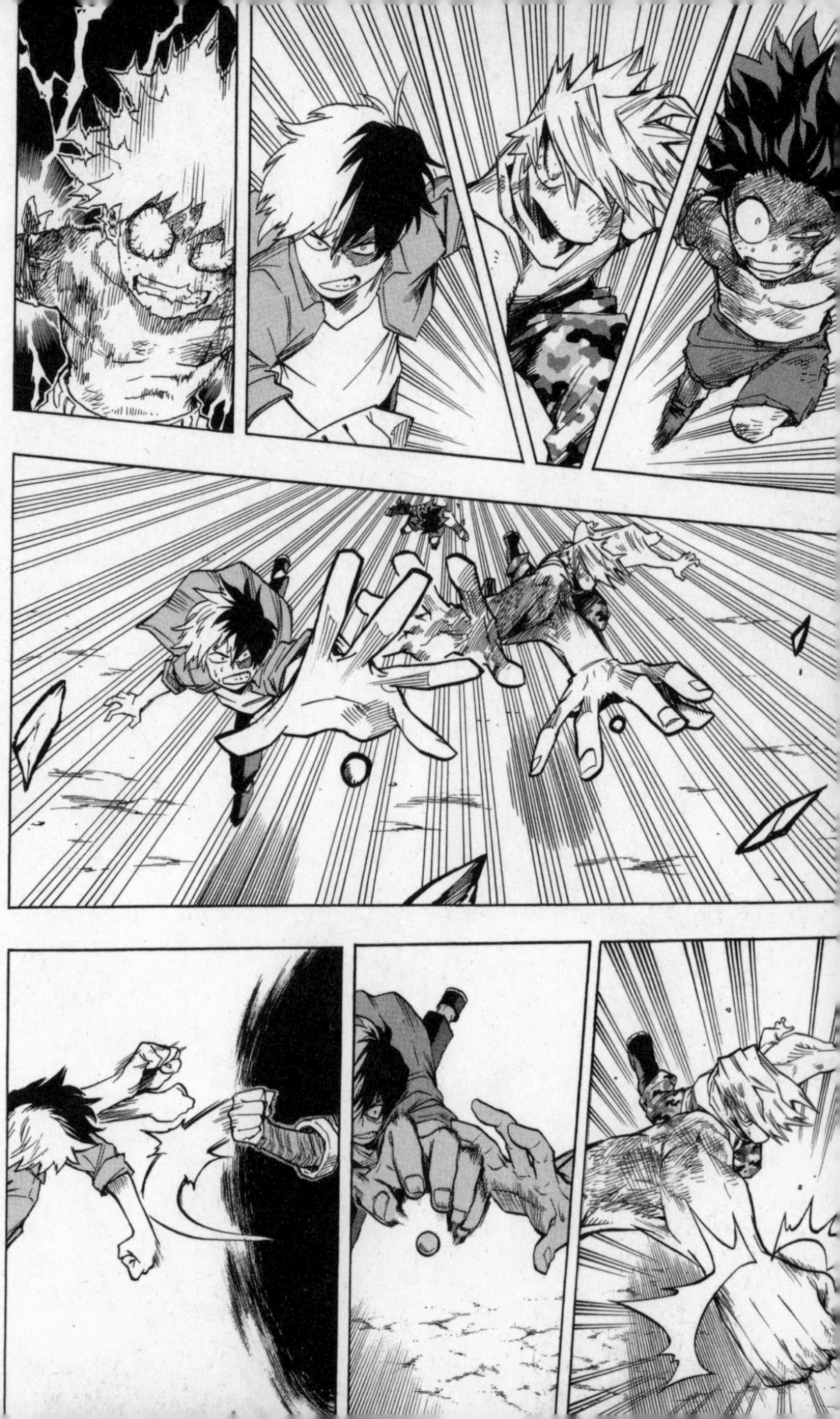

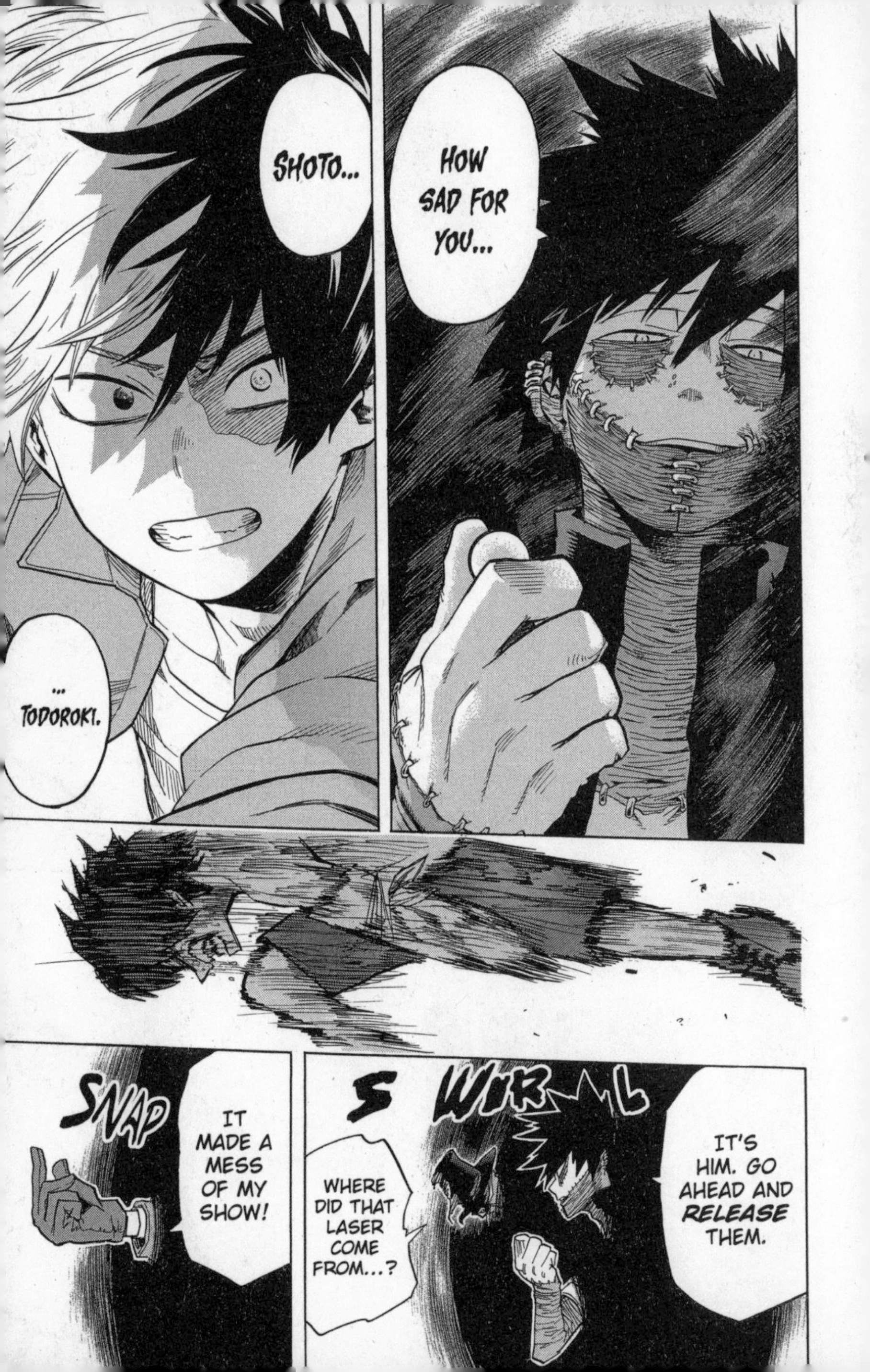
HOW SAD FOR YOU...
SHOTO...
...TODOROKI.
IT'S HIM. GO AHEAD AND RELEASE THEM.
WHERE DID THAT LASER COME FROM...?
SNAP
IT MADE A MESS OF MY SHOW!

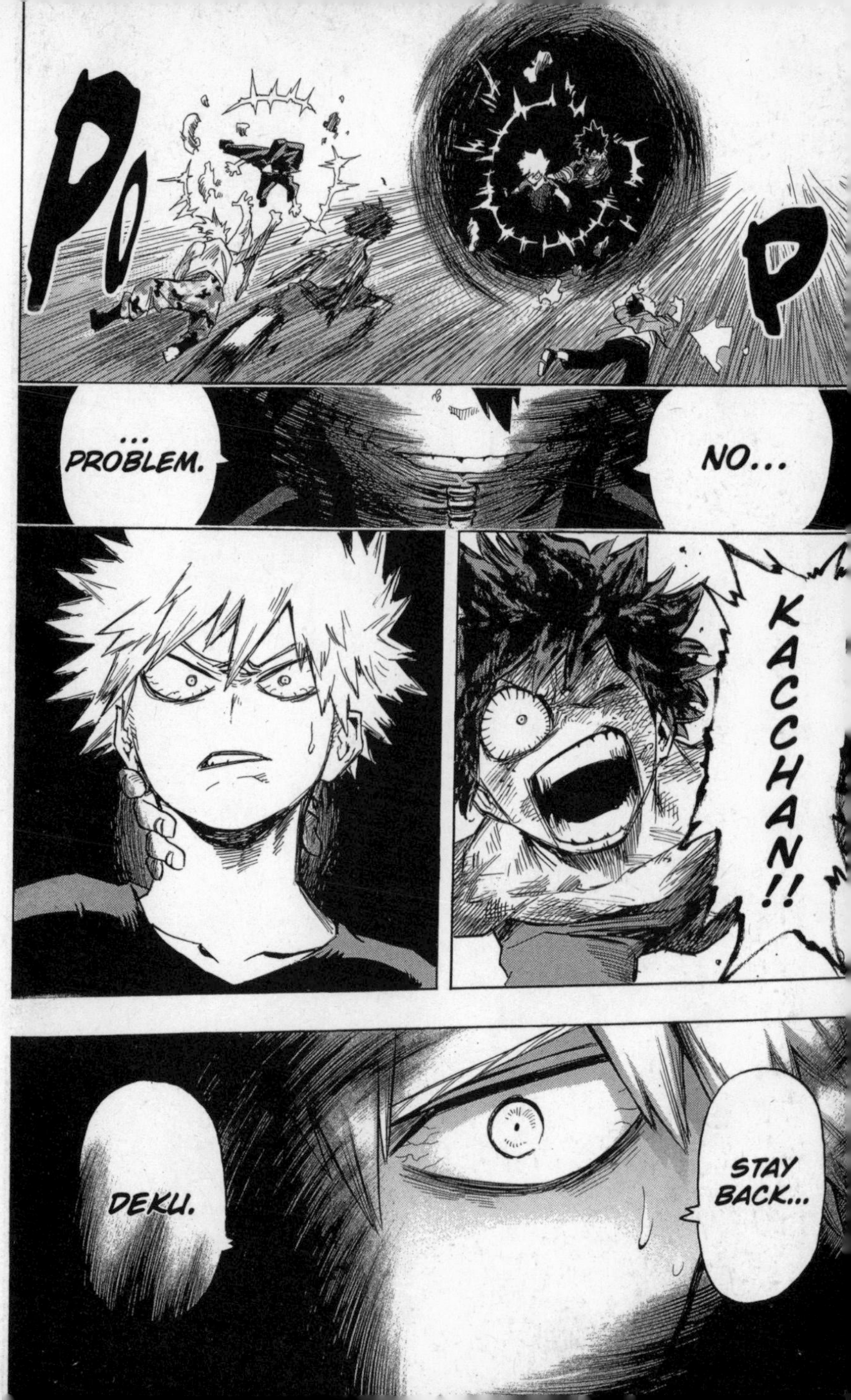
POP
NO...
...PROBLEM.
KACCHAN!!
STAY BACK...
DEKU.

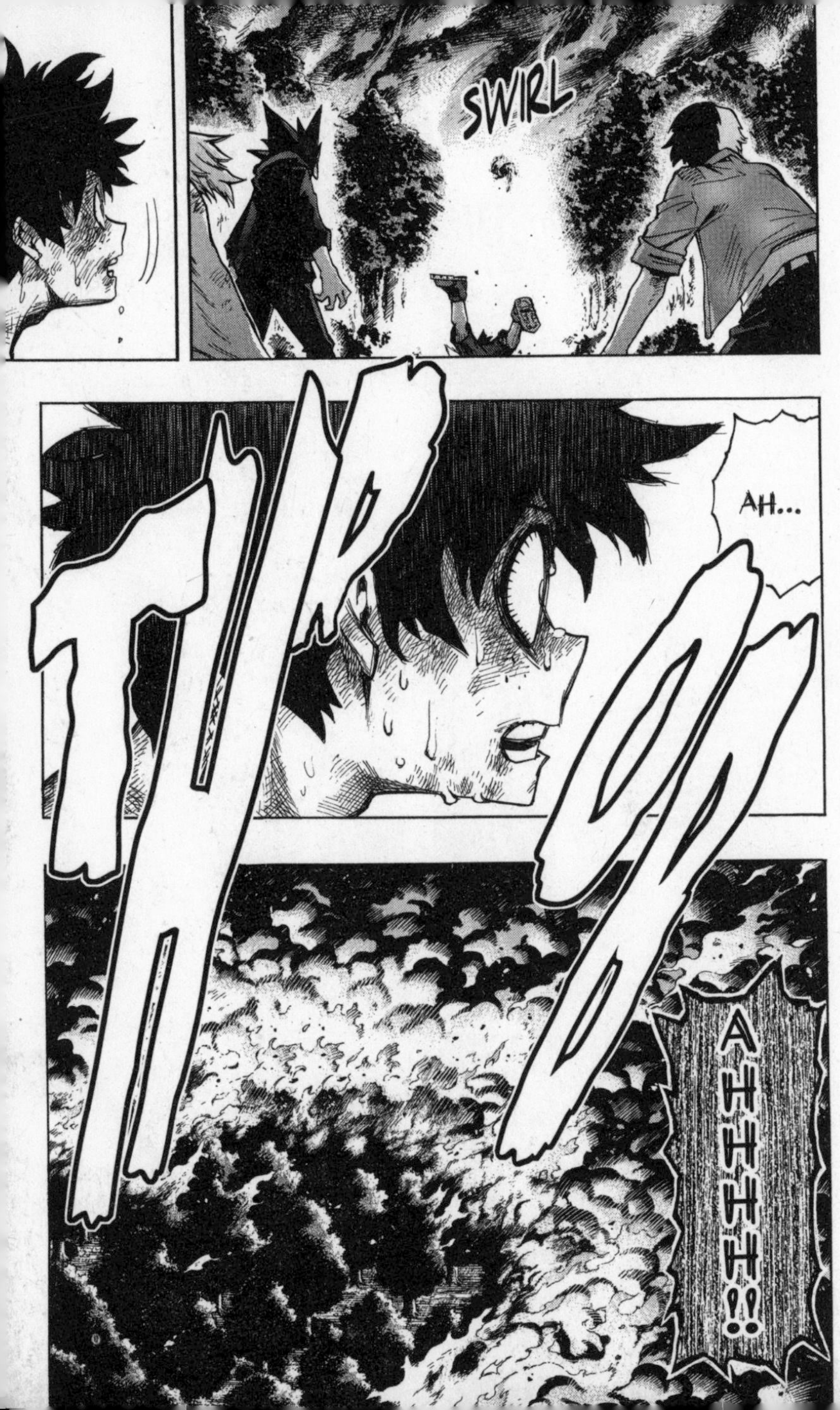
SWIRL
AH...
AHHHHHH!!

HERO

VLAD KING [30]
[SEKIJIRO KAN]

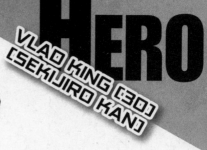

STREET CLOTHES

Birthday: 11/10
Height: 194 cm
Favorite Things: Tomatoes, cheese

BEHIND THE SCENES

Class B's homeroom teacher.

Unlike Aizawa, he actually gets along with his students.

He's got a dog.

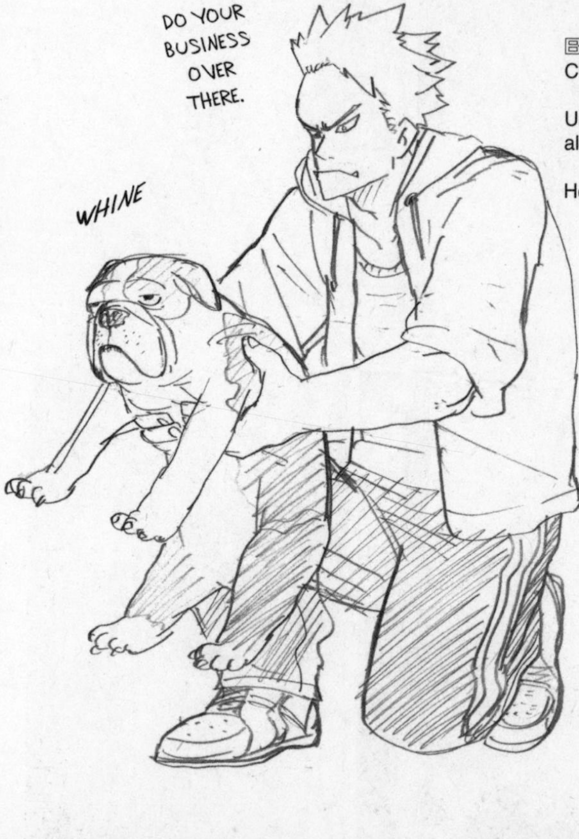

DO YOUR BUSINESS OVER THERE.
WHINE

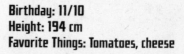

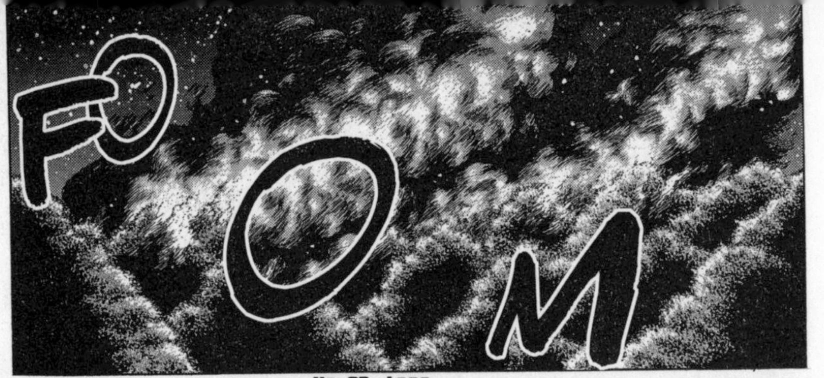
FOOM

No. 83 - Loss

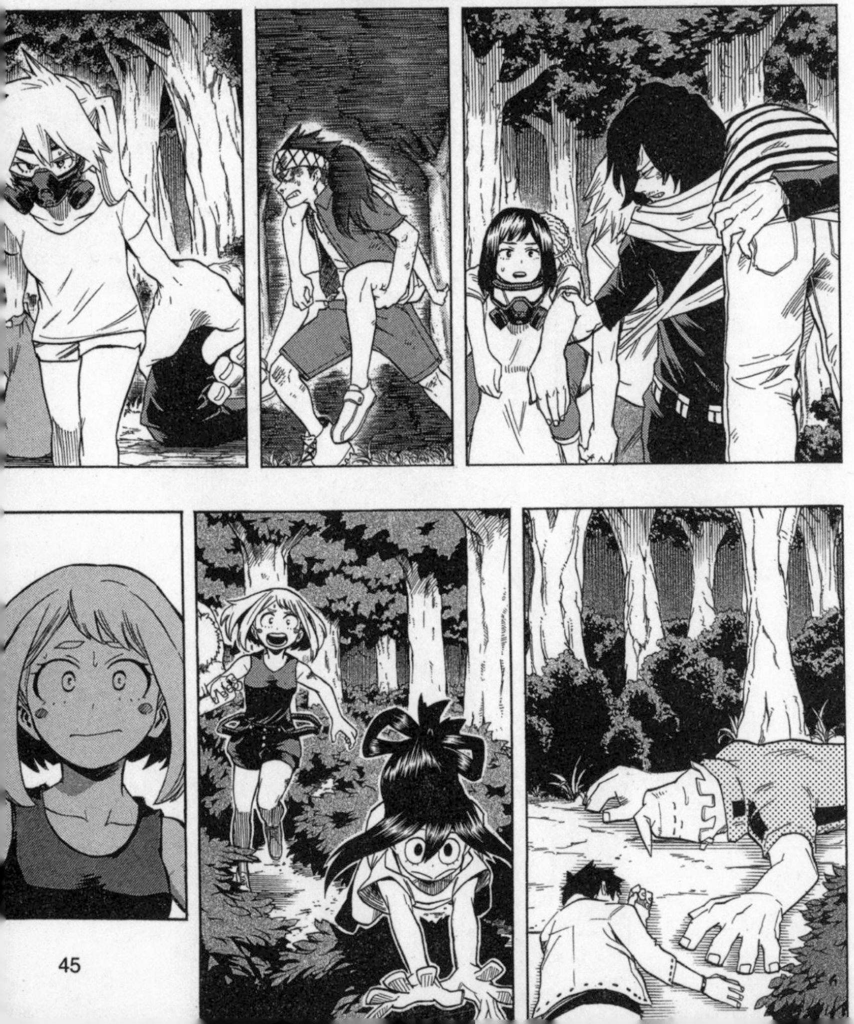

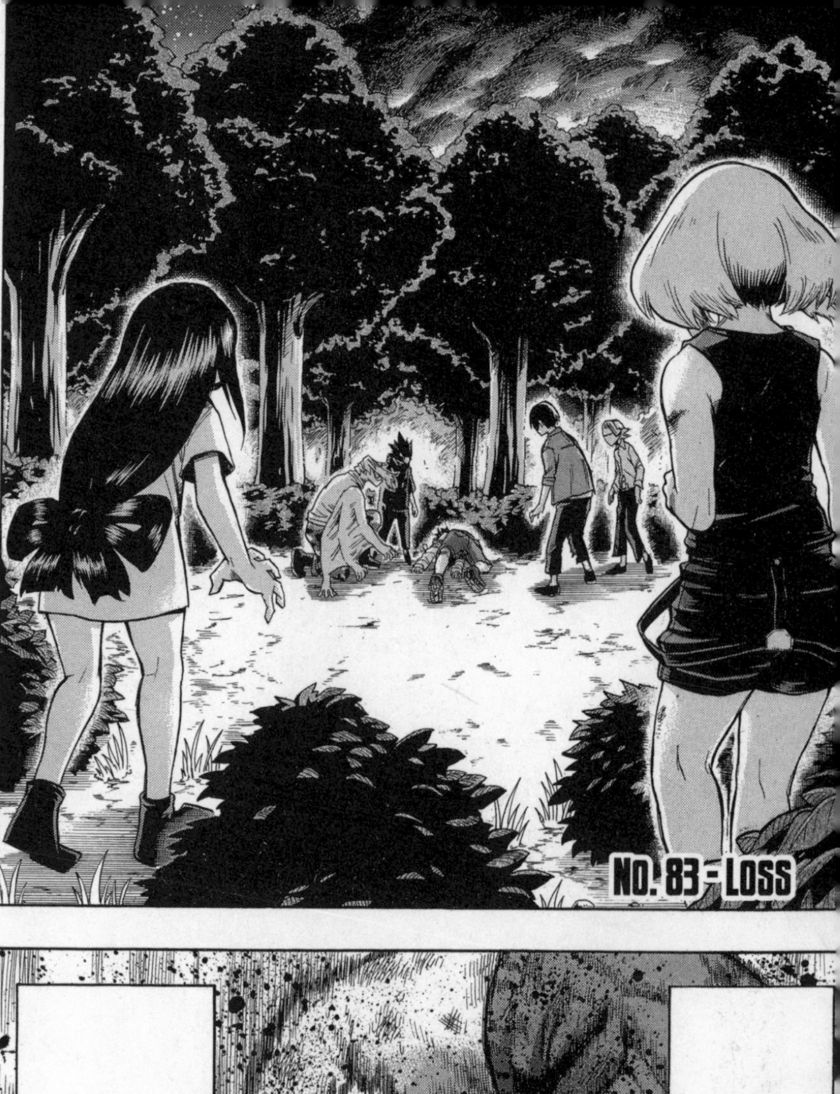
NO. 83 - LOSS

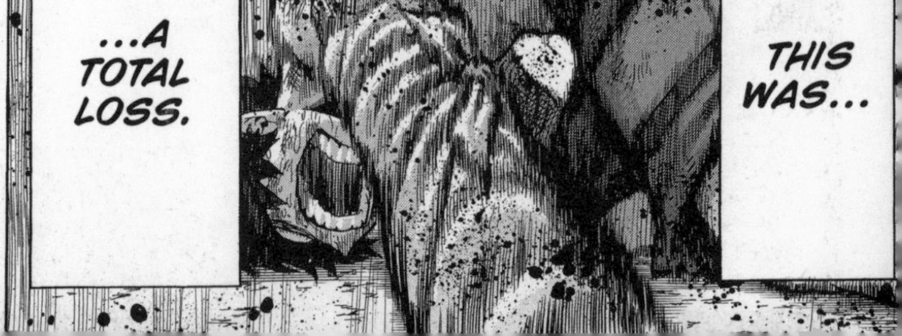
THIS WAS...
...A TOTAL LOSS.

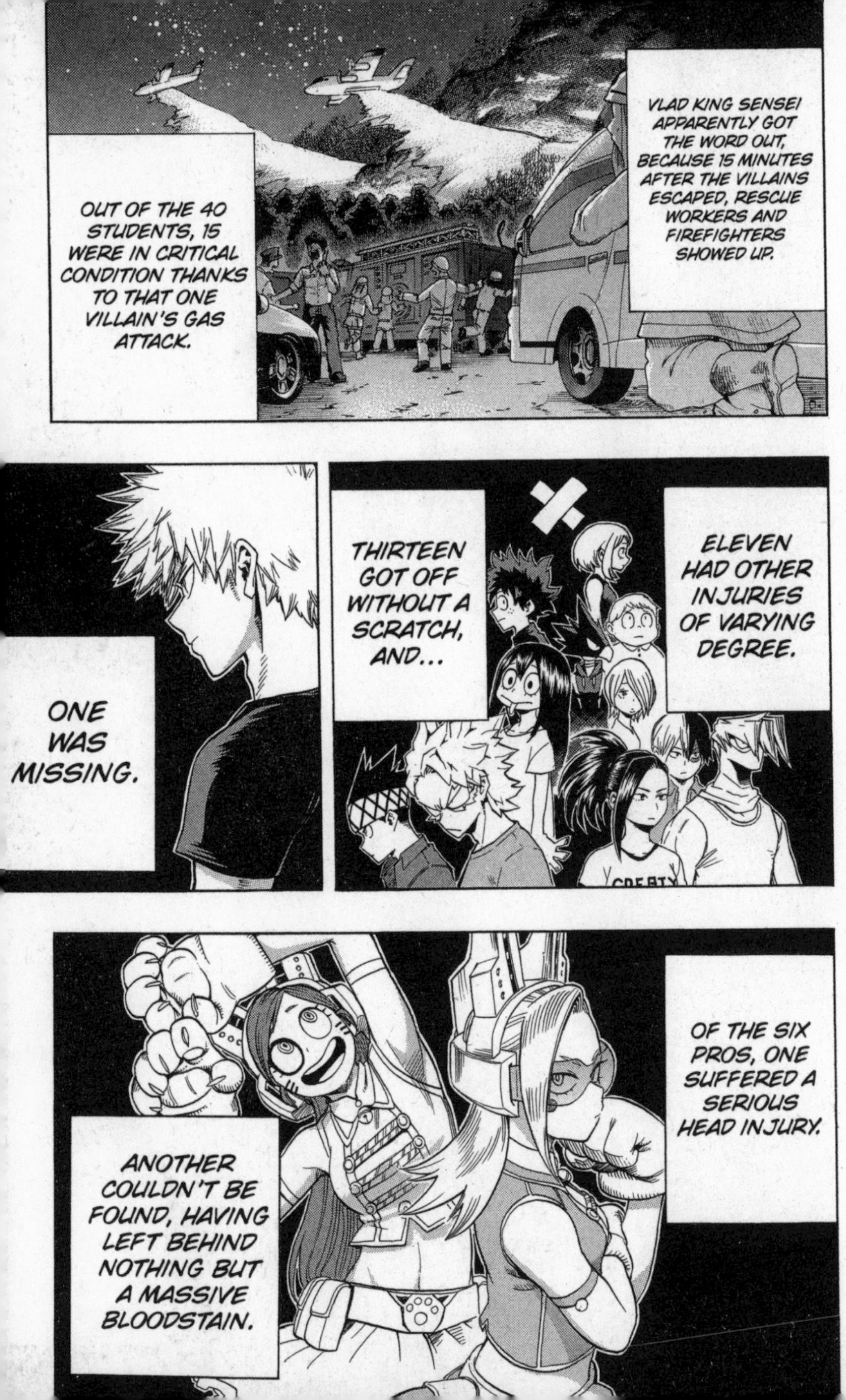
VLAD KING SENSEI APPARENTLY GOT THE WORD OUT, BECAUSE 15 MINUTES AFTER THE VILLAINS ESCAPED, RESCUE WORKERS AND FIREFIGHTERS SHOWED UP.
OUT OF THE 40 STUDENTS, 15 WERE IN CRITICAL CONDITION THANKS TO THAT ONE VILLAIN'S GAS ATTACK.
ELEVEN HAD OTHER INJURIES OF VARYING DEGREE.
THIRTEEN GOT OFF WITHOUT A SCRATCH, AND...
ONE WAS MISSING.
OF THE SIX PROS, ONE SUFFERED A SERIOUS HEAD INJURY.
ANOTHER COULDN'T BE FOUND, HAVING LEFT BEHIND NOTHING BUT A MASSIVE BLOODSTAIN.

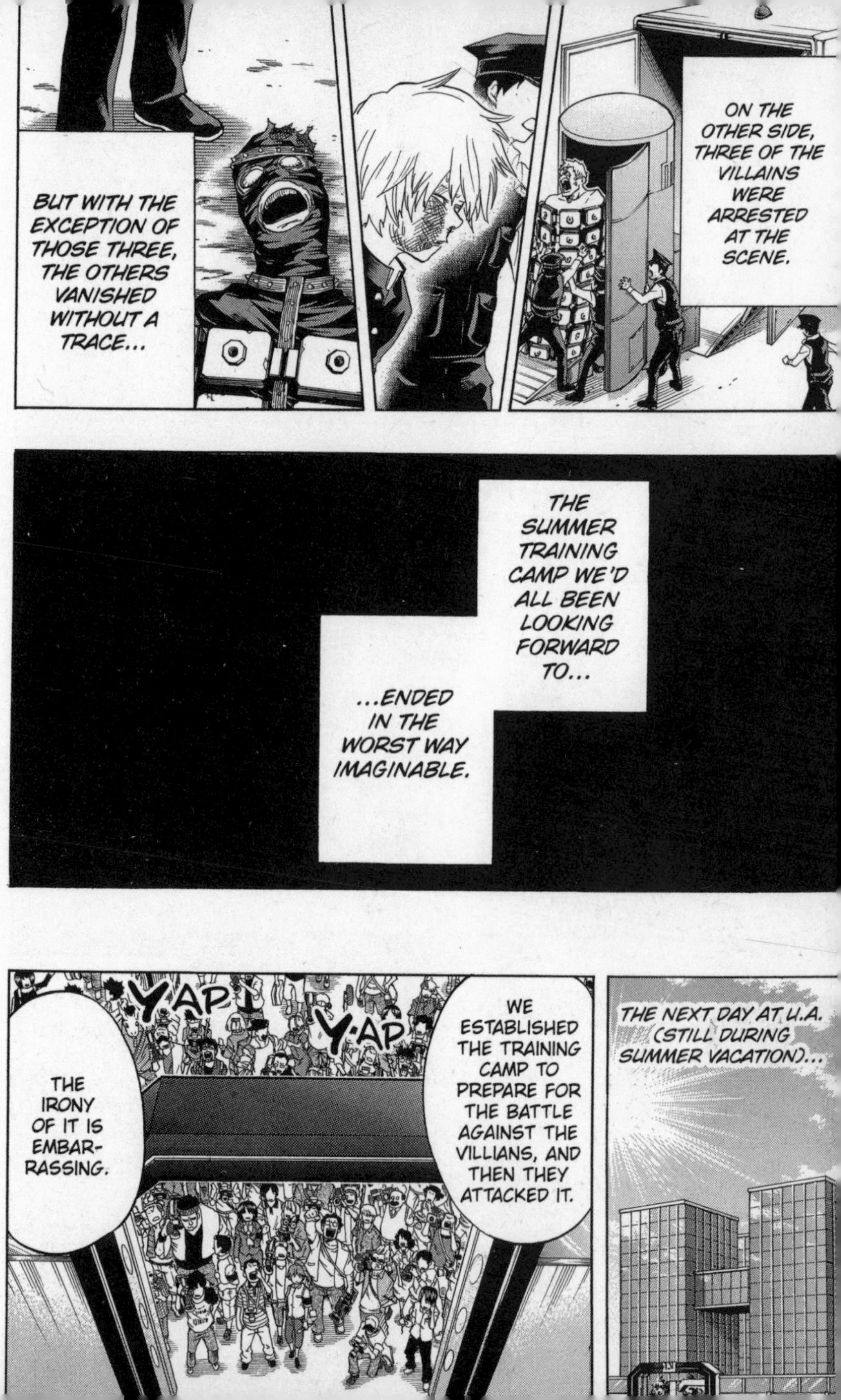
ON THE OTHER SIDE, THREE OF THE VILLAINS WERE ARRESTED AT THE SCENE.
BUT WITH THE EXCEPTION OF THOSE THREE, THE OTHERS VANISHED WITHOUT A TRACE...
THE SUMMER TRAINING CAMP WE'D ALL BEEN LOOKING FORWARD TO...
...ENDED IN THE WORST WAY IMAGINABLE.
THE NEXT DAY AT U.A. (STILL DURING SUMMER VACATION)...
Y-AP
WE ESTABLISHED THE TRAINING CAMP TO PREPARE FOR THE BATTLE AGAINST THE VILLIANS, AND THEN THEY ATTACKED IT.
YAP
THE IRONY OF IT IS EMBAR-RASSING.

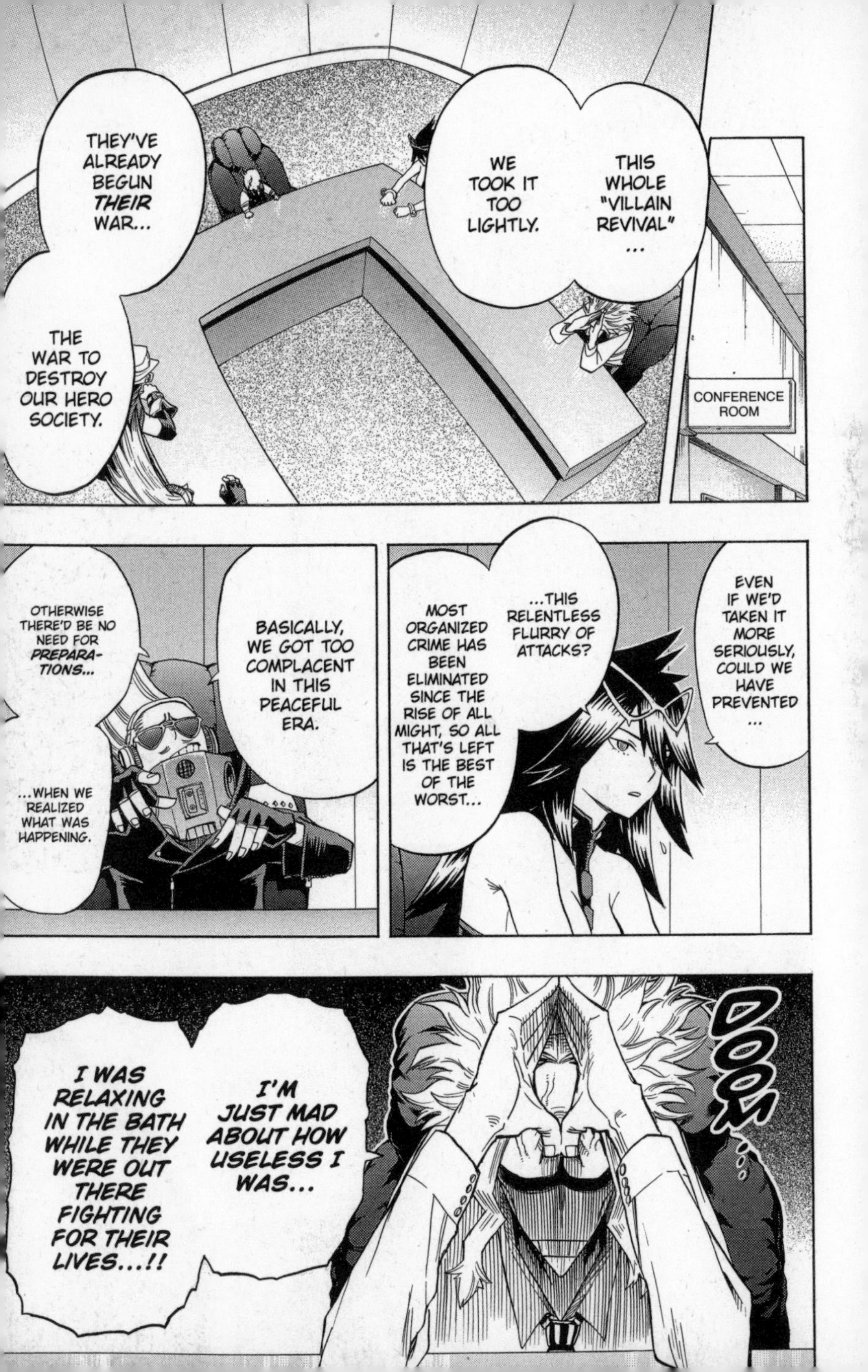
CONFERENCE ROOM
THIS WHOLE "VILLAIN REVIVAL"...
WE TOOK IT TOO LIGHTLY.
THEY'VE ALREADY BEGUN *THEIR* WAR...
THE WAR TO DESTROY OUR HERO SOCIETY.
EVEN IF WE'D TAKEN IT MORE SERIOUSLY, COULD WE HAVE PREVENTED...
...THIS RELENTLESS FLURRY OF ATTACKS?
MOST ORGANIZED CRIME HAS BEEN ELIMINATED SINCE THE RISE OF ALL MIGHT, SO ALL THAT'S LEFT IS THE BEST OF THE WORST...
BASICALLY, WE GOT TOO COMPLACENT IN THIS PEACEFUL ERA.
OTHERWISE THERE'D BE NO NEED FOR *PREPARATIONS*...
...WHEN WE REALIZED WHAT WAS HAPPENING.
DOOM...
I'M JUST MAD ABOUT HOW USELESS I WAS...
I WAS RELAXING IN THE BATH WHILE THEY WERE OUT THERE FIGHTING FOR THEIR LIVES...!!

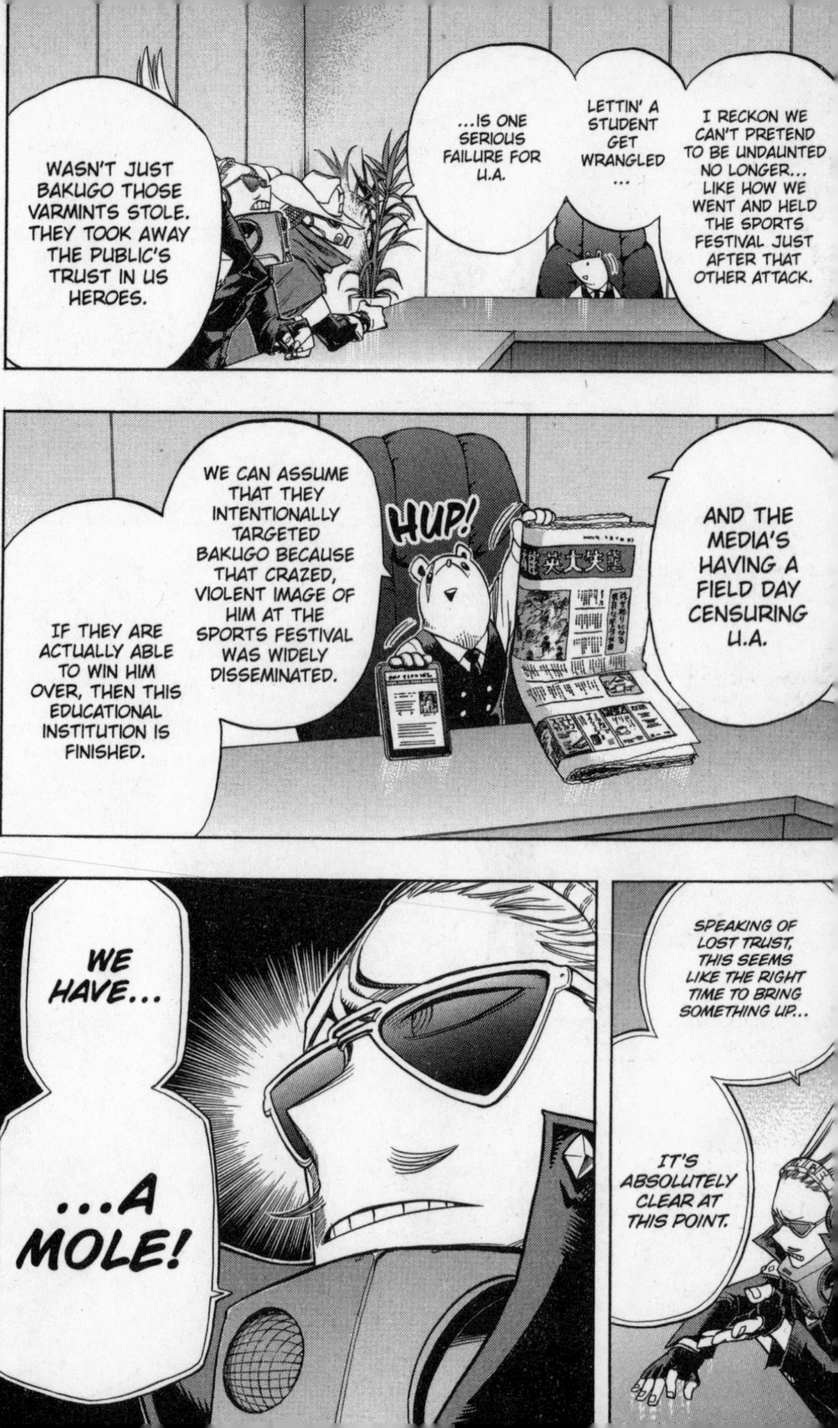
I RECKON WE CAN'T PRETEND TO BE UNDAUNTED NO LONGER... LIKE HOW WE WENT AND HELD THE SPORTS FESTIVAL JUST AFTER THAT OTHER ATTACK.
LETTIN' A STUDENT GET WRANGLED...
...IS ONE SERIOUS FAILURE FOR U.A.
WASN'T JUST BAKUGO THOSE VARMINTS STOLE. THEY TOOK AWAY THE PUBLIC'S TRUST IN US HEROES.
AND THE MEDIA'S HAVING A FIELD DAY CENSURING U.A.
HUP!
WE CAN ASSUME THAT THEY INTENTIONALLY TARGETED BAKUGO BECAUSE THAT CRAZED, VIOLENT IMAGE OF HIM AT THE SPORTS FESTIVAL WAS WIDELY DISSEMINATED.
IF THEY ARE ACTUALLY ABLE TO WIN HIM OVER, THEN THIS EDUCATIONAL INSTITUTION IS FINISHED.
SPEAKING OF LOST TRUST, THIS SEEMS LIKE THE RIGHT TIME TO BRING SOMETHING UP...
IT'S ABSOLUTELY CLEAR AT THIS POINT.
WE HAVE...
...A MOLE!

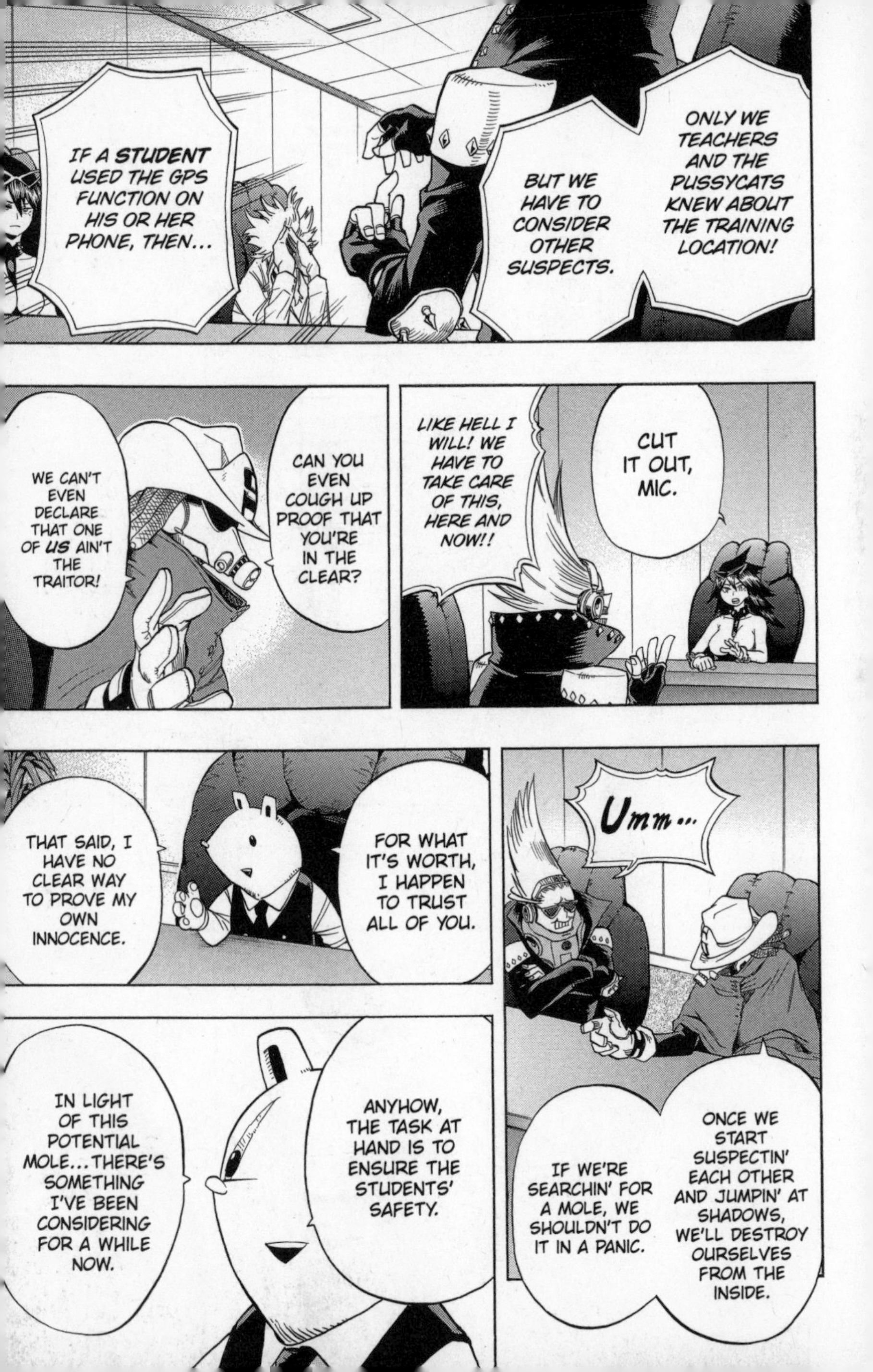
ONLY WE TEACHERS AND THE PUSSYCATS KNEW ABOUT THE TRAINING LOCATION!
BUT WE HAVE TO CONSIDER OTHER SUSPECTS.
IF A STUDENT USED THE GPS FUNCTION ON HIS OR HER PHONE, THEN...
CUT IT OUT, MIC.
LIKE HELL I WILL! WE HAVE TO TAKE CARE OF THIS, HERE AND NOW!!
CAN YOU EVEN COUGH UP PROOF THAT YOU'RE IN THE CLEAR?
WE CAN'T EVEN DECLARE THAT ONE OF US AIN'T THE TRAITOR!
Umm...
ONCE WE START SUSPECTIN' EACH OTHER AND JUMPIN' AT SHADOWS, WE'LL DESTROY OURSELVES FROM THE INSIDE.
IF WE'RE SEARCHIN' FOR A MOLE, WE SHOULDN'T DO IT IN A PANIC.
FOR WHAT IT'S WORTH, I HAPPEN TO TRUST ALL OF YOU.
THAT SAID, I HAVE NO CLEAR WAY TO PROVE MY OWN INNOCENCE.
ANYHOW, THE TASK AT HAND IS TO ENSURE THE STUDENTS' SAFETY.
IN LIGHT OF THIS POTENTIAL MOLE...THERE'S SOMETHING I'VE BEEN CONSIDERING FOR A WHILE NOW.

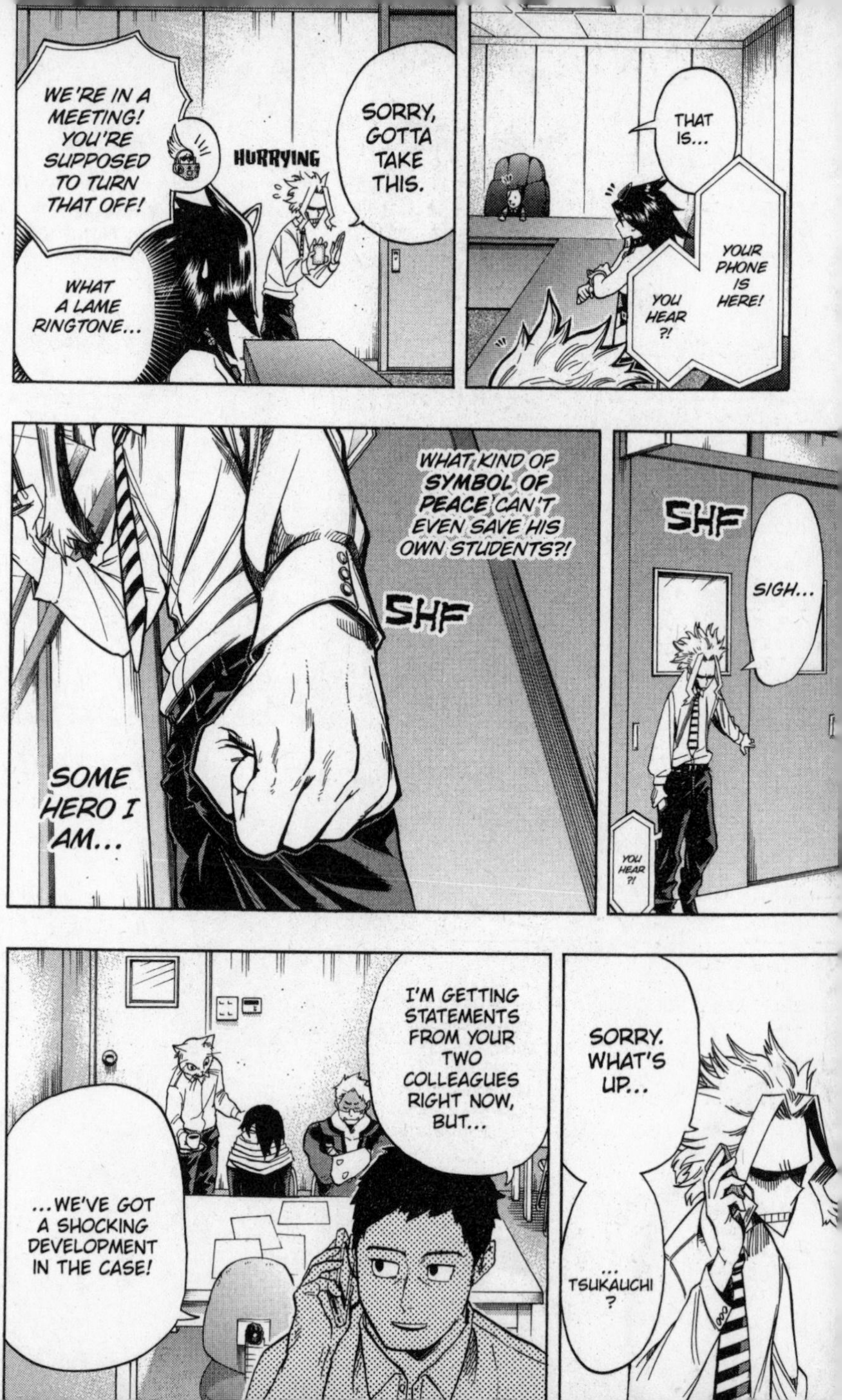
THAT IS...
YOUR PHONE IS HERE!
YOU HEAR ?!
SORRY, GOTTA TAKE THIS.
HURRYING
WE'RE IN A MEETING! YOU'RE SUPPOSED TO TURN THAT OFF!
WHAT A LAME RINGTONE...
SHF
SIGH...
YOU HEAR ?!
WHAT KIND OF SYMBOL OF PEACE CAN'T EVEN SAVE HIS OWN STUDENTS?!
SHF
SOME HERO I AM...
SORRY. WHAT'S UP...
...TSUKAUCHI?
I'M GETTING STATEMENTS FROM YOUR TWO COLLEAGUES RIGHT NOW, BUT...
...WE'VE GOT A SHOCKING DEVELOPMENT IN THE CASE!

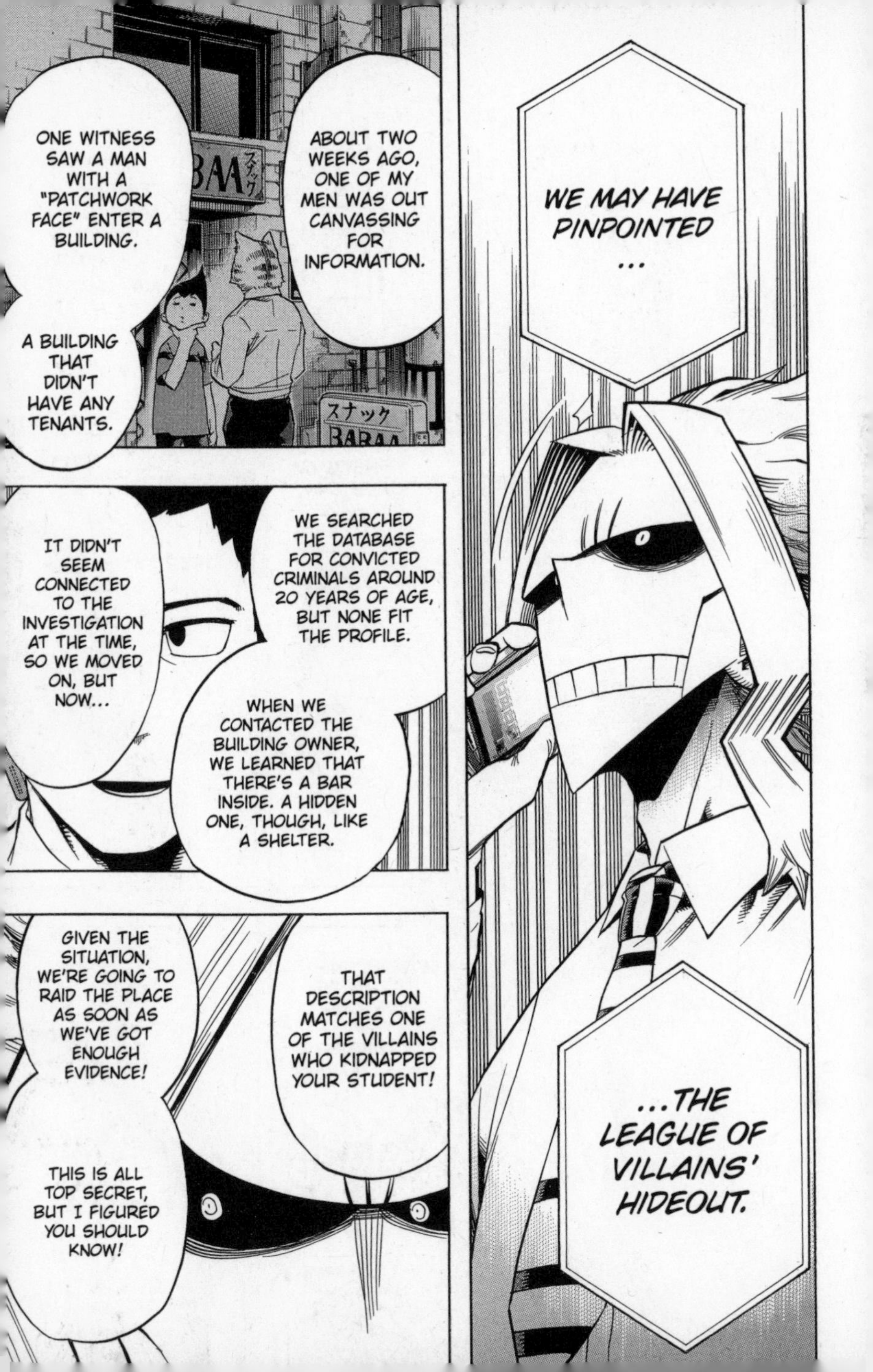
WE MAY HAVE PINPOINTED ...
...THE LEAGUE OF VILLAINS' HIDEOUT.
ABOUT TWO WEEKS AGO, ONE OF MY MEN WAS OUT CANVASSING FOR INFORMATION.
ONE WITNESS SAW A MAN WITH A "PATCHWORK FACE" ENTER A BUILDING.
A BUILDING THAT DIDN'T HAVE ANY TENANTS.
スナック
WE SEARCHED THE DATABASE FOR CONVICTED CRIMINALS AROUND 20 YEARS OF AGE, BUT NONE FIT THE PROFILE.
IT DIDN'T SEEM CONNECTED TO THE INVESTIGATION AT THE TIME, SO WE MOVED ON, BUT NOW...
WHEN WE CONTACTED THE BUILDING OWNER, WE LEARNED THAT THERE'S A BAR INSIDE. A HIDDEN ONE, THOUGH, LIKE A SHELTER.
THAT DESCRIPTION MATCHES ONE OF THE VILLAINS WHO KIDNAPPED YOUR STUDENT!
GIVEN THE SITUATION, WE'RE GOING TO RAID THE PLACE AS SOON AS WE'VE GOT ENOUGH EVIDENCE!
THIS IS ALL TOP SECRET, BUT I FIGURED YOU SHOULD KNOW!

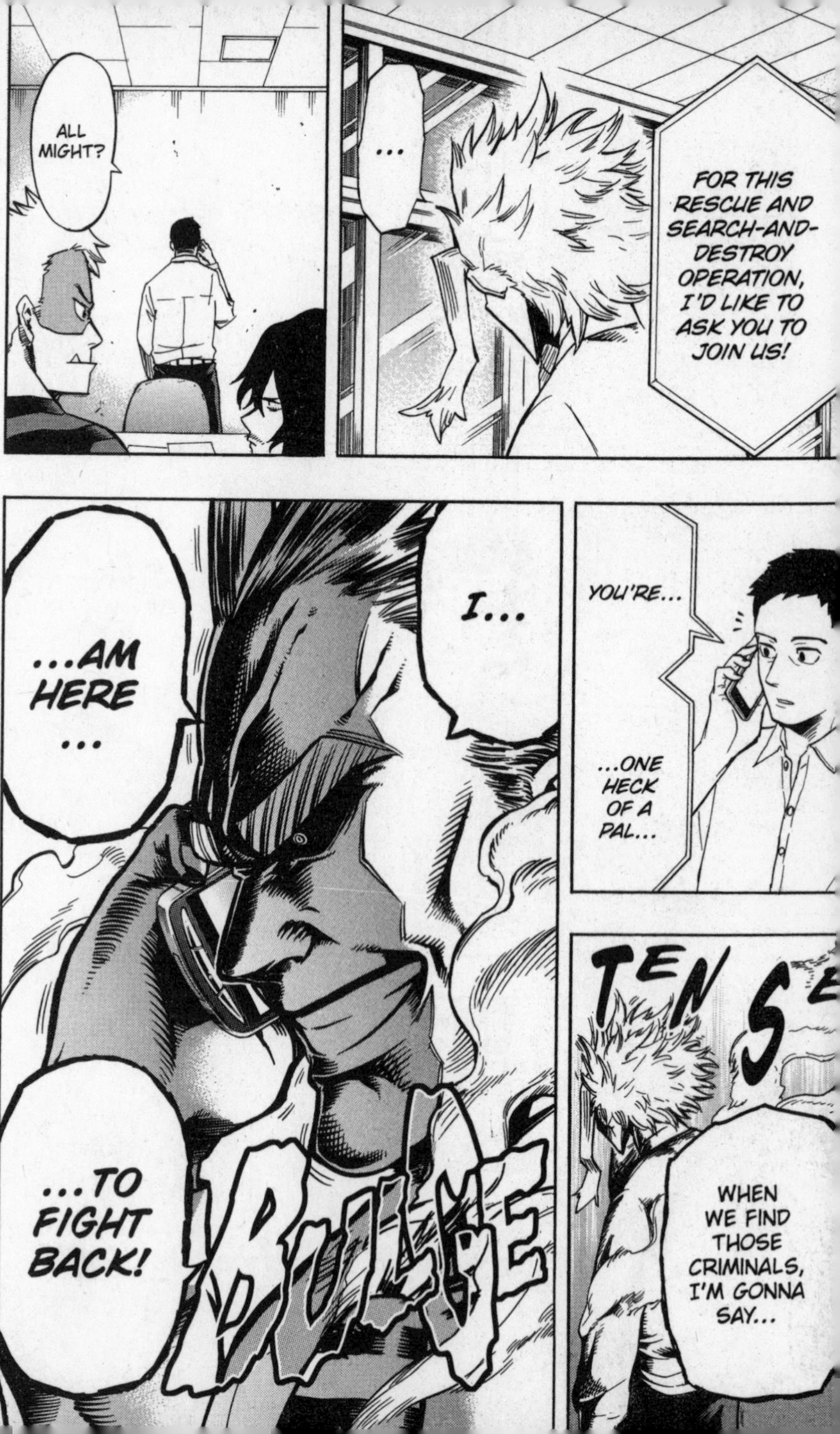
FOR THIS RESCUE AND SEARCH-AND-DESTROY OPERATION, I'D LIKE TO ASK YOU TO JOIN US!
...
ALL MIGHT?
YOU'RE...
...ONE HECK OF A PAL...
TENSE
WHEN WE FIND THOSE CRIMINALS, I'M GONNA SAY...
I...
...AM HERE...
...TO FIGHT BACK!
BULGE

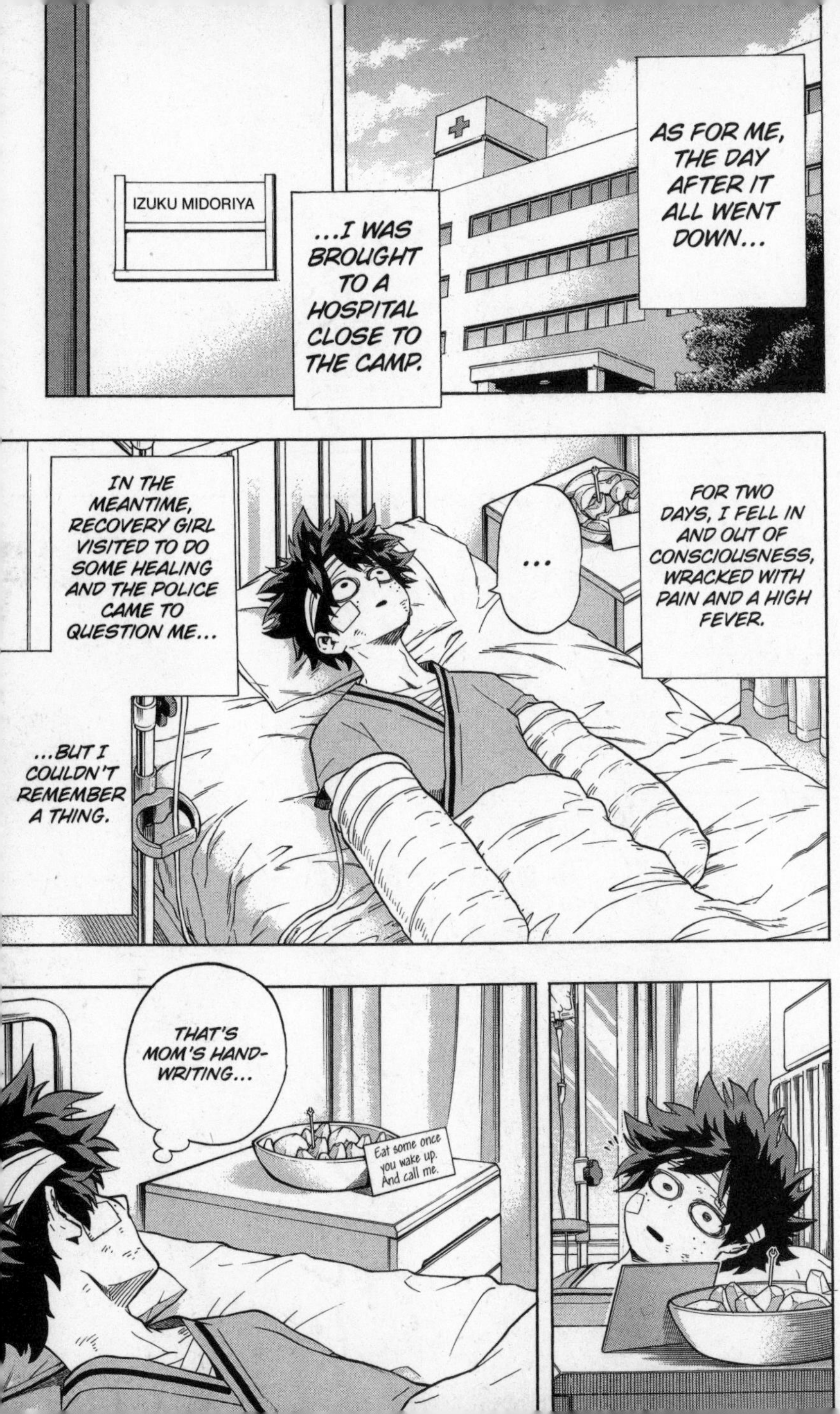
AS FOR ME, THE DAY AFTER IT ALL WENT DOWN...
...I WAS BROUGHT TO A HOSPITAL CLOSE TO THE CAMP.
IZUKU MIDORIYA
FOR TWO DAYS, I FELL IN AND OUT OF CONSCIOUSNESS, WRACKED WITH PAIN AND A HIGH FEVER.
...
IN THE MEANTIME, RECOVERY GIRL VISITED TO DO SOME HEALING AND THE POLICE CAME TO QUESTION ME...
...BUT I COULDN'T REMEMBER A THING.
THAT'S MOM'S HAND-WRITING...
Eat some once you wake up. And call me.

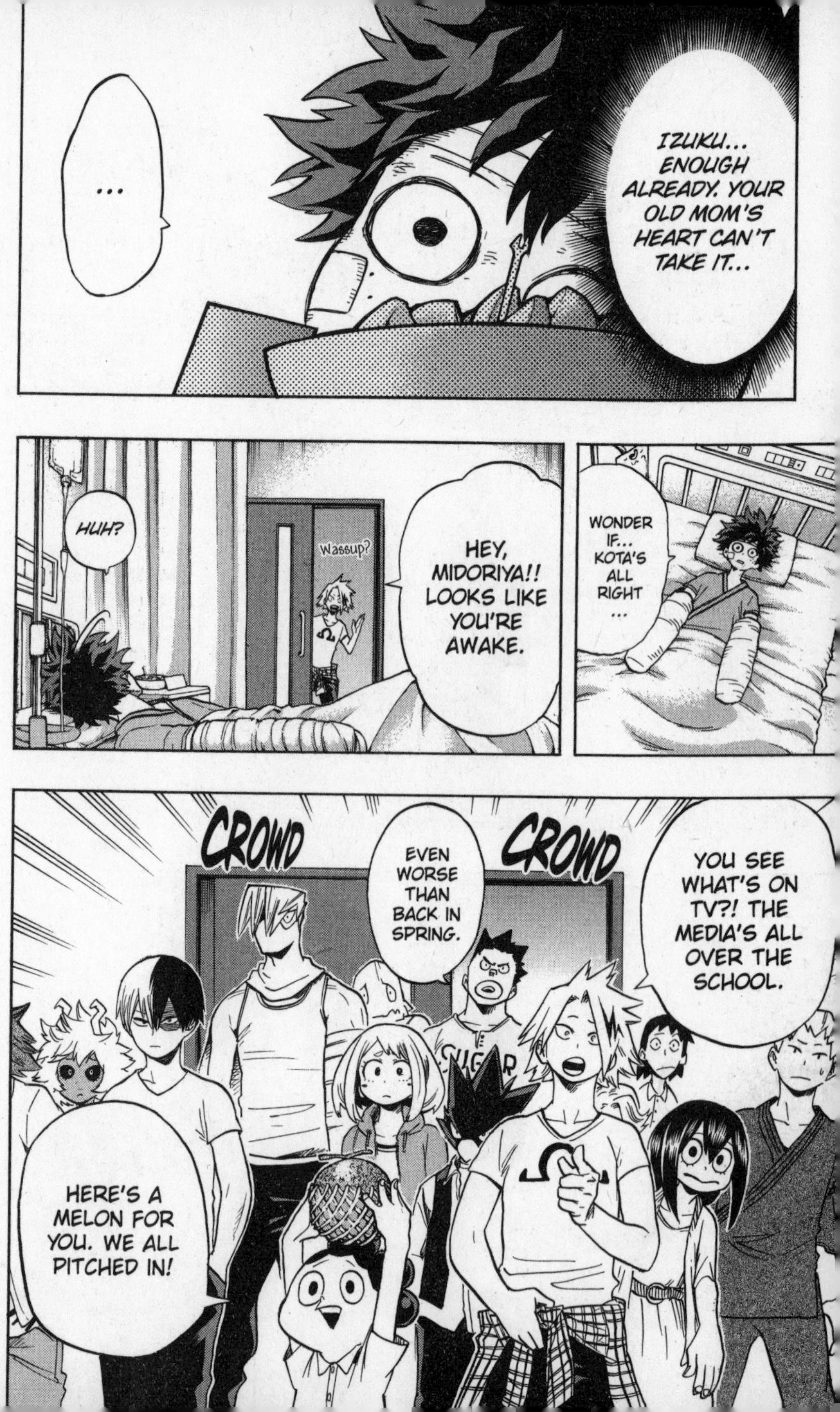
IZUKU... ENOUGH ALREADY. YOUR OLD MOM'S HEART CAN'T TAKE IT...
...
WONDER IF... KOTA'S ALL RIGHT ...
HEY, MIDORIYA!! LOOKS LIKE YOU'RE AWAKE.
Wassup?
HUH?
CROWD
CROWD
YOU SEE WHAT'S ON TV?! THE MEDIA'S ALL OVER THE SCHOOL.
EVEN WORSE THAN BACK IN SPRING.
HERE'S A MELON FOR YOU. WE ALL PITCHED IN!

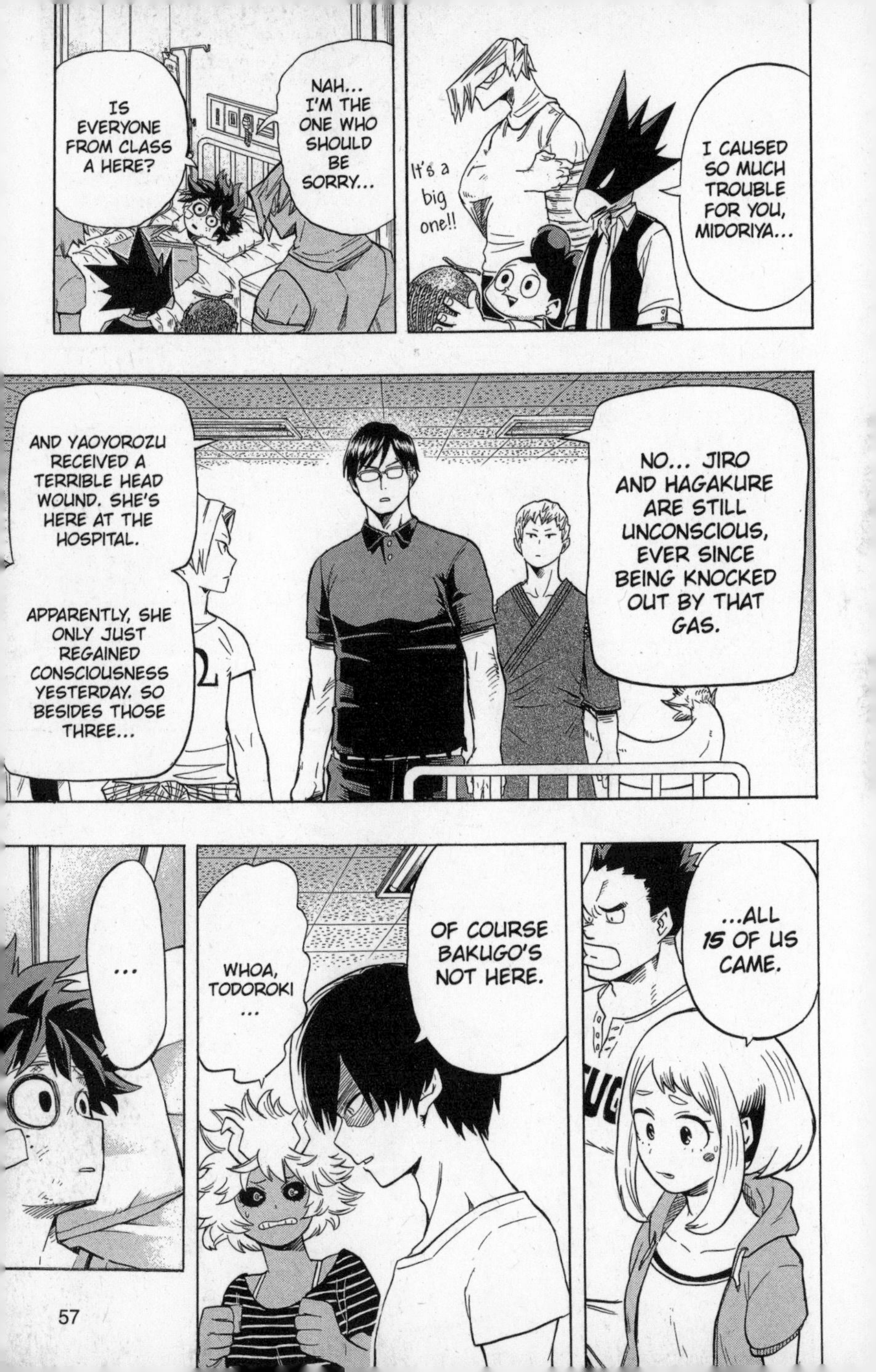
I CAUSED SO MUCH TROUBLE FOR YOU, MIDORIYA...
It's a big one!!
NAH... I'M THE ONE WHO SHOULD BE SORRY...
IS EVERYONE FROM CLASS A HERE?
NO... JIRO AND HAGAKURE ARE STILL UNCONSCIOUS, EVER SINCE BEING KNOCKED OUT BY THAT GAS.
AND YAOYOROZU RECEIVED A TERRIBLE HEAD WOUND. SHE'S HERE AT THE HOSPITAL.
APPARENTLY, SHE ONLY JUST REGAINED CONSCIOUSNESS YESTERDAY. SO BESIDES THOSE THREE...
...ALL 15 OF US CAME.
OF COURSE BAKUGO'S NOT HERE.
WHOA, TODOROKI ...
...

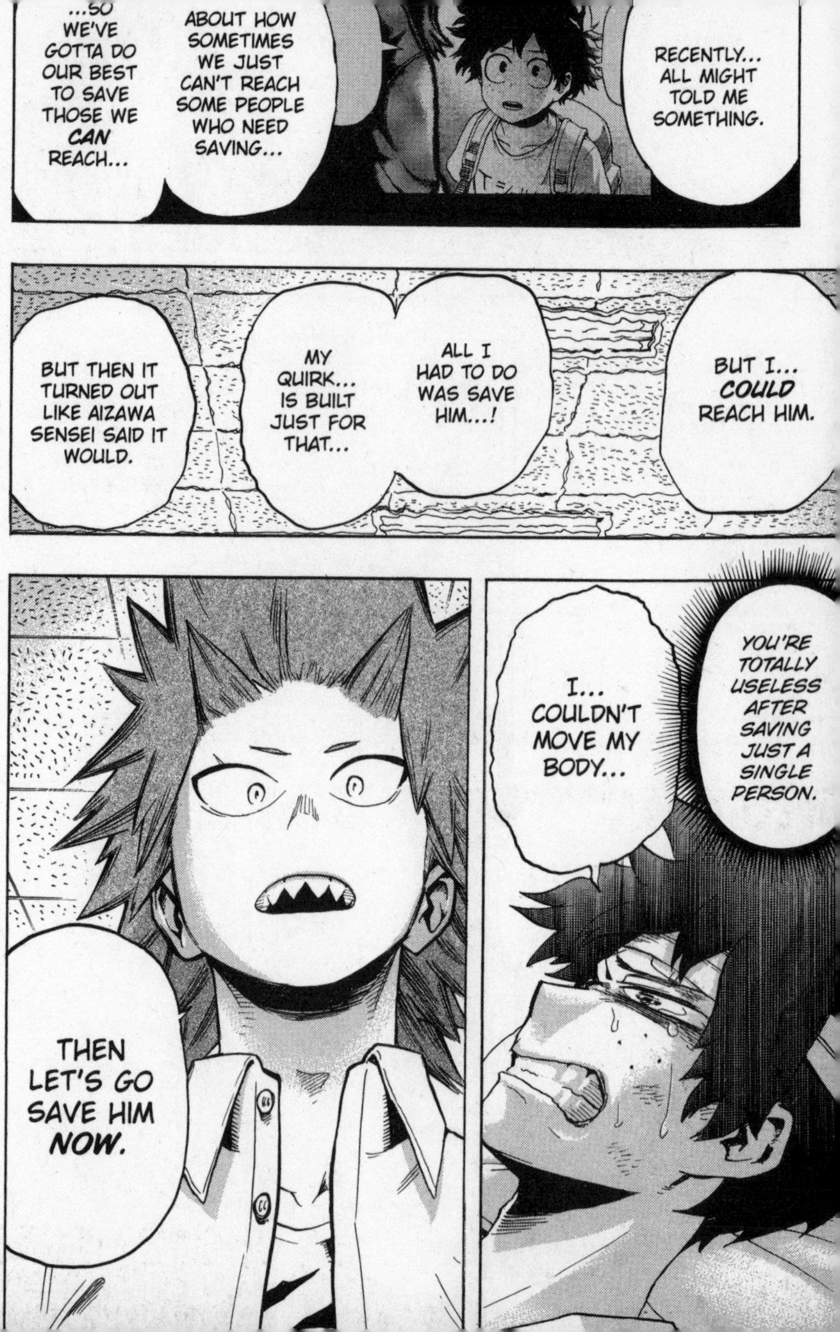
RECENTLY... ALL MIGHT TOLD ME SOMETHING.
ABOUT HOW SOMETIMES WE JUST CAN'T REACH SOME PEOPLE WHO NEED SAVING...
...SO WE'VE GOTTA DO OUR BEST TO SAVE THOSE WE *CAN* REACH...
BUT I... *COULD* REACH HIM.
ALL I HAD TO DO WAS SAVE HIM...!
MY QUIRK... IS BUILT JUST FOR THAT...
BUT THEN IT TURNED OUT LIKE AIZAWA SENSEI SAID IT WOULD.
YOU'RE TOTALLY USELESS AFTER SAVING JUST A SINGLE PERSON.
I... COULDN'T MOVE MY BODY...
THEN LET'S GO SAVE HIM *NOW.*

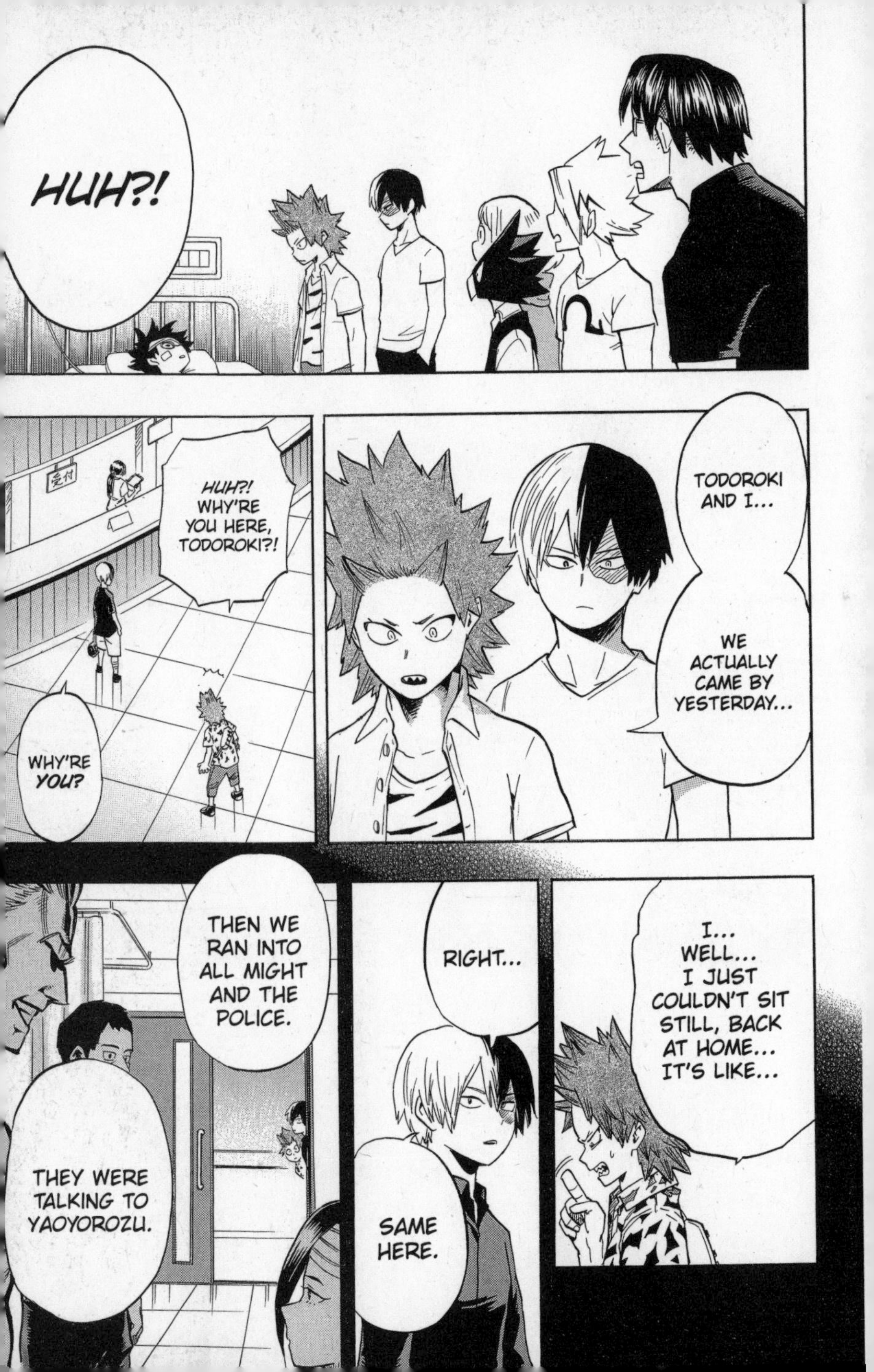
HUH?!
TODOROKI AND I...
WE ACTUALLY CAME BY YESTERDAY...
HUH?! WHY'RE YOU HERE, TODOROKI?!
受付
WHY'RE *YOU?*
I... WELL... I JUST COULDN'T SIT STILL, BACK AT HOME... IT'S LIKE...
RIGHT...
SAME HERE.
THEN WE RAN INTO ALL MIGHT AND THE POLICE.
THEY WERE TALKING TO YAOYOROZU.

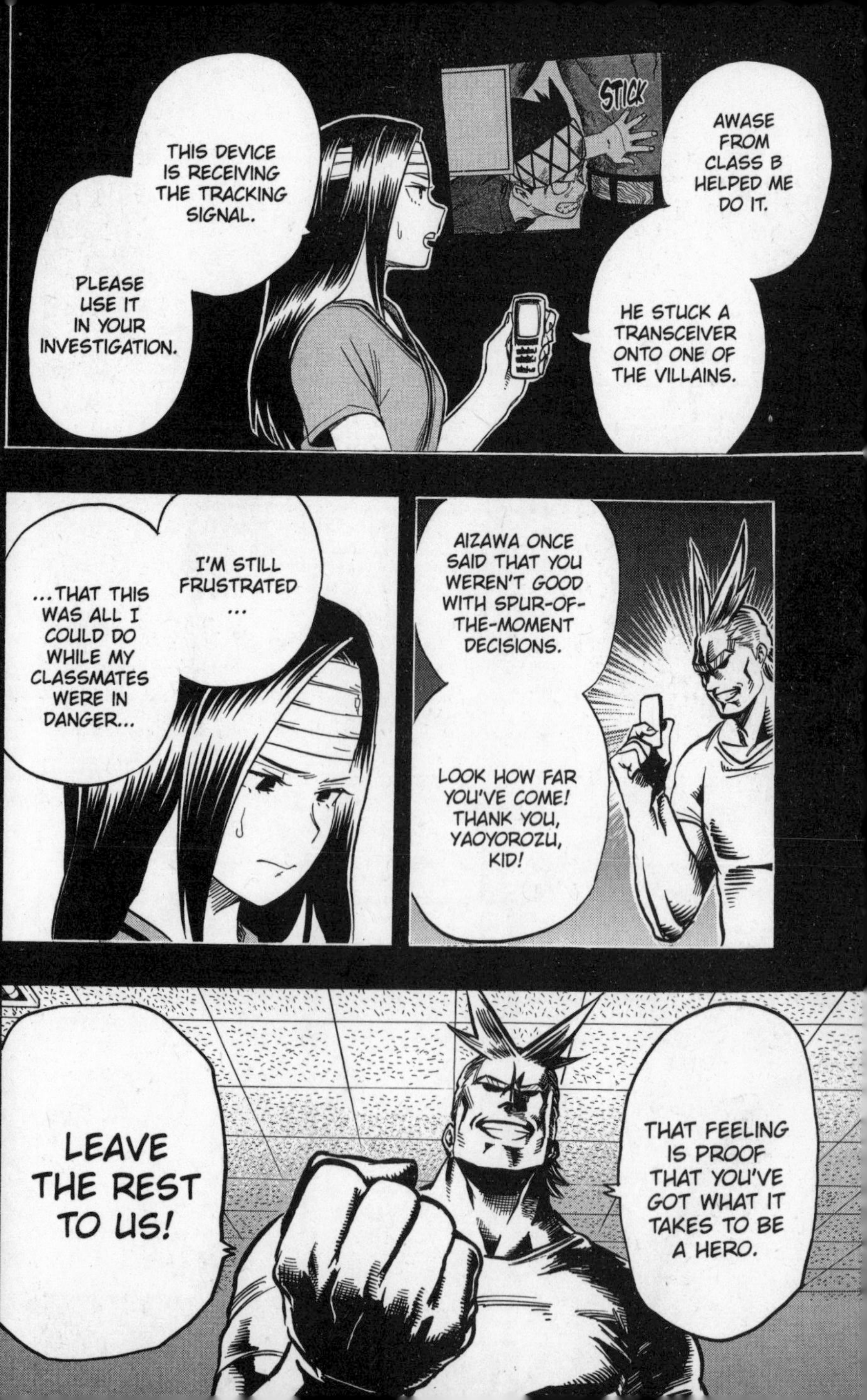
AWASE FROM CLASS B HELPED ME DO IT.
HE STUCK A TRANSCEIVER ONTO ONE OF THE VILLAINS.
STICK
THIS DEVICE IS RECEIVING THE TRACKING SIGNAL.
PLEASE USE IT IN YOUR INVESTIGATION.
AIZAWA ONCE SAID THAT YOU WEREN'T GOOD WITH SPUR-OF-THE-MOMENT DECISIONS.
LOOK HOW FAR YOU'VE COME! THANK YOU, YAOYOROZU, KID!
I'M STILL FRUSTRATED ...
...THAT THIS WAS ALL I COULD DO WHILE MY CLASSMATES WERE IN DANGER...
THAT FEELING IS PROOF THAT YOU'VE GOT WHAT IT TAKES TO BE A HERO.
LEAVE THE REST TO US!

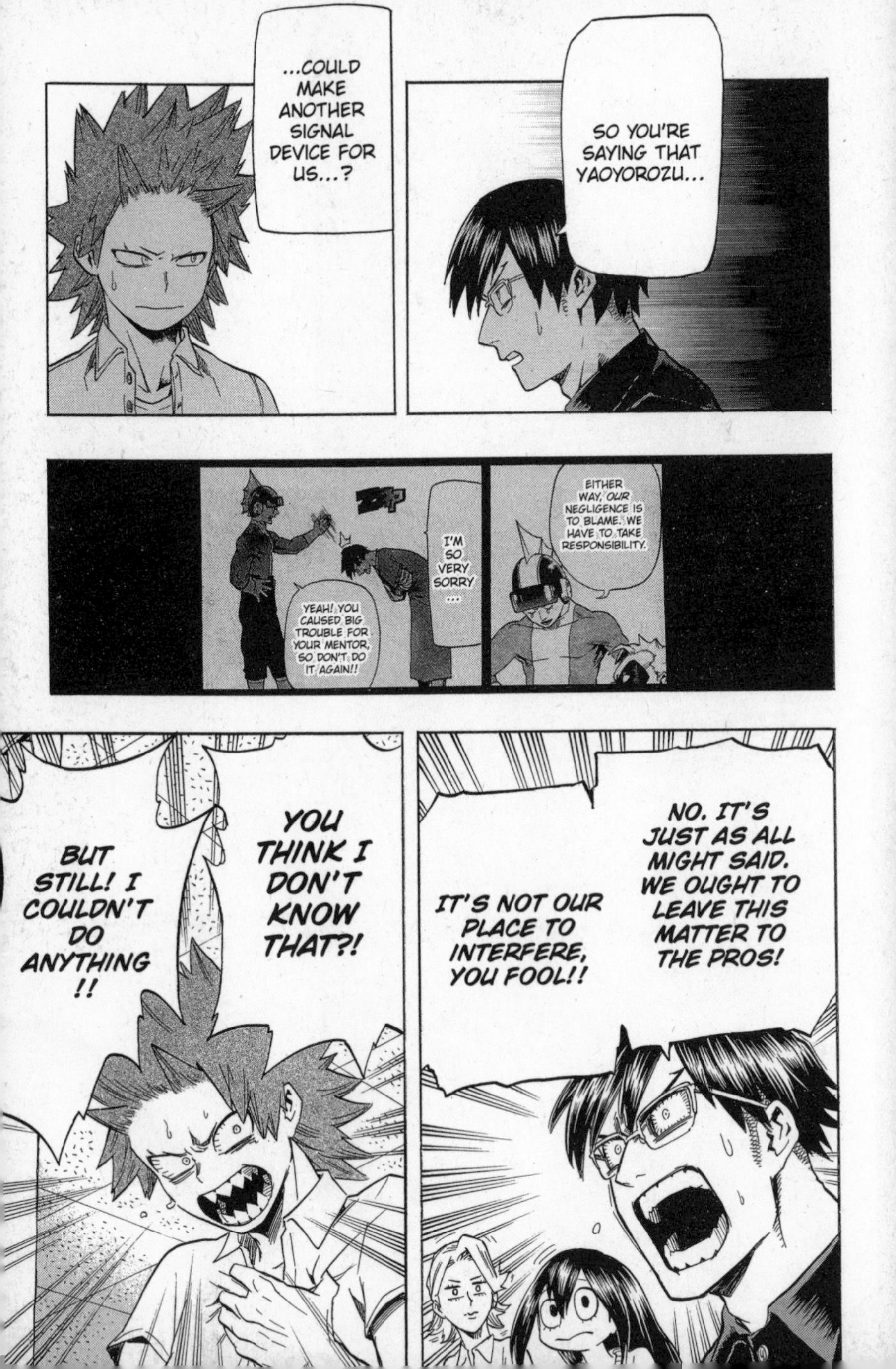
SO YOU'RE SAYING THAT YAOYOROZU...
...COULD MAKE ANOTHER SIGNAL DEVICE FOR US...?
EITHER WAY, OUR NEGLIGENCE IS TO BLAME. WE HAVE TO TAKE RESPONSIBILITY.
I'M SO VERY SORRY...
YEAH! YOU CAUSED BIG TROUBLE FOR YOUR MENTOR, SO DON'T DO IT AGAIN!!
NO. IT'S JUST AS ALL MIGHT SAID. WE OUGHT TO LEAVE THIS MATTER TO THE PROS!
IT'S NOT OUR PLACE TO INTERFERE, YOU FOOL!!
YOU THINK I DON'T KNOW THAT?!
BUT STILL! I COULDN'T DO ANYTHING!!

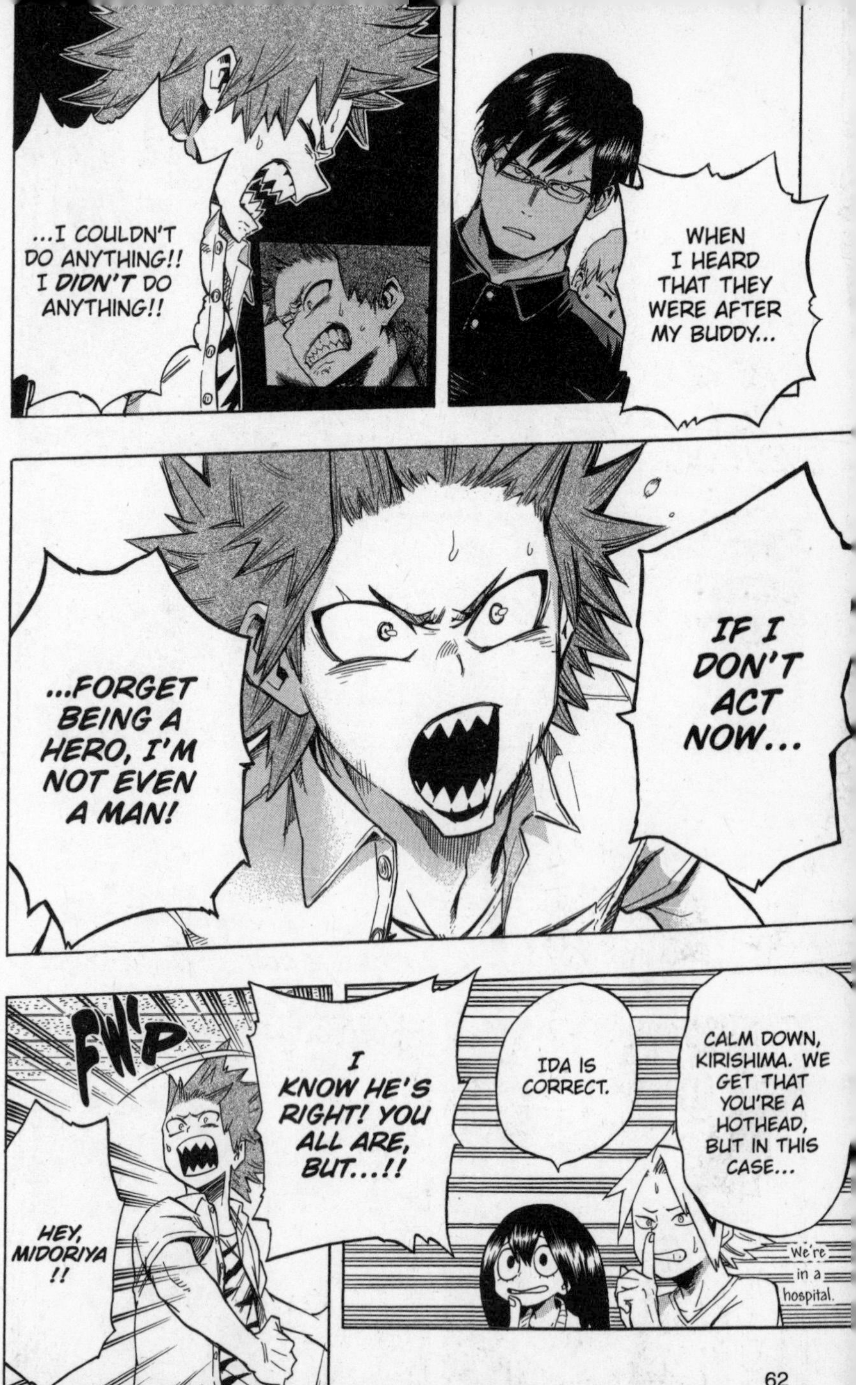
WHEN I HEARD THAT THEY WERE AFTER MY BUDDY...
...I COULDN'T DO ANYTHING!! I DIDN'T DO ANYTHING!!
IF I DON'T ACT NOW...
...FORGET BEING A HERO, I'M NOT EVEN A MAN!
CALM DOWN, KIRISHIMA. WE GET THAT YOU'RE A HOTHEAD, BUT IN THIS CASE...
IDA IS CORRECT.
We're in a hospital.
FWP
I KNOW HE'S RIGHT! YOU ALL ARE, BUT...!!
HEY, MIDORIYA!!

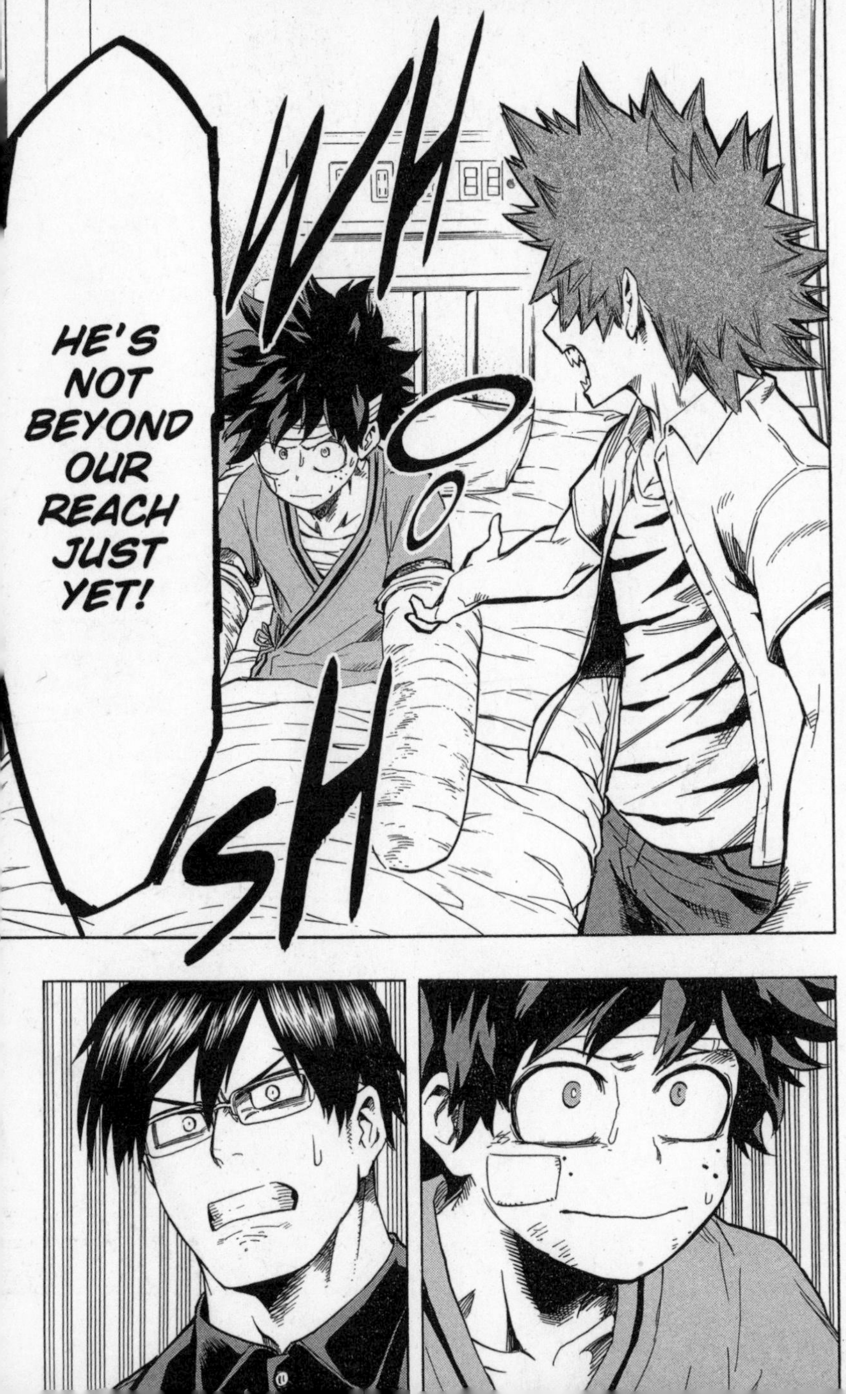
HE'S NOT BEYOND OUR REACH JUST YET!
WHOOSH

HERO

KOSEI TSUBURABA (16)

STREET CLOTHES

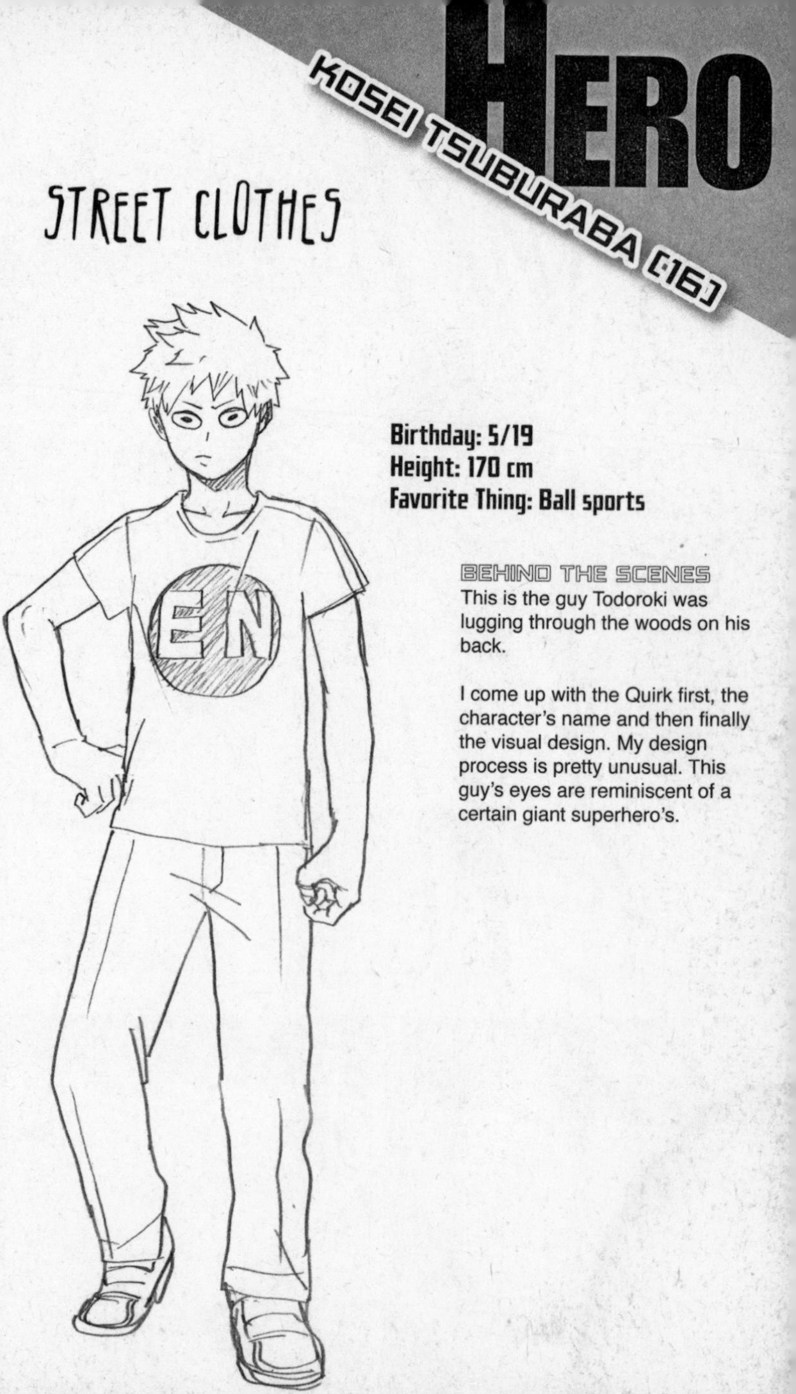
EN

Birthday: 5/19
Height: 170 cm
Favorite Thing: Ball sports

BEHIND THE SCENES

This is the guy Todoroki was lugging through the woods on his back.

I come up with the Quirk first, the character's name and then finally the visual design. My design process is pretty unusual. This guy's eyes are reminiscent of a certain giant superhero's.

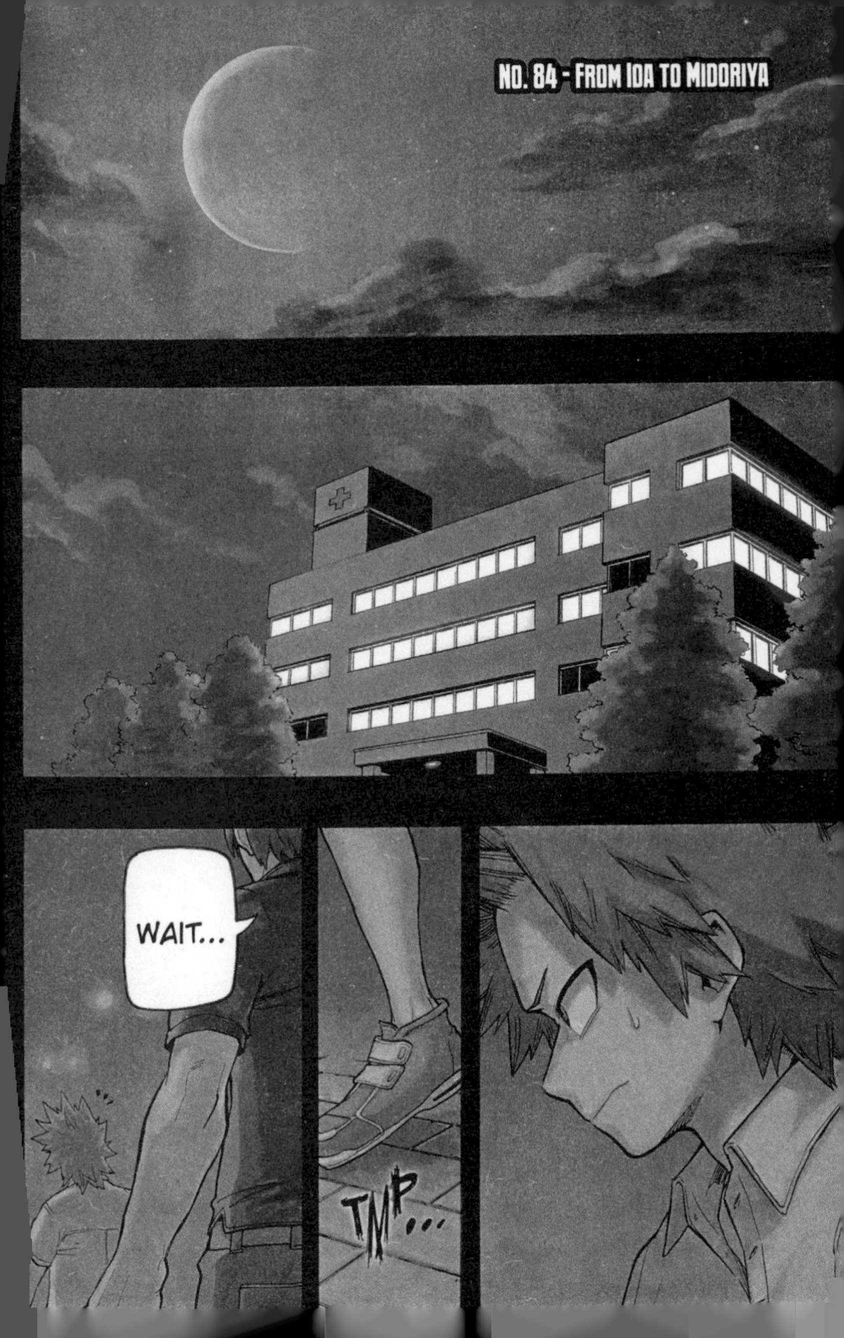
No. 84 - From Ida to Midoriya
TMP...
WAIT...

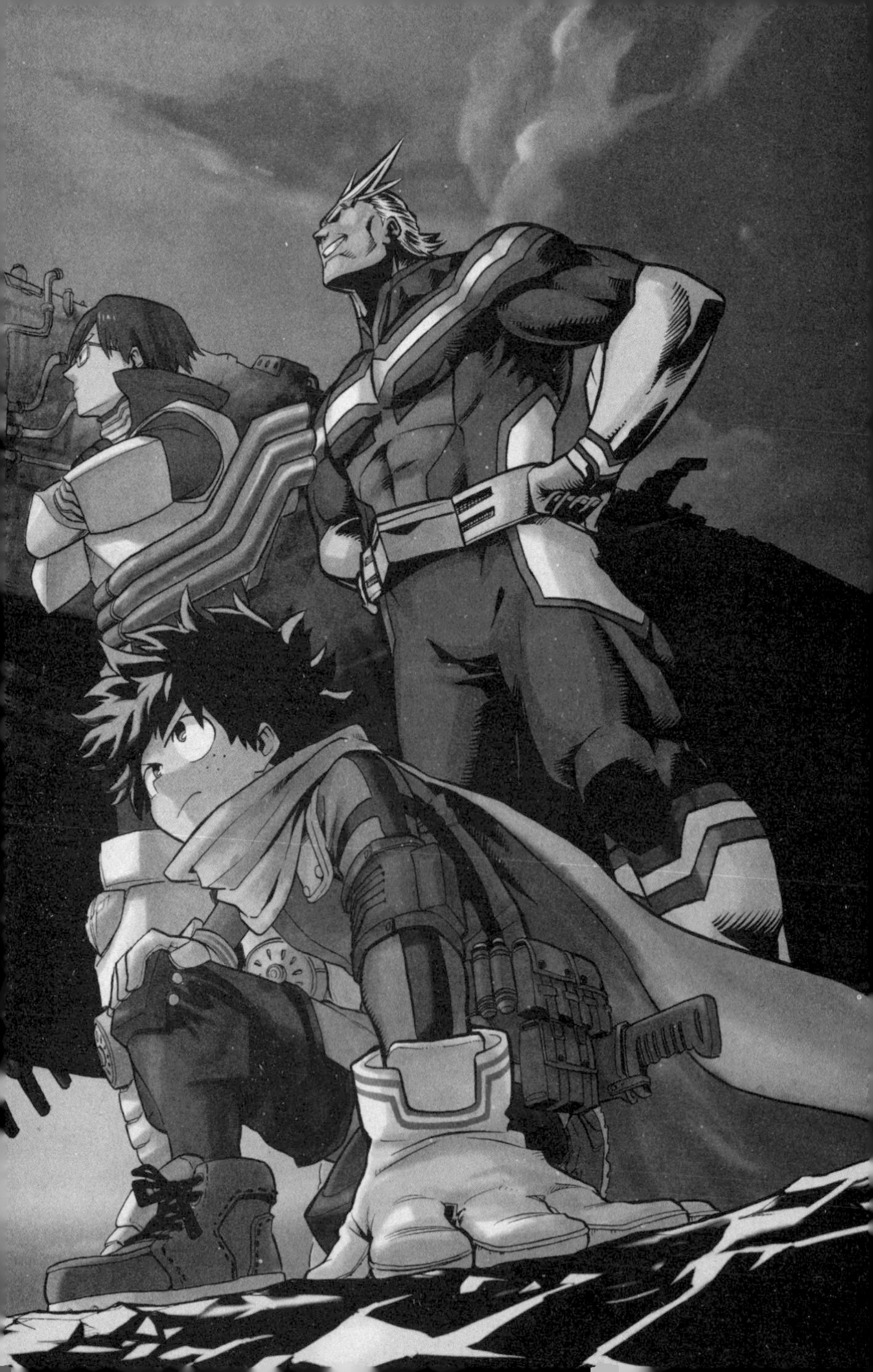

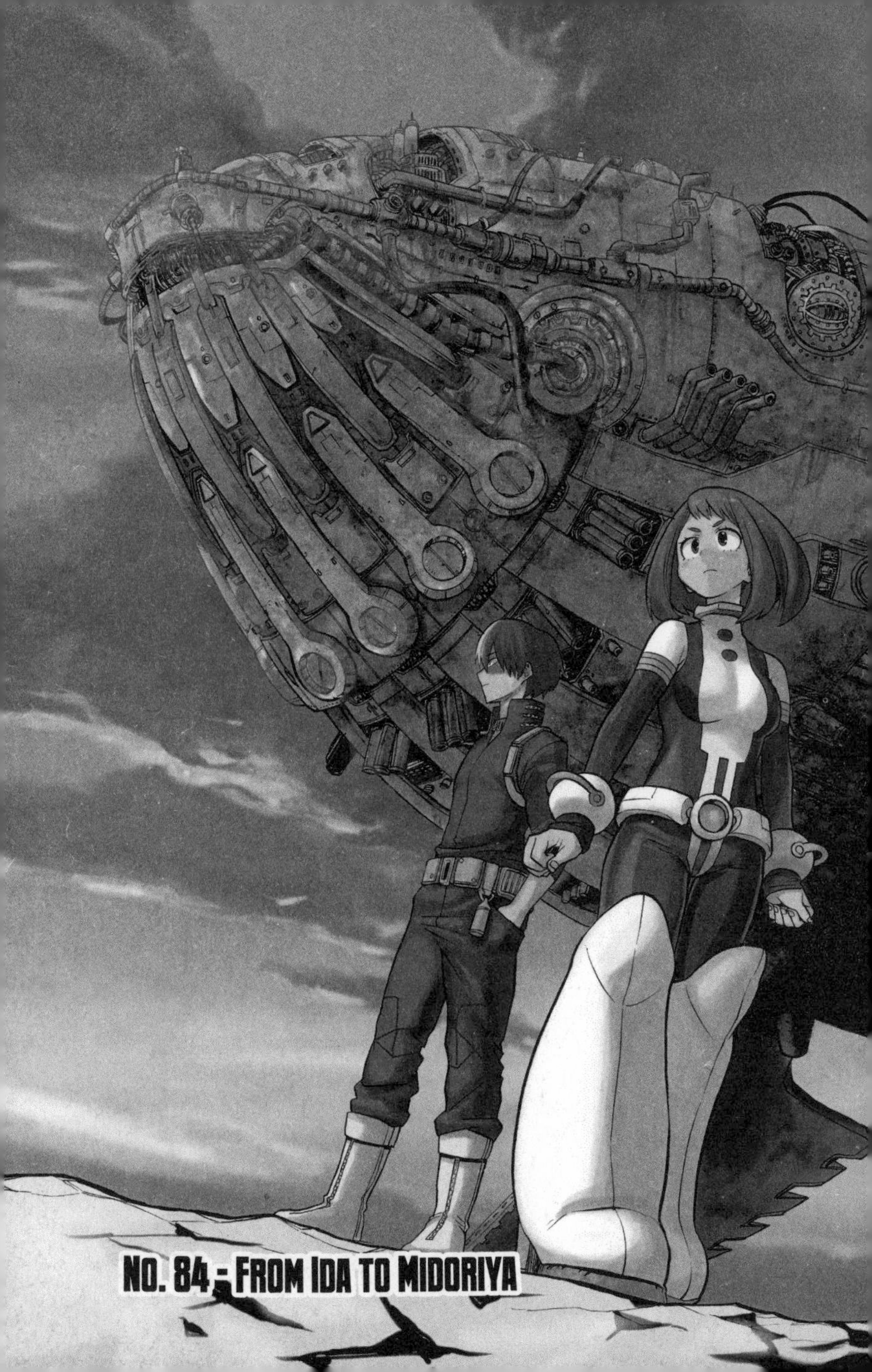
No. 84 - From Ida to Midoriya

MY HERO ACADEMIA

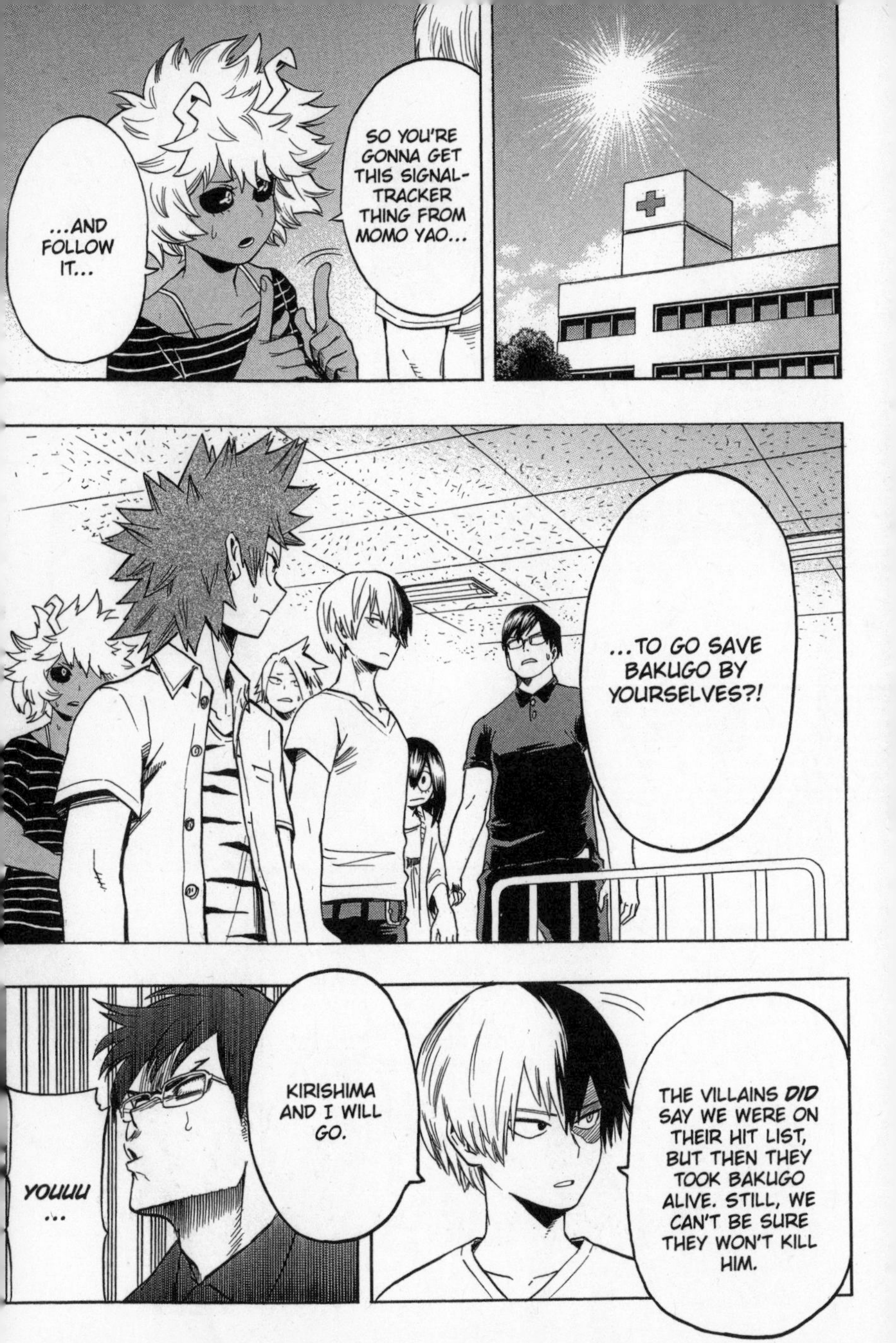
SO YOU'RE GONNA GET THIS SIGNAL-TRACKER THING FROM MOMO YAO...
...AND FOLLOW IT...
...TO GO SAVE BAKUGO BY YOURSELVES?!
THE VILLAINS DID SAY WE WERE ON THEIR HIT LIST, BUT THEN THEY TOOK BAKUGO ALIVE. STILL, WE CAN'T BE SURE THEY WON'T KILL HIM.
KIRISHIMA AND I WILL GO.
YOUUU...

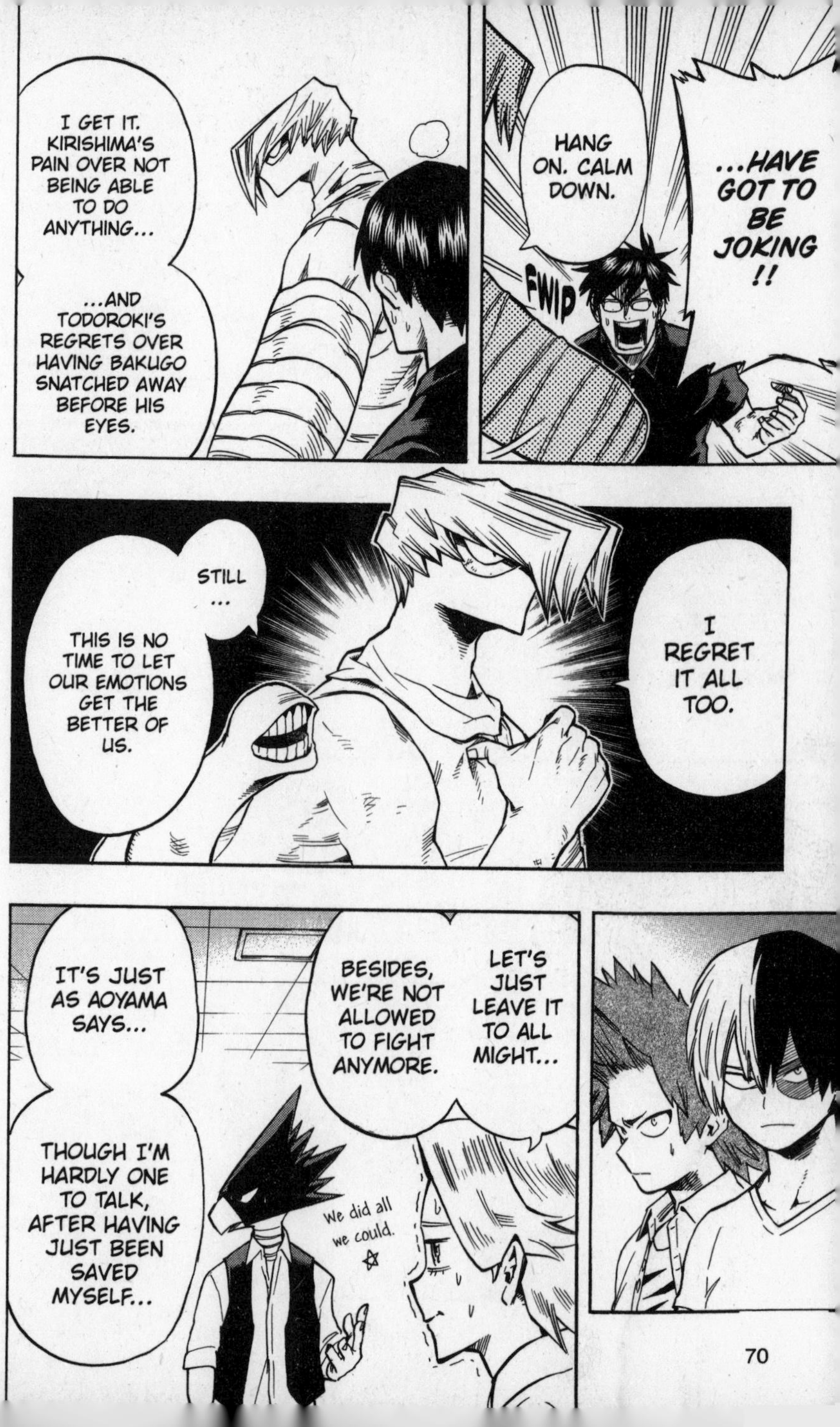
...HAVE GOT TO BE JOKING!!
FWIP
HANG ON. CALM DOWN.
I GET IT. KIRISHIMA'S PAIN OVER NOT BEING ABLE TO DO ANYTHING...
...AND TODOROKI'S REGRETS OVER HAVING BAKUGO SNATCHED AWAY BEFORE HIS EYES.
I REGRET IT ALL TOO.
STILL...
THIS IS NO TIME TO LET OUR EMOTIONS GET THE BETTER OF US.
LET'S JUST LEAVE IT TO ALL MIGHT...
BESIDES, WE'RE NOT ALLOWED TO FIGHT ANYMORE.
IT'S JUST AS AOYAMA SAYS...
THOUGH I'M HARDLY ONE TO TALK, AFTER HAVING JUST BEEN SAVED MYSELF...
We did all we could. ☆

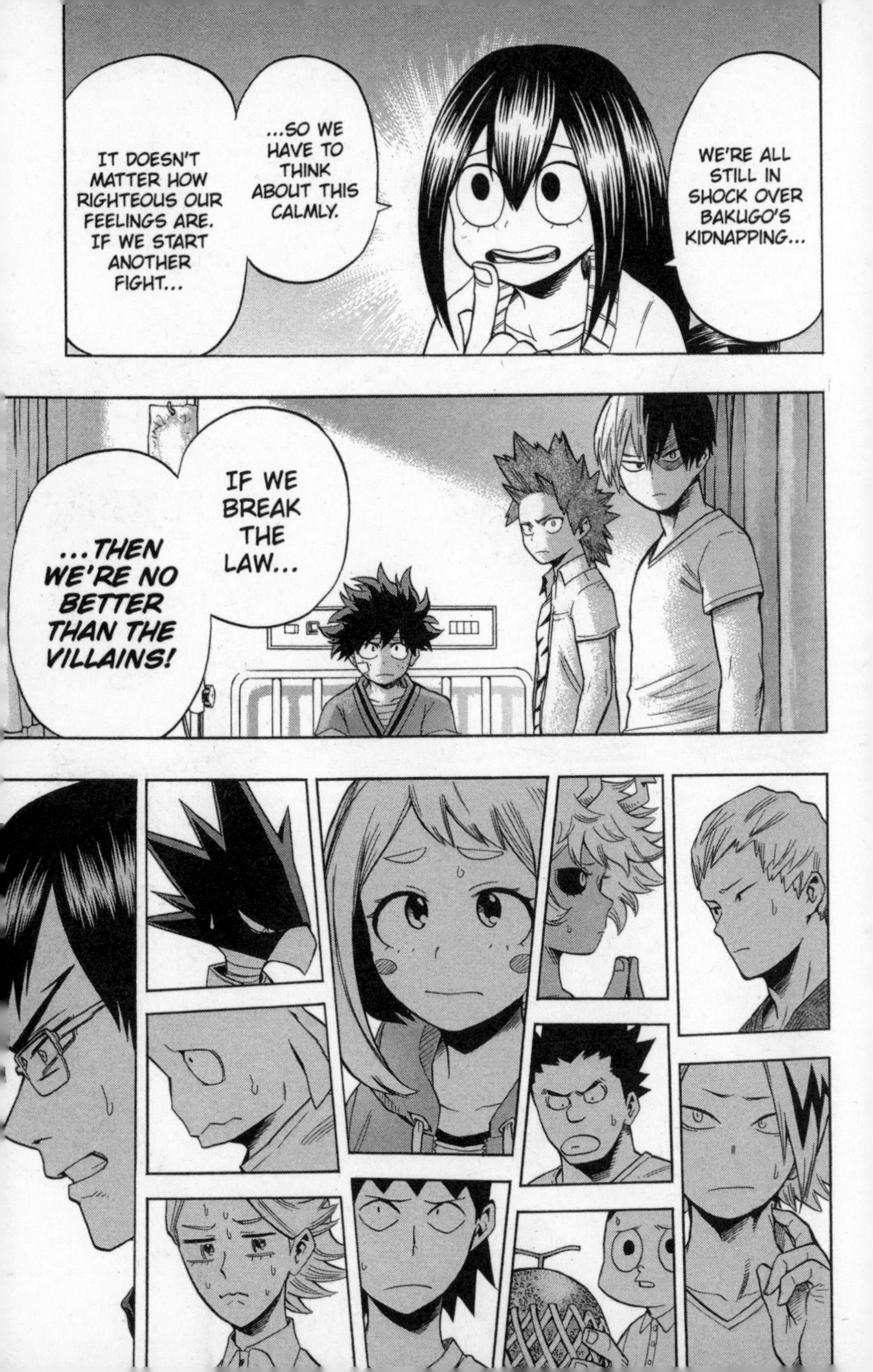
WE'RE ALL STILL IN SHOCK OVER BAKUGO'S KIDNAPPING...
...SO WE HAVE TO THINK ABOUT THIS CALMLY.
IT DOESN'T MATTER HOW RIGHTEOUS OUR FEELINGS ARE. IF WE START ANOTHER FIGHT...
IF WE BREAK THE LAW...
...THEN WE'RE NO BETTER THAN THE VILLAINS!

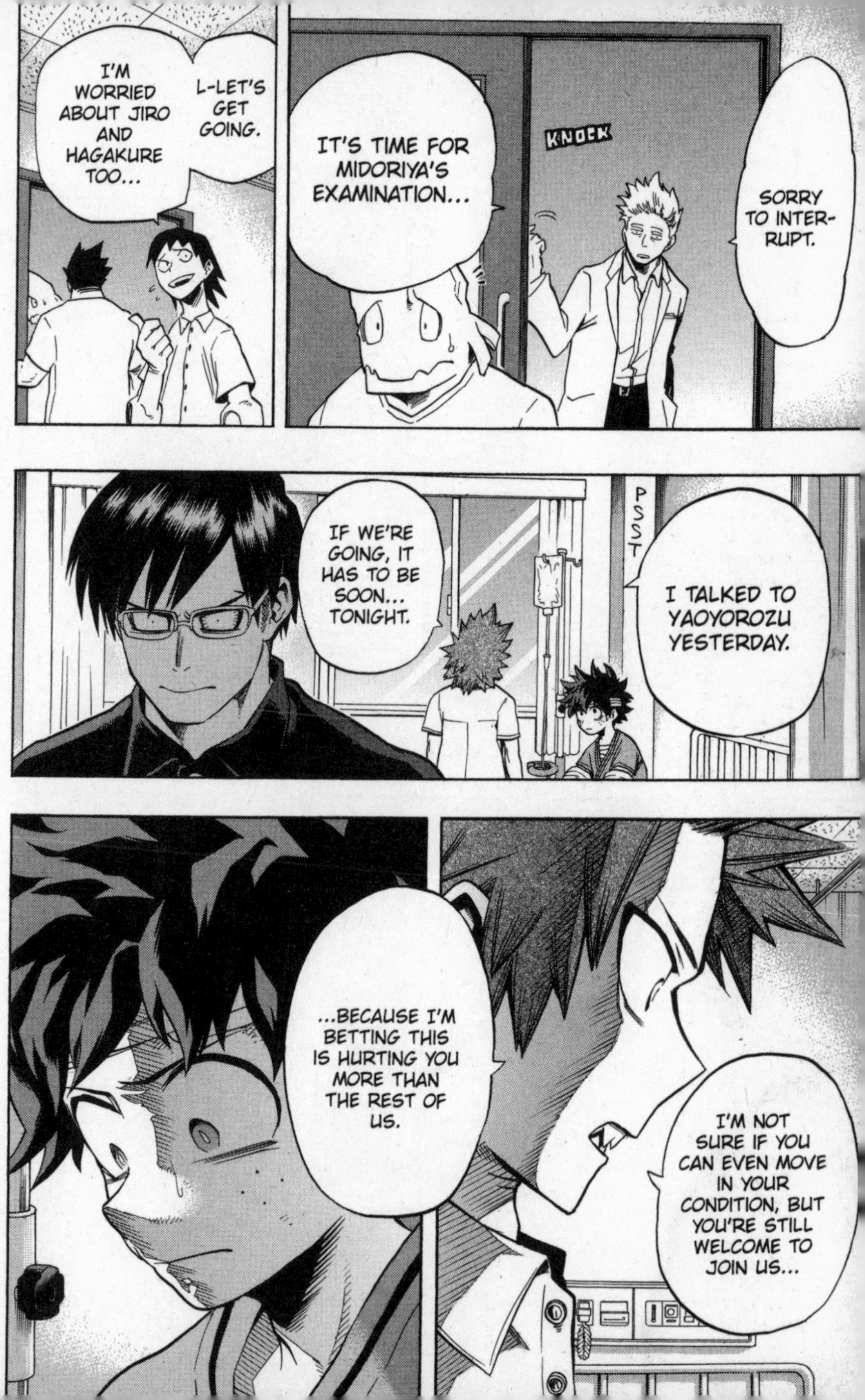
KNOCK
SORRY TO INTER-RUPT.
IT'S TIME FOR MIDORIYA'S EXAMINATION...
L-LET'S GET GOING.
I'M WORRIED ABOUT JIRO AND HAGAKURE TOO...
PSST
I TALKED TO YAOYOROZU YESTERDAY.
IF WE'RE GOING, IT HAS TO BE SOON... TONIGHT.
I'M NOT SURE IF YOU CAN EVEN MOVE IN YOUR CONDITION, BUT YOU'RE STILL WELCOME TO JOIN US...
...BECAUSE I'M BETTING THIS IS HURTING YOU MORE THAN THE REST OF US.

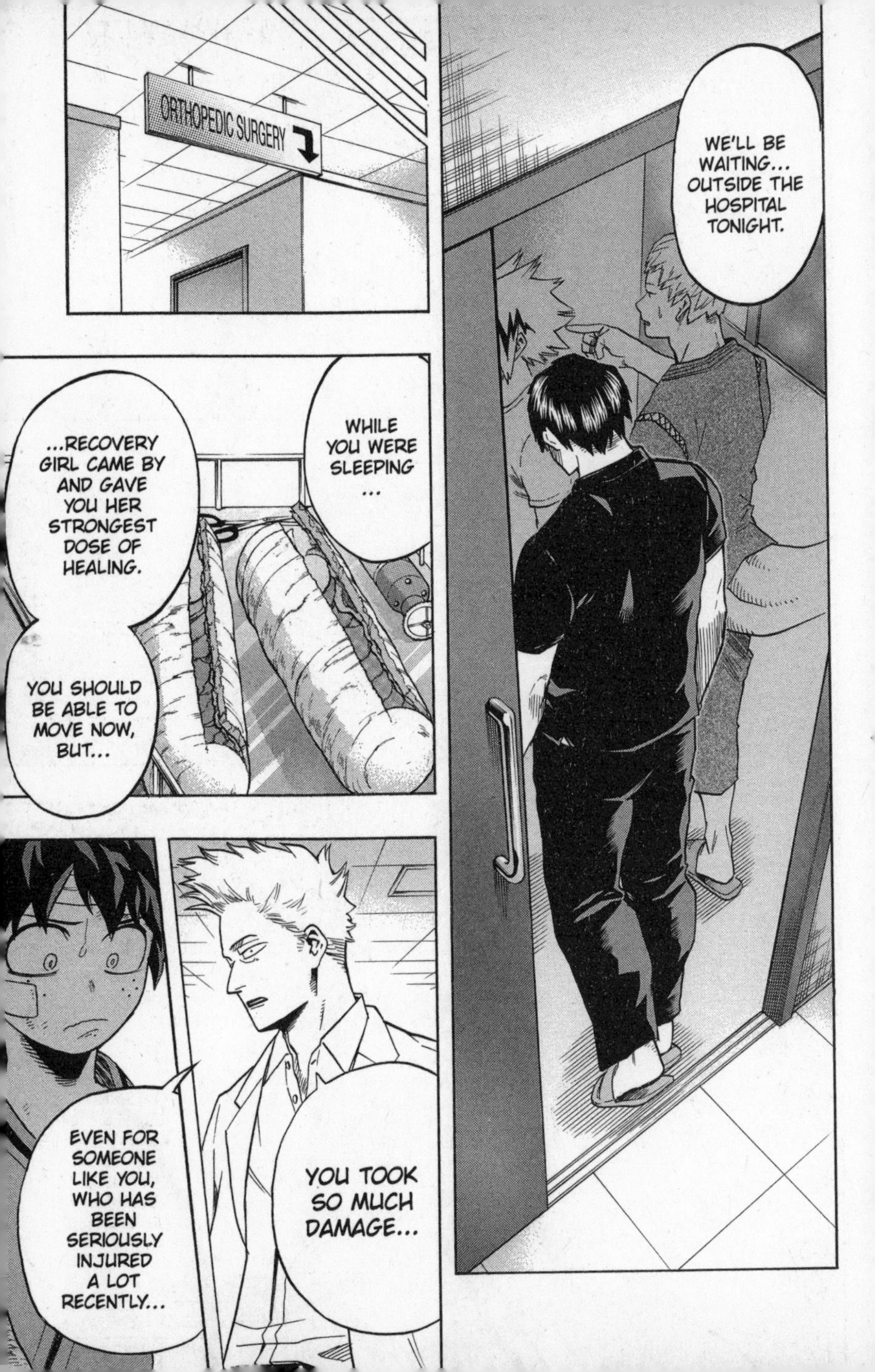
WE'LL BE WAITING... OUTSIDE THE HOSPITAL TONIGHT.
ORTHOPEDIC SURGERY
WHILE YOU WERE SLEEPING...
...RECOVERY GIRL CAME BY AND GAVE YOU HER STRONGEST DOSE OF HEALING.
YOU SHOULD BE ABLE TO MOVE NOW, BUT...
EVEN FOR SOMEONE LIKE YOU, WHO HAS BEEN SERIOUSLY INJURED A LOT RECENTLY...
YOU TOOK SO MUCH DAMAGE...

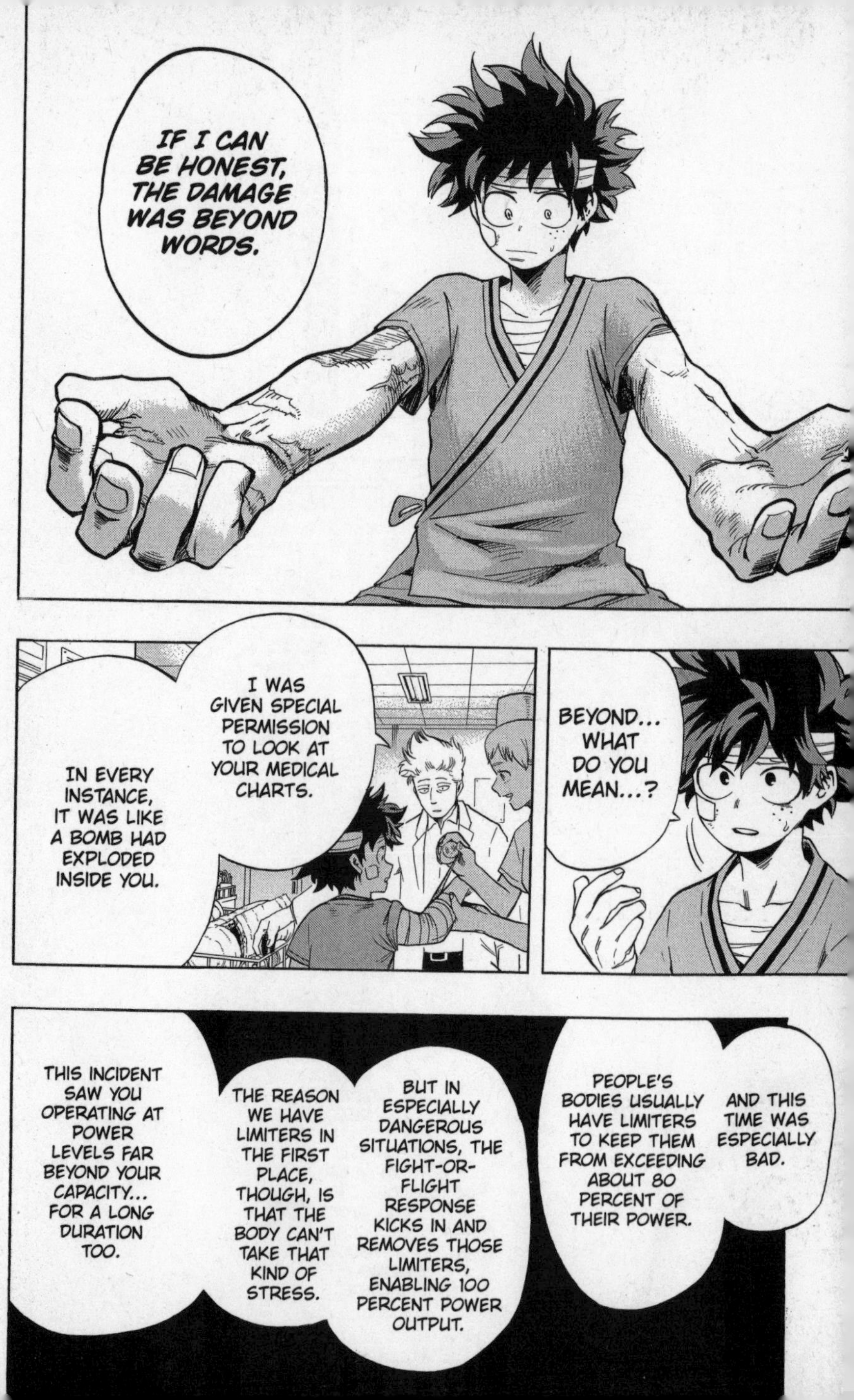
IF I CAN BE HONEST, THE DAMAGE WAS BEYOND WORDS.
BEYOND... WHAT DO YOU MEAN...?
I WAS GIVEN SPECIAL PERMISSION TO LOOK AT YOUR MEDICAL CHARTS.
IN EVERY INSTANCE, IT WAS LIKE A BOMB HAD EXPLODED INSIDE YOU.
AND THIS TIME WAS ESPECIALLY BAD.
PEOPLE'S BODIES USUALLY HAVE LIMITERS TO KEEP THEM FROM EXCEEDING ABOUT 80 PERCENT OF THEIR POWER.
BUT IN ESPECIALLY DANGEROUS SITUATIONS, THE FIGHT-OR-FLIGHT RESPONSE KICKS IN AND REMOVES THOSE LIMITERS, ENABLING 100 PERCENT POWER OUTPUT.
THE REASON WE HAVE LIMITERS IN THE FIRST PLACE, THOUGH, IS THAT THE BODY CAN'T TAKE THAT KIND OF STRESS.
THIS INCIDENT SAW YOU OPERATING AT POWER LEVELS FAR BEYOND YOUR CAPACITY... FOR A LONG DURATION TOO.

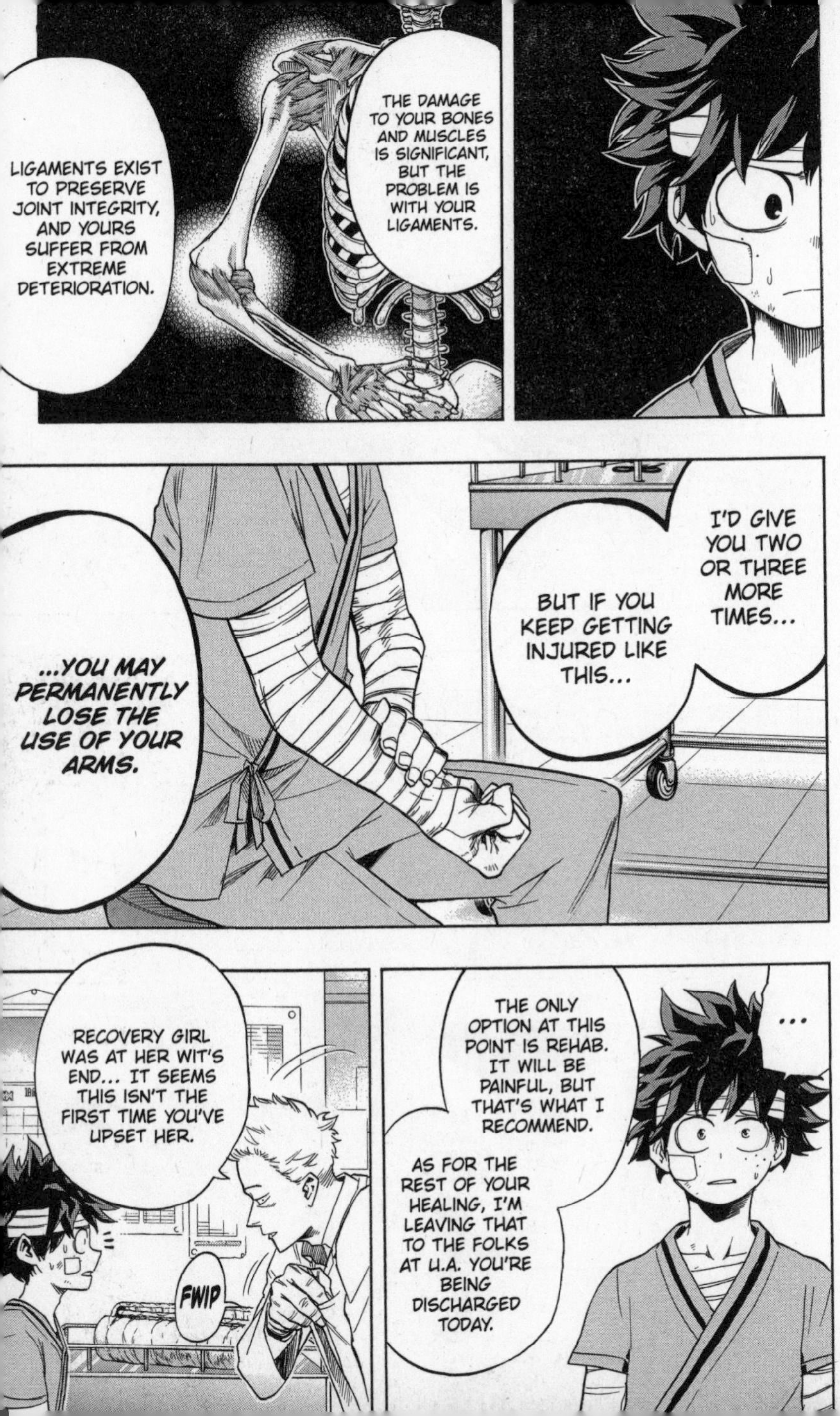
THE DAMAGE TO YOUR BONES AND MUSCLES IS SIGNIFICANT, BUT THE PROBLEM IS WITH YOUR LIGAMENTS.
LIGAMENTS EXIST TO PRESERVE JOINT INTEGRITY, AND YOURS SUFFER FROM EXTREME DETERIORATION.
I'D GIVE YOU TWO OR THREE MORE TIMES...
BUT IF YOU KEEP GETTING INJURED LIKE THIS...
...YOU MAY PERMANENTLY LOSE THE USE OF YOUR ARMS.
...
THE ONLY OPTION AT THIS POINT IS REHAB. IT WILL BE PAINFUL, BUT THAT'S WHAT I RECOMMEND.
AS FOR THE REST OF YOUR HEALING, I'M LEAVING THAT TO THE FOLKS AT U.A. YOU'RE BEING DISCHARGED TODAY.
RECOVERY GIRL WAS AT HER WIT'S END... IT SEEMS THIS ISN'T THE FIRST TIME YOU'VE UPSET HER.
FWIP

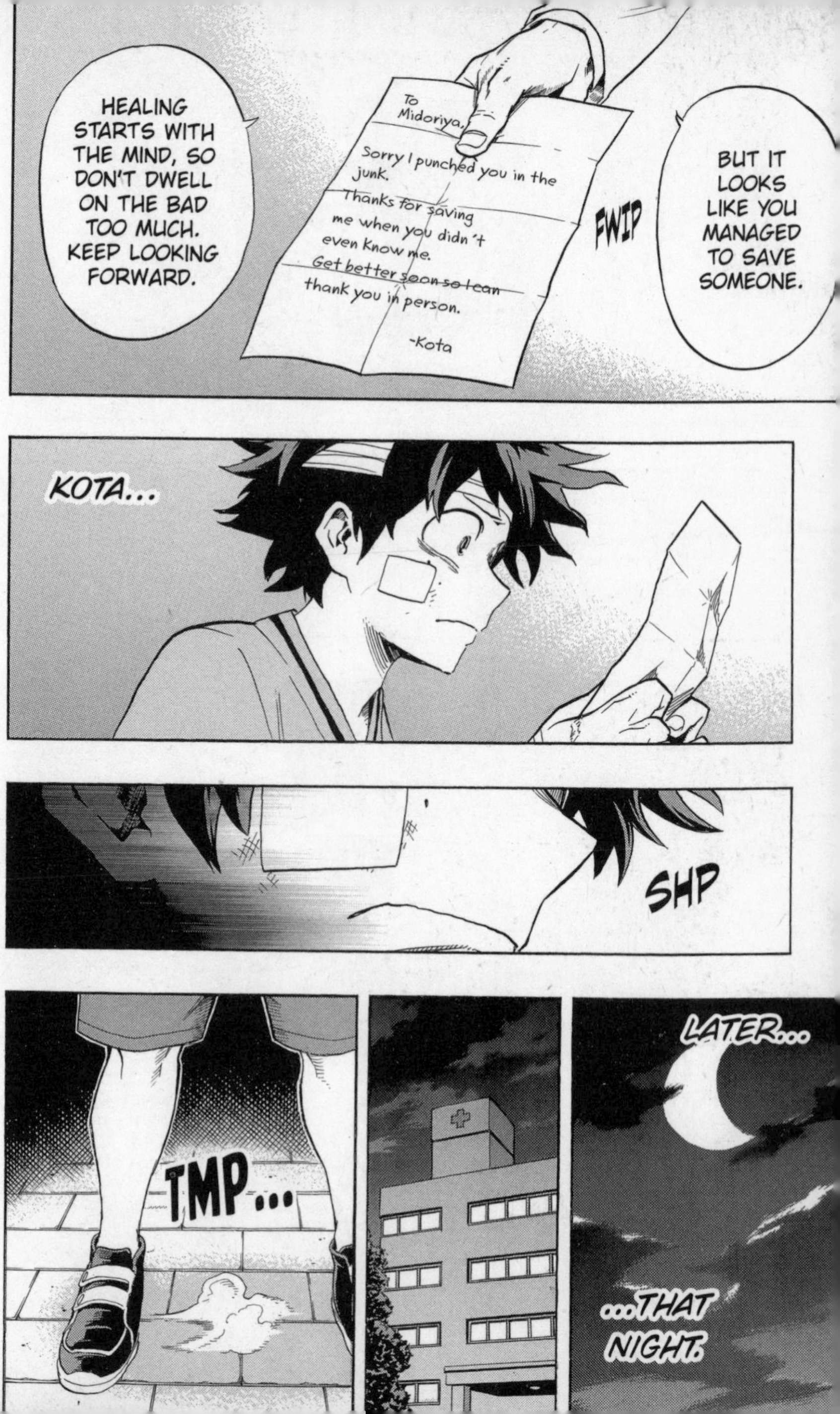

BUT IT LOOKS LIKE YOU MANAGED TO SAVE SOMEONE.
FWIP
To Midoriya,
Sorry I punched you in the junk.
Thanks for saving me when you didn't even know me.
Get better soon so I can thank you in person.
-Kota
HEALING STARTS WITH THE MIND, SO DON'T DWELL ON THE BAD TOO MUCH. KEEP LOOKING FORWARD.
KOTA...
SHP
LATER...
...THAT NIGHT.
TMP...

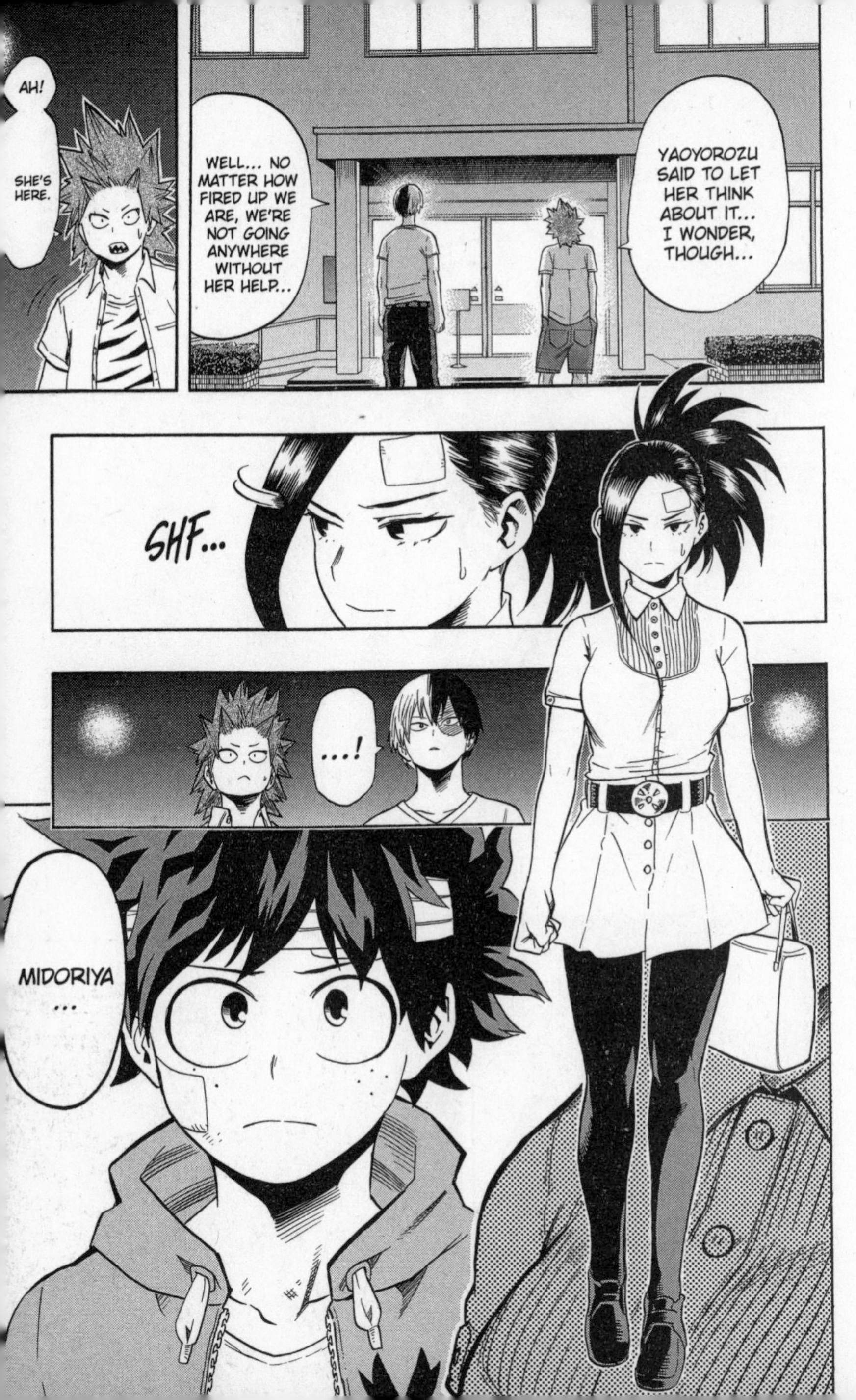

YAOYOROZU SAID TO LET HER THINK ABOUT IT... I WONDER, THOUGH...
WELL... NO MATTER HOW FIRED UP WE ARE, WE'RE NOT GOING ANYWHERE WITHOUT HER HELP...
AH!
SHE'S HERE.
SHF...
...!
MIDORIYA ...

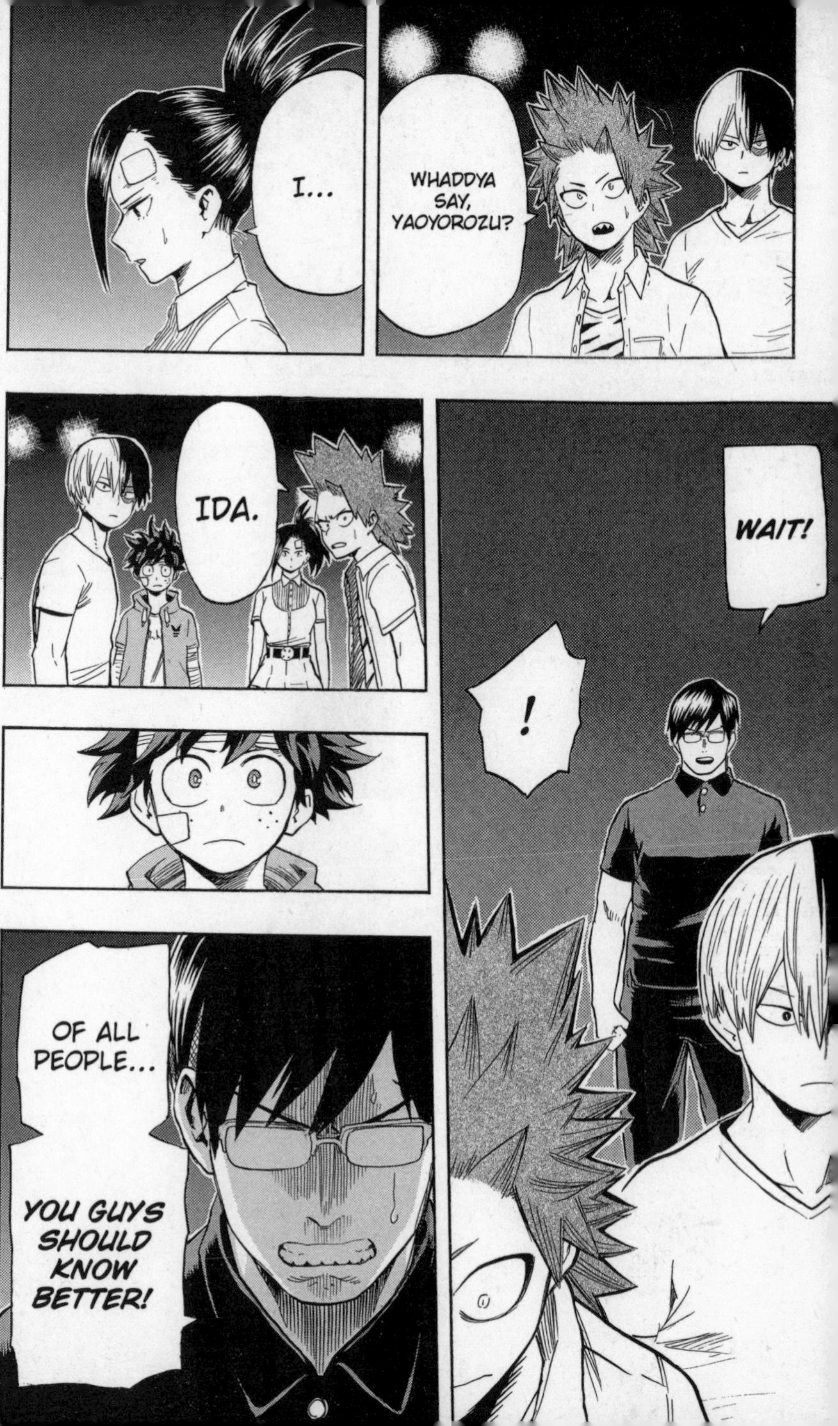
WHADDYA SAY, YAOYOROZU?
I...
WAIT!
!
IDA.
OF ALL PEOPLE...
YOU GUYS SHOULD KNOW BETTER!

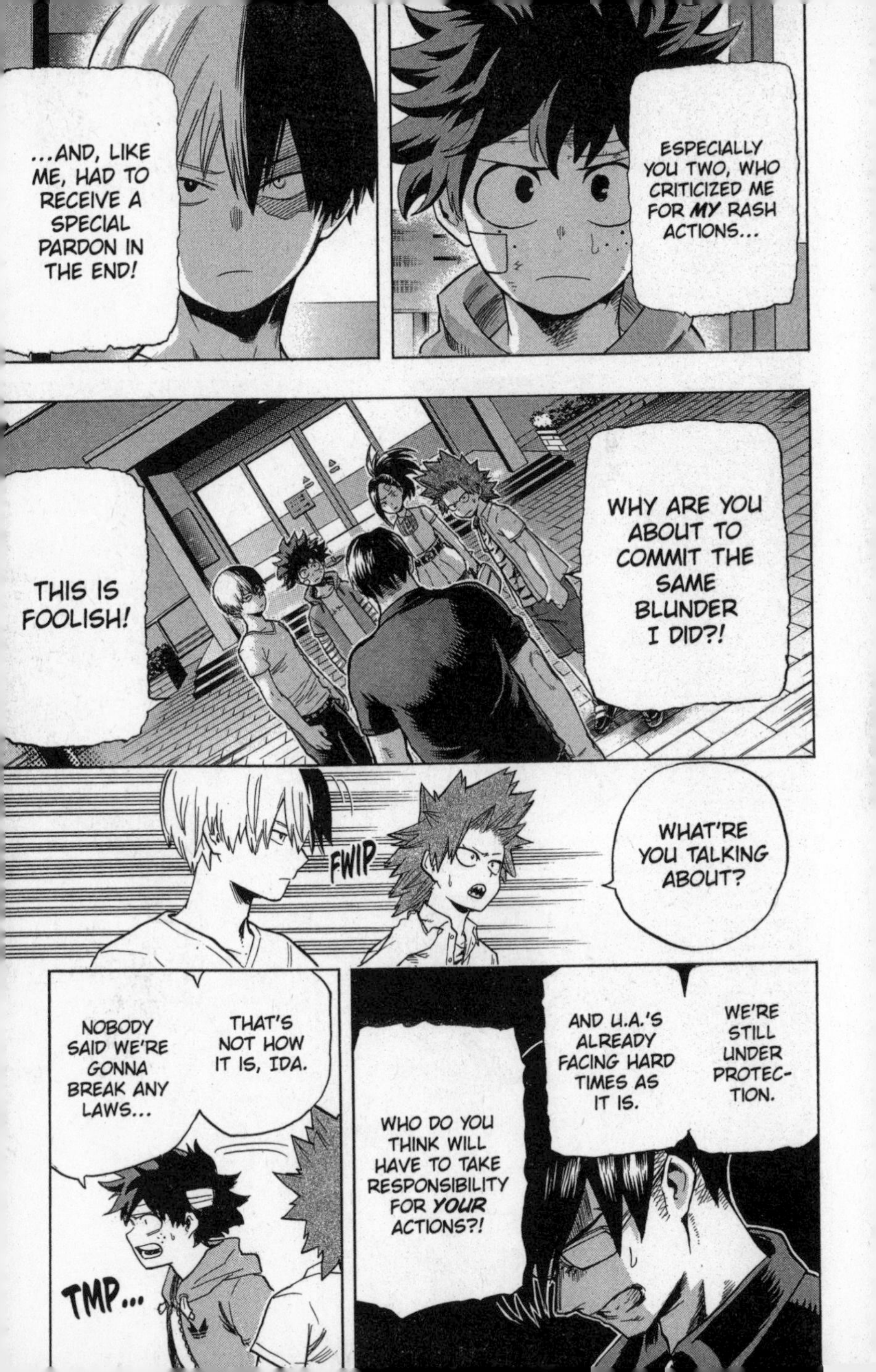
ESPECIALLY YOU TWO, WHO CRITICIZED ME FOR *MY* RASH ACTIONS...
...AND, LIKE ME, HAD TO RECEIVE A SPECIAL PARDON IN THE END!
WHY ARE YOU ABOUT TO COMMIT THE SAME BLUNDER I DID?!
THIS IS FOOLISH!
WHAT'RE YOU TALKING ABOUT?
FWIP
WE'RE STILL UNDER PROTECTION.
AND U.A.'S ALREADY FACING HARD TIMES AS IT IS.
WHO DO YOU THINK WILL HAVE TO TAKE RESPONSIBILITY FOR *YOUR* ACTIONS?!
THAT'S NOT HOW IT IS, IDA.
NOBODY SAID WE'RE GONNA BREAK ANY LAWS...
TMP...

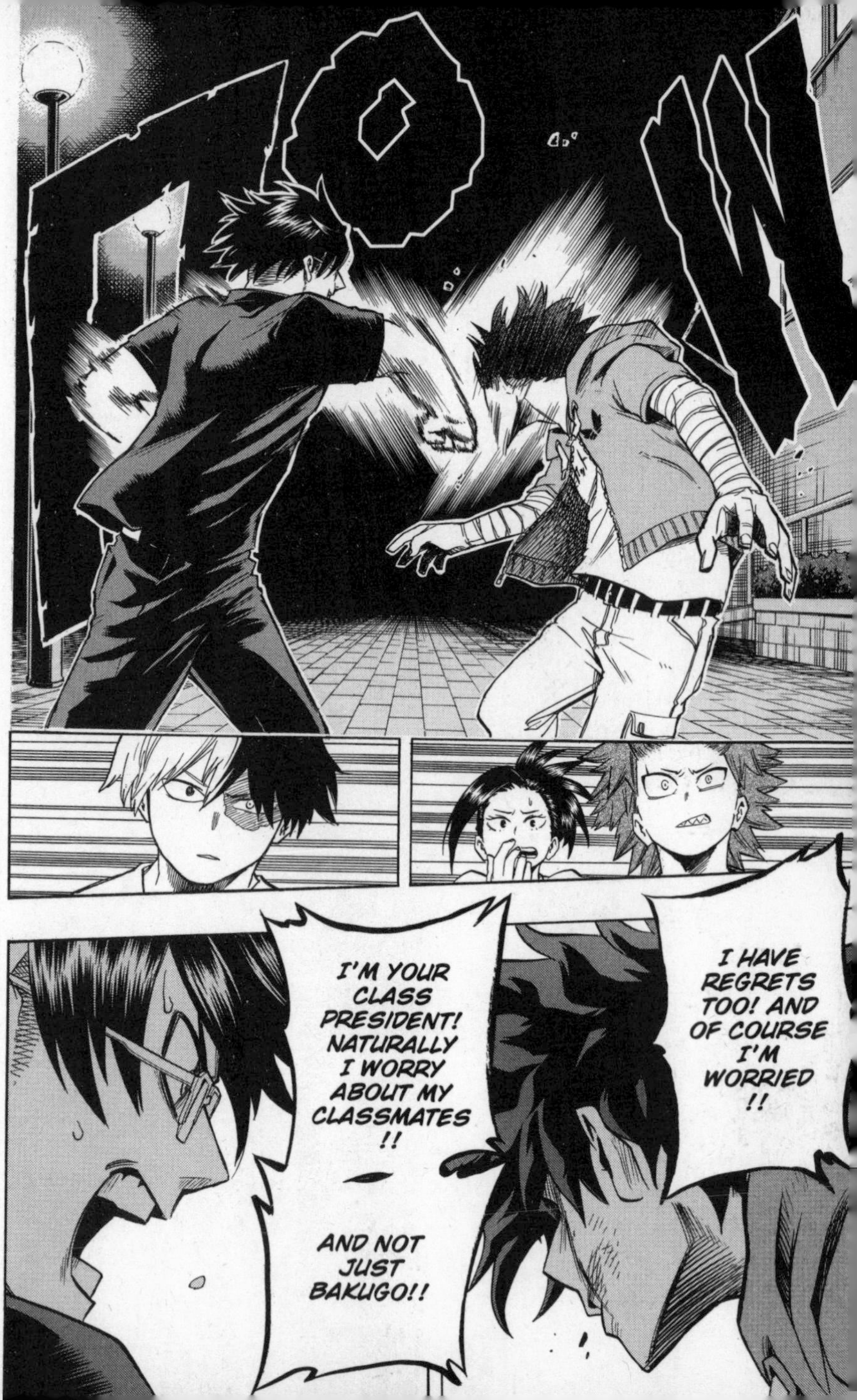
I HAVE REGRETS TOO! AND OF COURSE I'M WORRIED!!
I'M YOUR CLASS PRESIDENT! NATURALLY I WORRY ABOUT MY CLASSMATES!!
AND NOT JUST BAKUGO!!

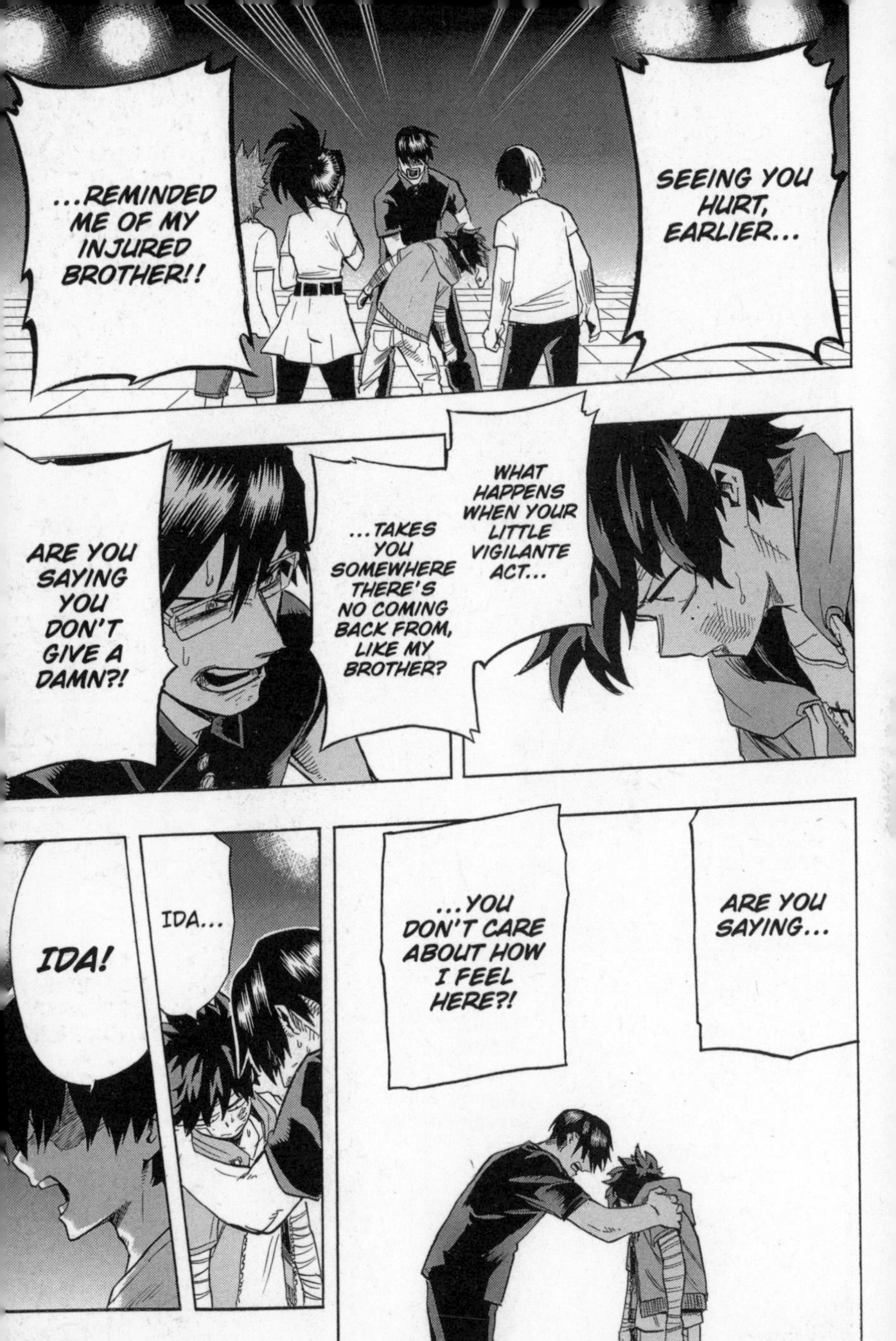
SEEING YOU HURT, EARLIER...
...REMINDED ME OF MY INJURED BROTHER!!
WHAT HAPPENS WHEN YOUR LITTLE VIGILANTE ACT...
...TAKES YOU SOMEWHERE THERE'S NO COMING BACK FROM, LIKE MY BROTHER?
ARE YOU SAYING YOU DON'T GIVE A DAMN?!
ARE YOU SAYING...
...YOU DON'T CARE ABOUT HOW I FEEL HERE?!
IDA...
IDA!

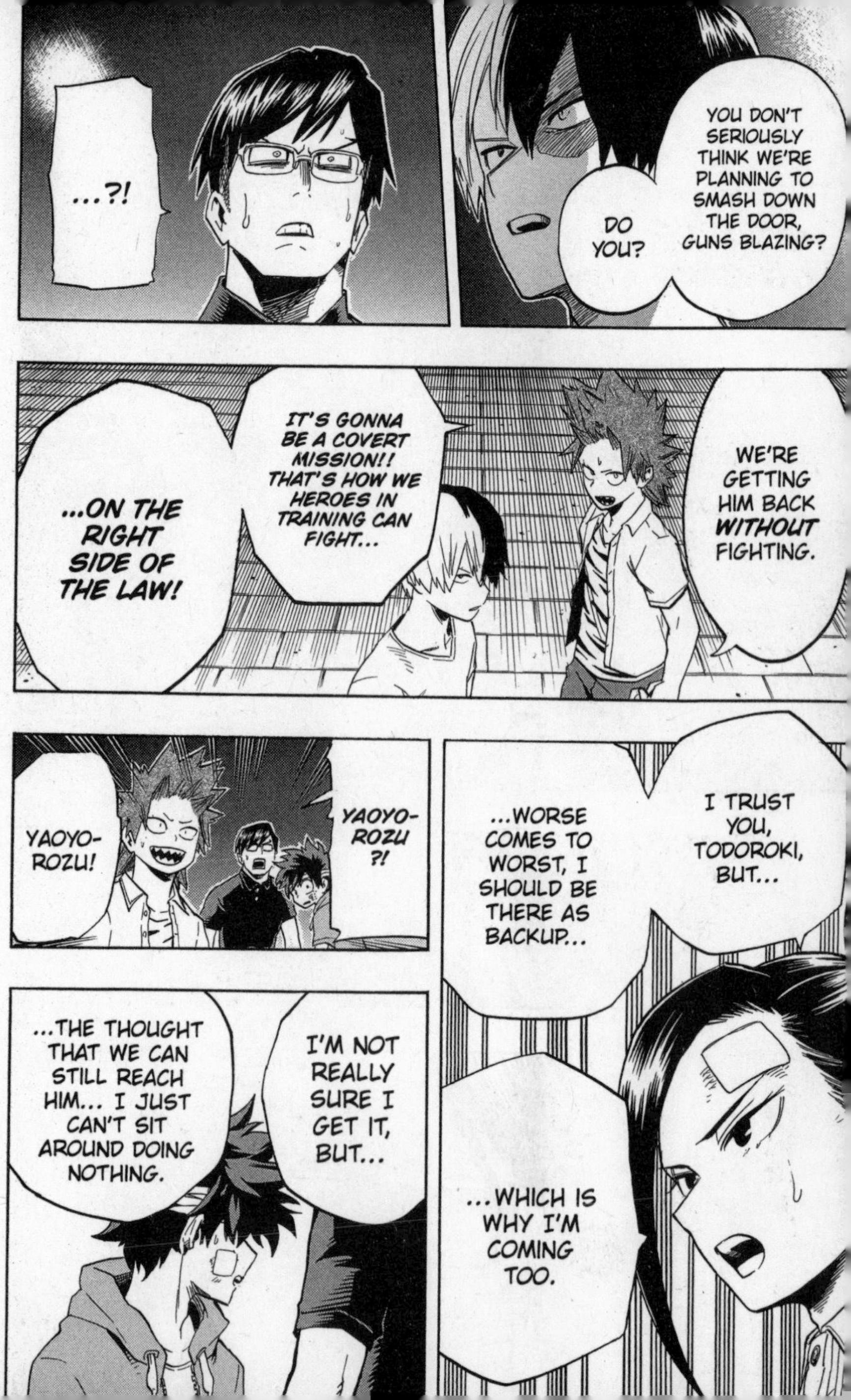
YOU DON'T SERIOUSLY THINK WE'RE PLANNING TO SMASH DOWN THE DOOR, GUNS BLAZING?
DO YOU?
...?!
WE'RE GETTING HIM BACK WITHOUT FIGHTING.
IT'S GONNA BE A COVERT MISSION!! THAT'S HOW WE HEROES IN TRAINING CAN FIGHT...
...ON THE RIGHT SIDE OF THE LAW!
I TRUST YOU, TODOROKI, BUT...
...WORSE COMES TO WORST, I SHOULD BE THERE AS BACKUP...
...WHICH IS WHY I'M COMING TOO.
YAOYO-ROZU ?!
YAOYO-ROZU!
I'M NOT REALLY SURE I GET IT, BUT...
...THE THOUGHT THAT WE CAN STILL REACH HIM... I JUST CAN'T SIT AROUND DOING NOTHING.

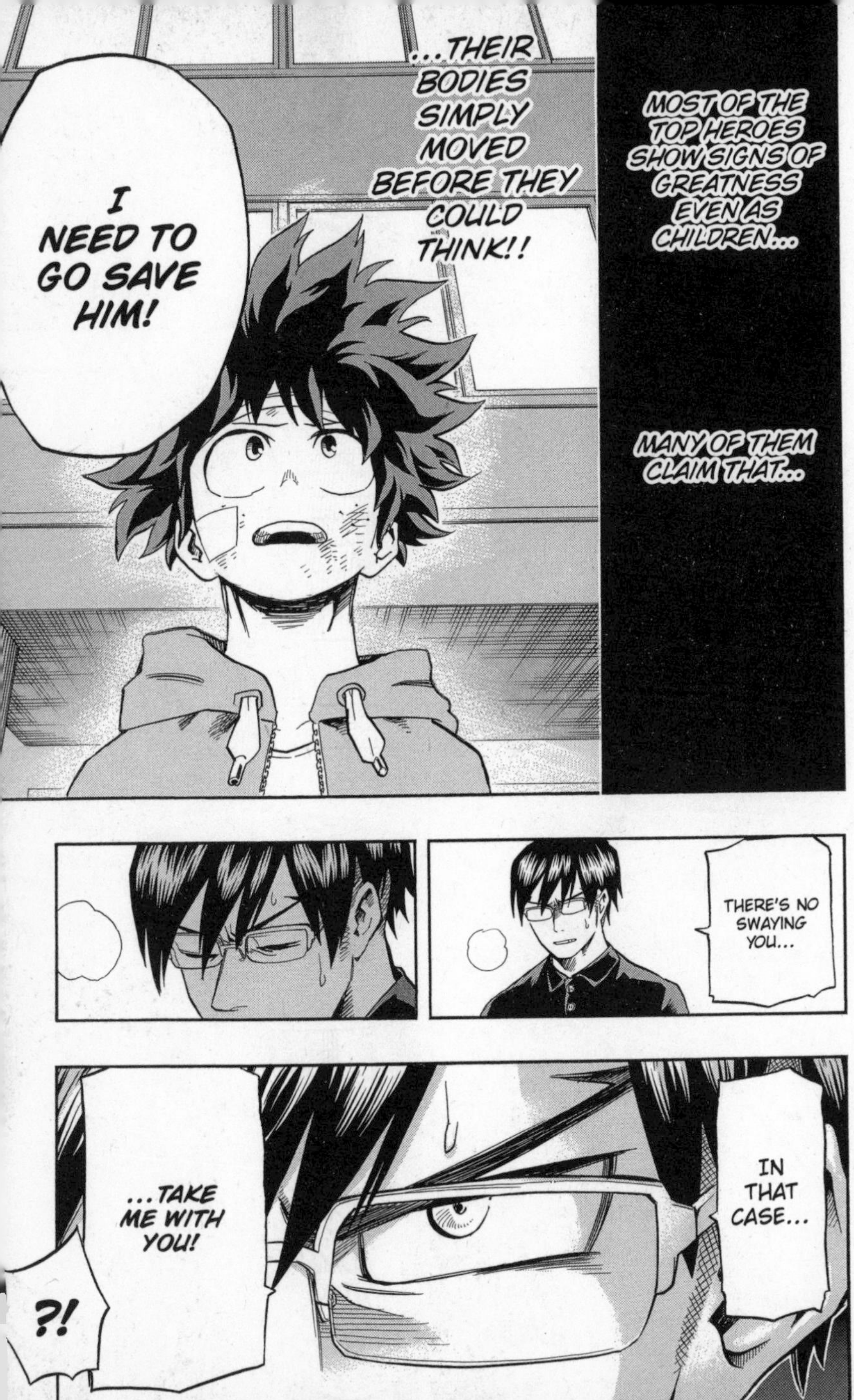
MOST OF THE TOP HEROES SHOW SIGNS OF GREATNESS EVEN AS CHILDREN...
MANY OF THEM CLAIM THAT...
...THEIR BODIES SIMPLY MOVED BEFORE THEY COULD THINK!!
I NEED TO GO SAVE HIM!
THERE'S NO SWAYING YOU...
IN THAT CASE...
...TAKE ME WITH YOU!
?!

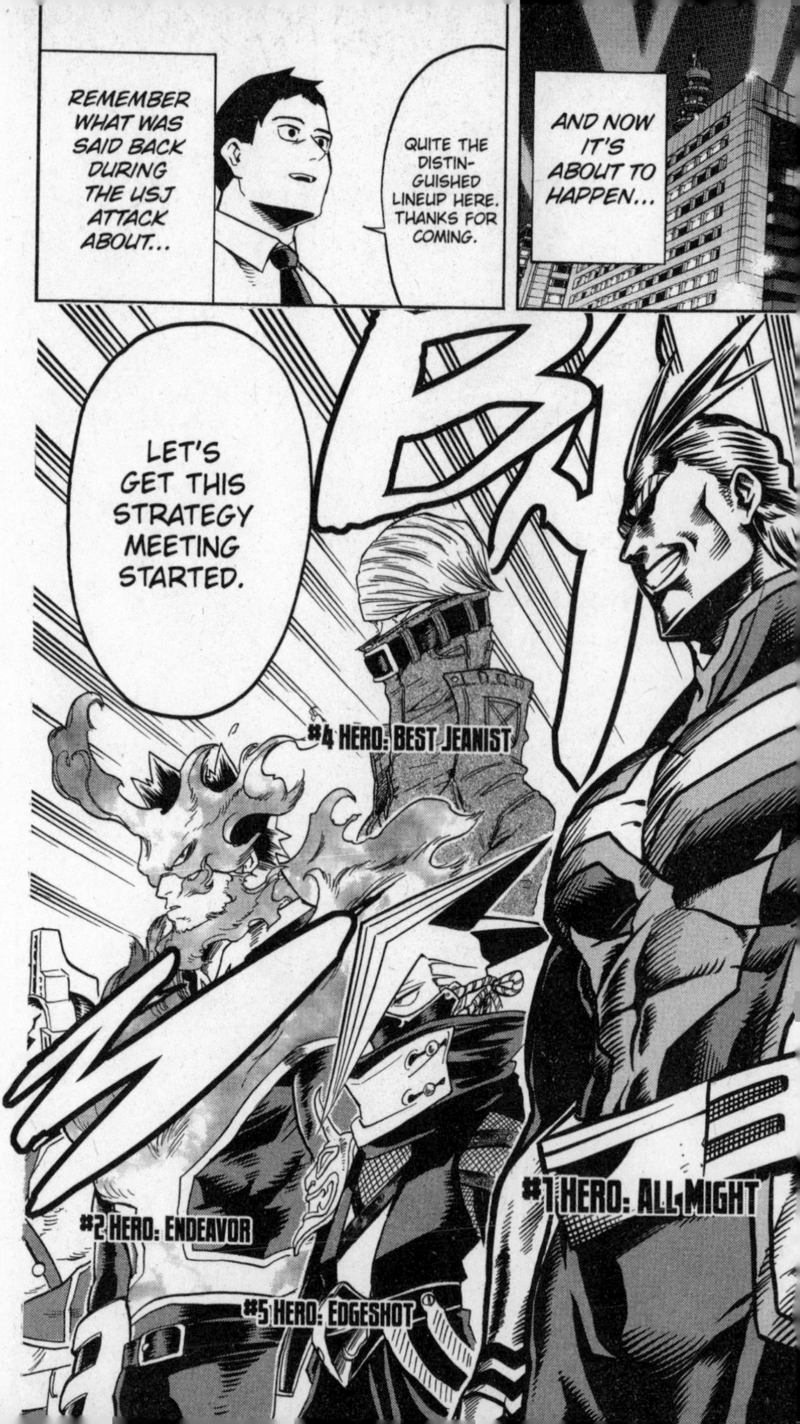
AND NOW IT'S ABOUT TO HAPPEN...
QUITE THE DISTIN-GUISHED LINEUP HERE. THANKS FOR COMING.
REMEMBER WHAT WAS SAID BACK DURING THE USJ ATTACK ABOUT...
LET'S GET THIS STRATEGY MEETING STARTED.
#4 HERO: BEST JEANIST
#1 HERO: ALL MIGHT
#2 HERO: ENDEAVOR
#5 HERO: EDGESHOT

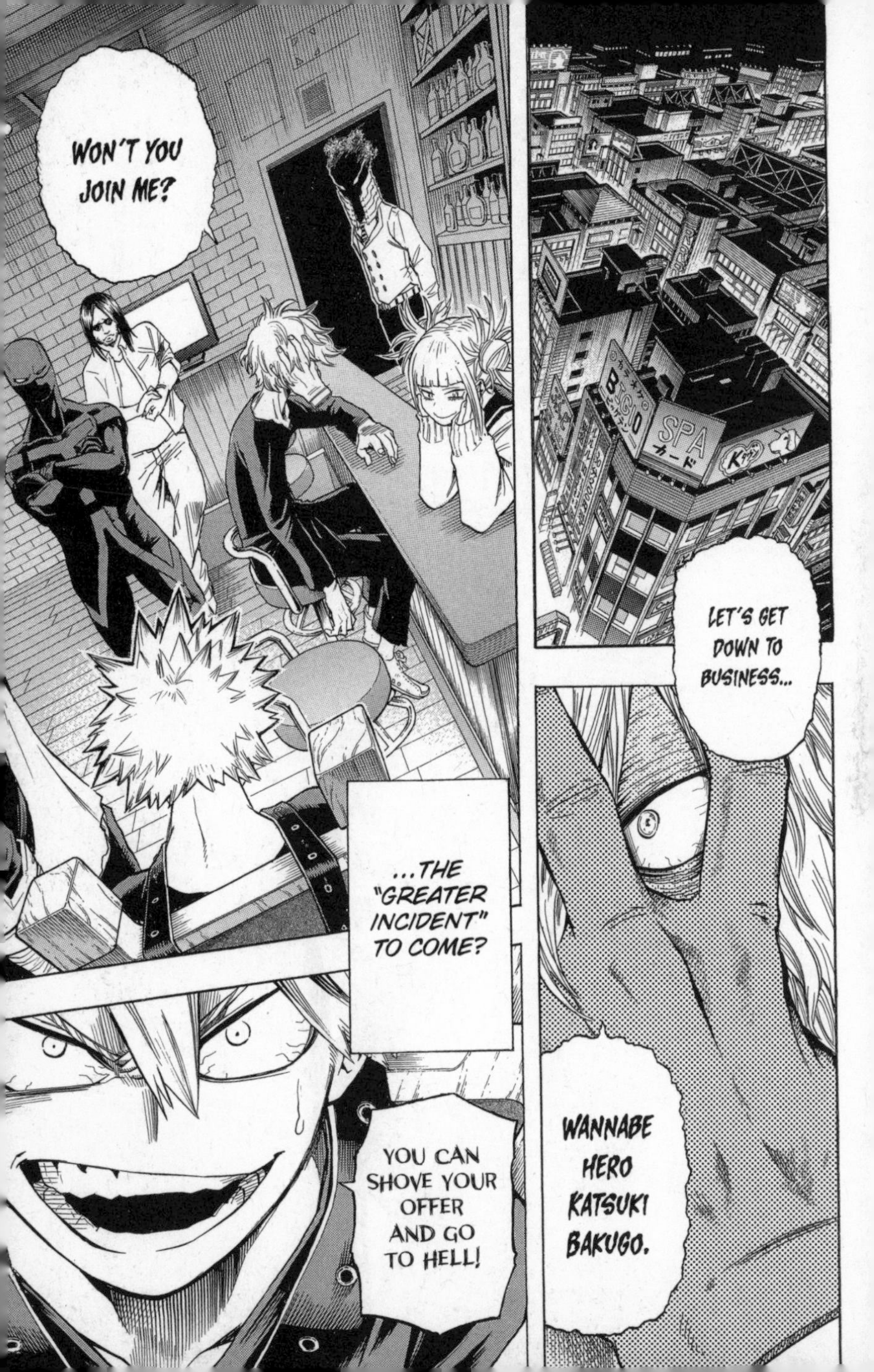
LET'S GET DOWN TO BUSINESS...
WANNABE HERO KATSUKI BAKUGO.
WON'T YOU JOIN ME?
...THE "GREATER INCIDENT" TO COME?
YOU CAN SHOVE YOUR OFFER AND GO TO HELL!
SPA
カード

COME TO THINK OF IT...

I never formally introduced Present Mic's civilian clothing or real name, so here it is. Incidentally, the word "HAGE" on the headphones he's always wearing is the brand name. It's not because he himself is *hage* (bald).

Hizashi Yamada

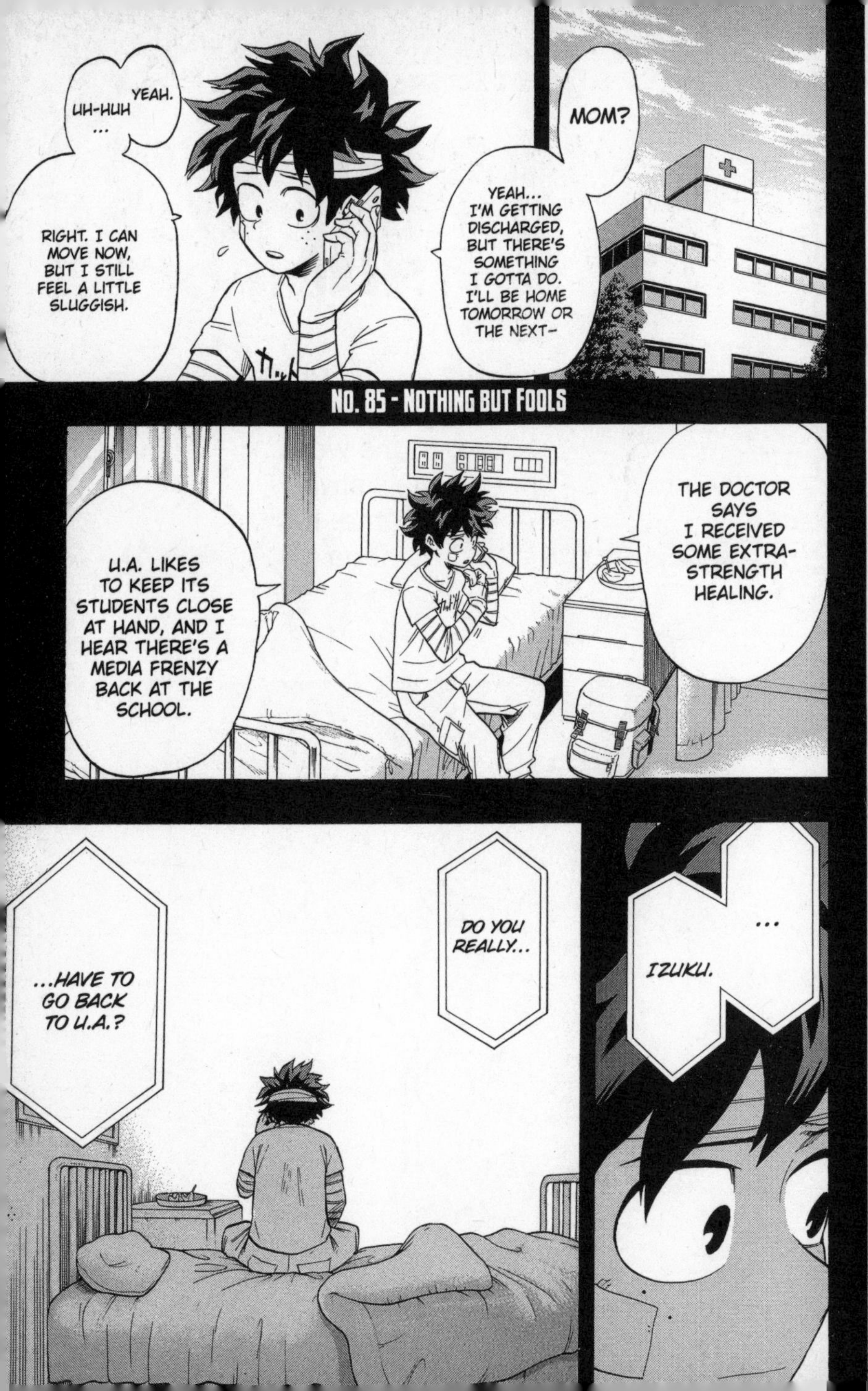
MOM?
YEAH... I'M GETTING DISCHARGED, BUT THERE'S SOMETHING I GOTTA DO. I'LL BE HOME TOMORROW OR THE NEXT–
YEAH. UH-HUH ...
RIGHT. I CAN MOVE NOW, BUT I STILL FEEL A LITTLE SLUGGISH.
NO. 85 - NOTHING BUT FOOLS
THE DOCTOR SAYS I RECEIVED SOME EXTRA-STRENGTH HEALING.
U.A. LIKES TO KEEP ITS STUDENTS CLOSE AT HAND, AND I HEAR THERE'S A MEDIA FRENZY BACK AT THE SCHOOL.
... IZUKU.
DO YOU REALLY...
...HAVE TO GO BACK TO U.A.?

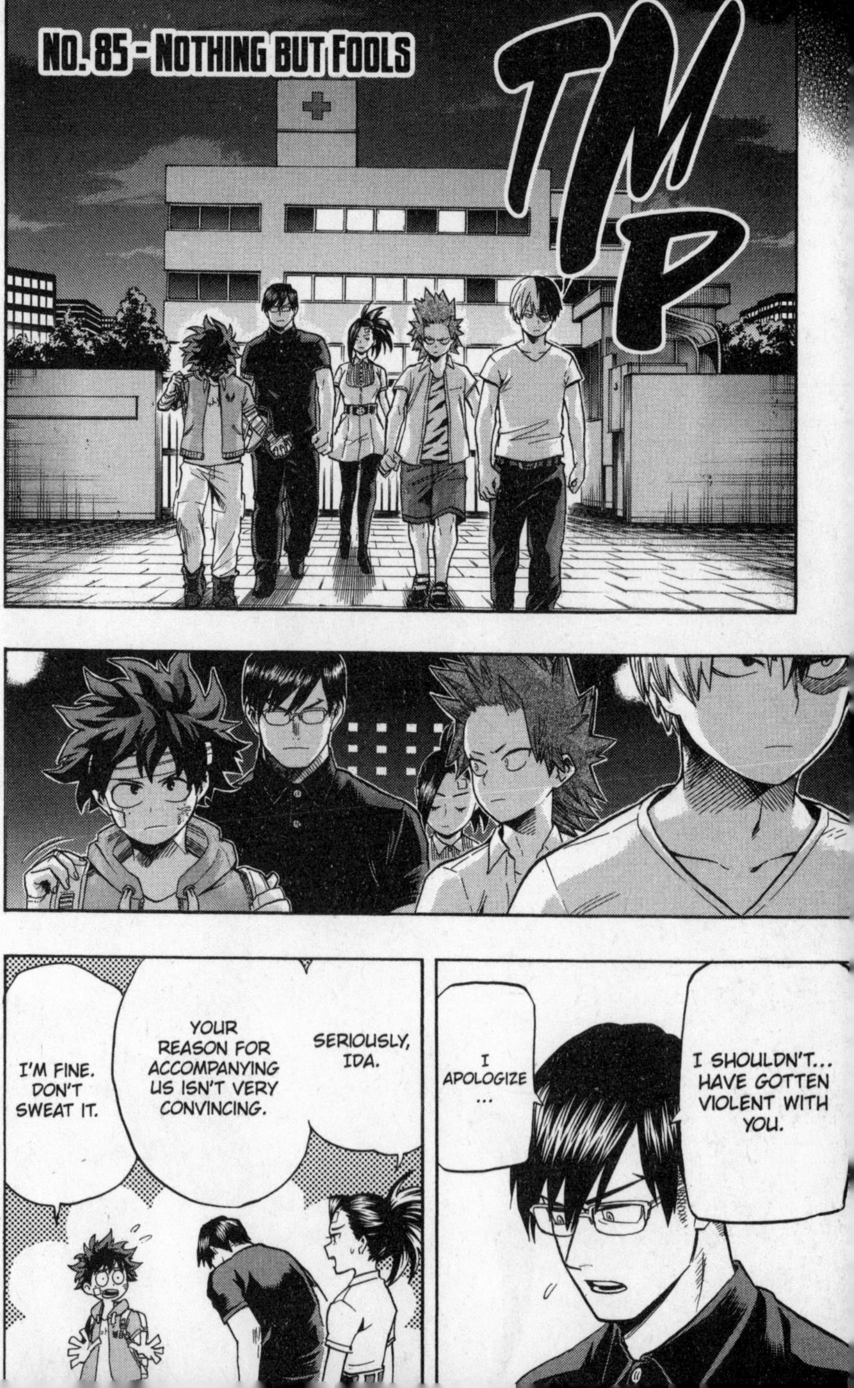
No. 85 - Nothing But Fools
TMP
I SHOULDN'T... HAVE GOTTEN VIOLENT WITH YOU.
I APOLOGIZE...
SERIOUSLY, IDA.
YOUR REASON FOR ACCOMPANYING US ISN'T VERY CONVINCING.
I'M FINE. DON'T SWEAT IT.

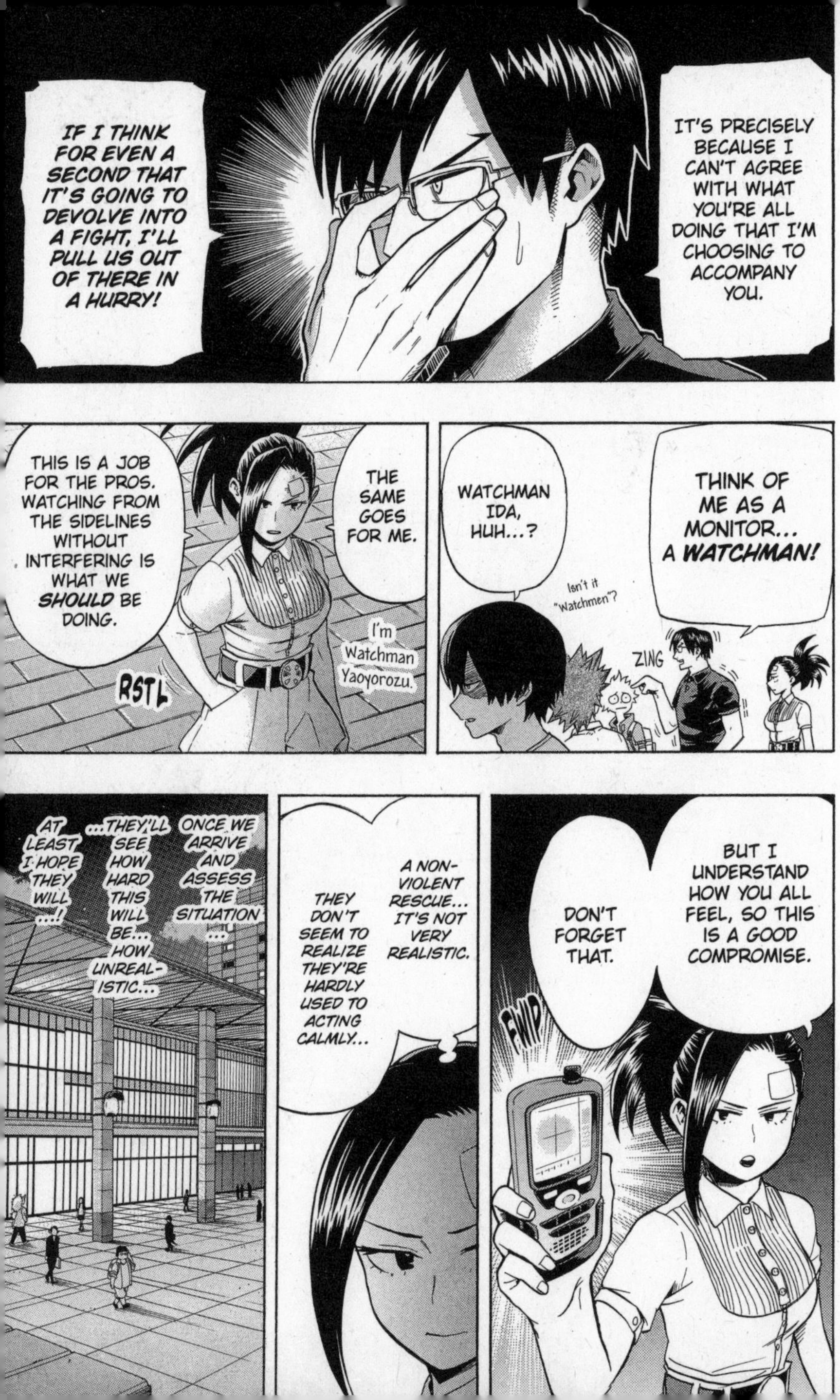
IT'S PRECISELY BECAUSE I CAN'T AGREE WITH WHAT YOU'RE ALL DOING THAT I'M CHOOSING TO ACCOMPANY YOU.
IF I THINK FOR EVEN A SECOND THAT IT'S GOING TO DEVOLVE INTO A FIGHT, I'LL PULL US OUT OF THERE IN A HURRY!
THINK OF ME AS A MONITOR... A WATCHMAN!
Isn't it "Watchmen"?
ZING
WATCHMAN IDA, HUH...?
THE SAME GOES FOR ME.
THIS IS A JOB FOR THE PROS. WATCHING FROM THE SIDELINES WITHOUT INTERFERING IS WHAT WE SHOULD BE DOING.
I'm Watchman Yaoyorozu.
RSTL
BUT I UNDERSTAND HOW YOU ALL FEEL, SO THIS IS A GOOD COMPROMISE.
DON'T FORGET THAT.
FWIP
A NON-VIOLENT RESCUE... IT'S NOT VERY REALISTIC.
THEY DON'T SEEM TO REALIZE THEY'RE HARDLY USED TO ACTING CALMLY...
ONCE WE ARRIVE AND ASSESS THE SITUATION...
...THEY'LL SEE HOW HARD THIS WILL BE... HOW UNREALISTIC...
AT LEAST I HOPE THEY WILL...!

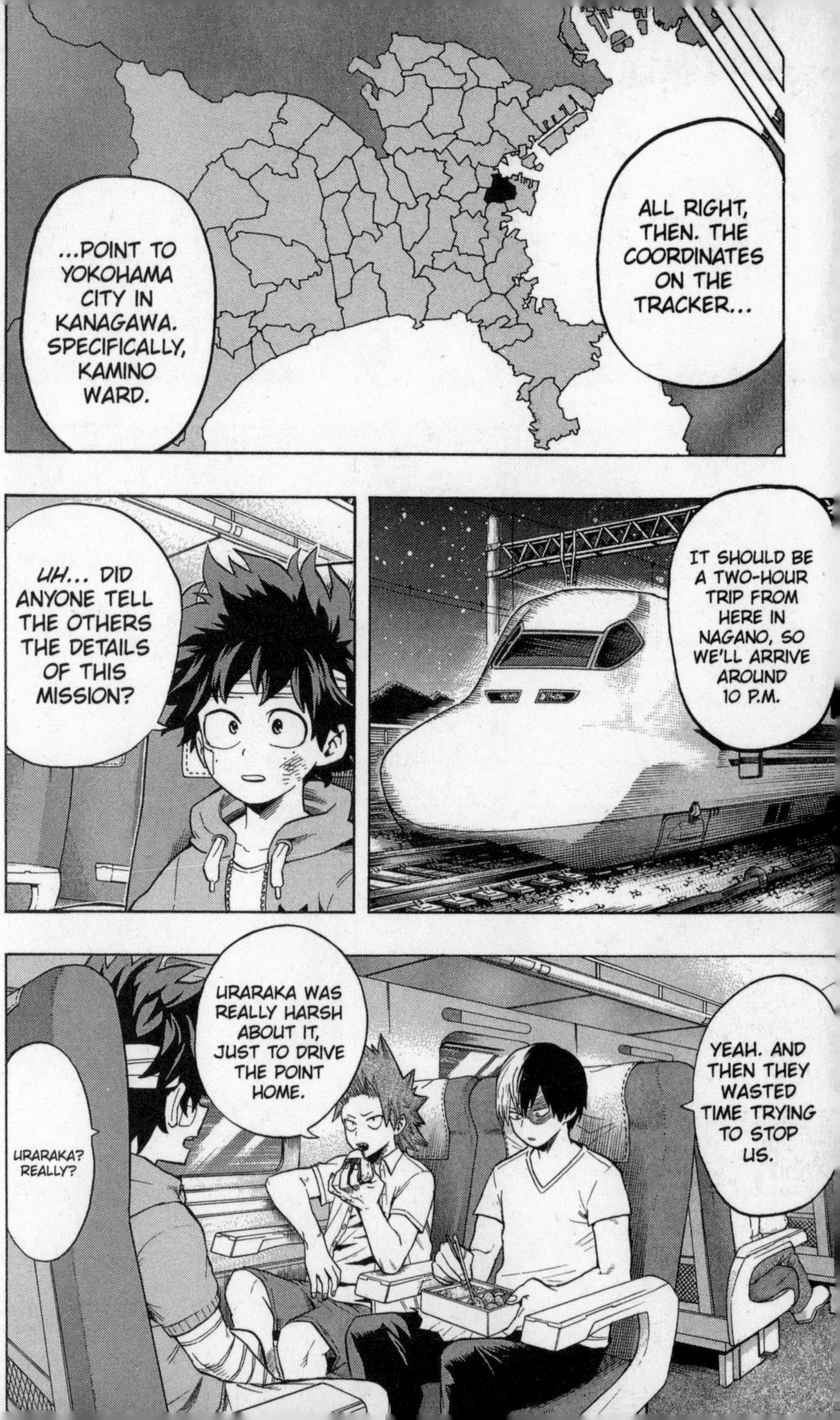
ALL RIGHT, THEN. THE COORDINATES ON THE TRACKER...
...POINT TO YOKOHAMA CITY IN KANAGAWA. SPECIFICALLY, KAMINO WARD.
IT SHOULD BE A TWO-HOUR TRIP FROM HERE IN NAGANO, SO WE'LL ARRIVE AROUND 10 P.M.
UH... DID ANYONE TELL THE OTHERS THE DETAILS OF THIS MISSION?
URARAKA WAS REALLY HARSH ABOUT IT, JUST TO DRIVE THE POINT HOME.
YEAH. AND THEN THEY WASTED TIME TRYING TO STOP US.
URARAKA? REALLY?

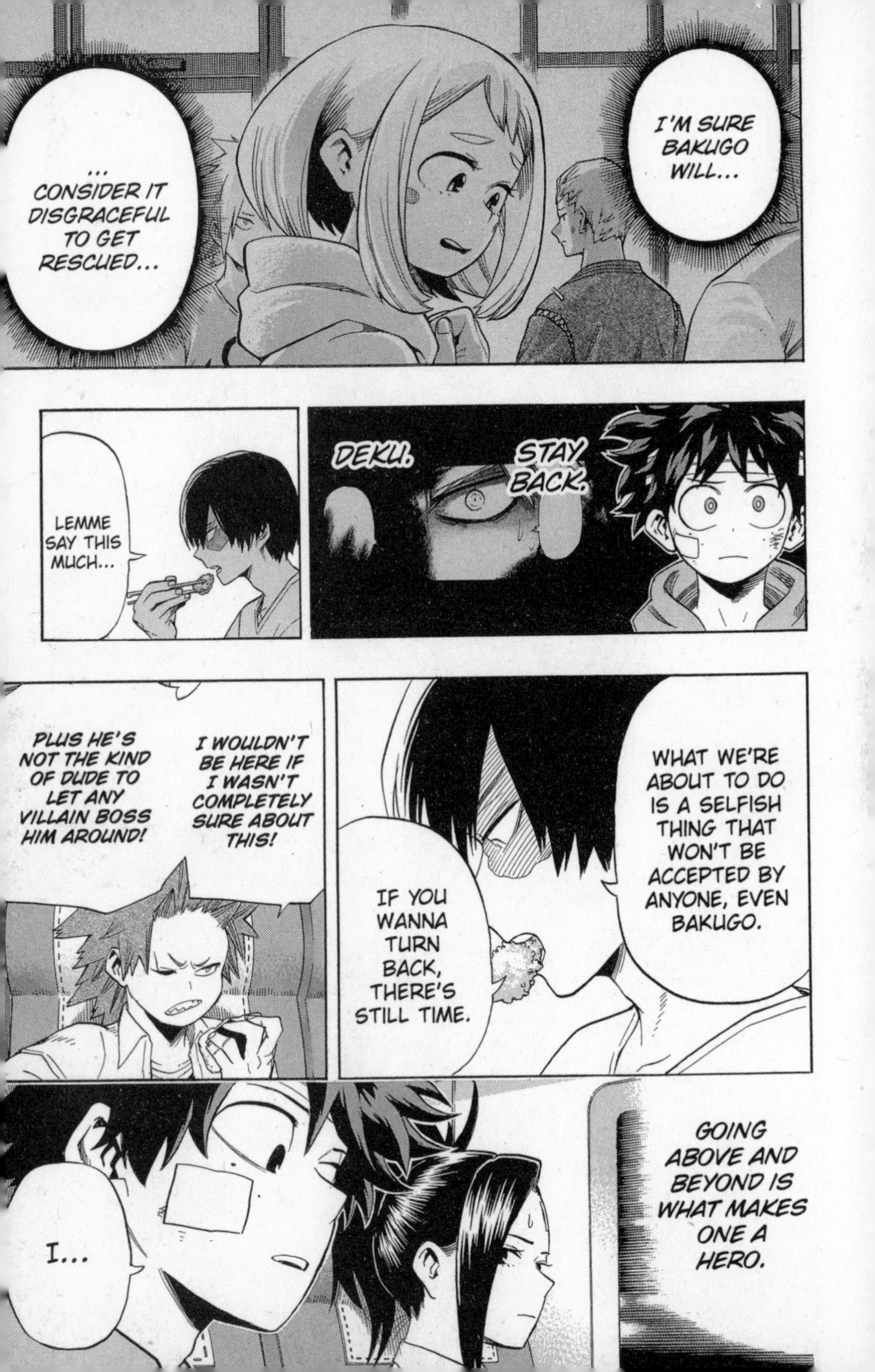
I'M SURE BAKUGO WILL...
... CONSIDER IT DISGRACEFUL TO GET RESCUED...
DEKU.
STAY BACK.
LEMME SAY THIS MUCH...
WHAT WE'RE ABOUT TO DO IS A SELFISH THING THAT WON'T BE ACCEPTED BY ANYONE, EVEN BAKUGO.
IF YOU WANNA TURN BACK, THERE'S STILL TIME.
I WOULDN'T BE HERE IF I WASN'T COMPLETELY SURE ABOUT THIS!
PLUS HE'S NOT THE KIND OF DUDE TO LET ANY VILLAIN BOSS HIM AROUND!
GOING ABOVE AND BEYOND IS WHAT MAKES ONE A HERO.
I...

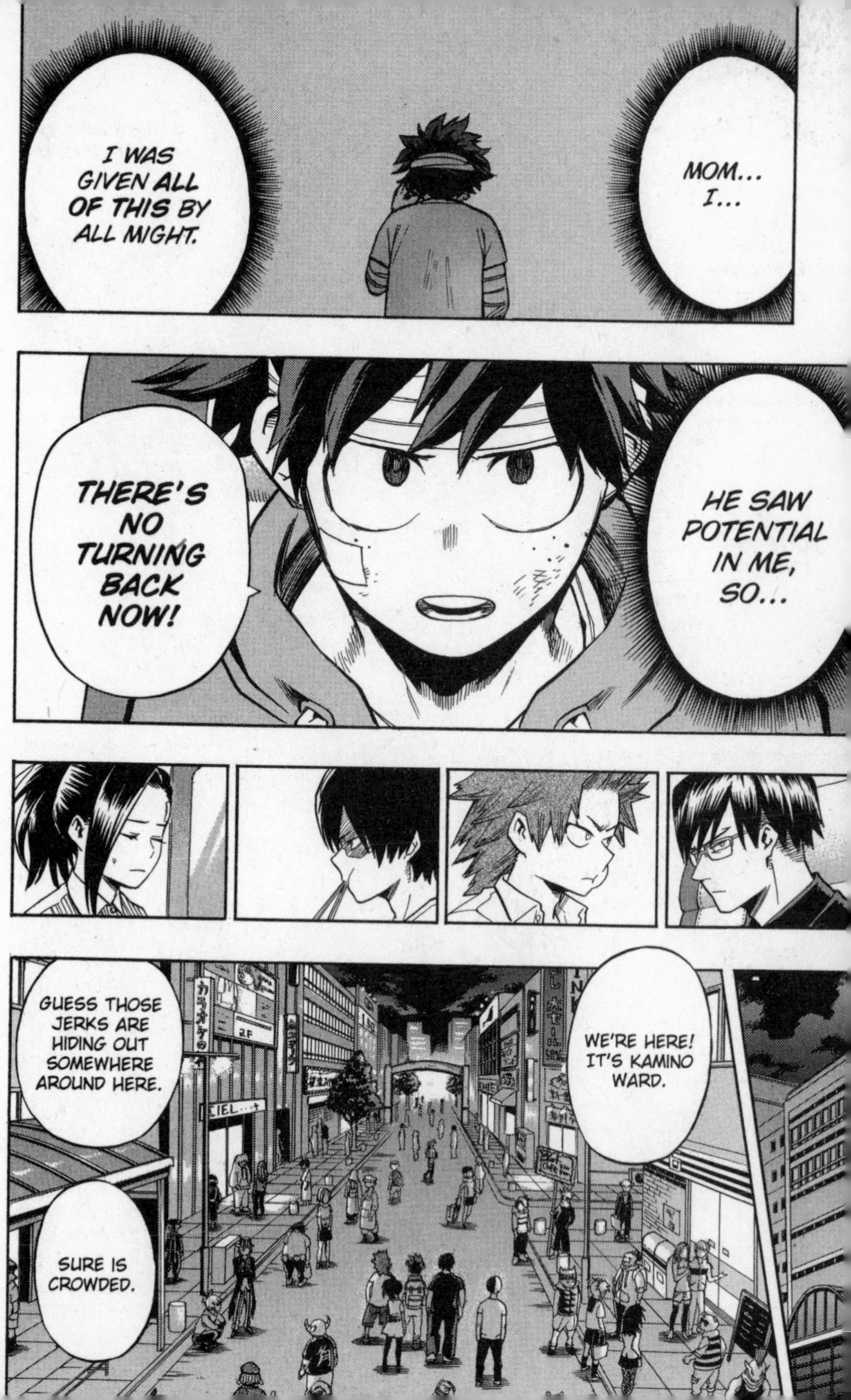
MOM... I...
I WAS GIVEN ALL OF THIS BY ALL MIGHT.
HE SAW POTENTIAL IN ME, SO...
THERE'S NO TURNING BACK NOW!
WE'RE HERE! IT'S KAMINO WARD.
GUESS THOSE JERKS ARE HIDING OUT SOMEWHERE AROUND HERE.
SURE IS CROWDED.
CIEL

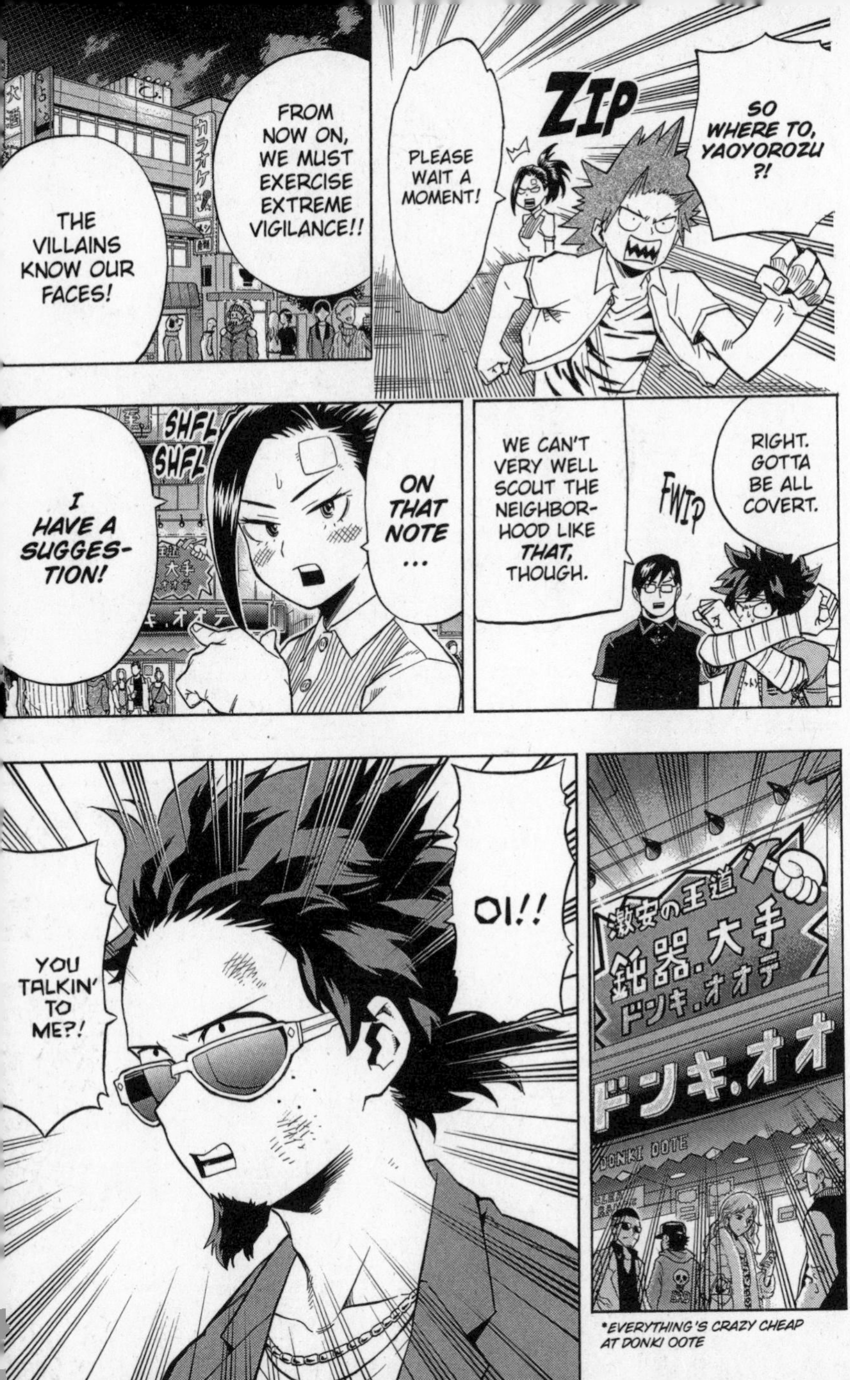
SO WHERE TO, YAOYOROZU ?!
ZIP
PLEASE WAIT A MOMENT!
FROM NOW ON, WE MUST EXERCISE EXTREME VIGILANCE!!
THE VILLAINS KNOW OUR FACES!
RIGHT. GOTTA BE ALL COVERT.
FWIP
WE CAN'T VERY WELL SCOUT THE NEIGHBOR-HOOD LIKE THAT, THOUGH.
ON THAT NOTE...
SHFL SHFL
I HAVE A SUGGES-TION!
激安の王道
鈍器.大手
ドンキ.オオテ
ドンキ.オオ
DONKI OOTE
OI!!
YOU TALKIN' TO ME?!

*EVERYTHING'S CRAZY CHEAP AT DONKI OOTE

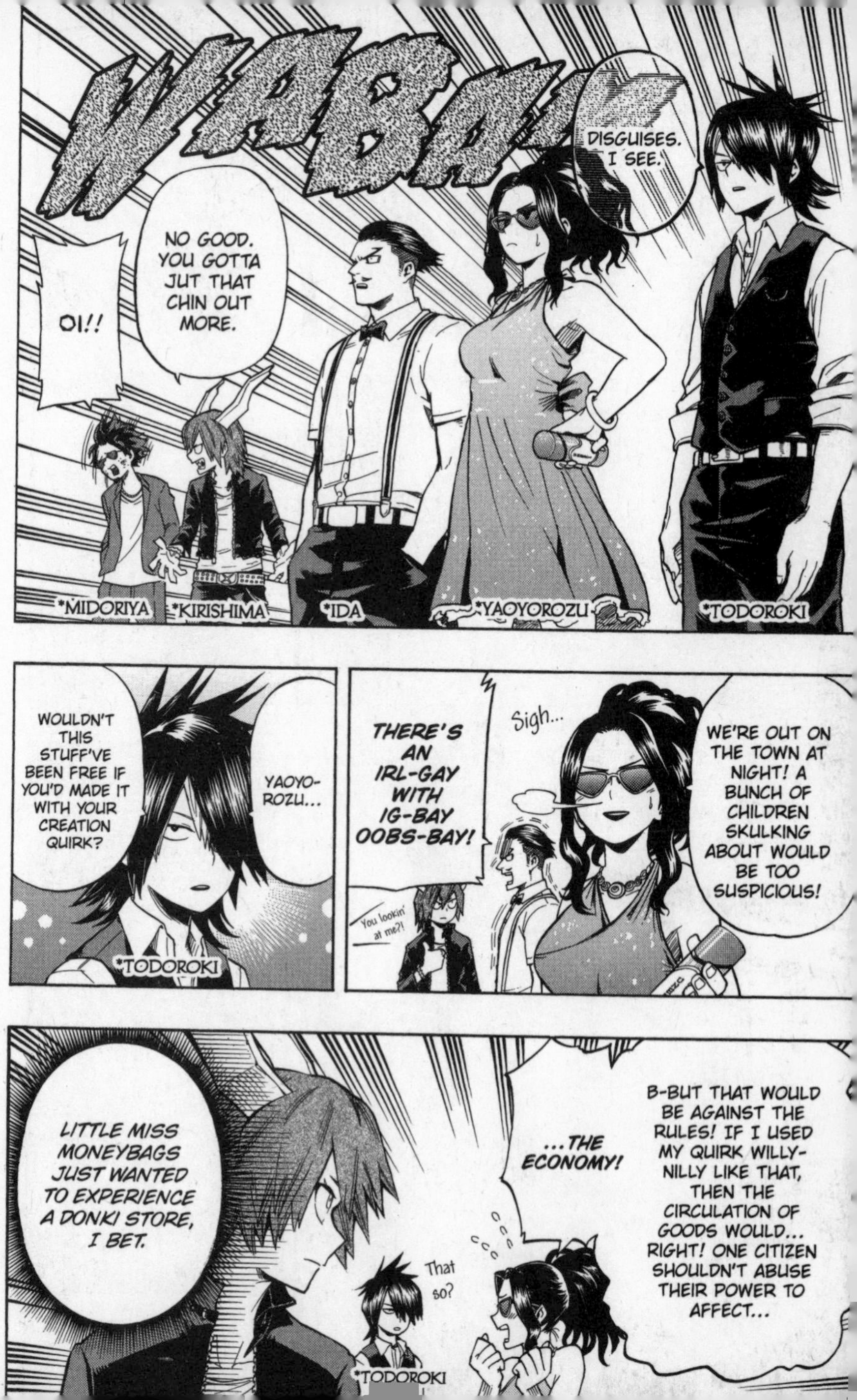
DISGUISES. I SEE.
WABAM
NO GOOD. YOU GOTTA JUT THAT CHIN OUT MORE.
OI!!
*TODOROKI
*YAOYOROZU
*IDA
*KIRISHIMA
*MIDORIYA
WE'RE OUT ON THE TOWN AT NIGHT! A BUNCH OF CHILDREN SKULKING ABOUT WOULD BE TOO SUSPICIOUS!
Sigh...
THERE'S AN IRL-GAY WITH IG-BAY OOBS-BAY!
You lookin' at me?!
YAOYO-ROZU...
WOULDN'T THIS STUFF'VE BEEN FREE IF YOU'D MADE IT WITH YOUR CREATION QUIRK?
*TODOROKI
B-BUT THAT WOULD BE AGAINST THE RULES! IF I USED MY QUIRK WILLY-NILLY LIKE THAT, THEN THE CIRCULATION OF GOODS WOULD... RIGHT! ONE CITIZEN SHOULDN'T ABUSE THEIR POWER TO AFFECT...
...THE ECONOMY!
That so?
LITTLE MISS MONEYBAGS JUST WANTED TO EXPERIENCE A DONKI STORE, I BET.
*TODOROKI

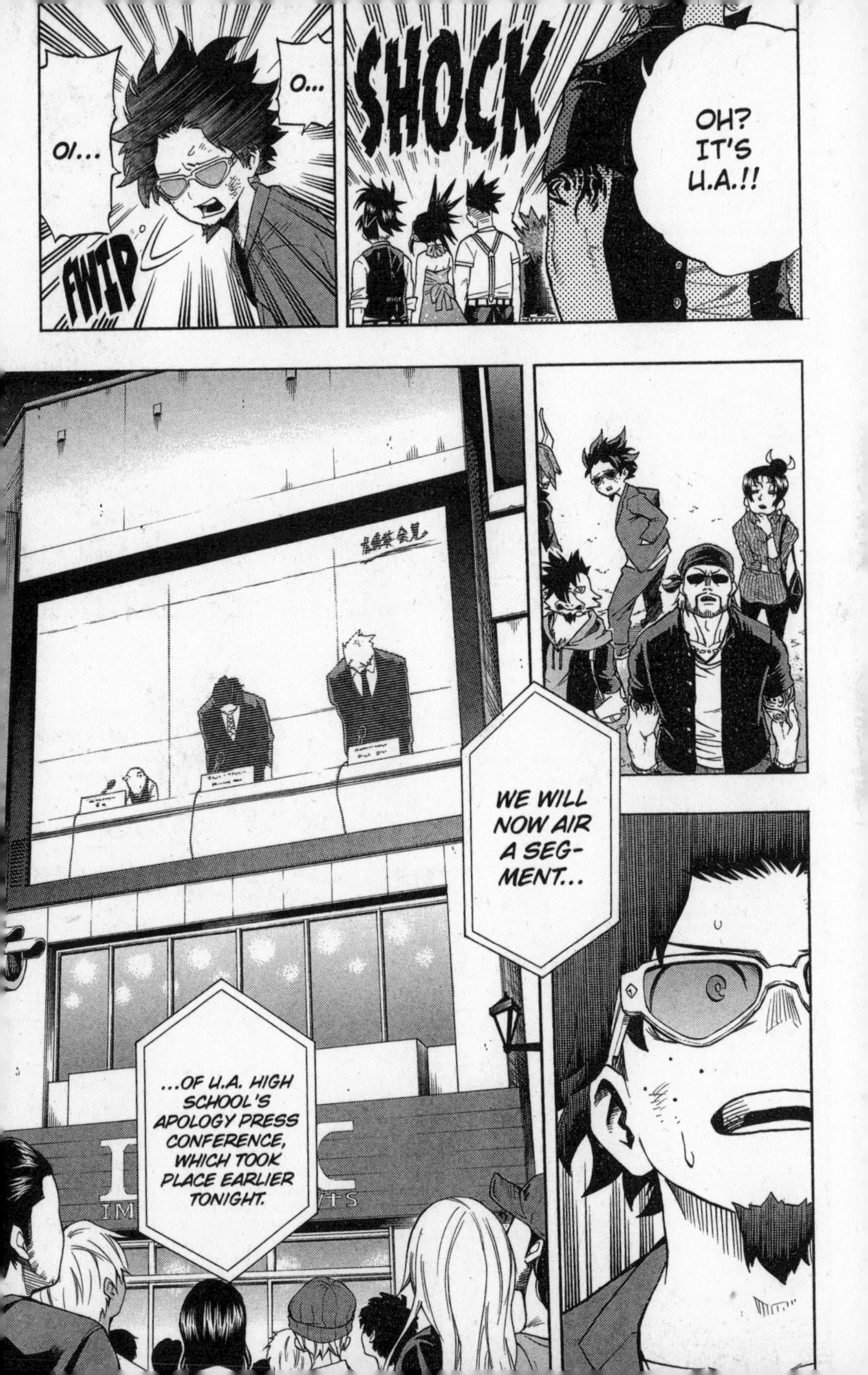
OH? IT'S U.A.!!
SHOCK
O...
OI...
FWIP
WE WILL NOW AIR A SEG-MENT...
...OF U.A. HIGH SCHOOL'S APOLOGY PRESS CONFERENCE, WHICH TOOK PLACE EARLIER TONIGHT.

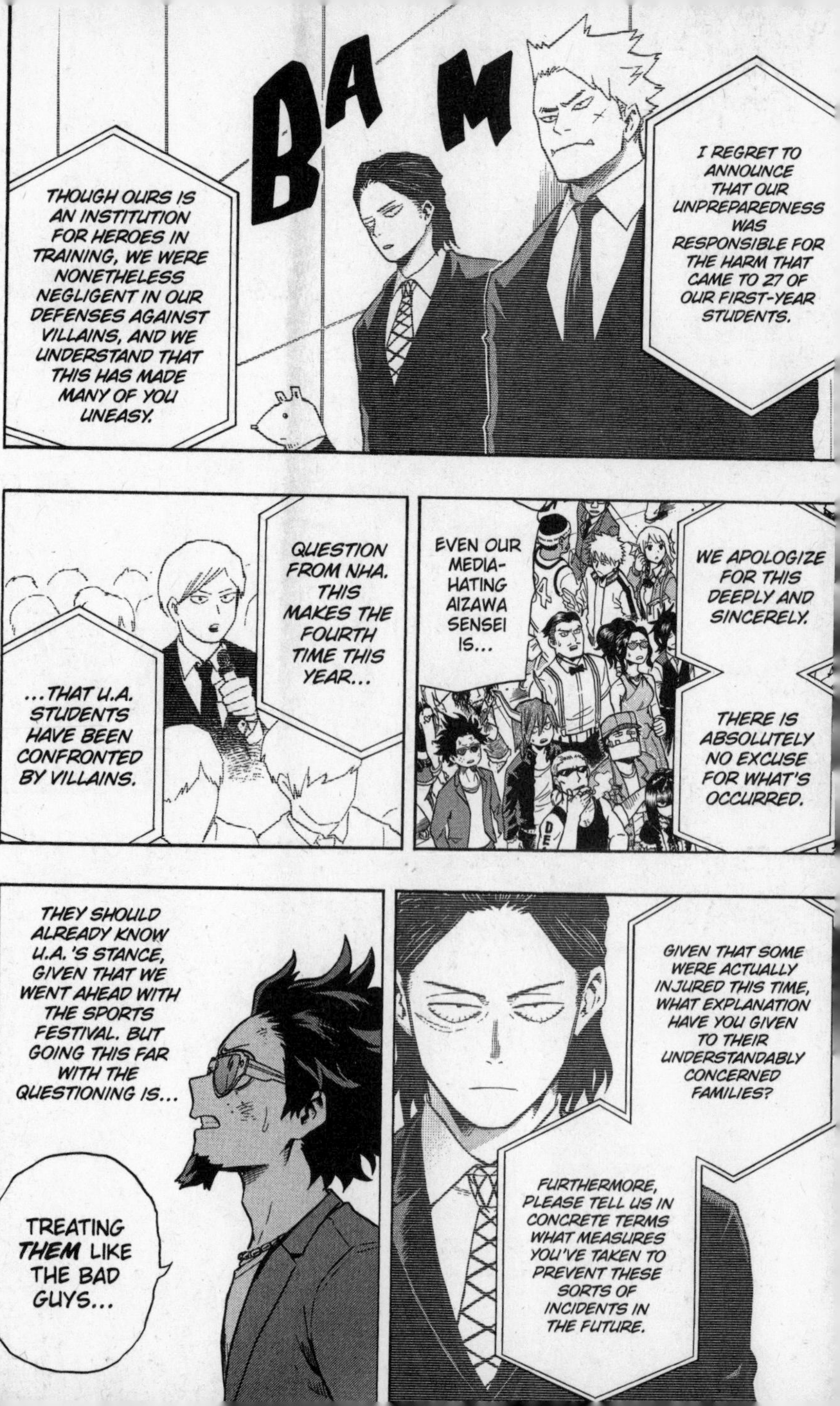
BAM
I REGRET TO ANNOUNCE THAT OUR UNPREPAREDNESS WAS RESPONSIBLE FOR THE HARM THAT CAME TO 27 OF OUR FIRST-YEAR STUDENTS.
THOUGH OURS IS AN INSTITUTION FOR HEROES IN TRAINING, WE WERE NONETHELESS NEGLIGENT IN OUR DEFENSES AGAINST VILLAINS, AND WE UNDERSTAND THAT THIS HAS MADE MANY OF YOU UNEASY.
WE APOLOGIZE FOR THIS DEEPLY AND SINCERELY.
EVEN OUR MEDIA-HATING AIZAWA SENSEI IS...
THERE IS ABSOLUTELY NO EXCUSE FOR WHAT'S OCCURRED.
QUESTION FROM NHA. THIS MAKES THE FOURTH TIME THIS YEAR...
...THAT U.A. STUDENTS HAVE BEEN CONFRONTED BY VILLAINS.
GIVEN THAT SOME WERE ACTUALLY INJURED THIS TIME, WHAT EXPLANATION HAVE YOU GIVEN TO THEIR UNDERSTANDABLY CONCERNED FAMILIES?
FURTHERMORE, PLEASE TELL US IN CONCRETE TERMS WHAT MEASURES YOU'VE TAKEN TO PREVENT THESE SORTS OF INCIDENTS IN THE FUTURE.
THEY SHOULD ALREADY KNOW U.A.'S STANCE, GIVEN THAT WE WENT AHEAD WITH THE SPORTS FESTIVAL. BUT GOING THIS FAR WITH THE QUESTIONING IS...
TREATING THEM LIKE THE BAD GUYS...

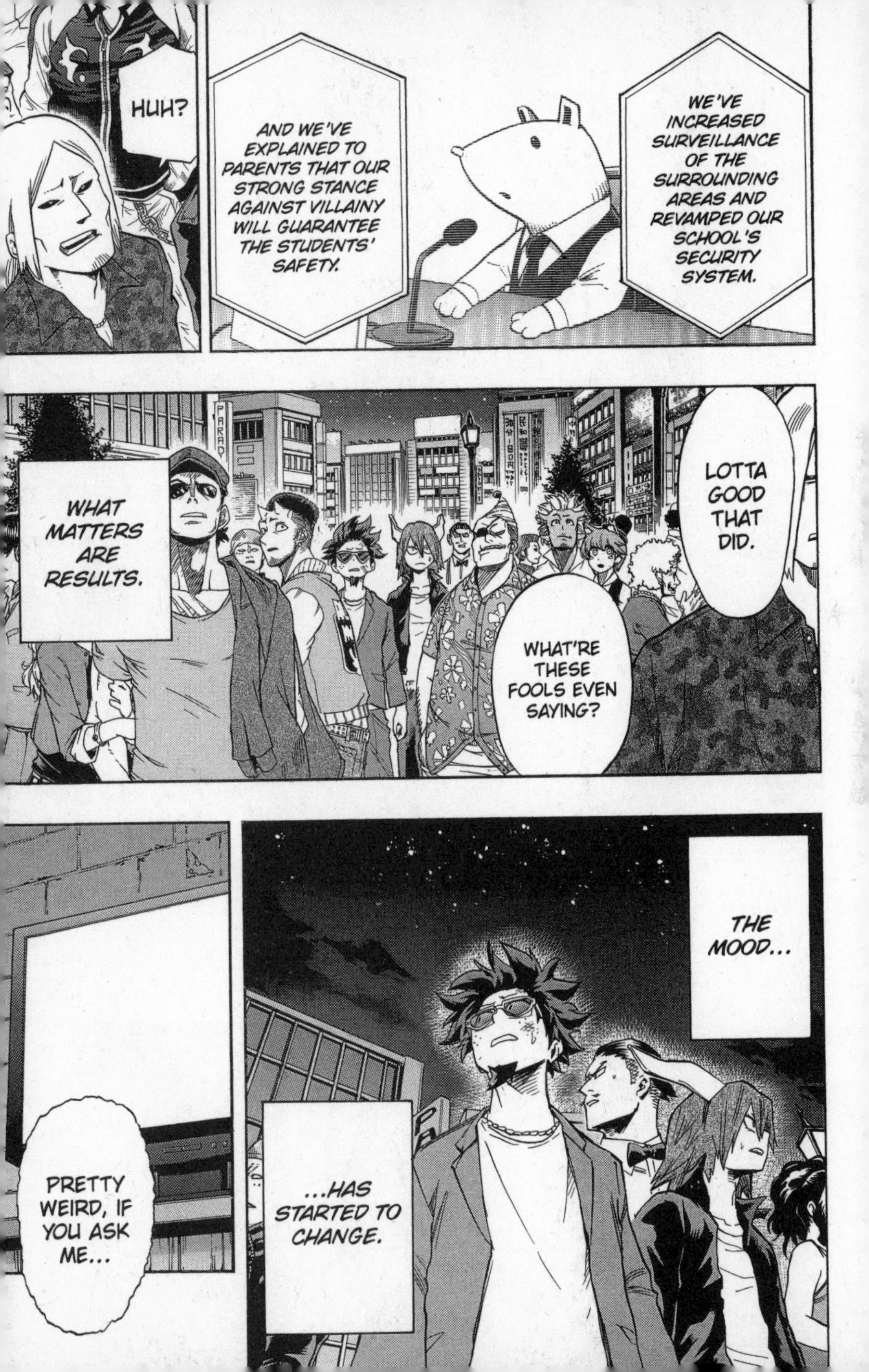
WE'VE INCREASED SURVEILLANCE OF THE SURROUNDING AREAS AND REVAMPED OUR SCHOOL'S SECURITY SYSTEM.
AND WE'VE EXPLAINED TO PARENTS THAT OUR STRONG STANCE AGAINST VILLAINY WILL GUARANTEE THE STUDENTS' SAFETY.
HUH?
LOTTA GOOD THAT DID.
WHAT'RE THESE FOOLS EVEN SAYING?
WHAT MATTERS ARE RESULTS.
THE MOOD...
...HAS STARTED TO CHANGE.
PRETTY WEIRD, IF YOU ASK ME...

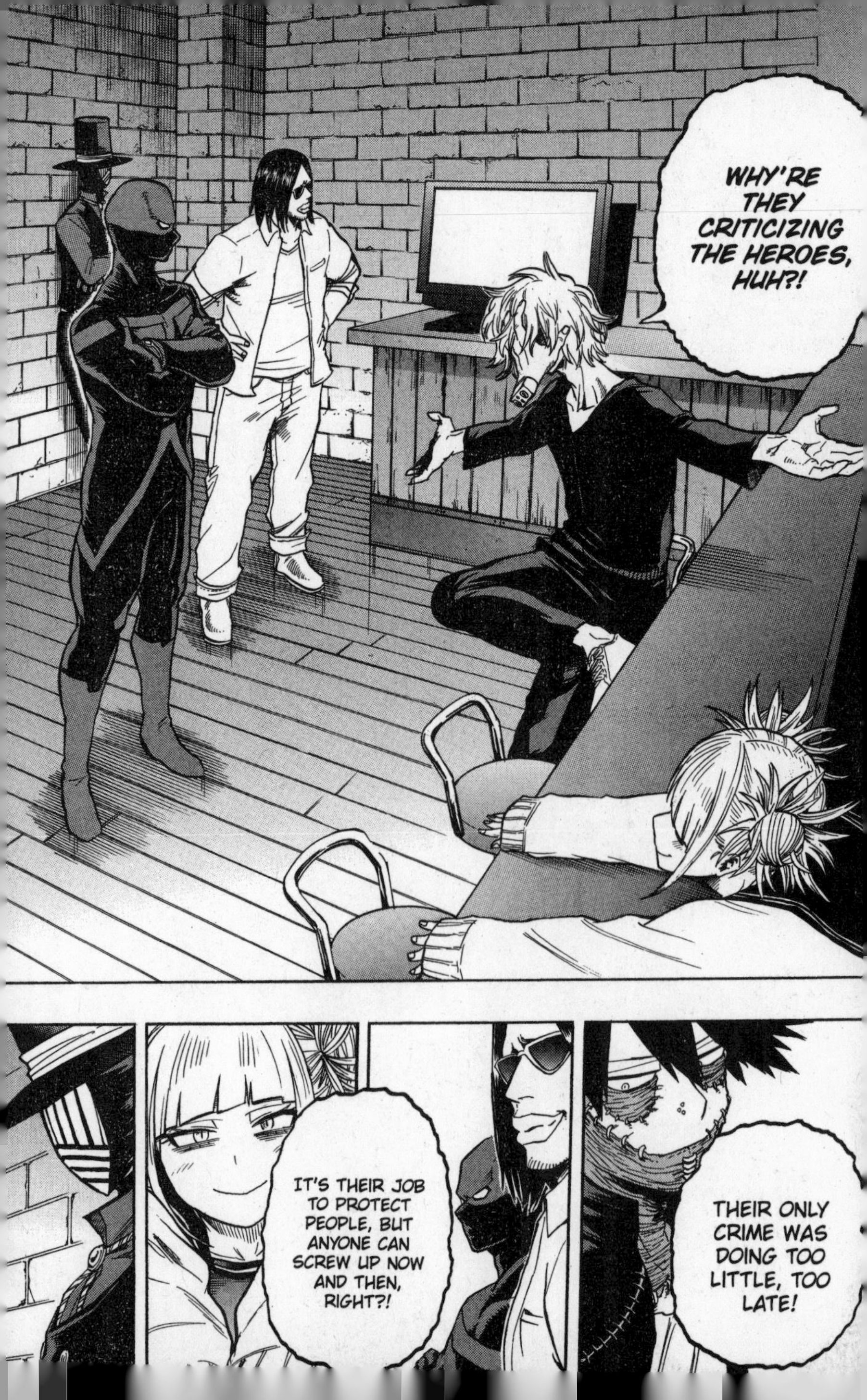
WHY'RE THEY CRITICIZING THE HEROES, HUH?!
THEIR ONLY CRIME WAS DOING TOO LITTLE, TOO LATE!
IT'S THEIR JOB TO PROTECT PEOPLE, BUT ANYONE CAN SCREW UP NOW AND THEN, RIGHT?!

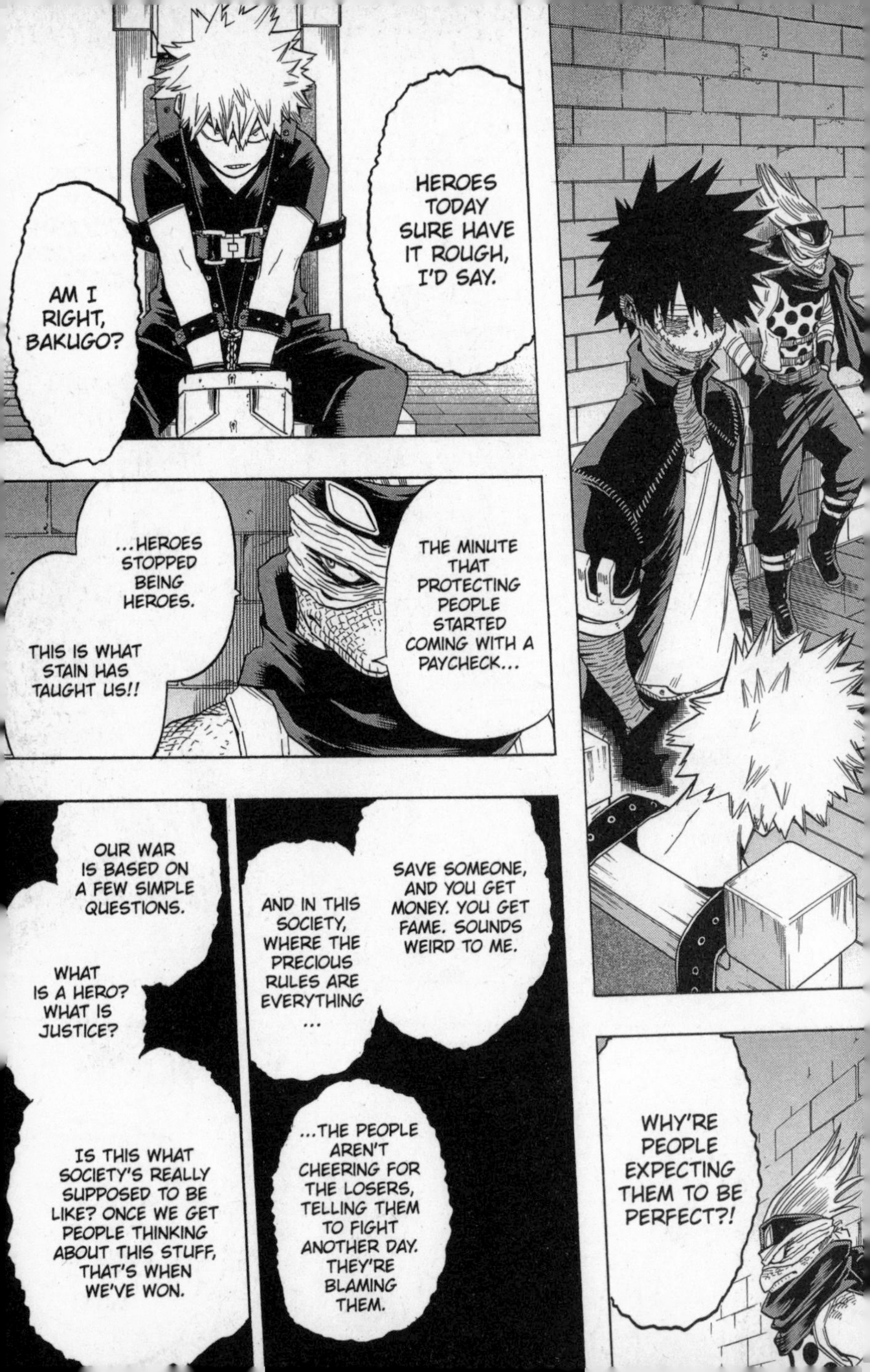
HEROES TODAY SURE HAVE IT ROUGH, I'D SAY.
AM I RIGHT, BAKUGO?
THE MINUTE THAT PROTECTING PEOPLE STARTED COMING WITH A PAYCHECK...
...HEROES STOPPED BEING HEROES.
THIS IS WHAT STAIN HAS TAUGHT US!!
WHY'RE PEOPLE EXPECTING THEM TO BE PERFECT?!
SAVE SOMEONE, AND YOU GET MONEY. YOU GET FAME. SOUNDS WEIRD TO ME.
AND IN THIS SOCIETY, WHERE THE PRECIOUS RULES ARE EVERYTHING ...
...THE PEOPLE AREN'T CHEERING FOR THE LOSERS, TELLING THEM TO FIGHT ANOTHER DAY. THEY'RE BLAMING THEM.
OUR WAR IS BASED ON A FEW SIMPLE QUESTIONS.
WHAT IS A HERO? WHAT IS JUSTICE?
IS THIS WHAT SOCIETY'S REALLY SUPPOSED TO BE LIKE? ONCE WE GET PEOPLE THINKING ABOUT THIS STUFF, THAT'S WHEN WE'VE WON.

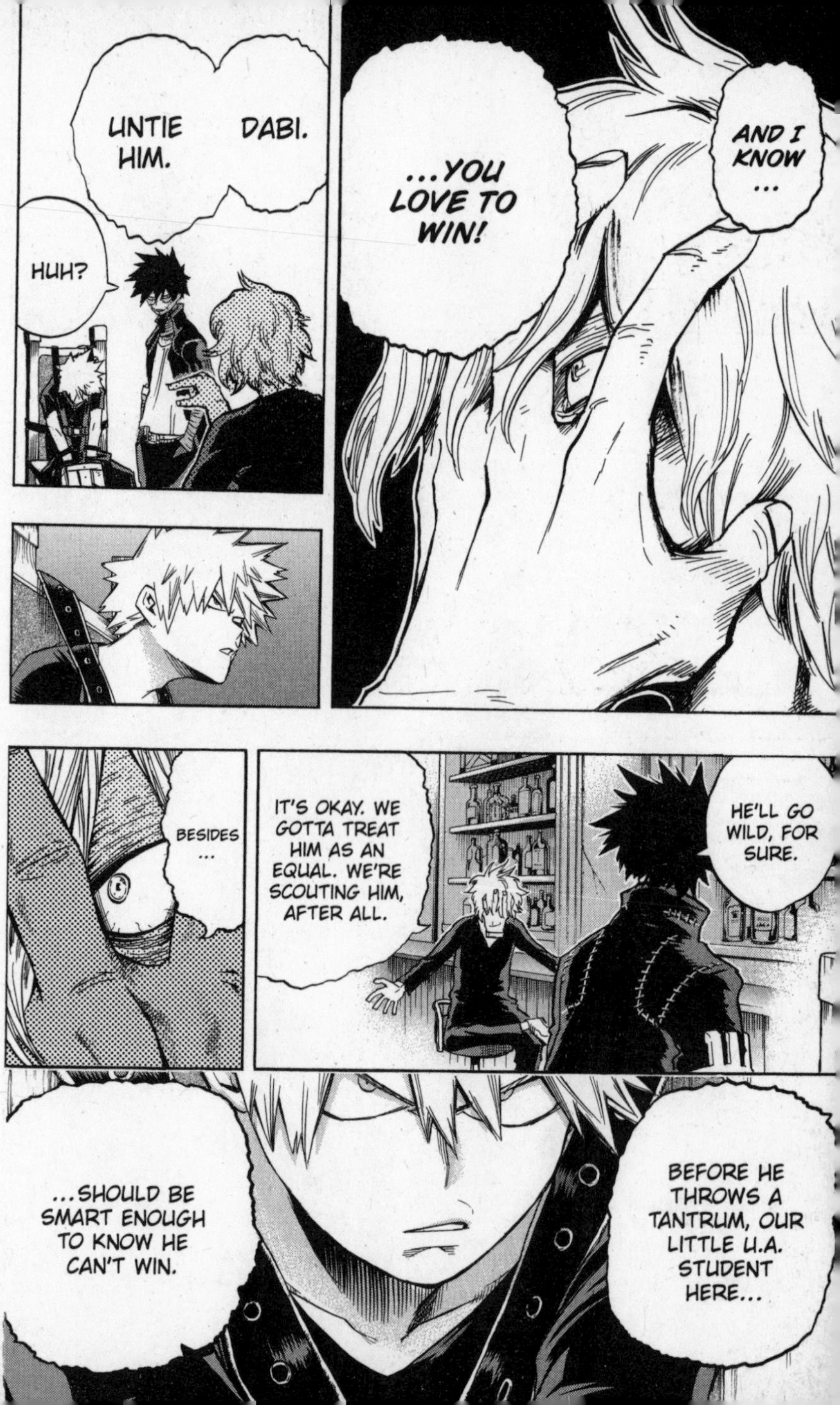
AND I KNOW ...
...YOU LOVE TO WIN!
DABI.
UNTIE HIM.
HUH?
HE'LL GO WILD, FOR SURE.
IT'S OKAY. WE GOTTA TREAT HIM AS AN EQUAL. WE'RE SCOUTING HIM, AFTER ALL.
BESIDES ...
BEFORE HE THROWS A TANTRUM, OUR LITTLE U.A. STUDENT HERE...
...SHOULD BE SMART ENOUGH TO KNOW HE CAN'T WIN.

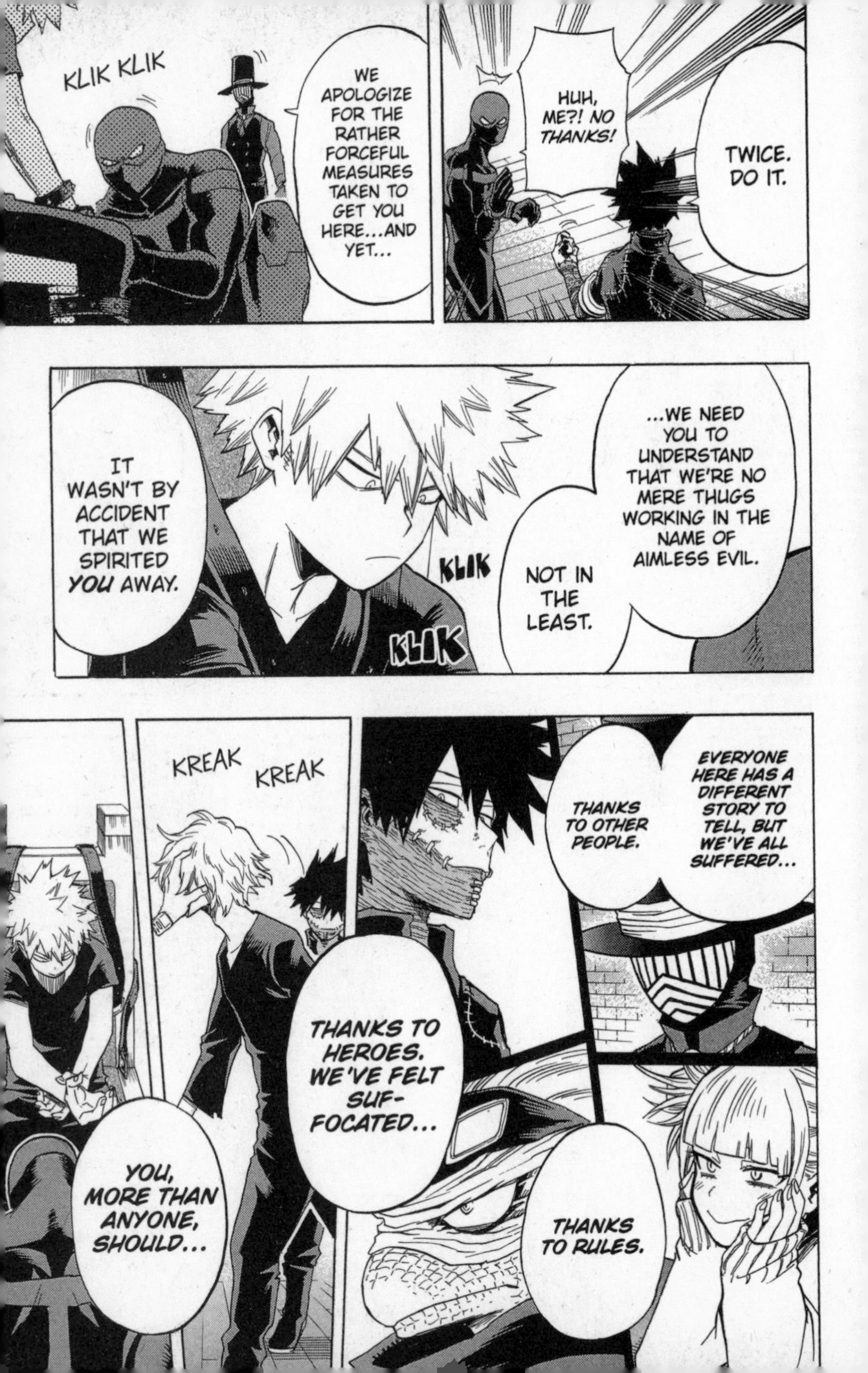
TWICE. DO IT.
HUH, ME?! NO THANKS!
WE APOLOGIZE FOR THE RATHER FORCEFUL MEASURES TAKEN TO GET YOU HERE...AND YET...
KLIK KLIK
...WE NEED YOU TO UNDERSTAND THAT WE'RE NO MERE THUGS WORKING IN THE NAME OF AIMLESS EVIL.
NOT IN THE LEAST.
KLIK
KLIK
IT WASN'T BY ACCIDENT THAT WE SPIRITED YOU AWAY.
EVERYONE HERE HAS A DIFFERENT STORY TO TELL, BUT WE'VE ALL SUFFERED...
THANKS TO OTHER PEOPLE.
THANKS TO RULES.
THANKS TO HEROES. WE'VE FELT SUF-FOCATED...
KREAK
KREAK
YOU, MORE THAN ANYONE, SHOULD...

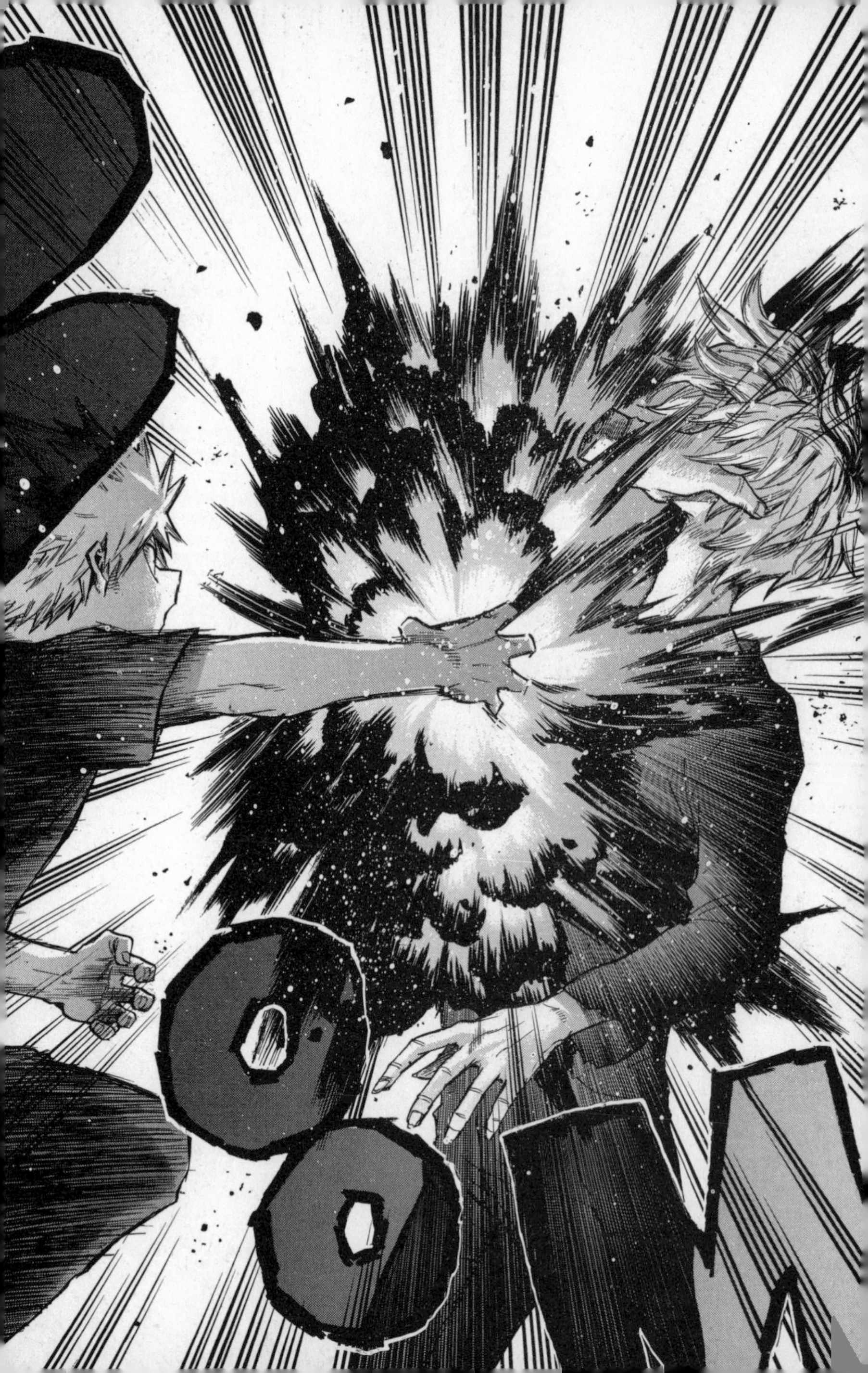
OOM

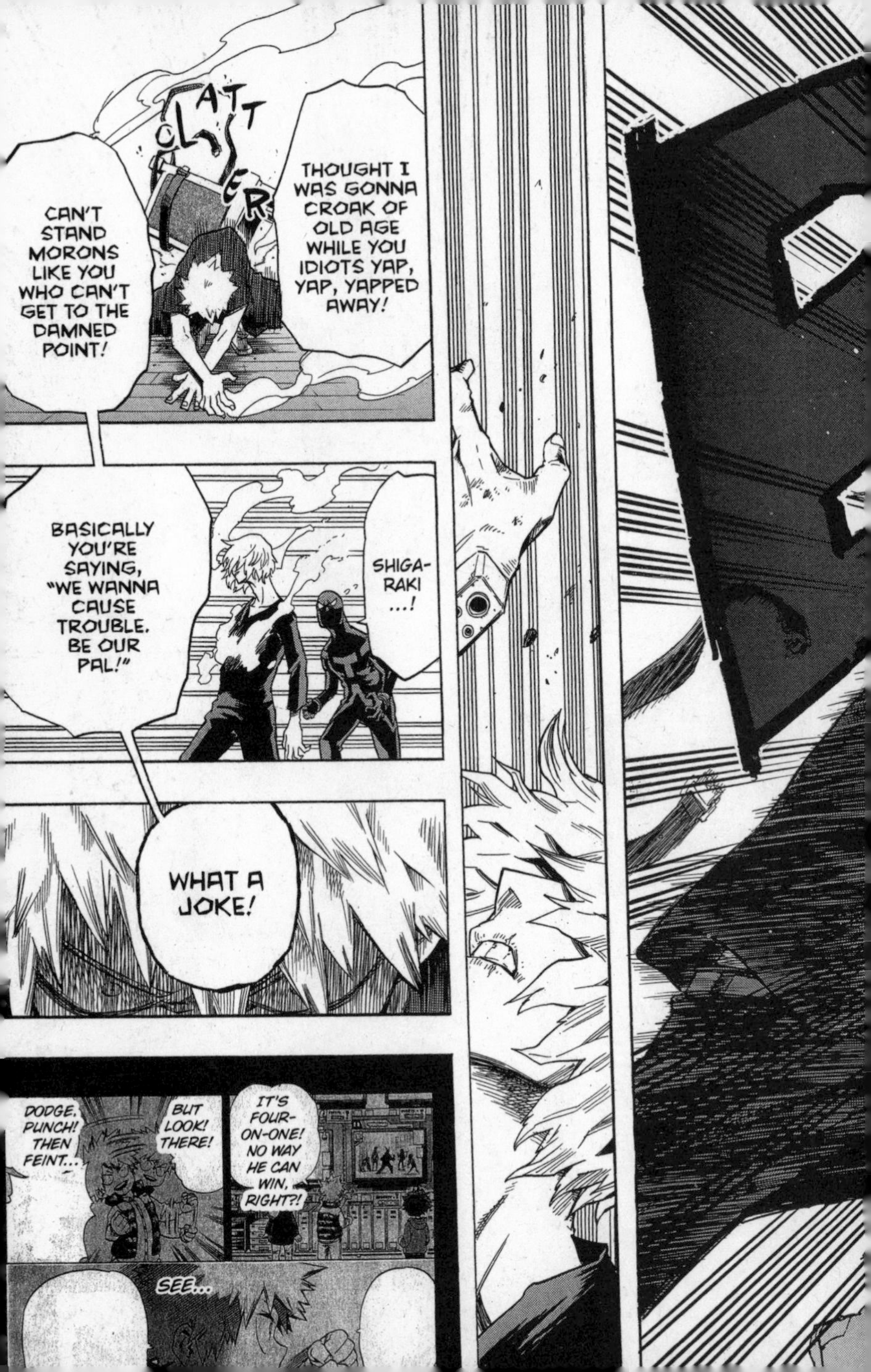
THOUGHT I WAS GONNA CROAK OF OLD AGE WHILE YOU IDIOTS YAP, YAP, YAPPED AWAY!
CLATTER
CAN'T STAND MORONS LIKE YOU WHO CAN'T GET TO THE DAMNED POINT!
SHIGA-RAKI ...!
BASICALLY YOU'RE SAYING, "WE WANNA CAUSE TROUBLE. BE OUR PAL!"
WHAT A JOKE!
IT'S FOUR-ON-ONE! NO WAY HE CAN WIN, RIGHT?!
BUT LOOK! THERE!
DODGE. PUNCH! THEN FEINT...
SEE...

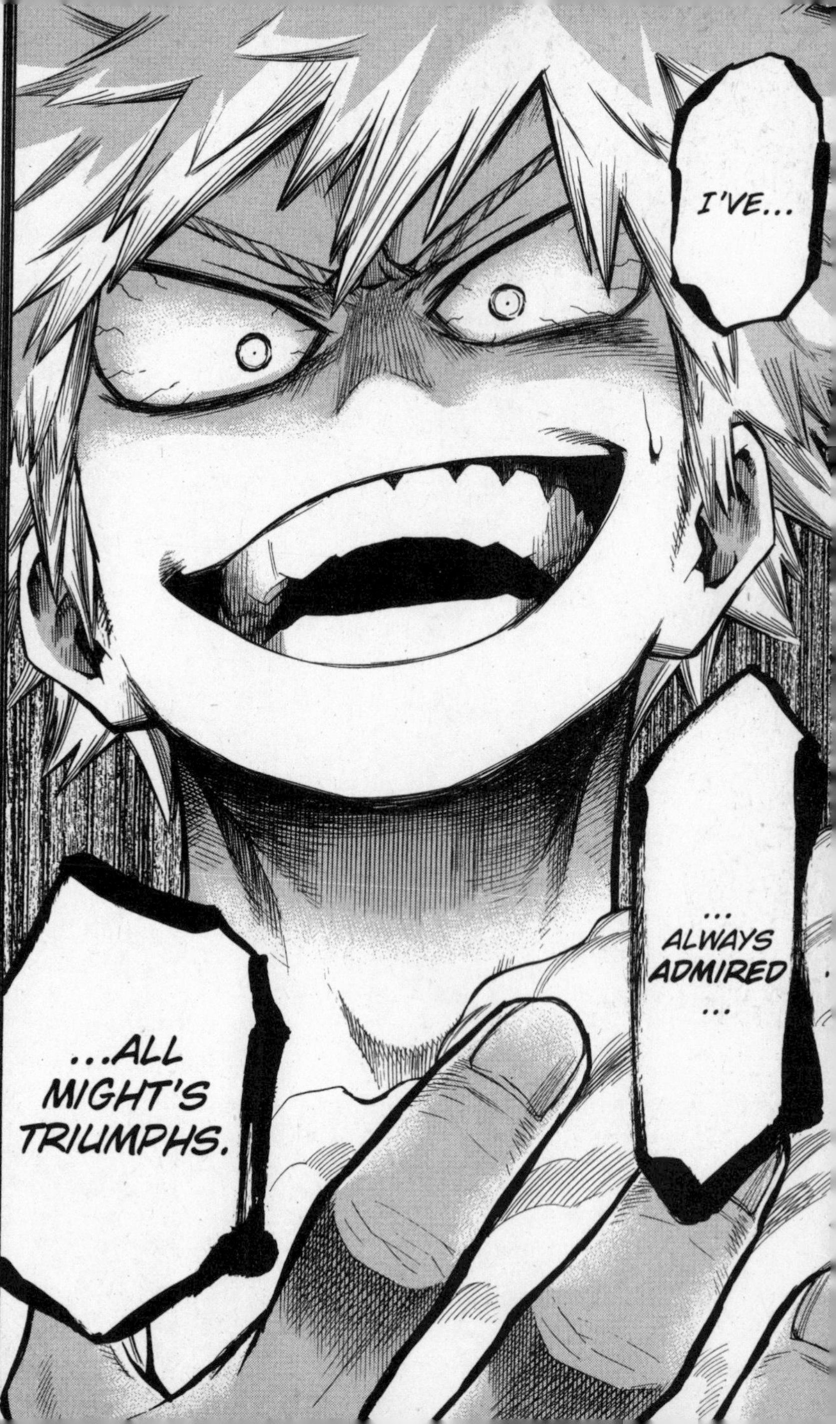
I'VE...
...ALWAYS ADMIRED...
...ALL MIGHT'S TRIUMPHS.

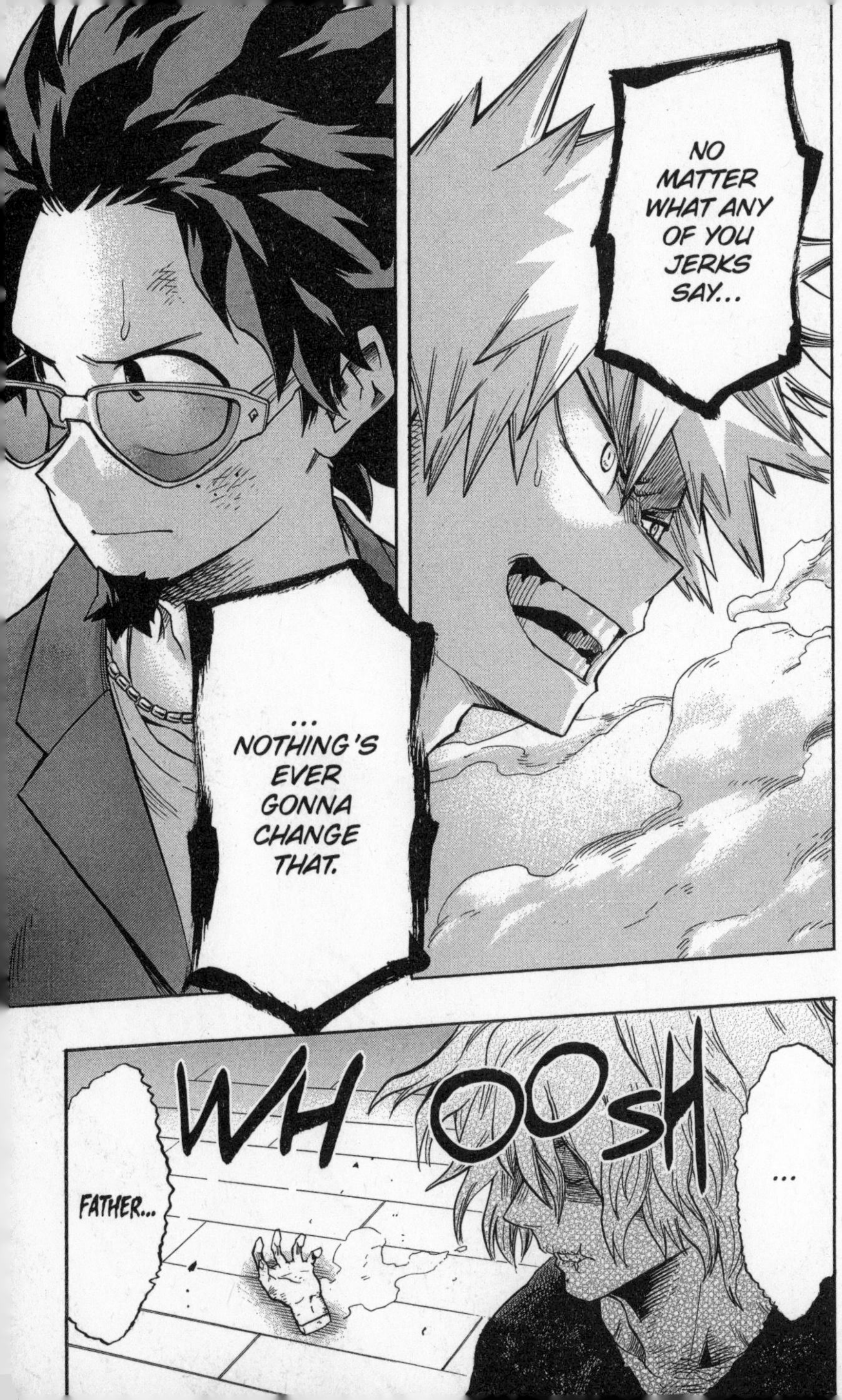
NO MATTER WHAT ANY OF YOU JERKS SAY...
... NOTHING'S EVER GONNA CHANGE THAT.
WHOOSH
...
FATHER...

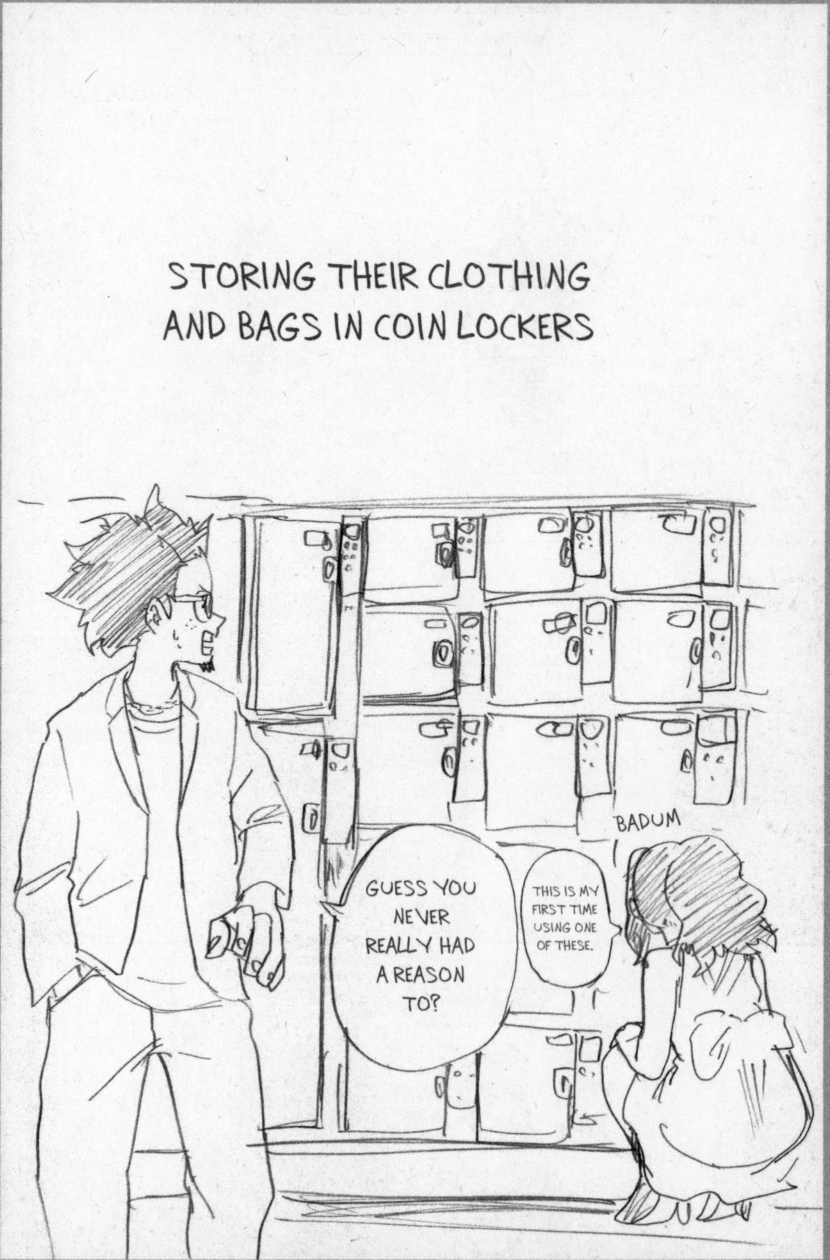
STORING THEIR CLOTHING AND BAGS IN COIN LOCKERS
BADUM
THIS IS MY FIRST TIME USING ONE OF THESE.
GUESS YOU NEVER REALLY HAD A REASON TO?

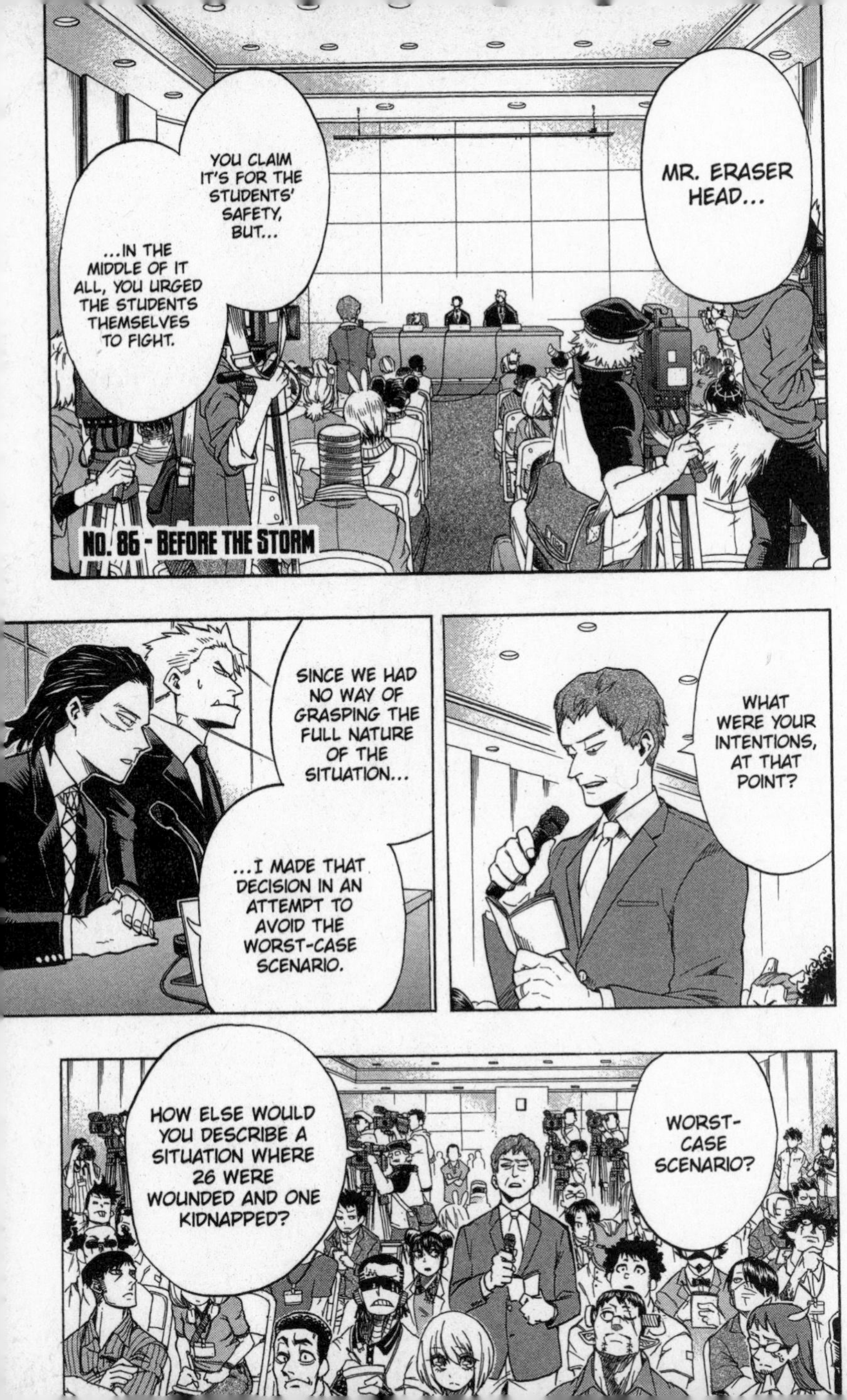
MR. ERASER HEAD...
YOU CLAIM IT'S FOR THE STUDENTS' SAFETY, BUT...
...IN THE MIDDLE OF IT ALL, YOU URGED THE STUDENTS THEMSELVES TO FIGHT.
No. 86 - Before the Storm
WHAT WERE YOUR INTENTIONS, AT THAT POINT?
SINCE WE HAD NO WAY OF GRASPING THE FULL NATURE OF THE SITUATION...
...I MADE THAT DECISION IN AN ATTEMPT TO AVOID THE WORST-CASE SCENARIO.
WORST-CASE SCENARIO?
HOW ELSE WOULD YOU DESCRIBE A SITUATION WHERE 26 WERE WOUNDED AND ONE KIDNAPPED?

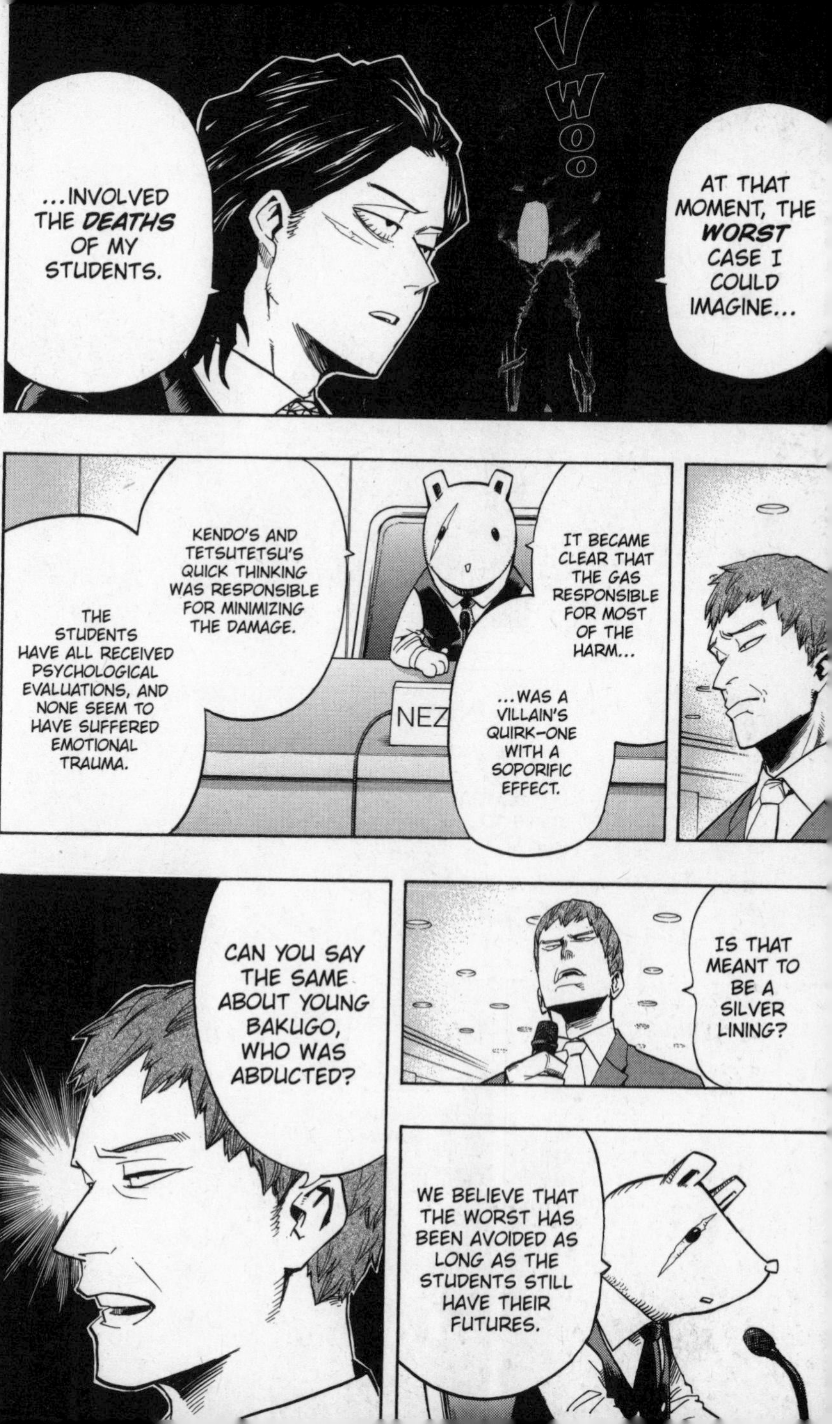
AT THAT MOMENT, THE WORST CASE I COULD IMAGINE...
VWOO
...INVOLVED THE DEATHS OF MY STUDENTS.
NEZ
IT BECAME CLEAR THAT THE GAS RESPONSIBLE FOR MOST OF THE HARM...
...WAS A VILLAIN'S QUIRK-ONE WITH A SOPORIFIC EFFECT.
KENDO'S AND TETSUTETSU'S QUICK THINKING WAS RESPONSIBLE FOR MINIMIZING THE DAMAGE.
THE STUDENTS HAVE ALL RECEIVED PSYCHOLOGICAL EVALUATIONS, AND NONE SEEM TO HAVE SUFFERED EMOTIONAL TRAUMA.
IS THAT MEANT TO BE A SILVER LINING?
WE BELIEVE THAT THE WORST HAS BEEN AVOIDED AS LONG AS THE STUDENTS STILL HAVE THEIR FUTURES.
CAN YOU SAY THE SAME ABOUT YOUNG BAKUGO, WHO WAS ABDUCTED?

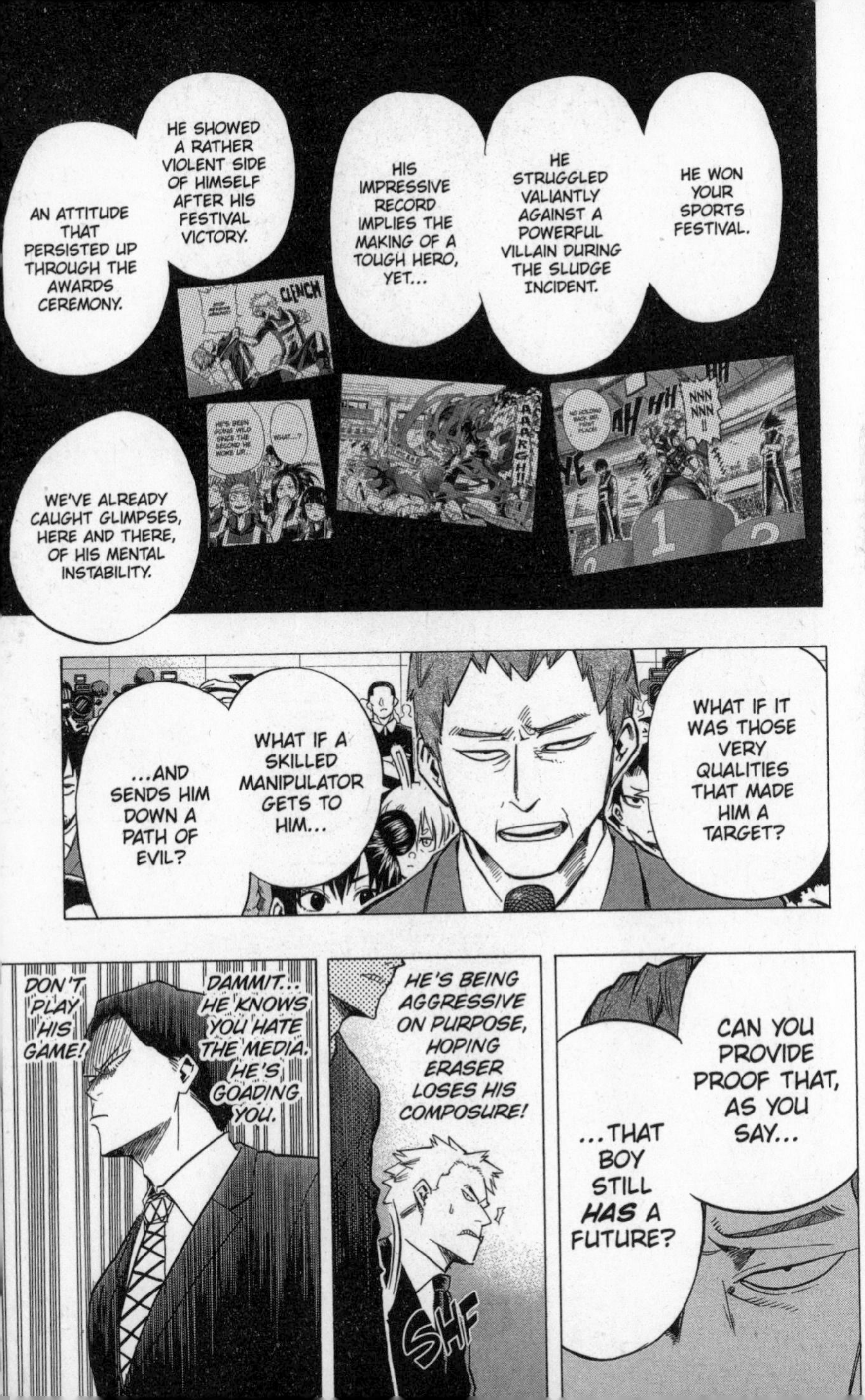
HE WON YOUR SPORTS FESTIVAL.
HE STRUGGLED VALIANTLY AGAINST A POWERFUL VILLAIN DURING THE SLUDGE INCIDENT.
HIS IMPRESSIVE RECORD IMPLIES THE MAKING OF A TOUGH HERO, YET...
HE SHOWED A RATHER VIOLENT SIDE OF HIMSELF AFTER HIS FESTIVAL VICTORY.
AN ATTITUDE THAT PERSISTED UP THROUGH THE AWARDS CEREMONY.
CLENCH
WE'VE ALREADY CAUGHT GLIMPSES, HERE AND THERE, OF HIS MENTAL INSTABILITY.
WHAT IF IT WAS THOSE VERY QUALITIES THAT MADE HIM A TARGET?
WHAT IF A SKILLED MANIPULATOR GETS TO HIM...
...AND SENDS HIM DOWN A PATH OF EVIL?
CAN YOU PROVIDE PROOF THAT, AS YOU SAY...
...THAT BOY STILL HAS A FUTURE?
HE'S BEING AGGRESSIVE ON PURPOSE, HOPING ERASER LOSES HIS COMPOSURE!
SHF
DAMMIT... HE KNOWS YOU HATE THE MEDIA. HE'S GOADING YOU.
DON'T PLAY HIS GAME!

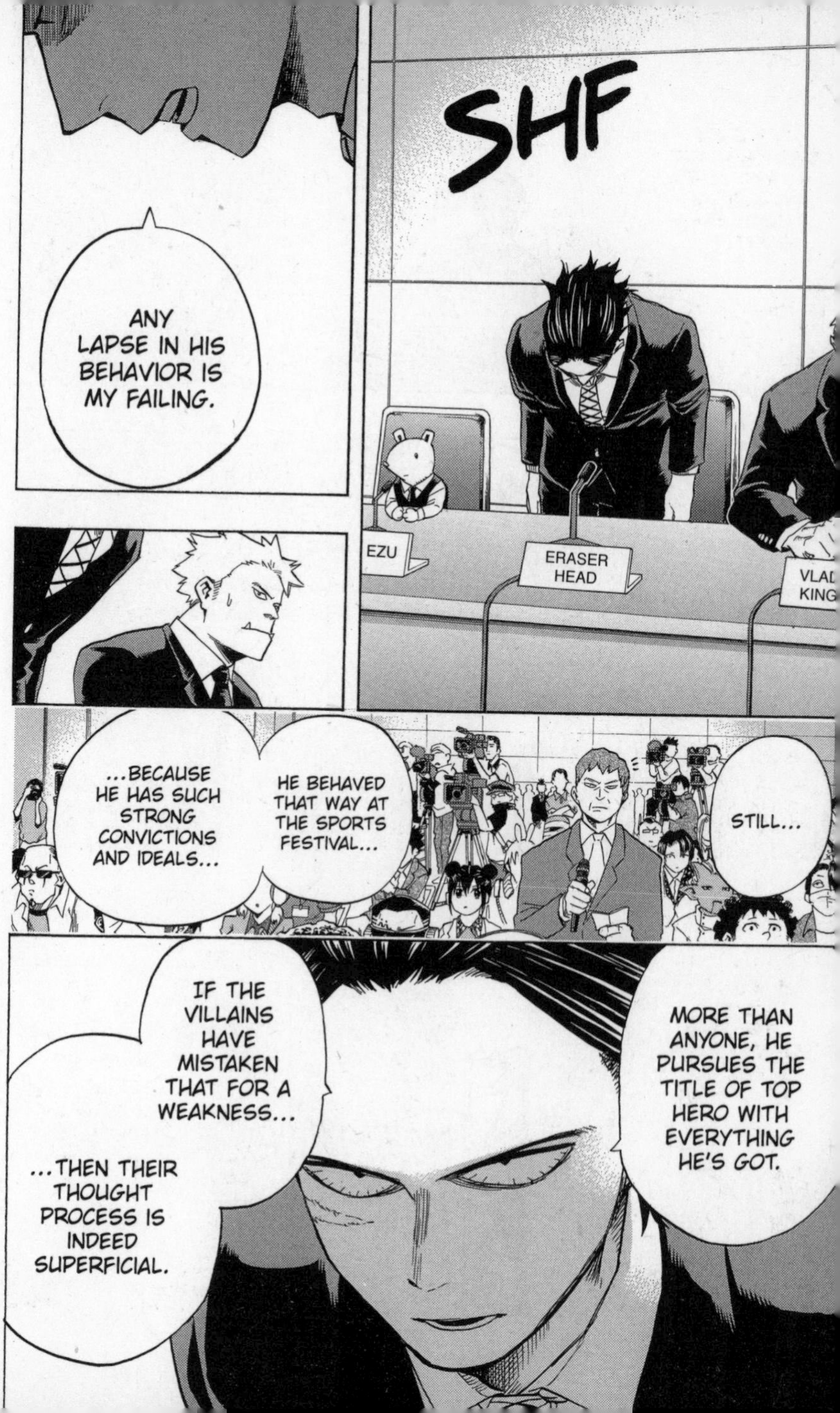
SHF
EZU
ERASER HEAD
ANY LAPSE IN HIS BEHAVIOR IS MY FAILING.
STILL...
HE BEHAVED THAT WAY AT THE SPORTS FESTIVAL...
...BECAUSE HE HAS SUCH STRONG CONVICTIONS AND IDEALS...
MORE THAN ANYONE, HE PURSUES THE TITLE OF TOP HERO WITH EVERYTHING HE'S GOT.
IF THE VILLAINS HAVE MISTAKEN THAT FOR A WEAKNESS...
...THEN THEIR THOUGHT PROCESS IS INDEED SUPERFICIAL.

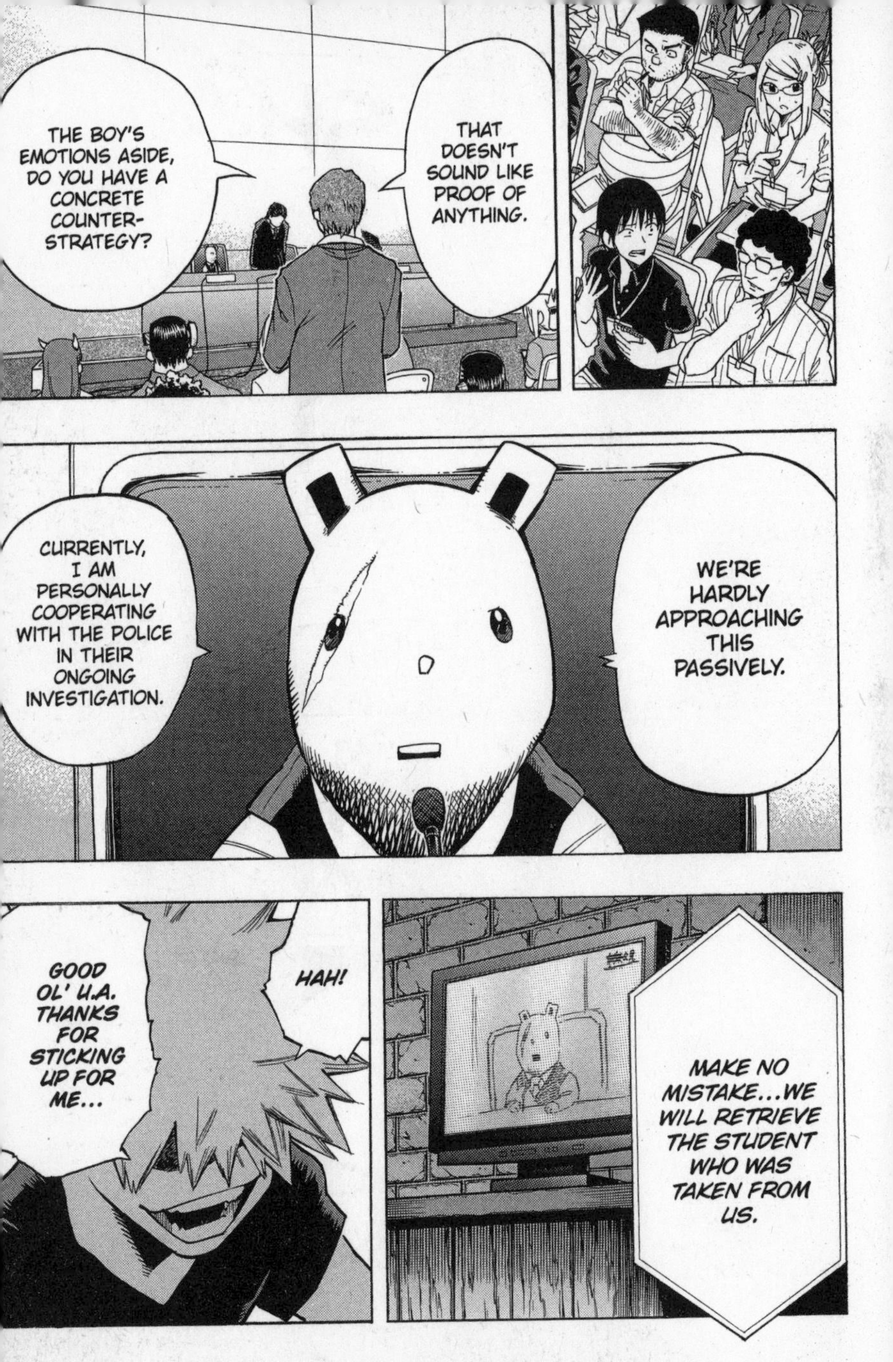
THAT DOESN'T SOUND LIKE PROOF OF ANYTHING.
THE BOY'S EMOTIONS ASIDE, DO YOU HAVE A CONCRETE COUNTER-STRATEGY?
WE'RE HARDLY APPROACHING THIS PASSIVELY.
CURRENTLY, I AM PERSONALLY COOPERATING WITH THE POLICE IN THEIR ONGOING INVESTIGATION.
MAKE NO MISTAKE...WE WILL RETRIEVE THE STUDENT WHO WAS TAKEN FROM US.
HAH!
GOOD OL' U.A. THANKS FOR STICKING UP FOR ME...

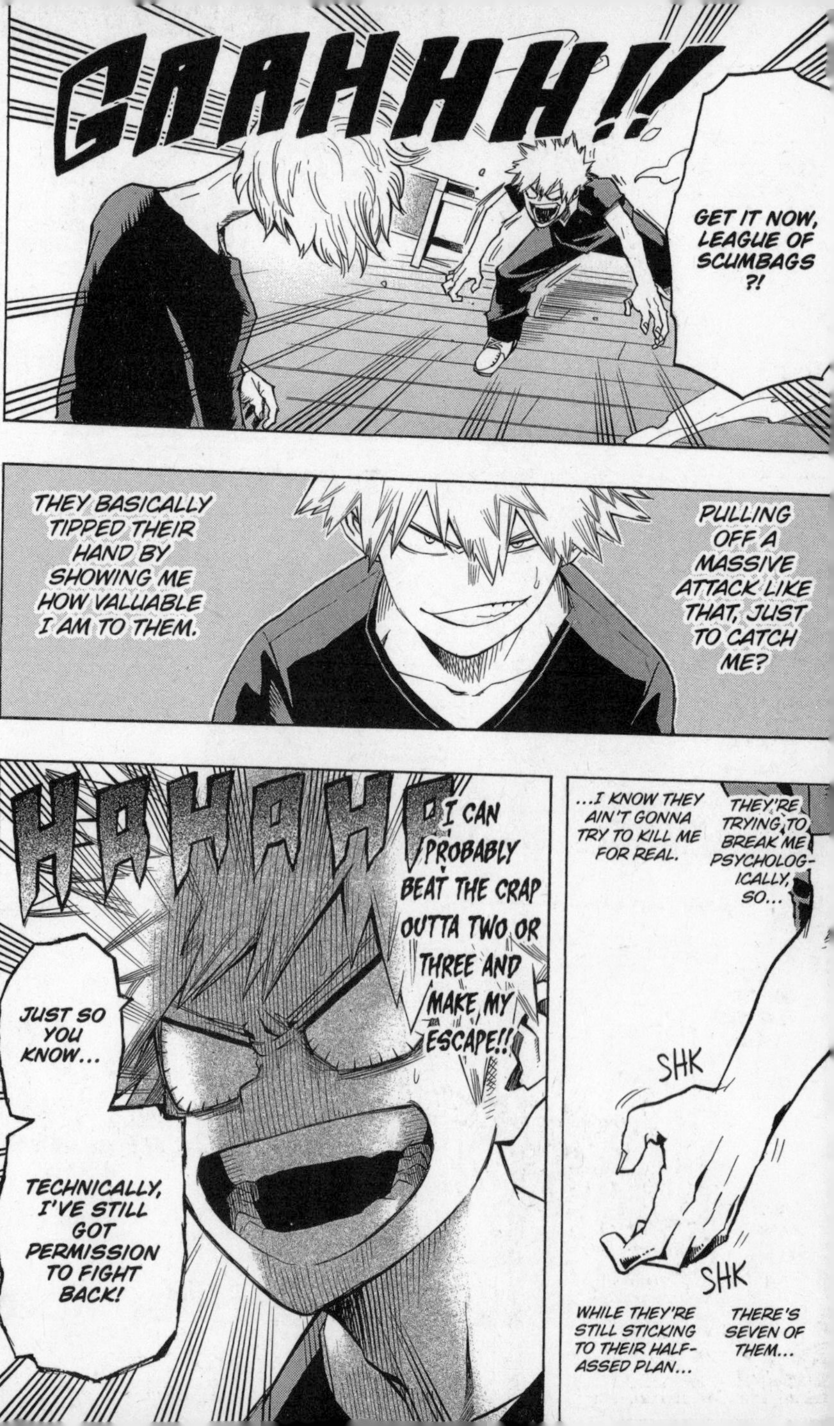
GAAAHHH!!
GET IT NOW, LEAGUE OF SCUMBAGS ?!
PULLING OFF A MASSIVE ATTACK LIKE THAT, JUST TO CATCH ME?
THEY BASICALLY TIPPED THEIR HAND BY SHOWING ME HOW VALUABLE I AM TO THEM.
THEY'RE TRYING TO BREAK ME PSYCHOLOG-ICALLY, SO...
...I KNOW THEY AIN'T GONNA TRY TO KILL ME FOR REAL.
SHK
SHK
THERE'S SEVEN OF THEM...
WHILE THEY'RE STILL STICKING TO THEIR HALF-ASSED PLAN...
HAHAHA
I CAN PROBABLY BEAT THE CRAP OUTTA TWO OR THREE AND MAKE MY ESCAPE!!
JUST SO YOU KNOW...
TECHNICALLY, I'VE STILL GOT PERMISSION TO FIGHT BACK!

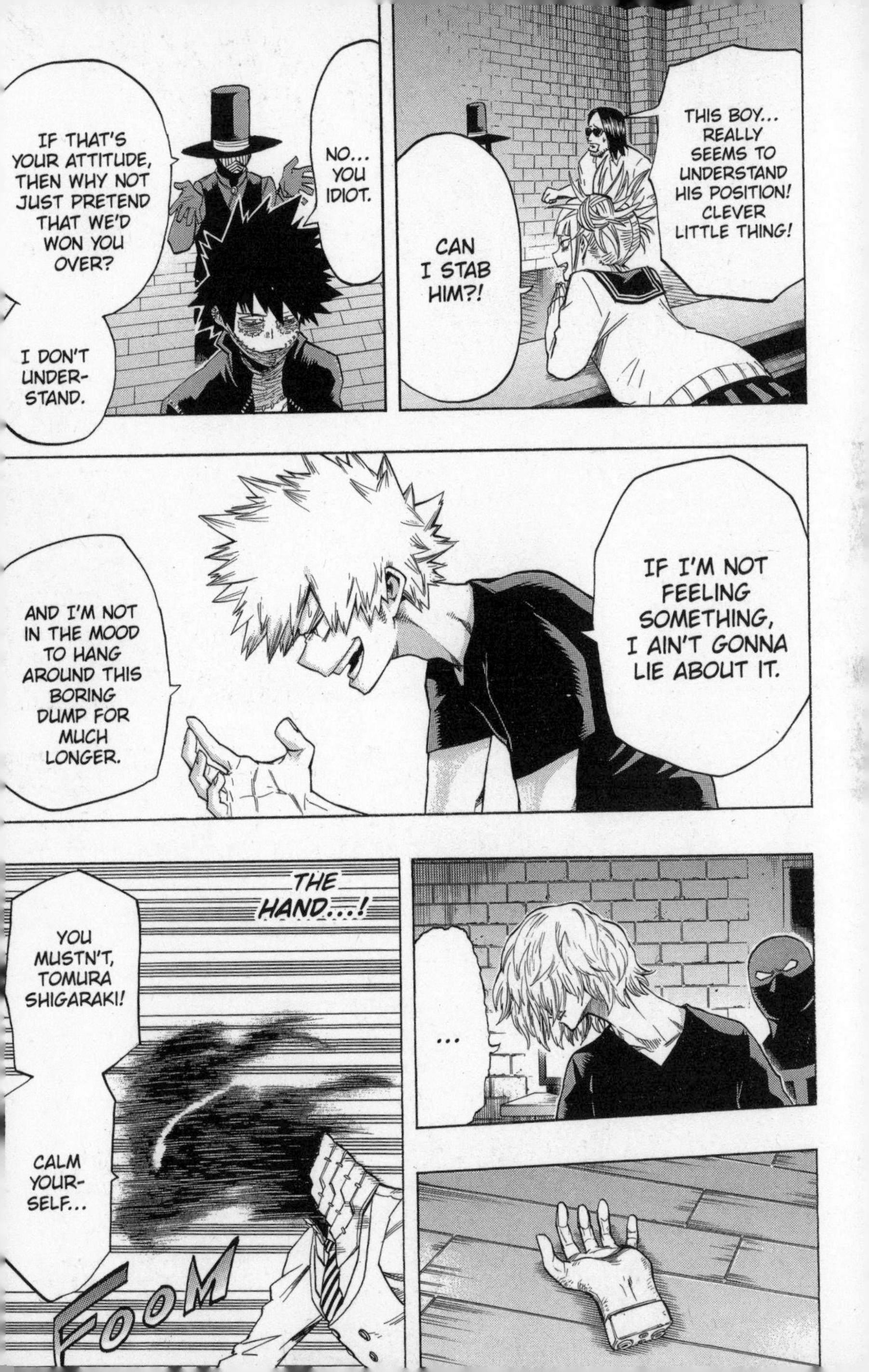
THIS BOY... REALLY SEEMS TO UNDERSTAND HIS POSITION! CLEVER LITTLE THING!
CAN I STAB HIM?!
NO... YOU IDIOT.
IF THAT'S YOUR ATTITUDE, THEN WHY NOT JUST PRETEND THAT WE'D WON YOU OVER?
I DON'T UNDER-STAND.
IF I'M NOT FEELING SOMETHING, I AIN'T GONNA LIE ABOUT IT.
AND I'M NOT IN THE MOOD TO HANG AROUND THIS BORING DUMP FOR MUCH LONGER.
...
THE HAND...!
YOU MUSTN'T, TOMURA SHIGARAKI!
CALM YOUR-SELF...
FOOM

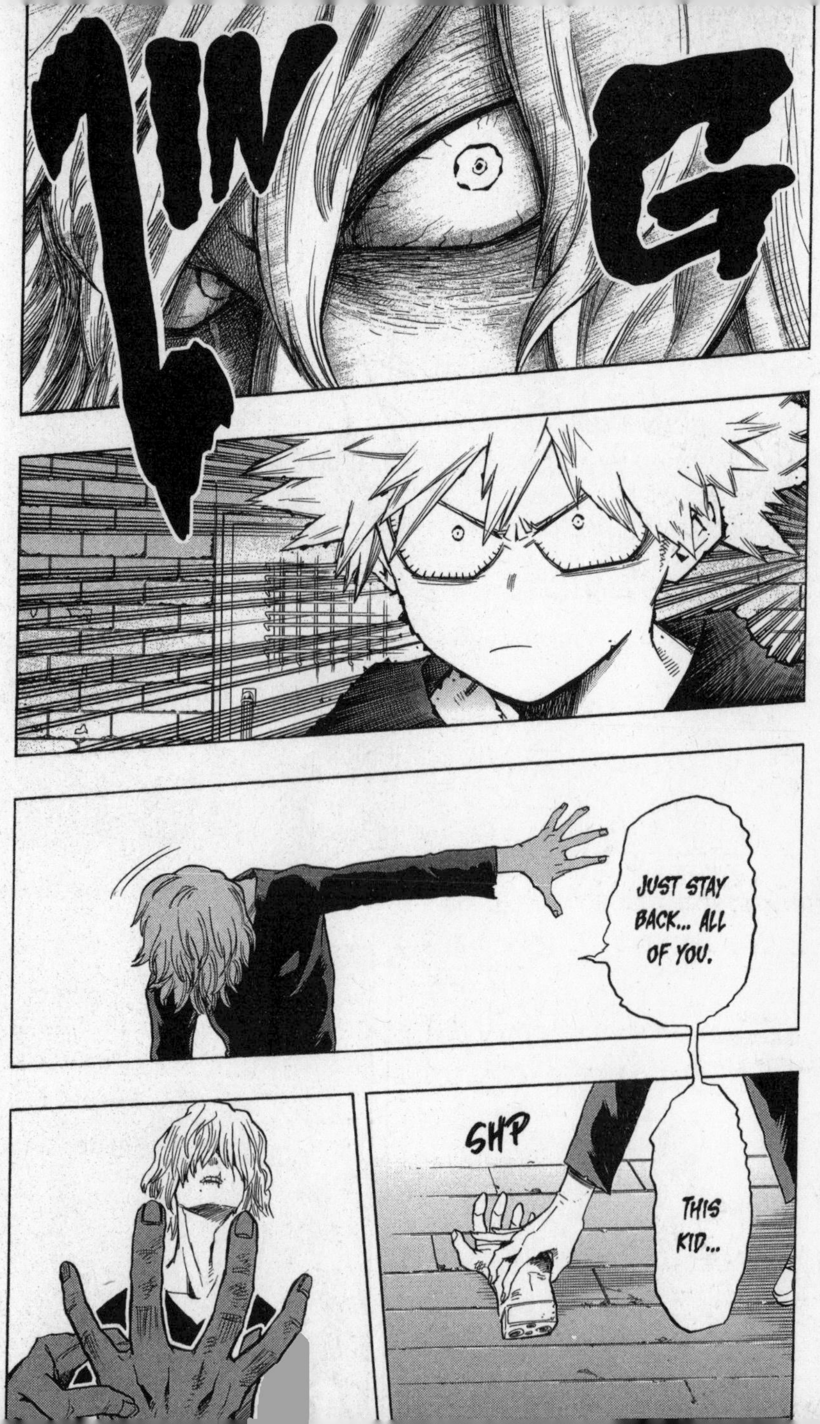
ZING
JUST STAY BACK... ALL OF YOU.
THIS KID...
SHP

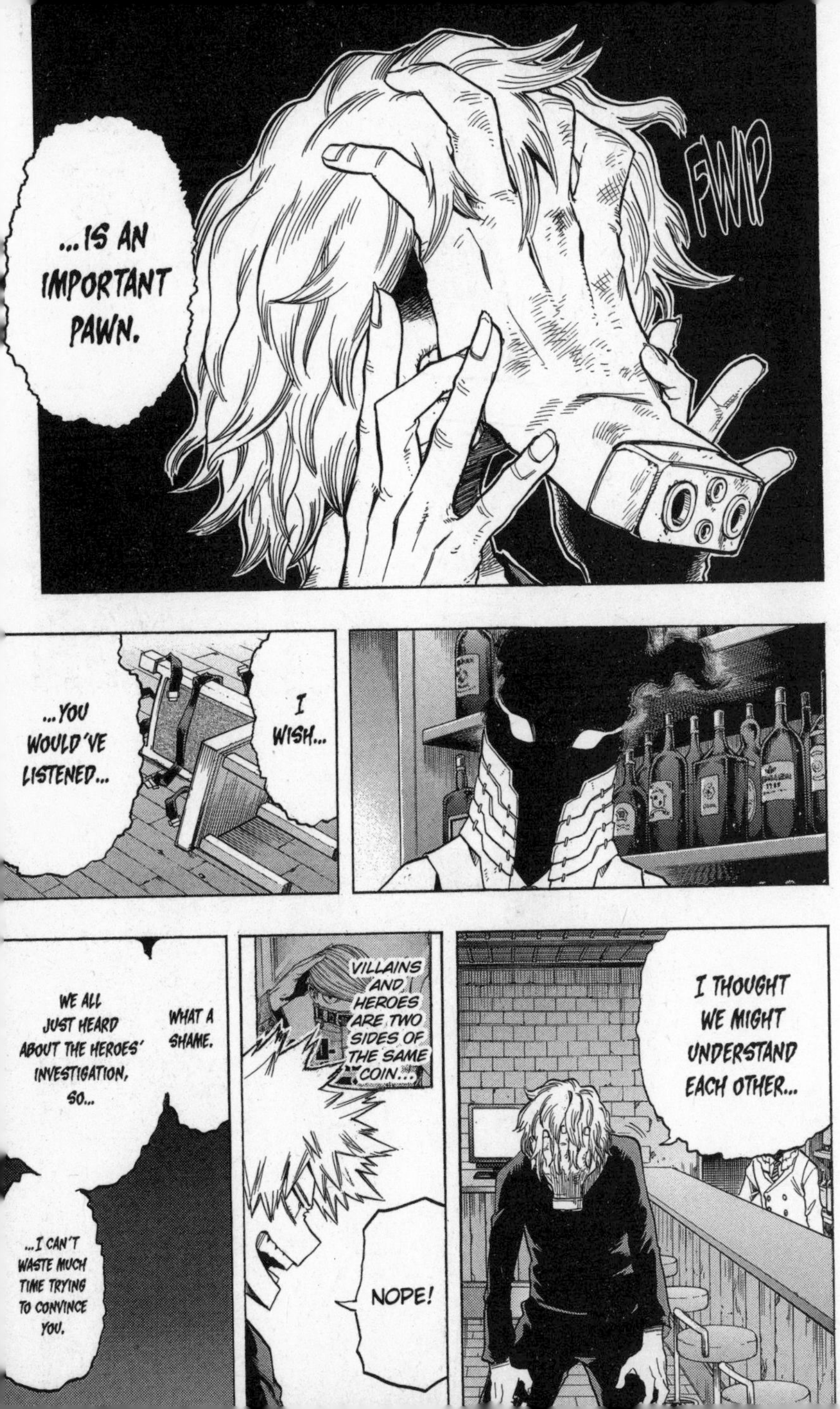
FWIP
...IS AN IMPORTANT PAWN.
I WISH...
...YOU WOULD'VE LISTENED...
I THOUGHT WE MIGHT UNDERSTAND EACH OTHER...
VILLAINS AND HEROES ARE TWO SIDES OF THE SAME COIN...
NOPE!
WHAT A SHAME.
WE ALL JUST HEARD ABOUT THE HEROES' INVESTIGATION, SO...
...I CAN'T WASTE MUCH TIME TRYING TO CONVINCE YOU.

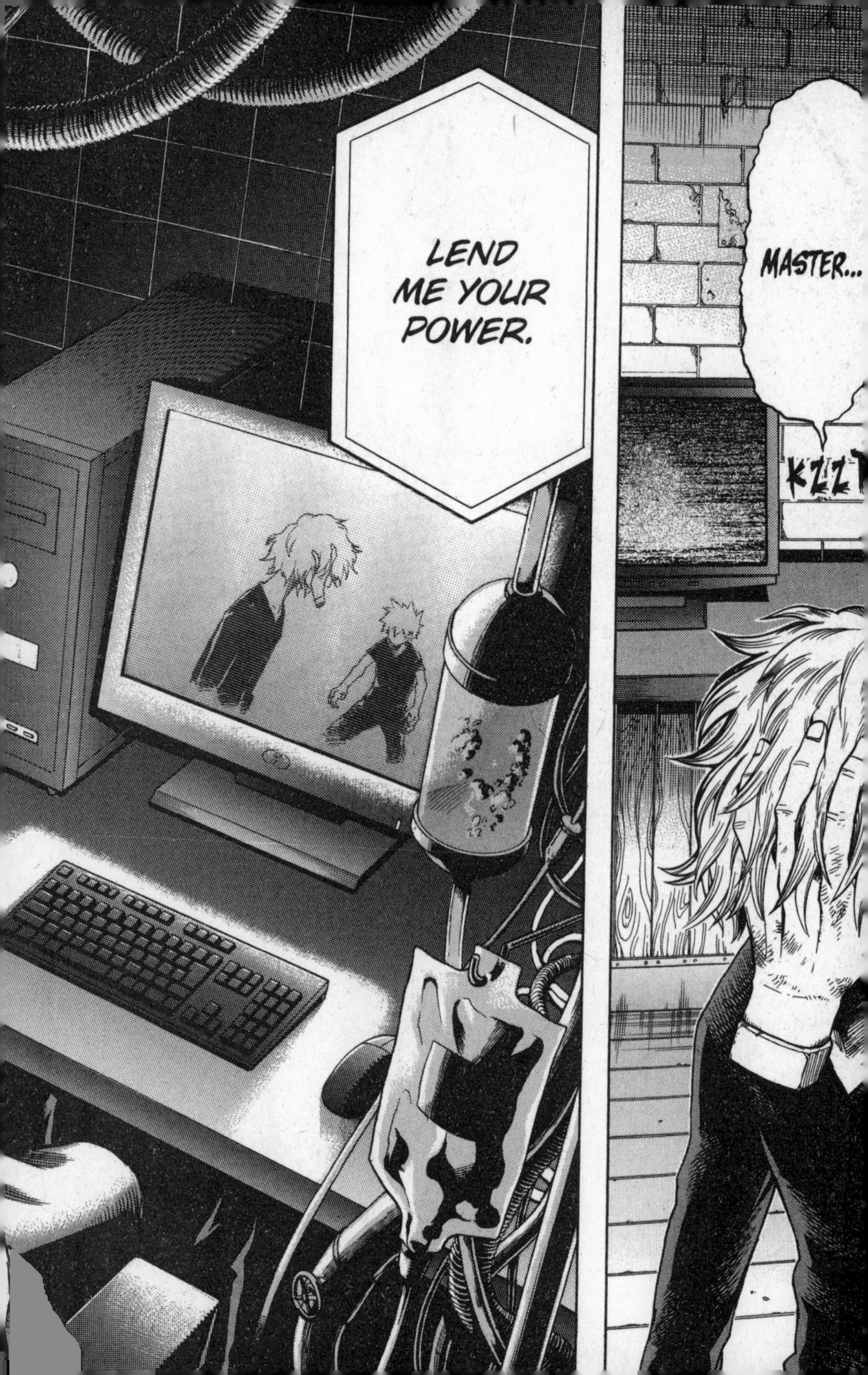
MASTER...
KZZ
LEND ME YOUR POWER.

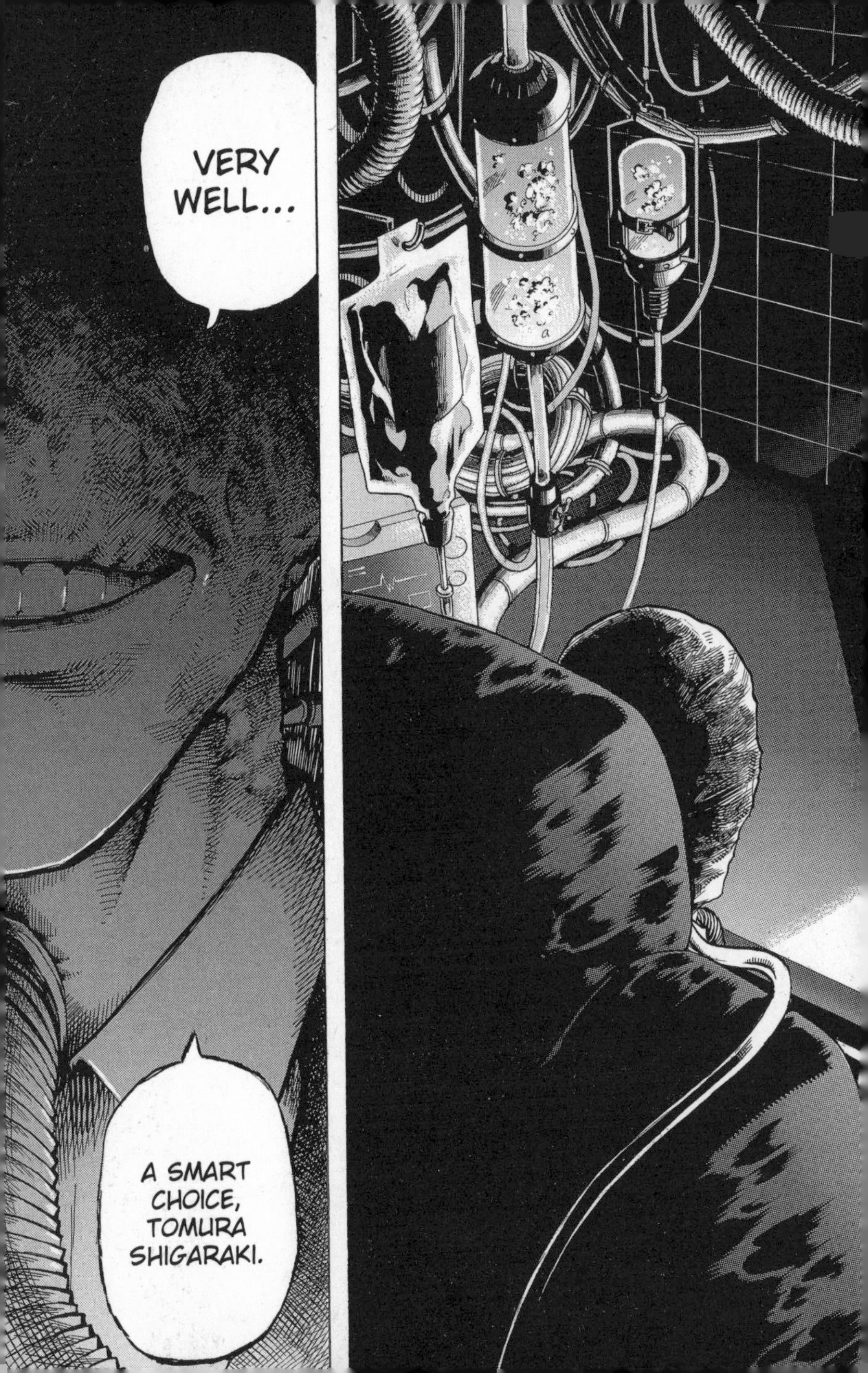
VERY WELL...
A SMART CHOICE, TOMURA SHIGARAKI.

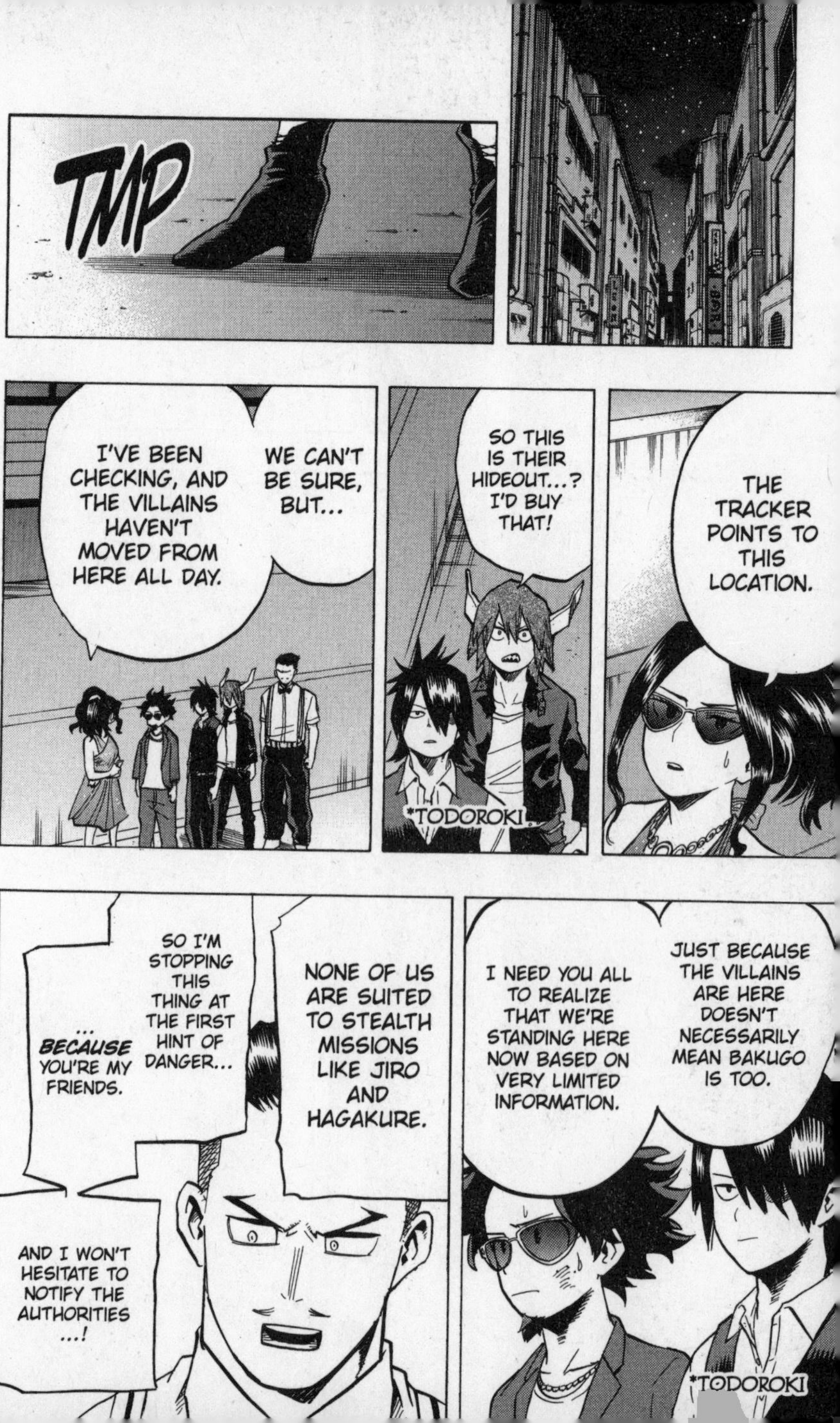
TMP
THE TRACKER POINTS TO THIS LOCATION.
SO THIS IS THEIR HIDEOUT...? I'D BUY THAT!
*TODOROKI
WE CAN'T BE SURE, BUT...
I'VE BEEN CHECKING, AND THE VILLAINS HAVEN'T MOVED FROM HERE ALL DAY.
JUST BECAUSE THE VILLAINS ARE HERE DOESN'T NECESSARILY MEAN BAKUGO IS TOO.
I NEED YOU ALL TO REALIZE THAT WE'RE STANDING HERE NOW BASED ON VERY LIMITED INFORMATION.
*TODOROKI
NONE OF US ARE SUITED TO STEALTH MISSIONS LIKE JIRO AND HAGAKURE.
SO I'M STOPPING THIS THING AT THE FIRST HINT OF DANGER...
...*BECAUSE* YOU'RE MY FRIENDS.
AND I WON'T HESITATE TO NOTIFY THE AUTHORITIES ...!

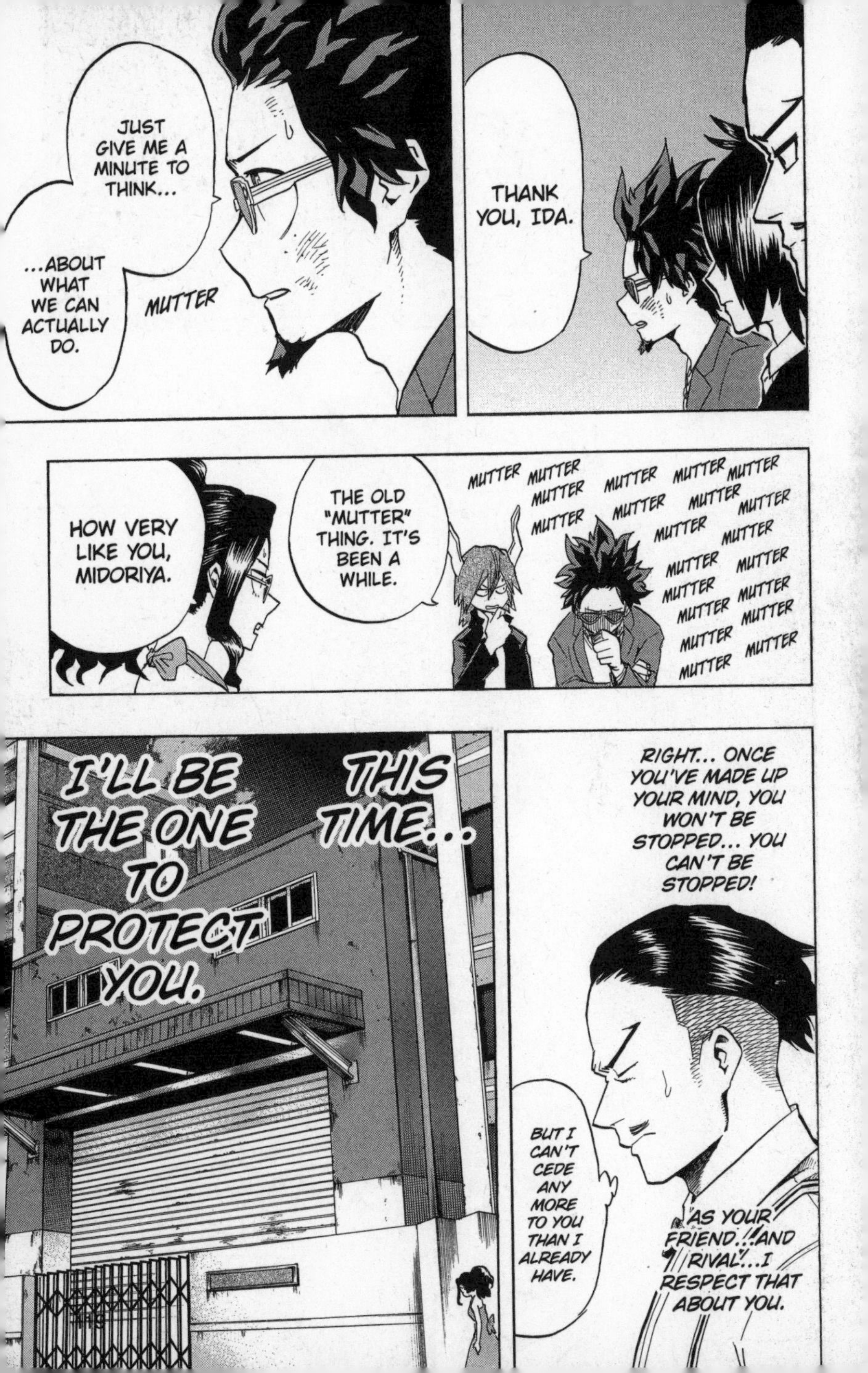
THANK YOU, IDA.
JUST GIVE ME A MINUTE TO THINK...
...ABOUT WHAT WE CAN ACTUALLY DO.
MUTTER
MUTTER MUTTER
THE OLD "MUTTER" THING. IT'S BEEN A WHILE.
HOW VERY LIKE YOU, MIDORIYA.
RIGHT... ONCE YOU'VE MADE UP YOUR MIND, YOU WON'T BE STOPPED... YOU CAN'T BE STOPPED!
AS YOUR FRIEND...AND RIVAL...I RESPECT THAT ABOUT YOU.
BUT I CAN'T CEDE ANY MORE TO YOU THAN I ALREADY HAVE.
THIS TIME...
I'LL BE THE ONE TO PROTECT YOU.

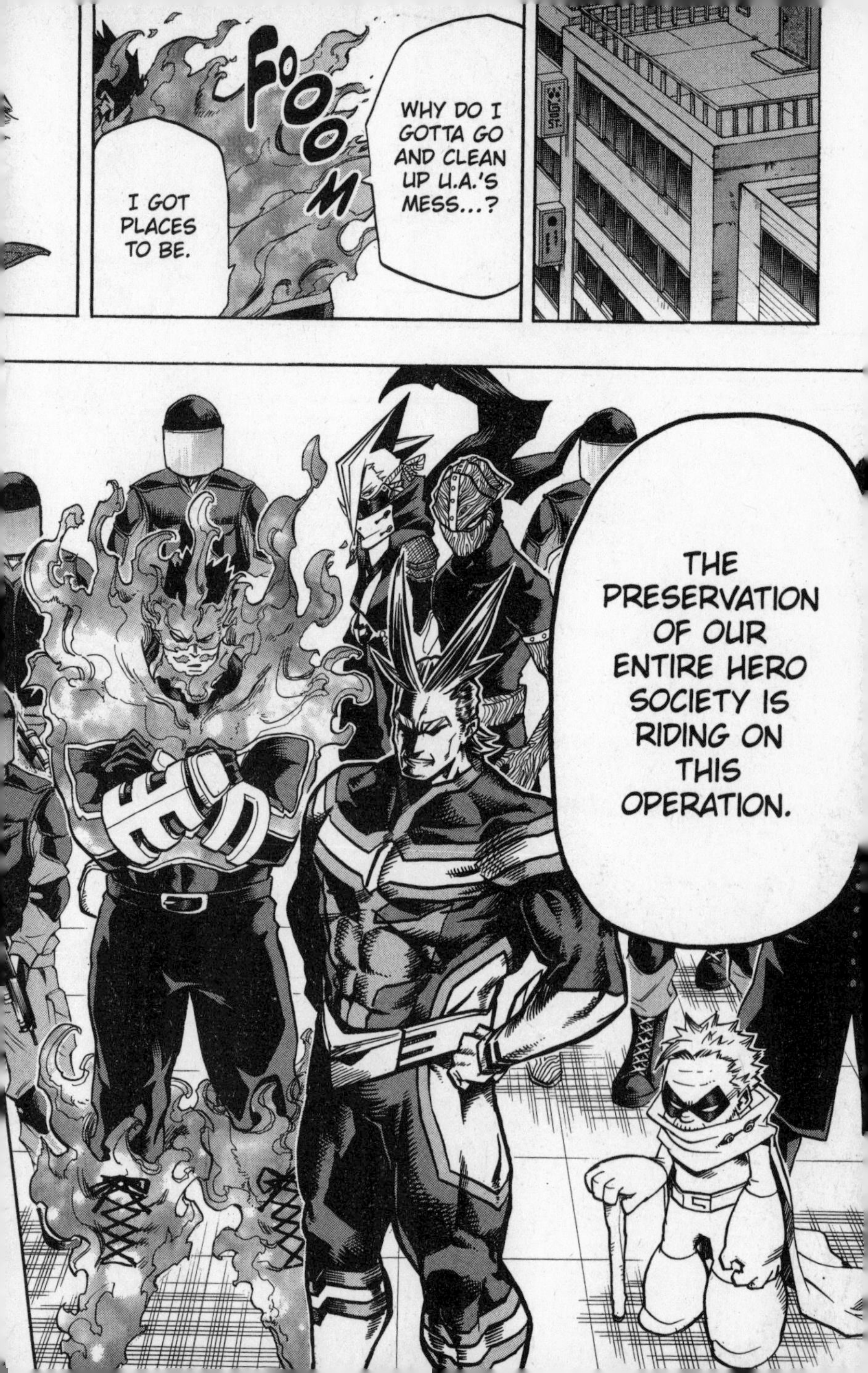
WHY DO I GOTTA GO AND CLEAN UP U.A.'S MESS...?
FOOOM
I GOT PLACES TO BE.
THE PRESERVATION OF OUR ENTIRE HERO SOCIETY IS RIDING ON THIS OPERATION.

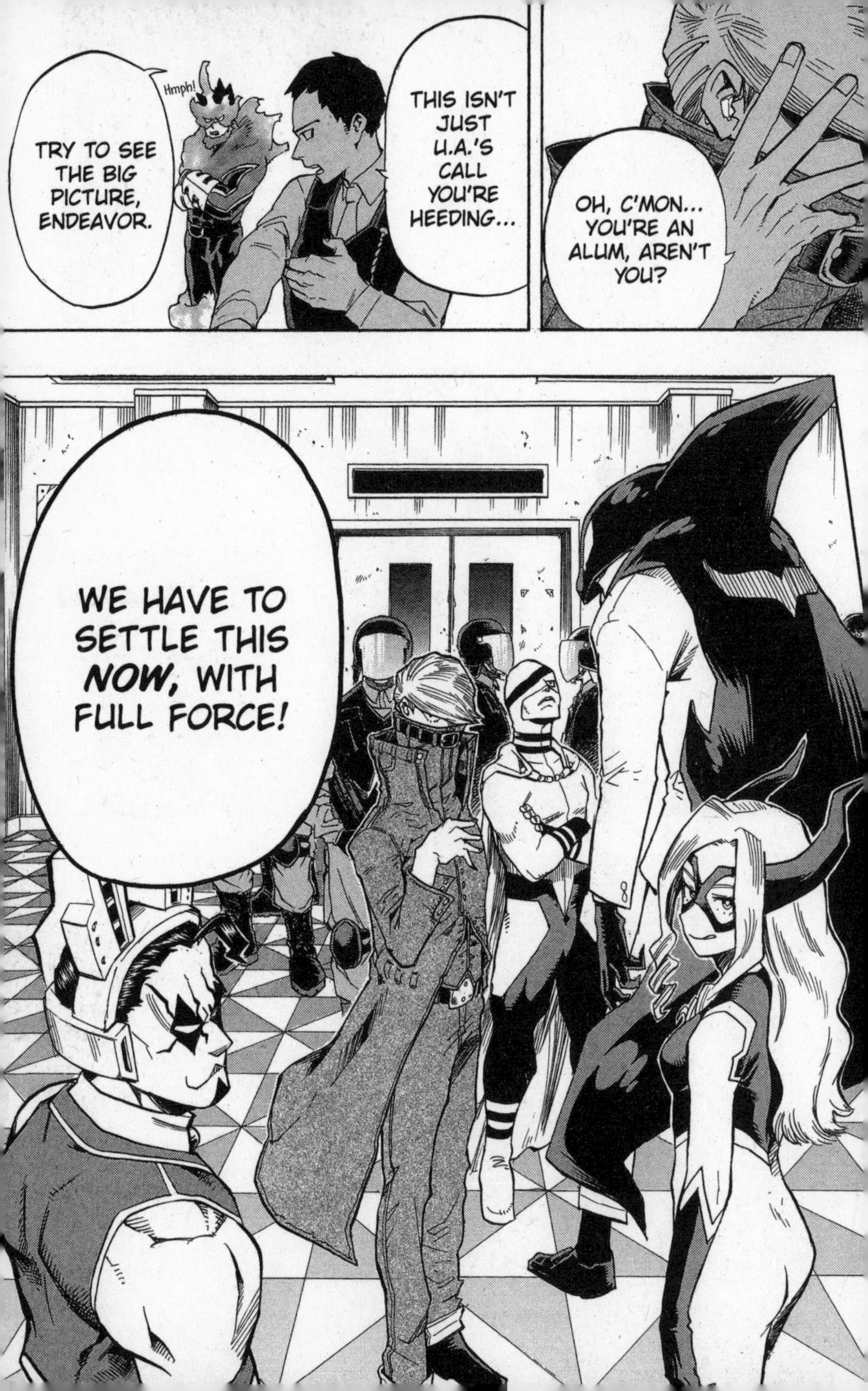
OH, C'MON... YOU'RE AN ALUM, AREN'T YOU?
THIS ISN'T JUST U.A.'S CALL YOU'RE HEEDING...
Hmph!
TRY TO SEE THE BIG PICTURE, ENDEAVOR.
WE HAVE TO SETTLE THIS *NOW,* WITH FULL FORCE!

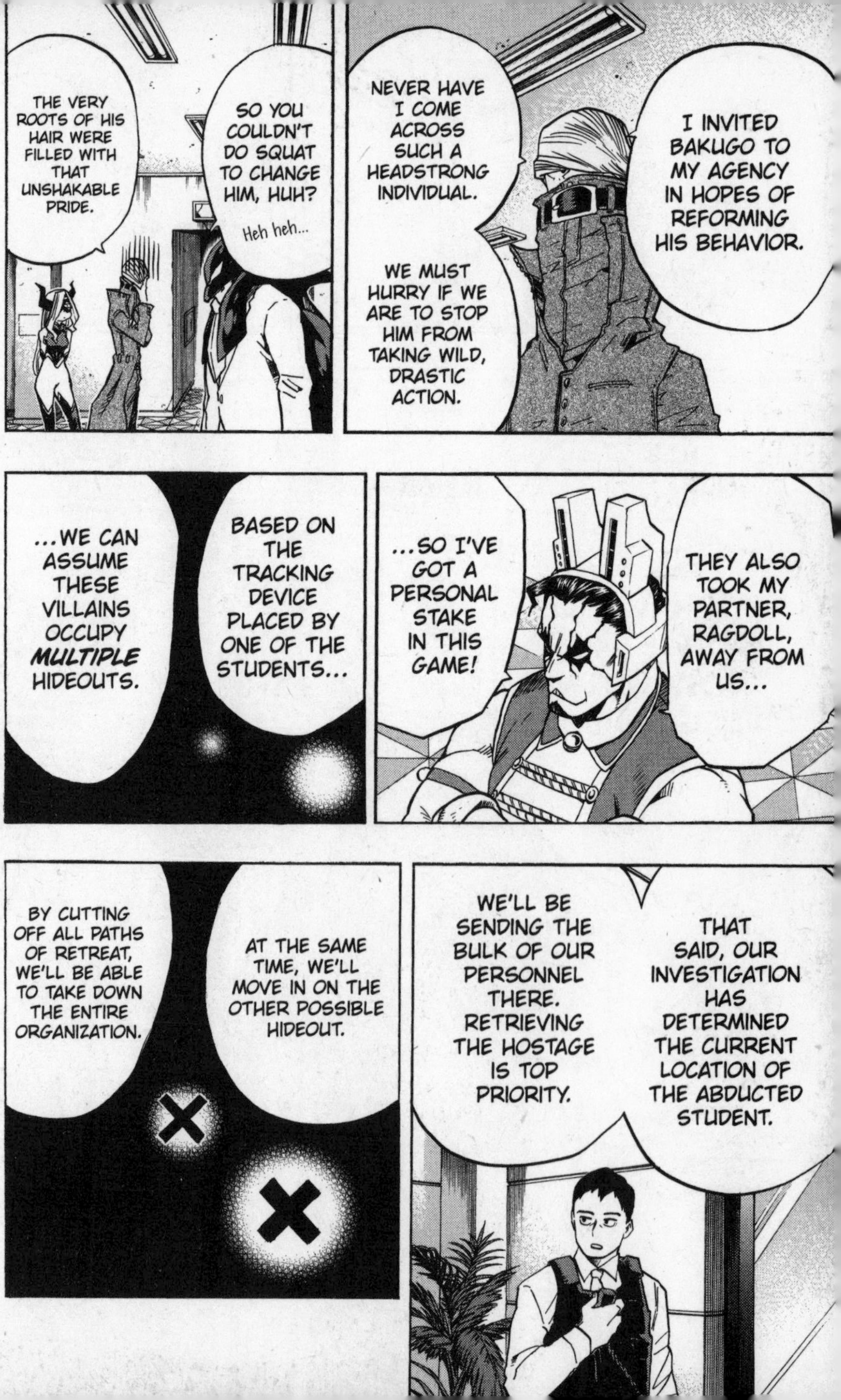
I INVITED BAKUGO TO MY AGENCY IN HOPES OF REFORMING HIS BEHAVIOR.
NEVER HAVE I COME ACROSS SUCH A HEADSTRONG INDIVIDUAL.
WE MUST HURRY IF WE ARE TO STOP HIM FROM TAKING WILD, DRASTIC ACTION.
SO YOU COULDN'T DO SQUAT TO CHANGE HIM, HUH?
Heh heh...
THE VERY ROOTS OF HIS HAIR WERE FILLED WITH THAT UNSHAKABLE PRIDE.
THEY ALSO TOOK MY PARTNER, RAGDOLL, AWAY FROM US...
...SO I'VE GOT A PERSONAL STAKE IN THIS GAME!
BASED ON THE TRACKING DEVICE PLACED BY ONE OF THE STUDENTS...
...WE CAN ASSUME THESE VILLAINS OCCUPY *MULTIPLE* HIDEOUTS.
THAT SAID, OUR INVESTIGATION HAS DETERMINED THE CURRENT LOCATION OF THE ABDUCTED STUDENT.
WE'LL BE SENDING THE BULK OF OUR PERSONNEL THERE. RETRIEVING THE HOSTAGE IS TOP PRIORITY.
AT THE SAME TIME, WE'LL MOVE IN ON THE OTHER POSSIBLE HIDEOUT.
BY CUTTING OFF ALL PATHS OF RETREAT, WE'LL BE ABLE TO TAKE DOWN THE ENTIRE ORGANIZATION.

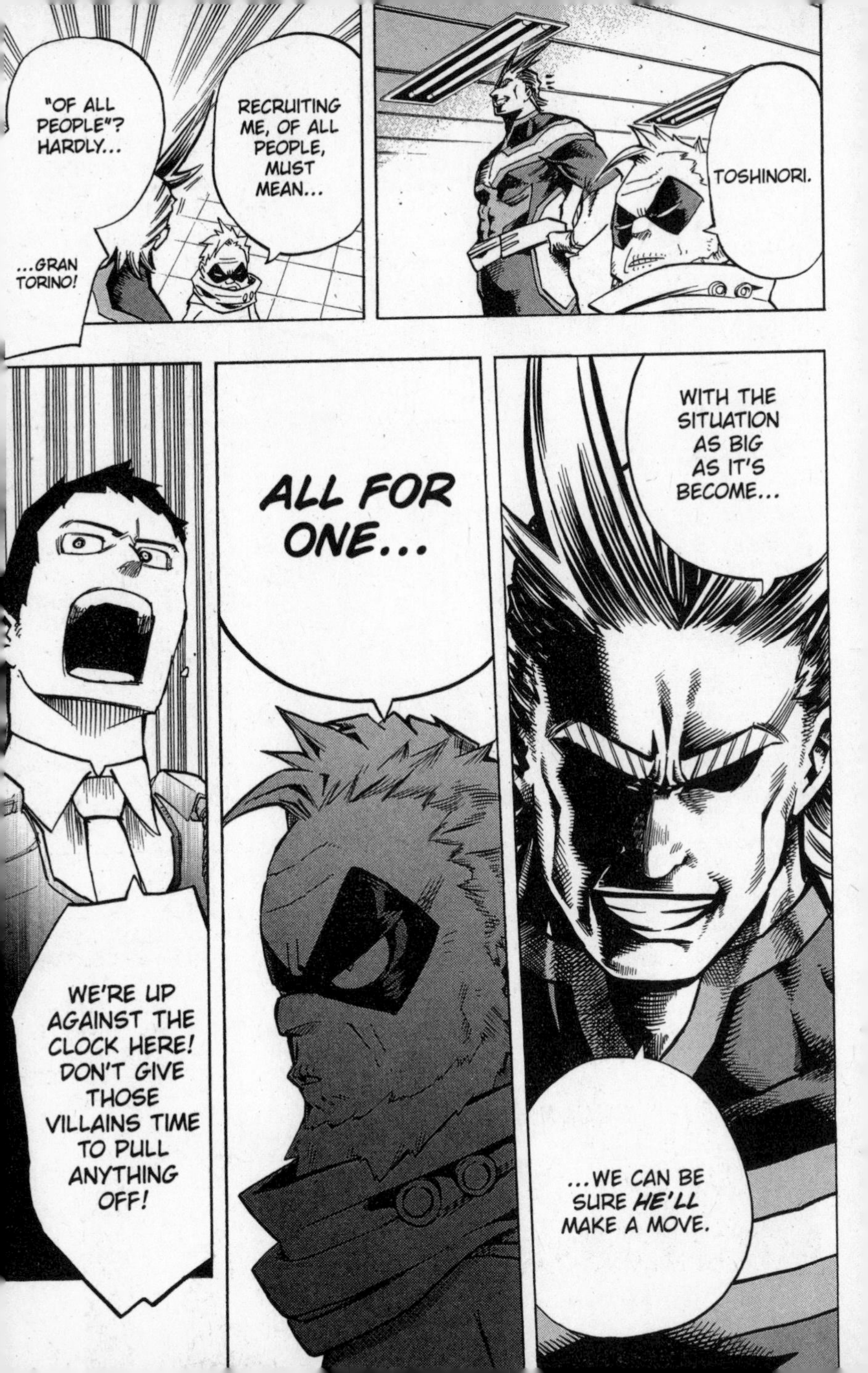
TOSHINORI.
RECRUITING ME, OF ALL PEOPLE, MUST MEAN...
"OF ALL PEOPLE"? HARDLY...
...GRAN TORINO!
WITH THE SITUATION AS BIG AS IT'S BECOME...
...WE CAN BE SURE *HE'LL* MAKE A MOVE.
ALL FOR ONE...
WE'RE UP AGAINST THE CLOCK HERE! DON'T GIVE THOSE VILLAINS TIME TO PULL ANYTHING OFF!

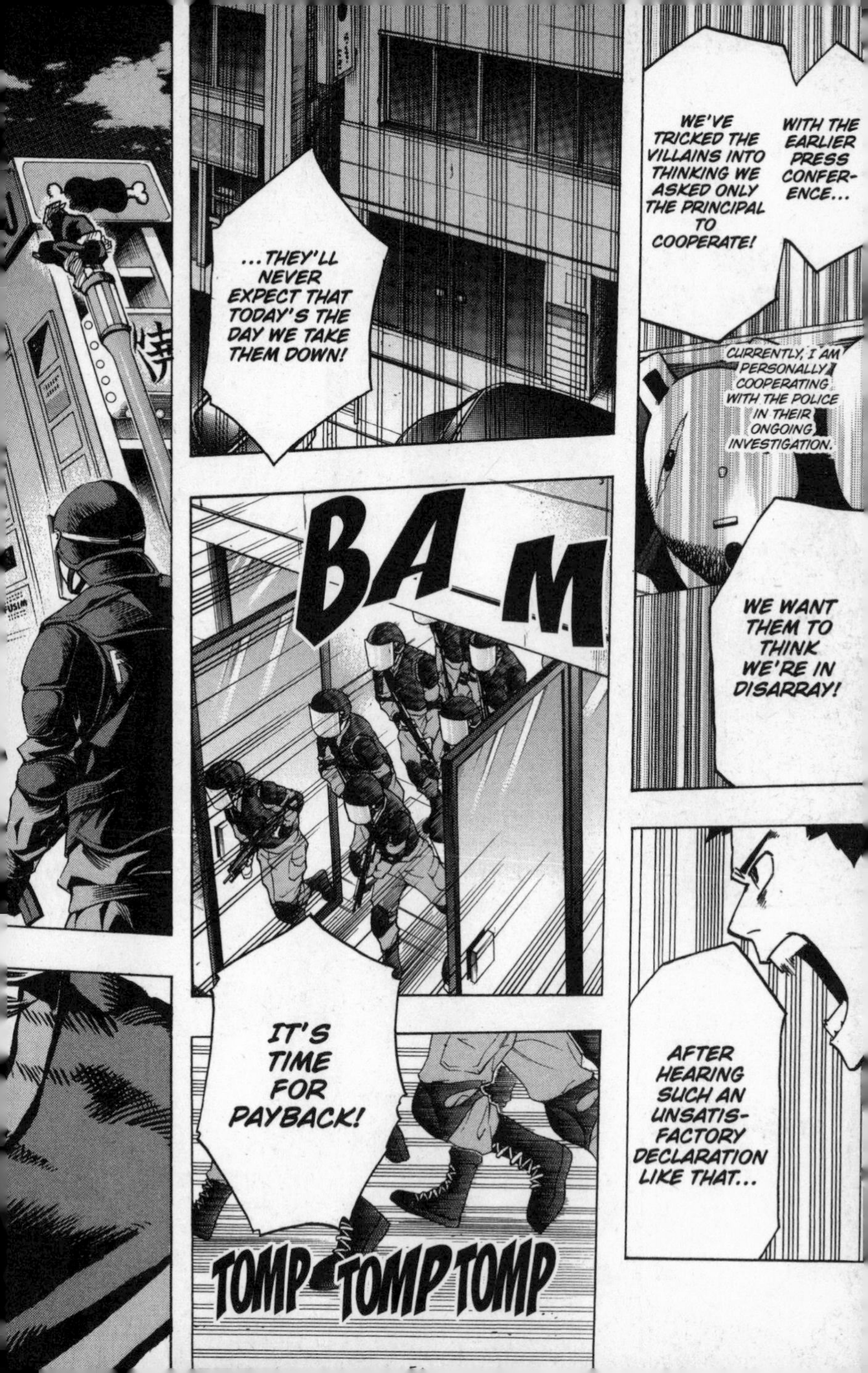
WITH THE EARLIER PRESS CONFERENCE...
WE'VE TRICKED THE VILLAINS INTO THINKING WE ASKED ONLY THE PRINCIPAL TO COOPERATE!
...THEY'LL NEVER EXPECT THAT TODAY'S THE DAY WE TAKE THEM DOWN!
CURRENTLY, I AM PERSONALLY COOPERATING WITH THE POLICE IN THEIR ONGOING INVESTIGATION.
WE WANT THEM TO THINK WE'RE IN DISARRAY!
BAM
AFTER HEARING SUCH AN UNSATIS-FACTORY DECLARATION LIKE THAT...
IT'S TIME FOR PAYBACK!
TOMP TOMP TOMP

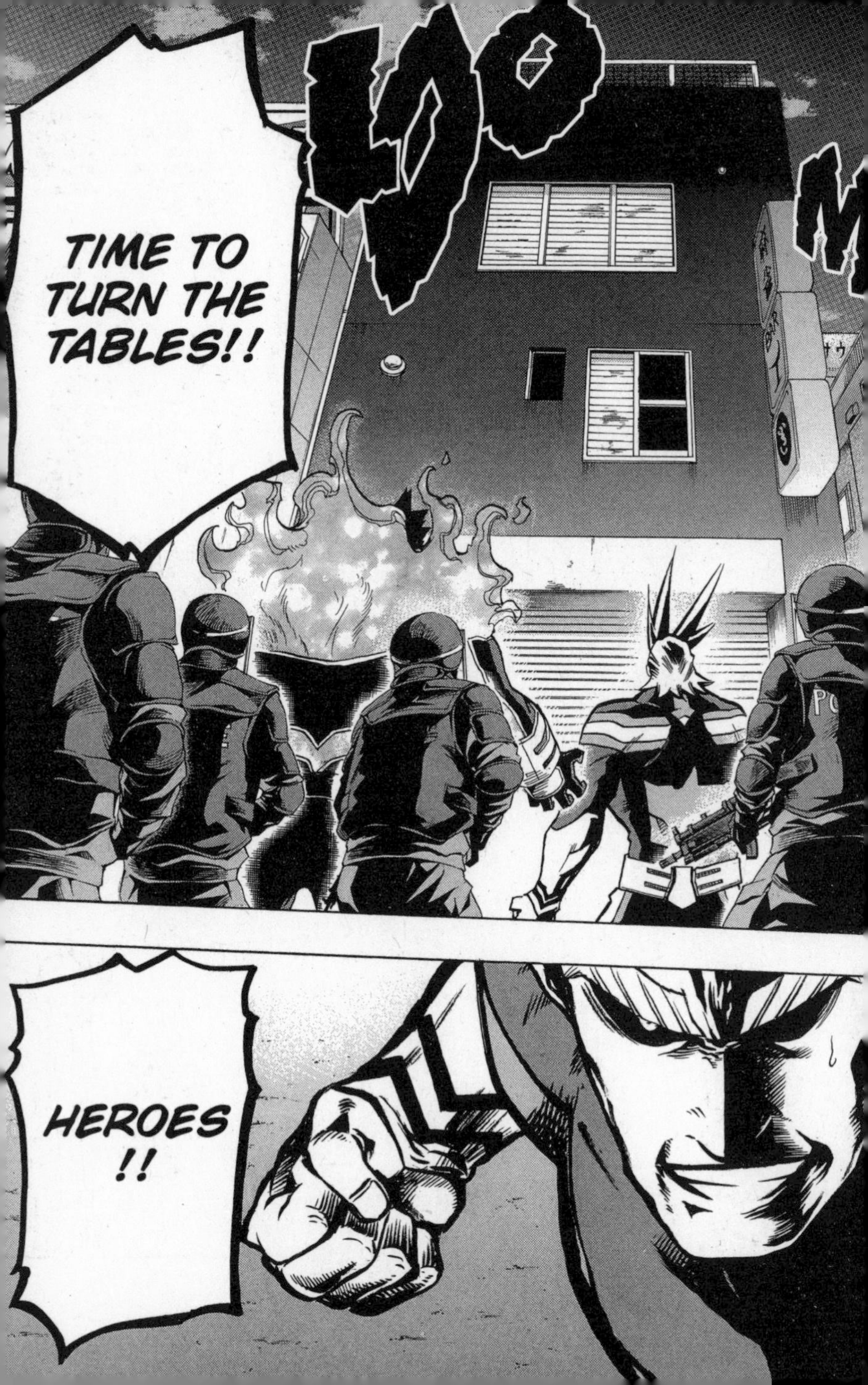
TIME TO TURN THE TABLES!!
HEROES !!

HERO

MT. LADY (23) (YU TAKEYAMA)

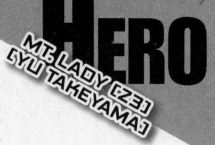

STREET CLOTHES

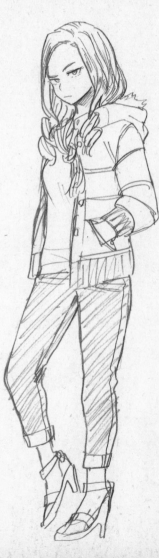

Birthday: 8/11
Height: 162 cm
Favorite Thing: Peaches

THE SUPPLEMENT

She started her own agency at a young age, and although her incident-resolution rate has earned her popularity, she always ends up destroying parts of the city, so it's hard for her finances to stay in the black.

She works even harder to earn more money, but then she ends up causing more destruction. It's a vicious cycle.

All that hard work caught the attention of some important people, which is why she was included in the mission featured in this volume.

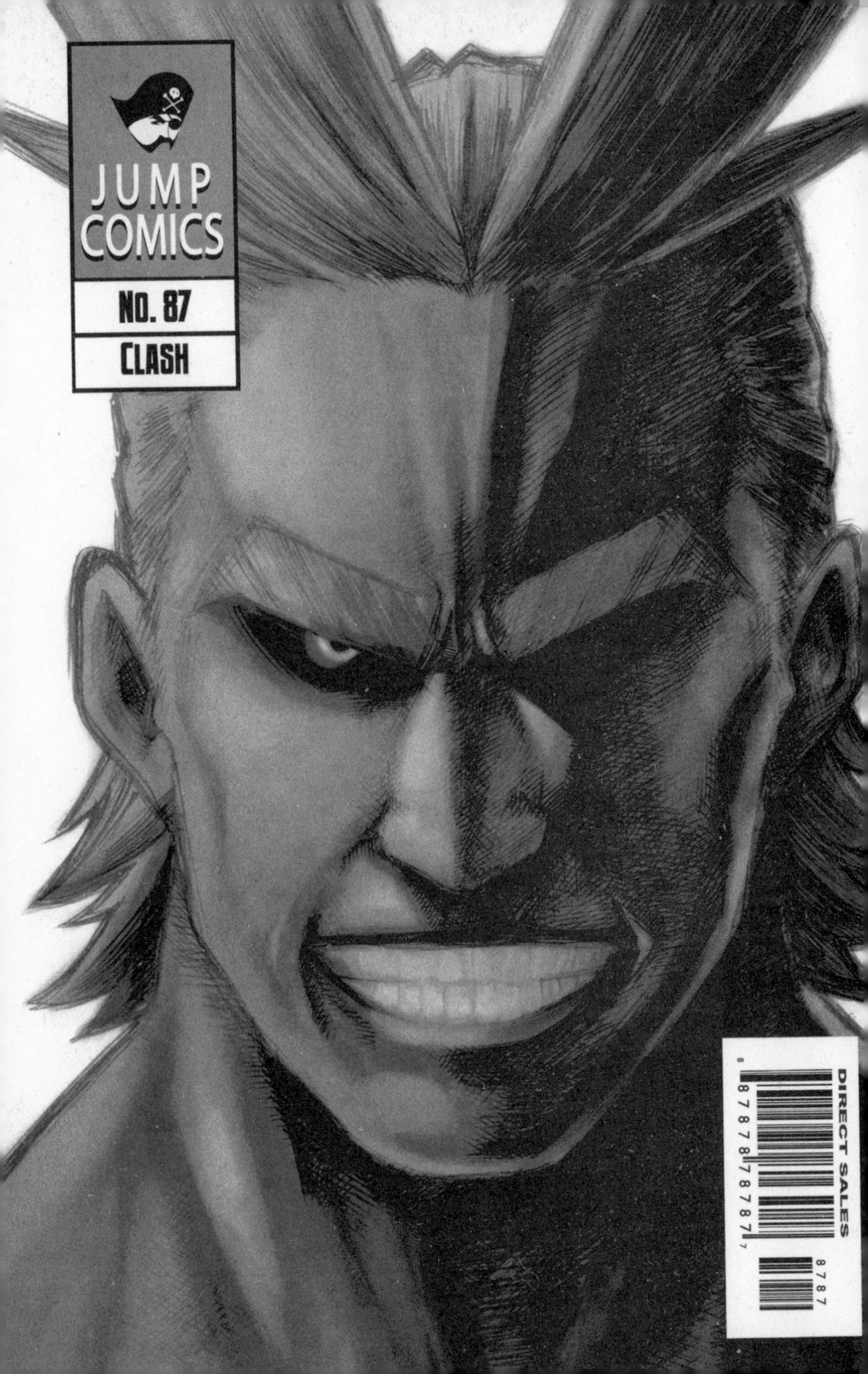
JUMP
COMICS
NO. 87
CLASH
DIRECT SALES

MY HERO ACADEMIA

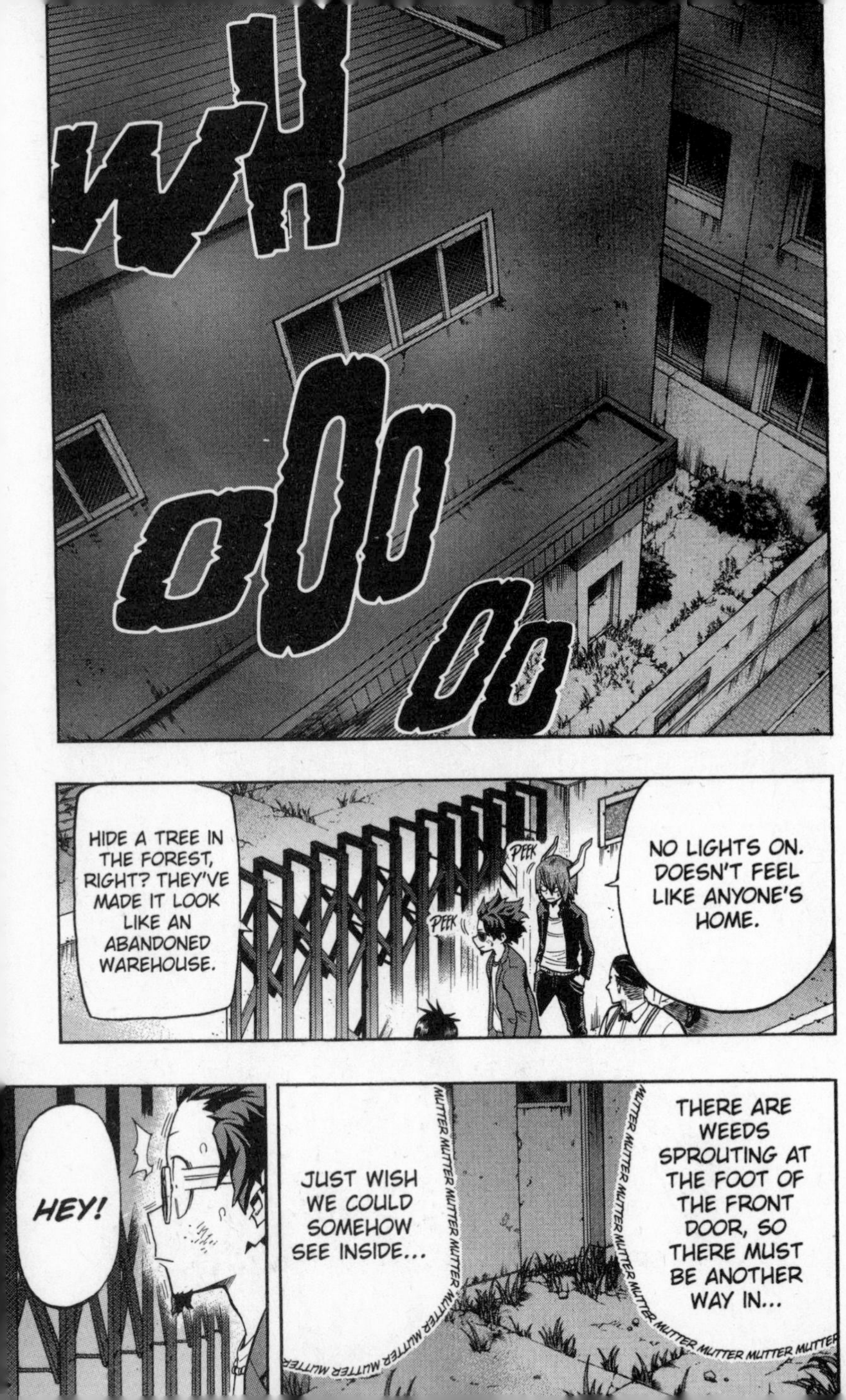
WHOOOOOO
NO LIGHTS ON. DOESN'T FEEL LIKE ANYONE'S HOME.
PEEK
PEEK
HIDE A TREE IN THE FOREST, RIGHT? THEY'VE MADE IT LOOK LIKE AN ABANDONED WAREHOUSE.
THERE ARE WEEDS SPROUTING AT THE FOOT OF THE FRONT DOOR, SO THERE MUST BE ANOTHER WAY IN...
JUST WISH WE COULD SOMEHOW SEE INSIDE...
MUTTER MUTTER MUTTER MUTTER MUTTER MUTTER MUTTER MUTTER
HEY!

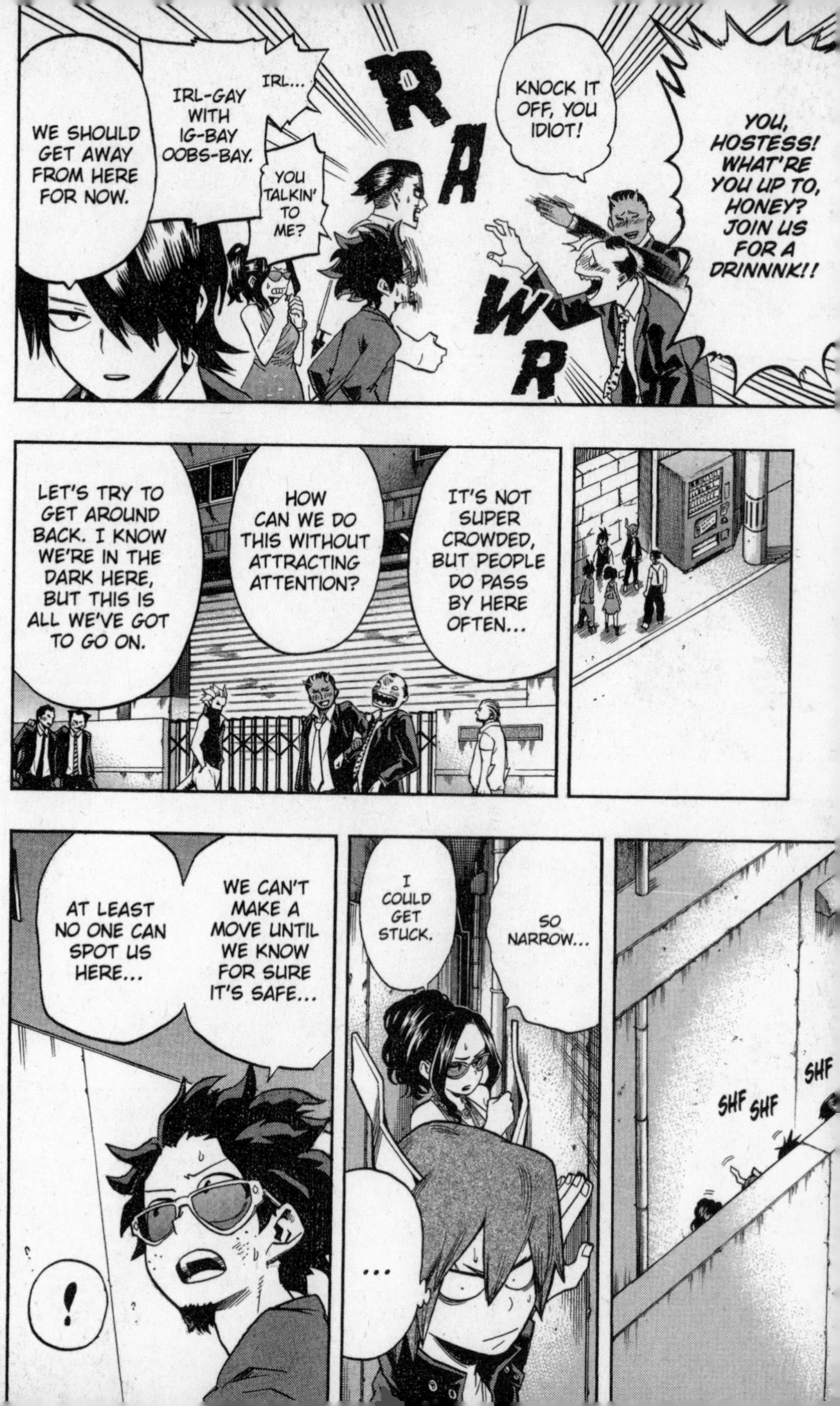
YOU, HOSTESS! WHAT'RE YOU UP TO, HONEY? JOIN US FOR A DRINNNK!!
KNOCK IT OFF, YOU IDIOT!
RAWR
YOU TALKIN' TO ME?
IRL...
IRL-GAY WITH IG-BAY OOBS-BAY.
WE SHOULD GET AWAY FROM HERE FOR NOW.
IT'S NOT SUPER CROWDED, BUT PEOPLE DO PASS BY HERE OFTEN...
HOW CAN WE DO THIS WITHOUT ATTRACTING ATTENTION?
LET'S TRY TO GET AROUND BACK. I KNOW WE'RE IN THE DARK HERE, BUT THIS IS ALL WE'VE GOT TO GO ON.
SHF
SHF SHF
SO NARROW...
I COULD GET STUCK.
...
WE CAN'T MAKE A MOVE UNTIL WE KNOW FOR SURE IT'S SAFE...
AT LEAST NO ONE CAN SPOT US HERE...
!

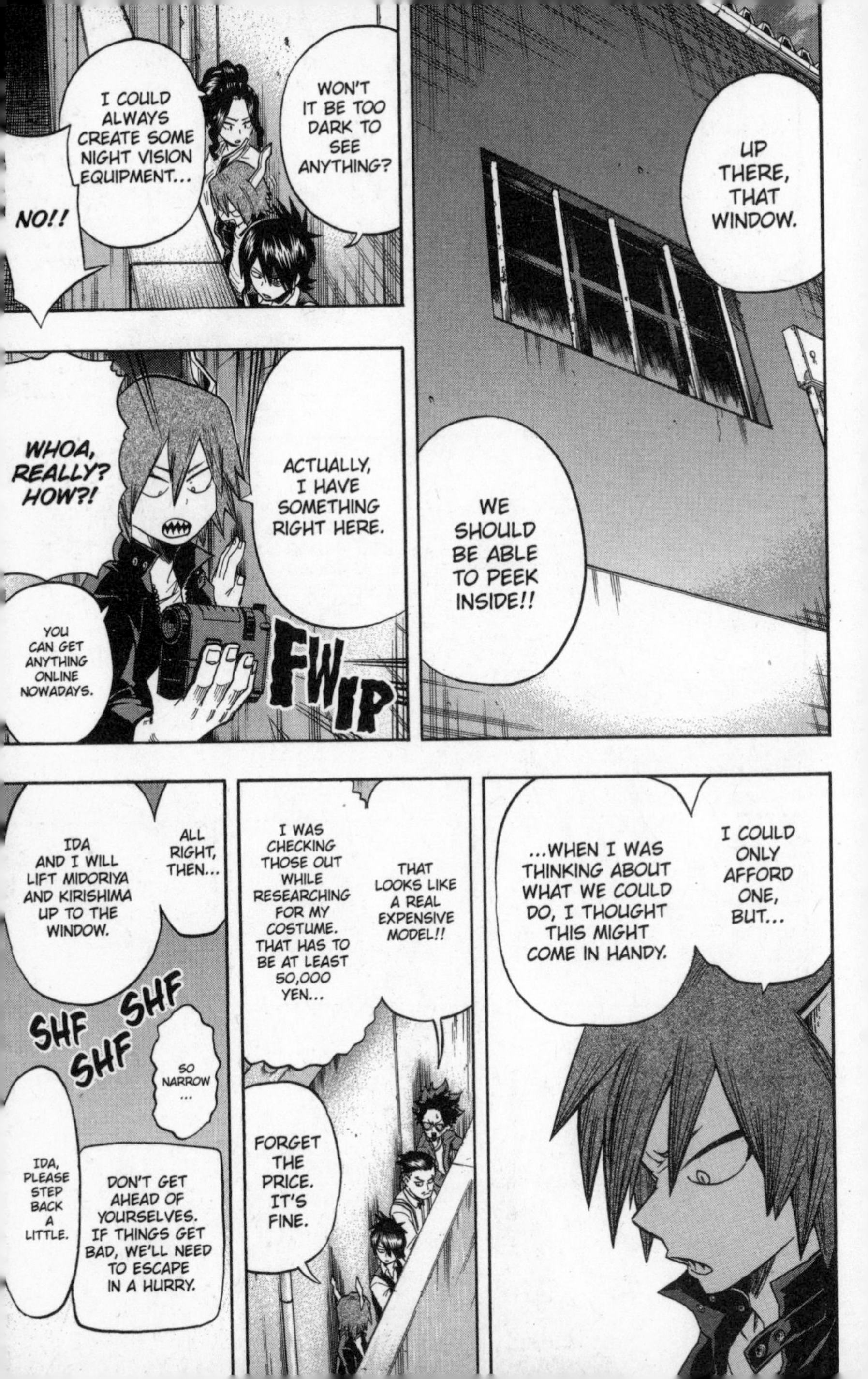
UP THERE, THAT WINDOW.
WE SHOULD BE ABLE TO PEEK INSIDE!!
WON'T IT BE TOO DARK TO SEE ANYTHING?
I COULD ALWAYS CREATE SOME NIGHT VISION EQUIPMENT...
NO!!
ACTUALLY, I HAVE SOMETHING RIGHT HERE.
FWIP
WHOA, REALLY? HOW?!
YOU CAN GET ANYTHING ONLINE NOWADAYS.
I COULD ONLY AFFORD ONE, BUT...
...WHEN I WAS THINKING ABOUT WHAT WE COULD DO, I THOUGHT THIS MIGHT COME IN HANDY.
THAT LOOKS LIKE A REAL EXPENSIVE MODEL!!
I WAS CHECKING THOSE OUT WHILE RESEARCHING FOR MY COSTUME. THAT HAS TO BE AT LEAST 50,000 YEN...
FORGET THE PRICE. IT'S FINE.
ALL RIGHT, THEN...
IDA AND I WILL LIFT MIDORIYA AND KIRISHIMA UP TO THE WINDOW.
SHF SHF SHF
SO NARROW...
DON'T GET AHEAD OF YOURSELVES. IF THINGS GET BAD, WE'LL NEED TO ESCAPE IN A HURRY.
IDA, PLEASE STEP BACK A LITTLE.

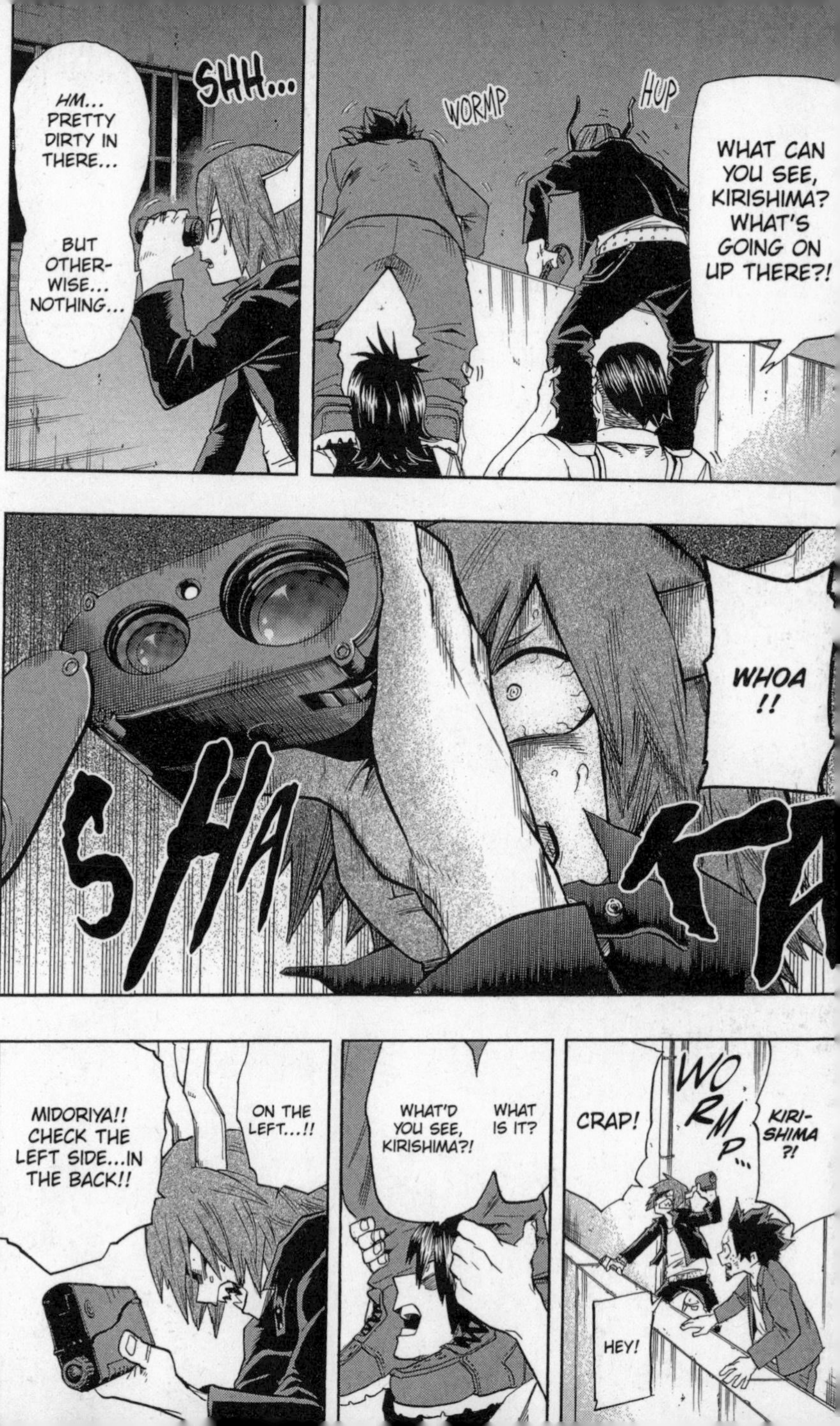
HUP
WHAT CAN YOU SEE, KIRISHIMA? WHAT'S GOING ON UP THERE?!
WORMP
SHH...
HM... PRETTY DIRTY IN THERE...
BUT OTHER-WISE... NOTHING...
WHOA!!
SHA
KA
KIRI-SHIMA?!
WORMP...
CRAP!
HEY!
WHAT IS IT?
WHAT'D YOU SEE, KIRISHIMA?!
ON THE LEFT...!!
MIDORIYA!! CHECK THE LEFT SIDE...IN THE BACK!!

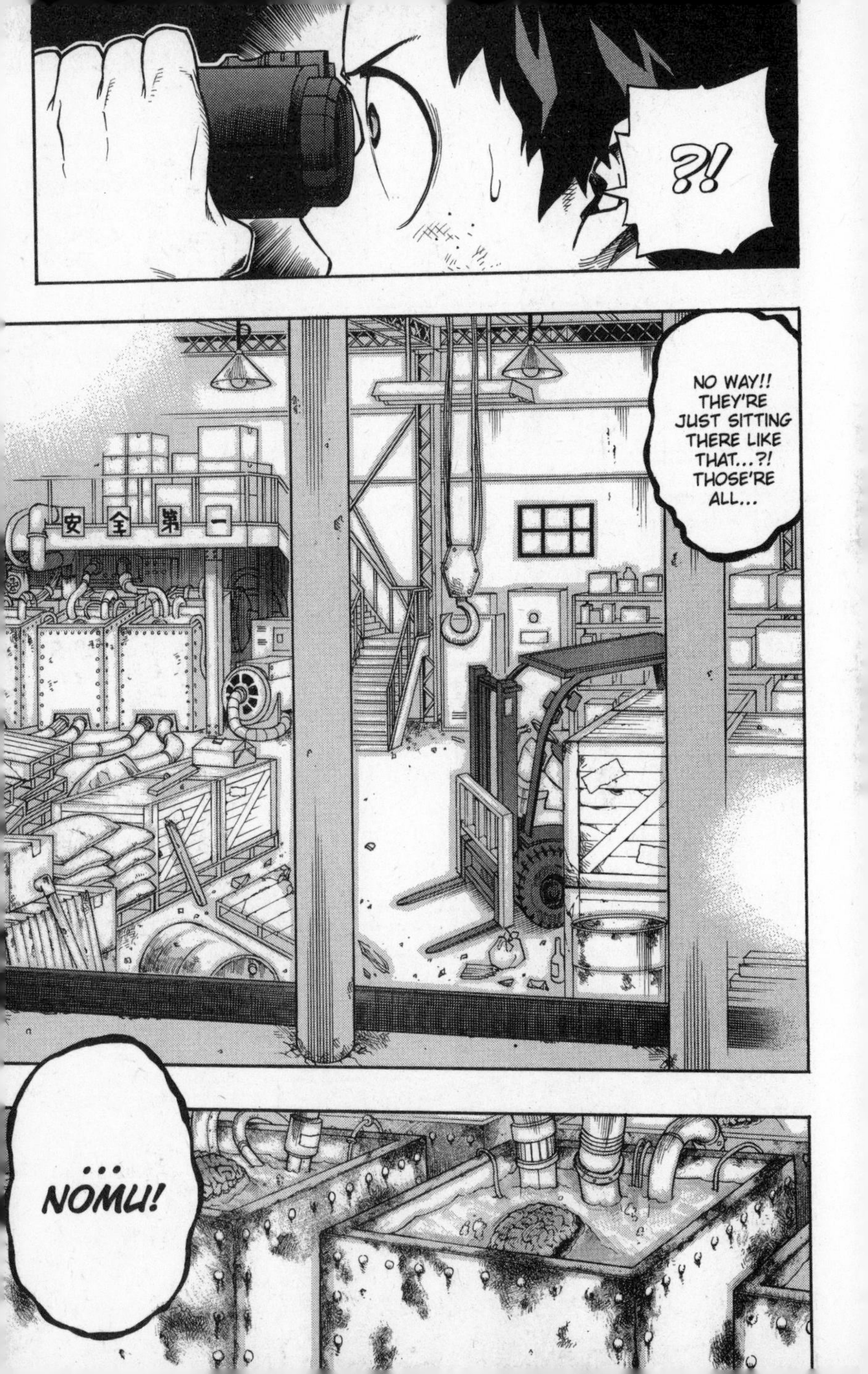
?!
NO WAY!! THEY'RE JUST SITTING THERE LIKE THAT...?! THOSE'RE ALL...
安全第一
...NOMU!

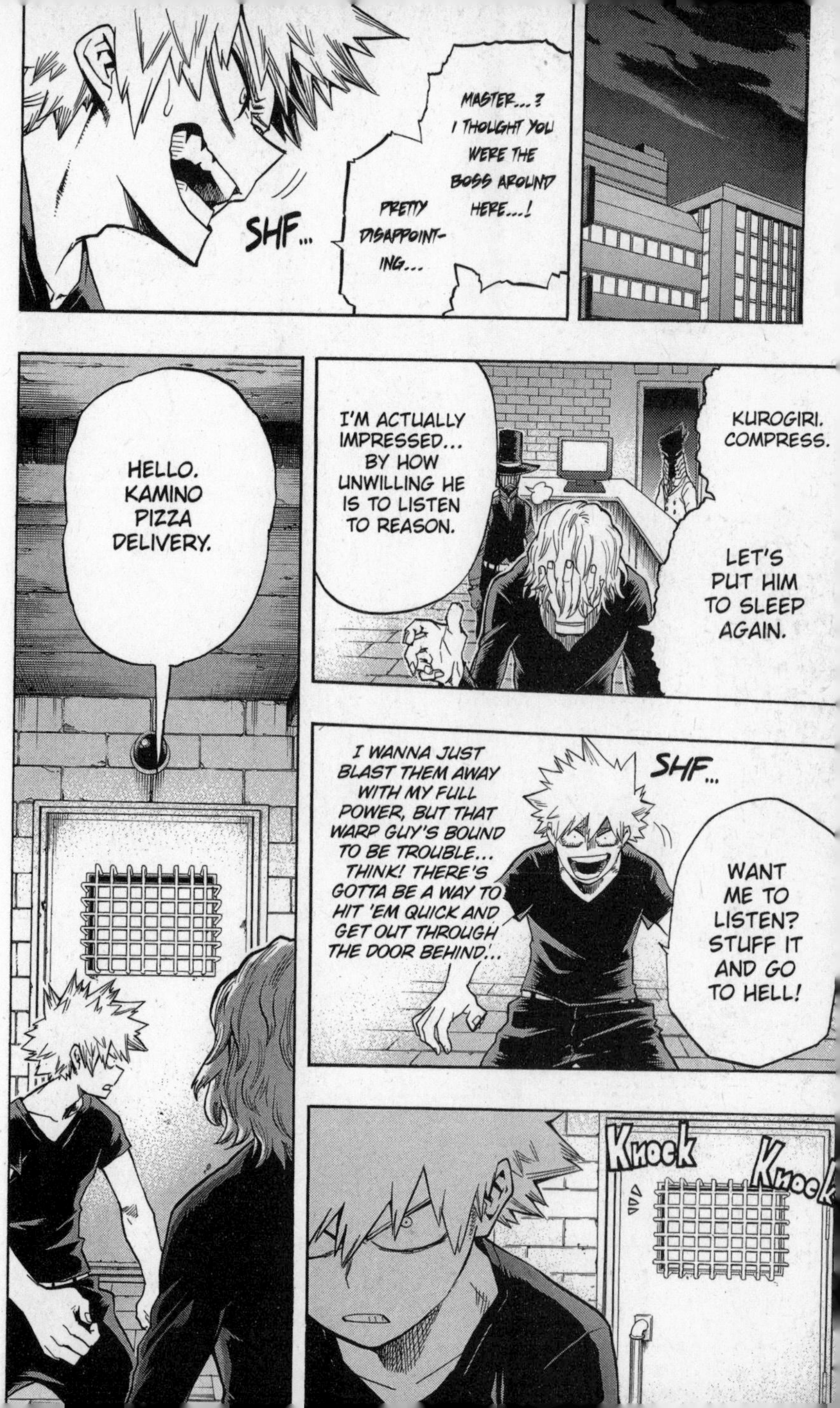
MASTER...?
I THOUGHT YOU WERE THE BOSS AROUND HERE...!
PRETTY DISAPPOINTING...
SHF...
KUROGIRI. COMPRESS.
LET'S PUT HIM TO SLEEP AGAIN.
I'M ACTUALLY IMPRESSED... BY HOW UNWILLING HE IS TO LISTEN TO REASON.
SHF...
WANT ME TO LISTEN? STUFF IT AND GO TO HELL!
I WANNA JUST BLAST THEM AWAY WITH MY FULL POWER, BUT THAT WARP GUY'S BOUND TO BE TROUBLE... THINK! THERE'S GOTTA BE A WAY TO HIT 'EM QUICK AND GET OUT THROUGH THE DOOR BEHIND...
Knock
Knock
HELLO. KAMINO PIZZA DELIVERY.

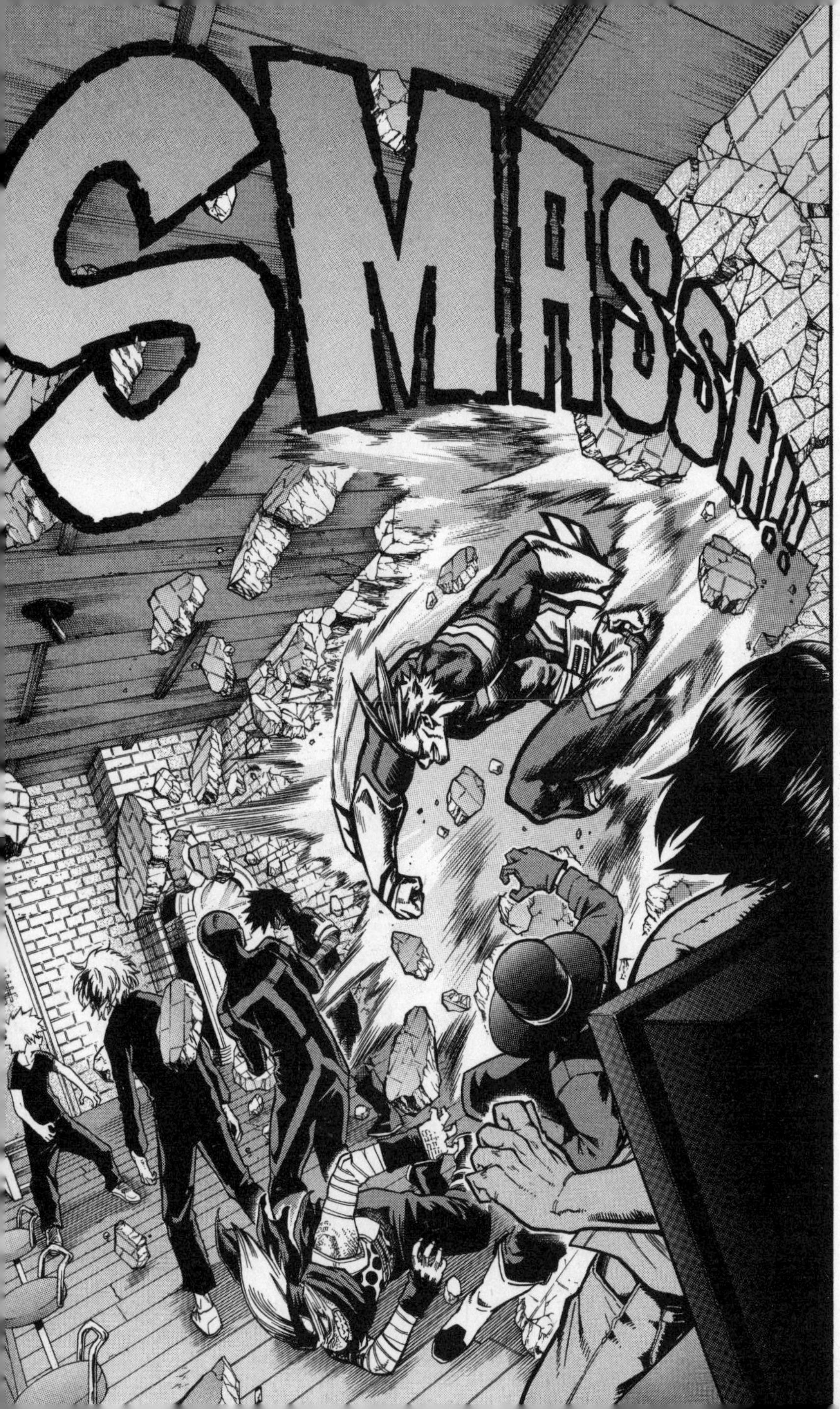
SMASH!!

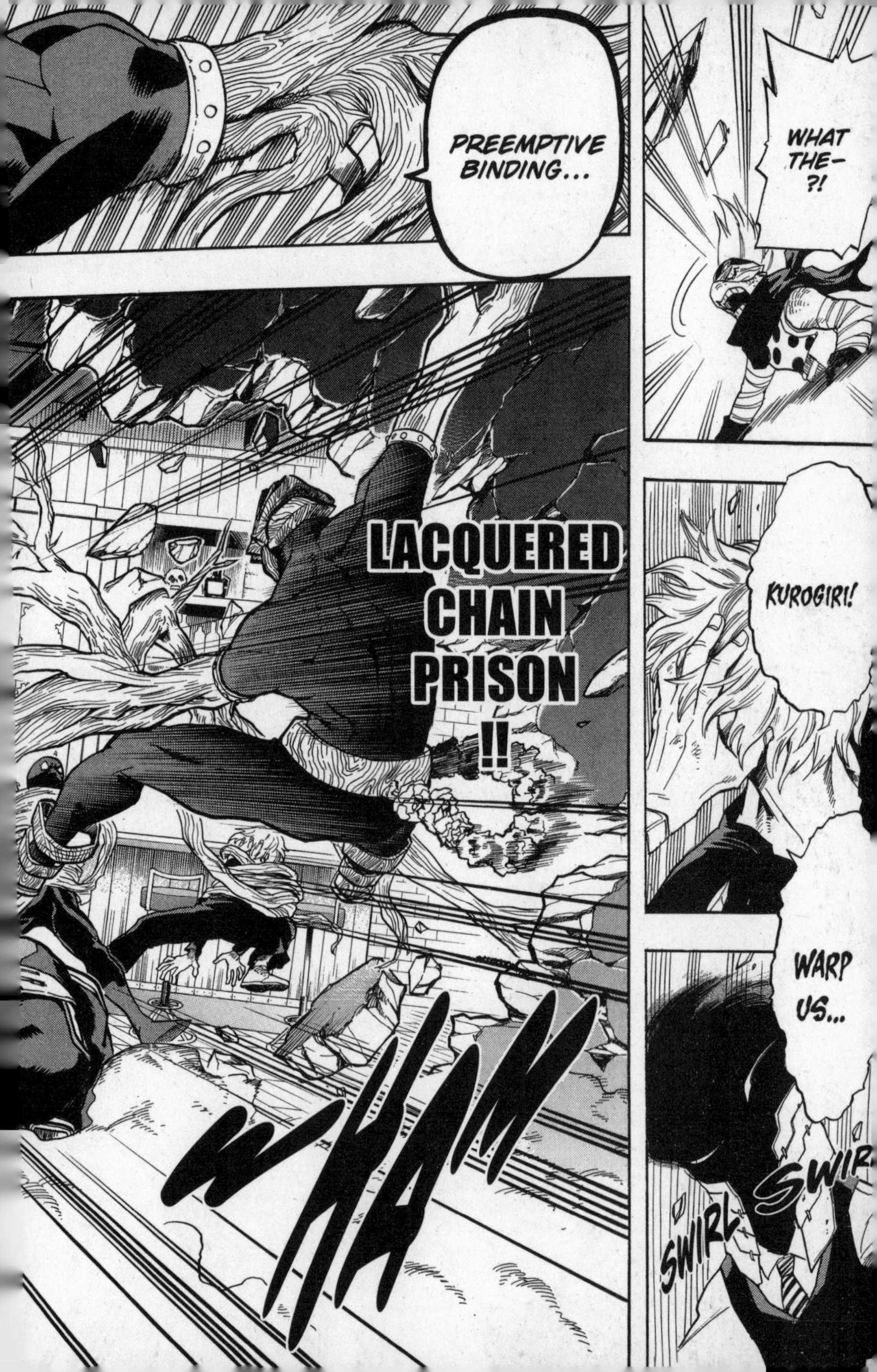
WHAT THE-?!
KUROGIRI!
WARP US...
SWIRL SWIRL
SWIRL
PREEMPTIVE BINDING...
LACQUERED CHAIN PRISON!!
WHAM

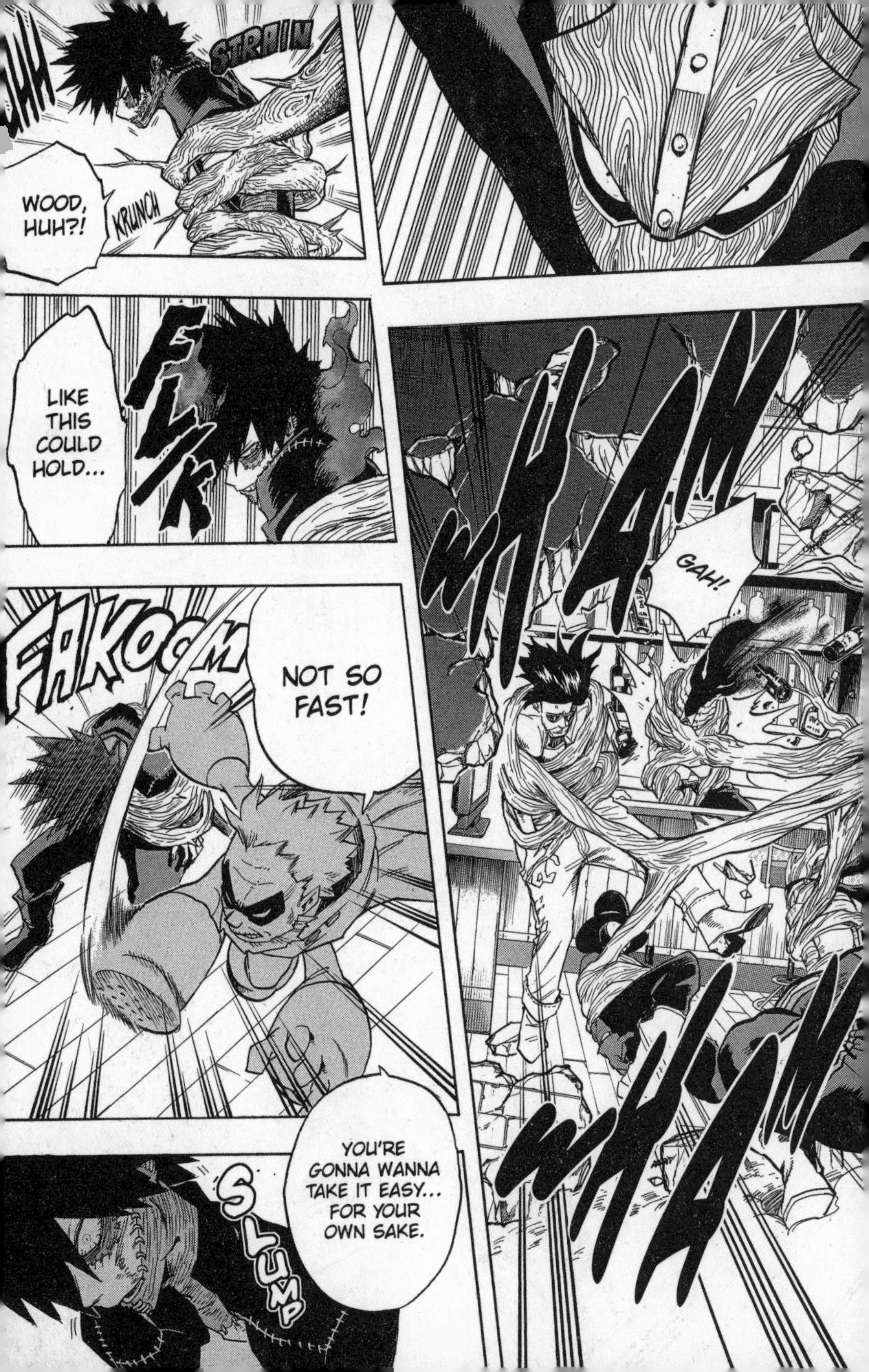
STRAIN
WOOD, HUH?!
KRUNCH
WHAM
GAH!
WHAM
LIKE THIS COULD HOLD...
FLK
NOT SO FAST!
FAKOOM
YOU'RE GONNA WANNA TAKE IT EASY... FOR YOUR OWN SAKE.
SLUMP

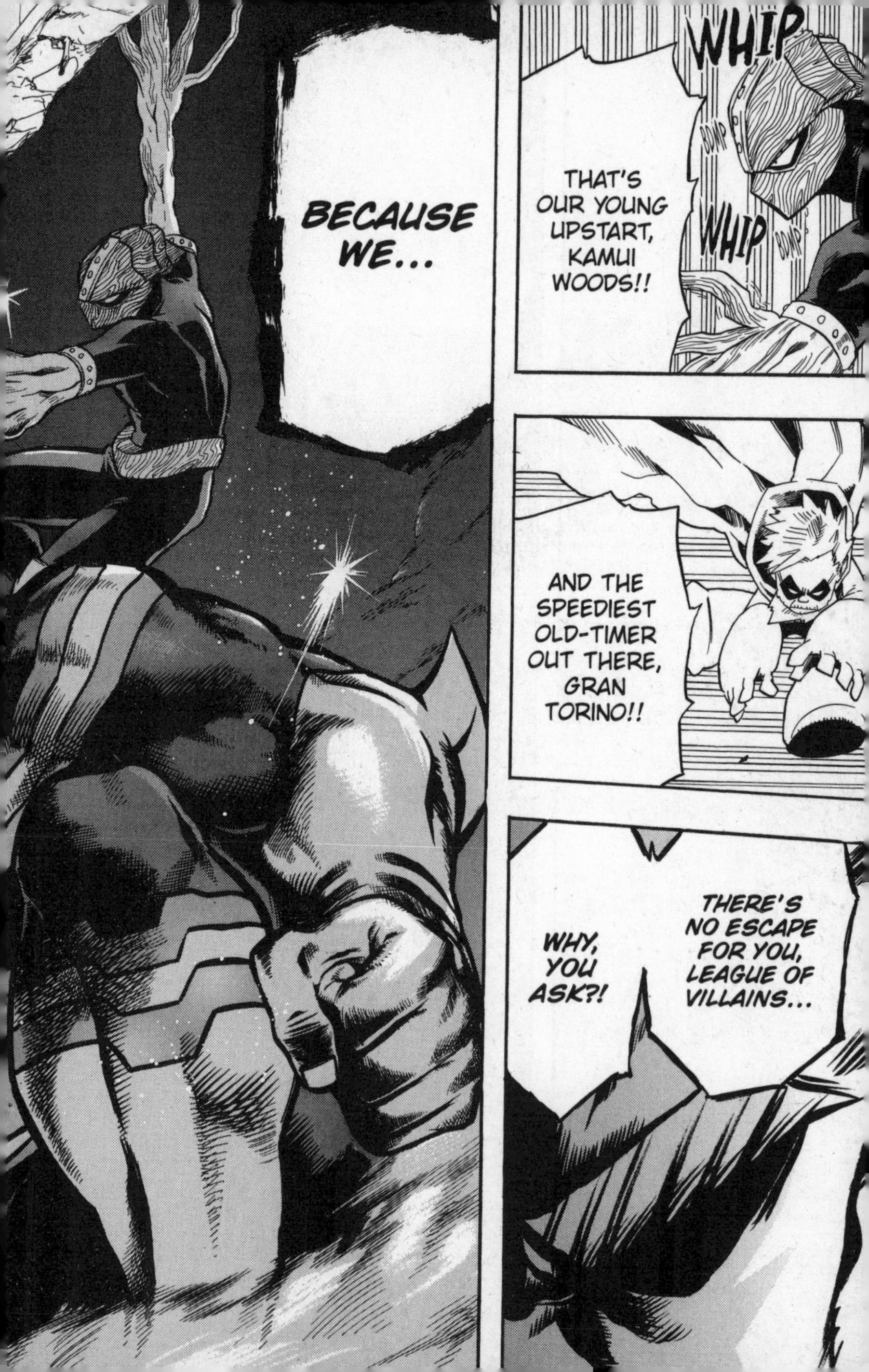
WHIP
BDMP
WHIP
BDMP
THAT'S OUR YOUNG UPSTART, KAMUI WOODS!!
AND THE SPEEDIEST OLD-TIMER OUT THERE, GRAN TORINO!!
THERE'S NO ESCAPE FOR YOU, LEAGUE OF VILLAINS...
WHY, YOU ASK?!
BECAUSE WE...

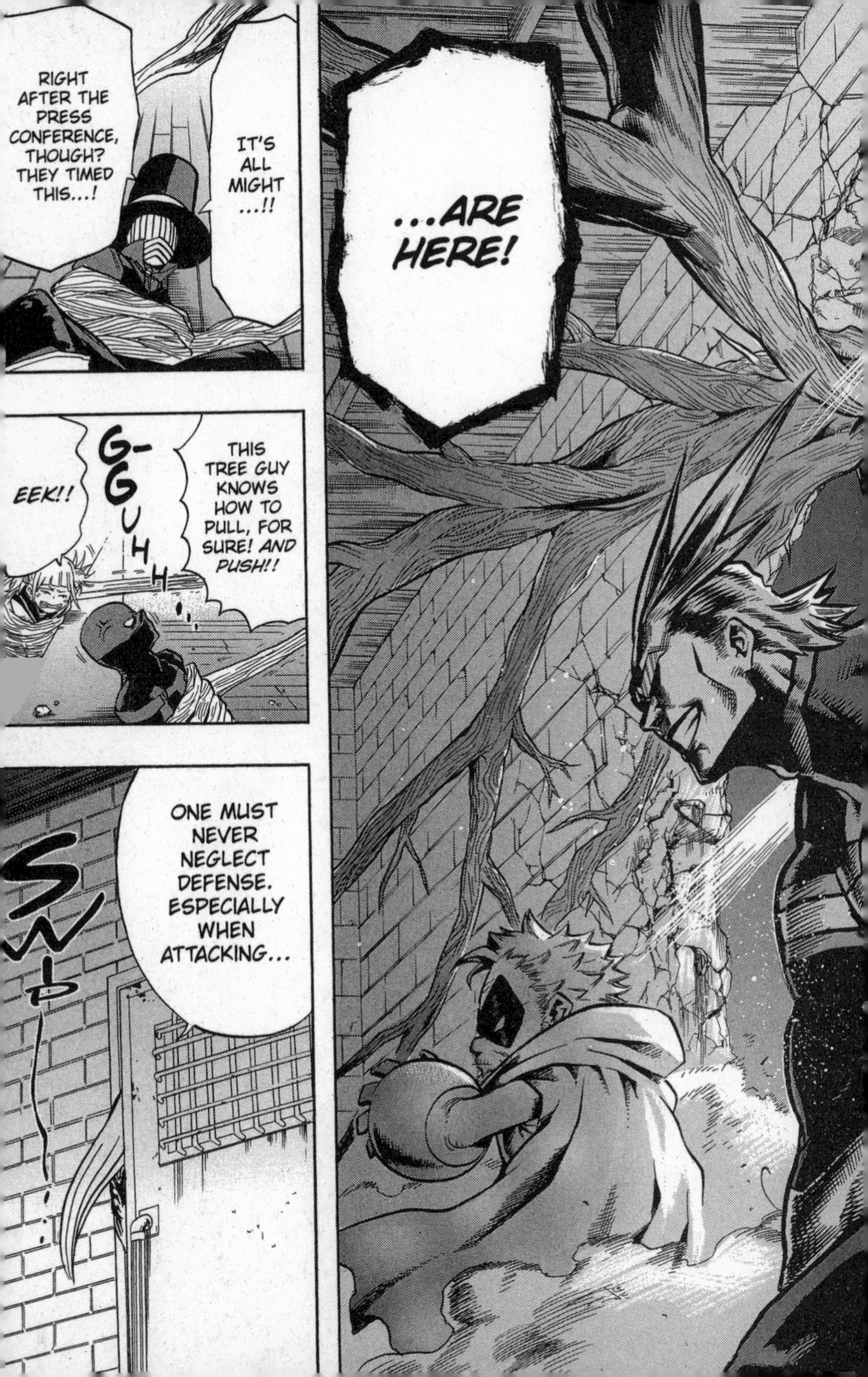
...ARE HERE!
IT'S ALL MIGHT ...!!
RIGHT AFTER THE PRESS CONFERENCE, THOUGH? THEY TIMED THIS...!
THIS TREE GUY KNOWS HOW TO PULL, FOR SURE! AND PUSH!!
G-GUHH
EEK!!
ONE MUST NEVER NEGLECT DEFENSE. ESPECIALLY WHEN ATTACKING...
SWIP

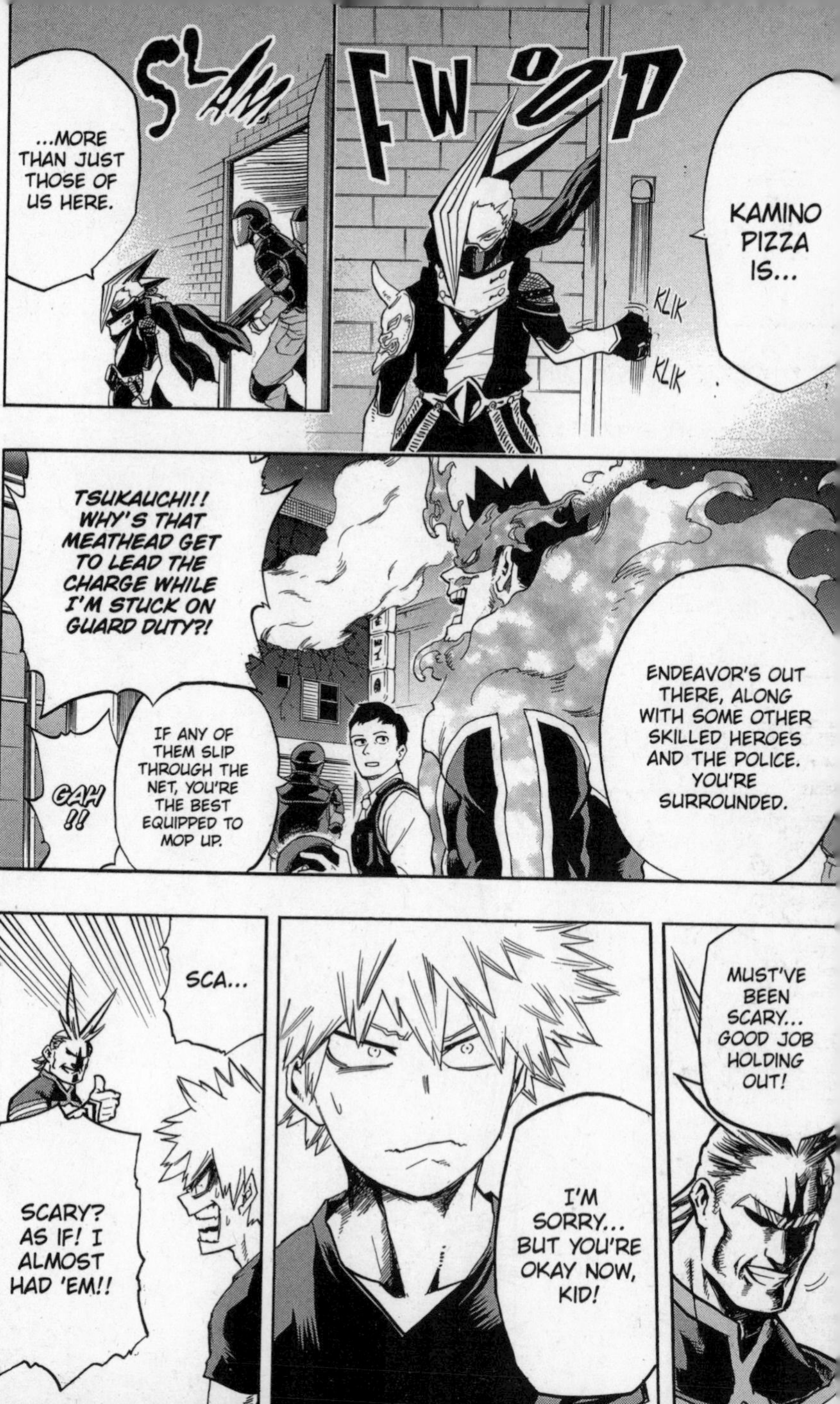
KAMINO PIZZA IS...
FWOOP
KLIK
KLIK
SLAM
...MORE THAN JUST THOSE OF US HERE.
ENDEAVOR'S OUT THERE, ALONG WITH SOME OTHER SKILLED HEROES AND THE POLICE. YOU'RE SURROUNDED.
TSUKAUCHI!! WHY'S THAT MEATHEAD GET TO LEAD THE CHARGE WHILE I'M STUCK ON GUARD DUTY?!
IF ANY OF THEM SLIP THROUGH THE NET, YOU'RE THE BEST EQUIPPED TO MOP UP.
GAH!!
MUST'VE BEEN SCARY... GOOD JOB HOLDING OUT!
I'M SORRY... BUT YOU'RE OKAY NOW, KID!
SCA...
SCARY? AS IF! I ALMOST HAD 'EM!!

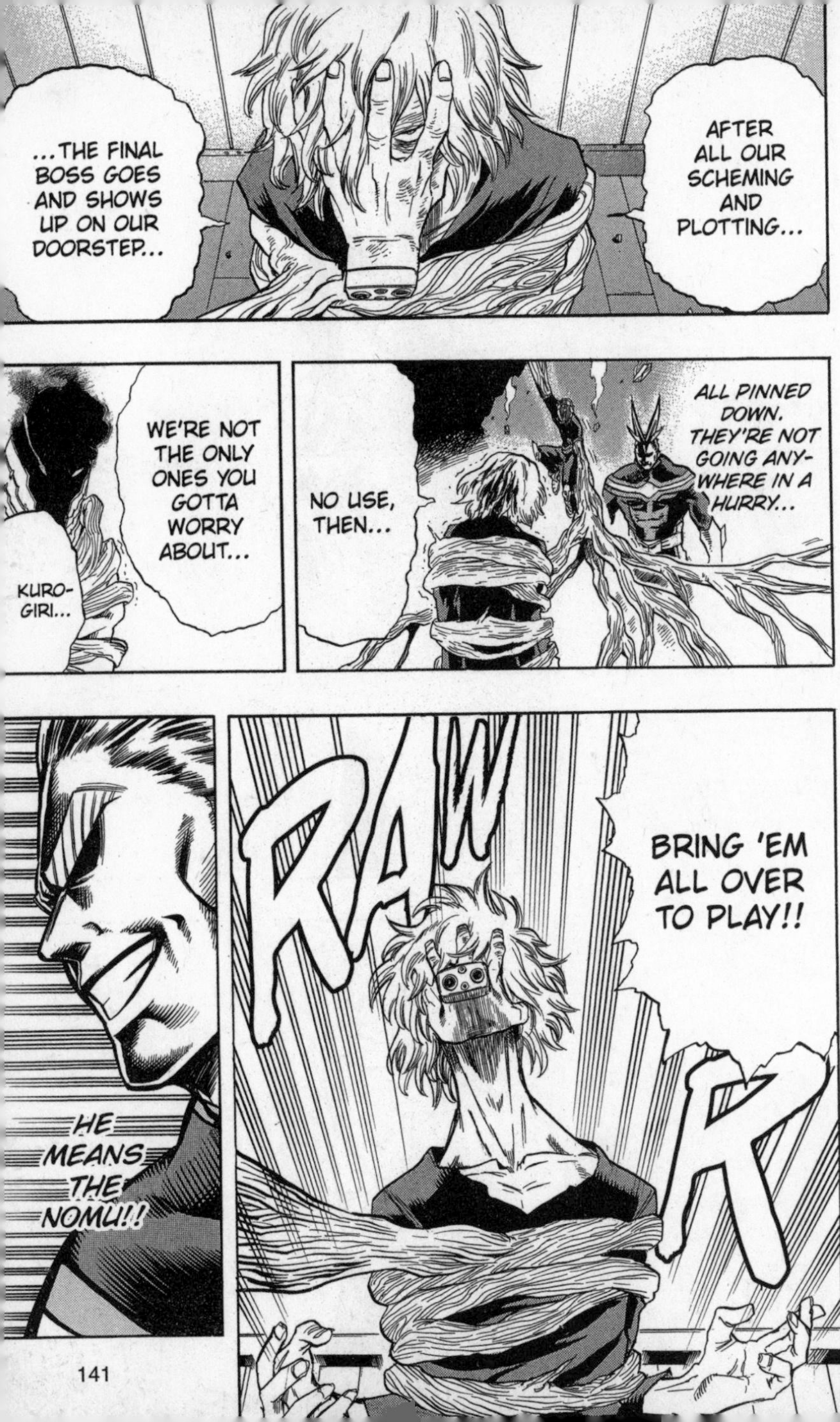
AFTER ALL OUR SCHEMING AND PLOTTING...
...THE FINAL BOSS GOES AND SHOWS UP ON OUR DOORSTEP...
ALL PINNED DOWN. THEY'RE NOT GOING ANY-WHERE IN A HURRY...
NO USE, THEN...
WE'RE NOT THE ONLY ONES YOU GOTTA WORRY ABOUT...
KURO-GIRI...
RAWR
BRING 'EM ALL OVER TO PLAY!!
HE MEANS THE NOMU!!

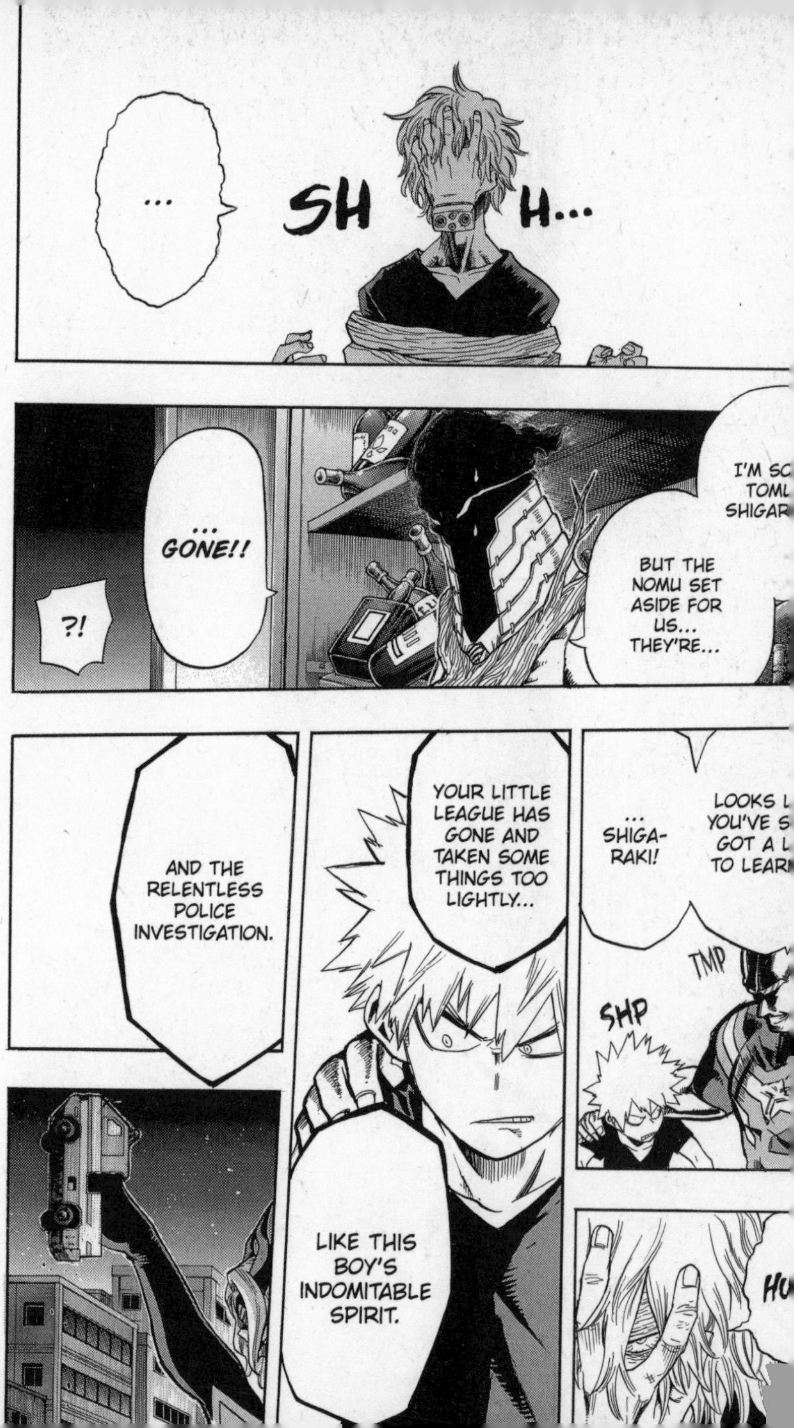
SH H...
...
I'M SC TOML SHIGAR
BUT THE NOMU SET ASIDE FOR US... THEY'RE...
... GONE!!
?!
LOOKS L YOU'VE S GOT A L TO LEAR
... SHIGA-RAKI!
TMP
SHP
HU
YOUR LITTLE LEAGUE HAS GONE AND TAKEN SOME THINGS TOO LIGHTLY...
LIKE THIS BOY'S INDOMITABLE SPIRIT.
AND THE RELENTLESS POLICE INVESTIGATION.

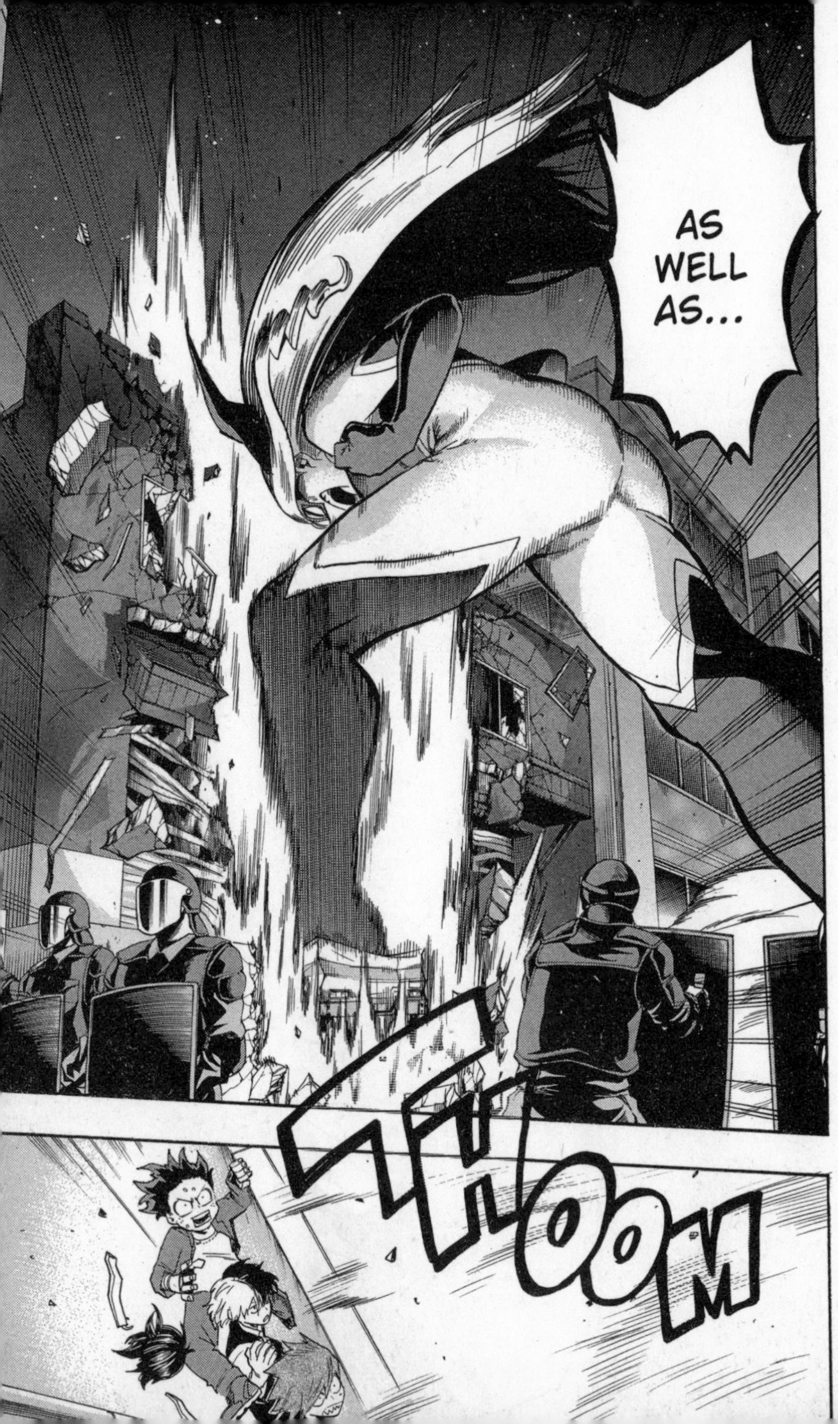
AS WELL AS...
THOOM

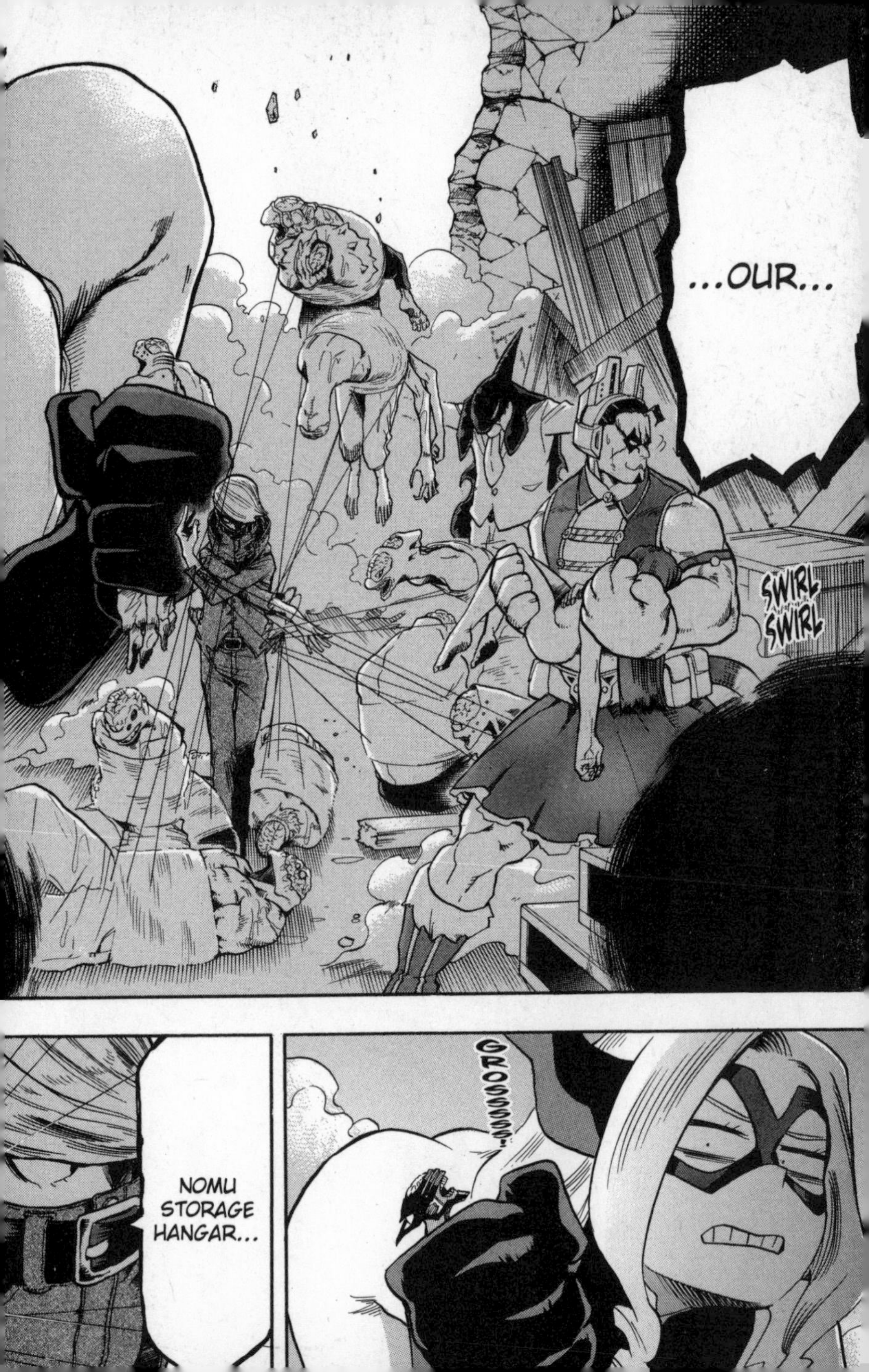
...OUR...
SWIRL SWIRL
GROSSSSSS!
NOMU STORAGE HANGAR...

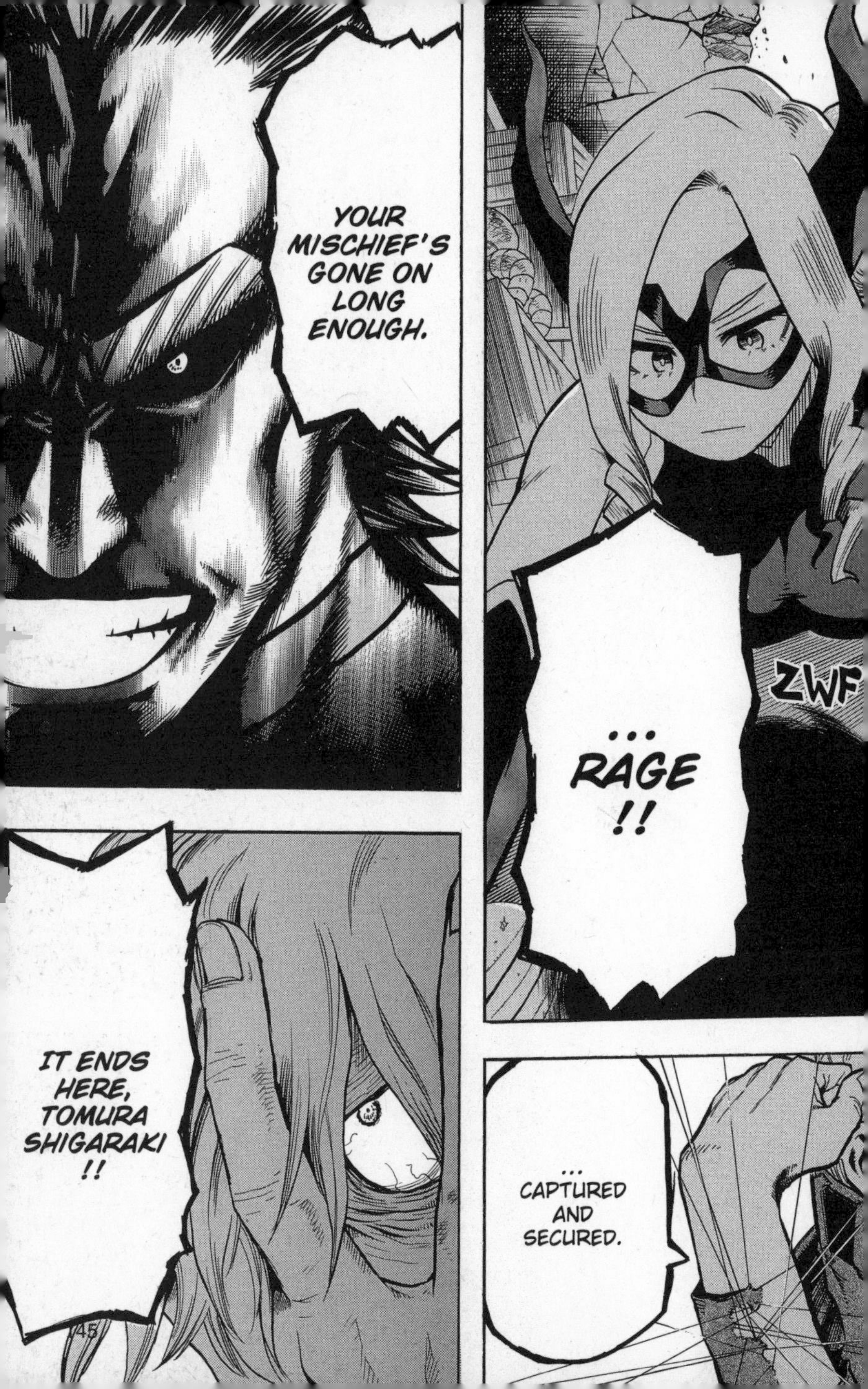
ZWF
...RAGE!!
YOUR MISCHIEF'S GONE ON LONG ENOUGH.
...CAPTURED AND SECURED.
IT ENDS HERE, TOMURA SHIGARAKI!!

HERO

KAMUI WOODS (29, SINCE HE STARTED COUNTING) (SHINJI NISHIYA)

STREET CLOTHES
(ALL MADE OF ORGANIC MATERIALS)

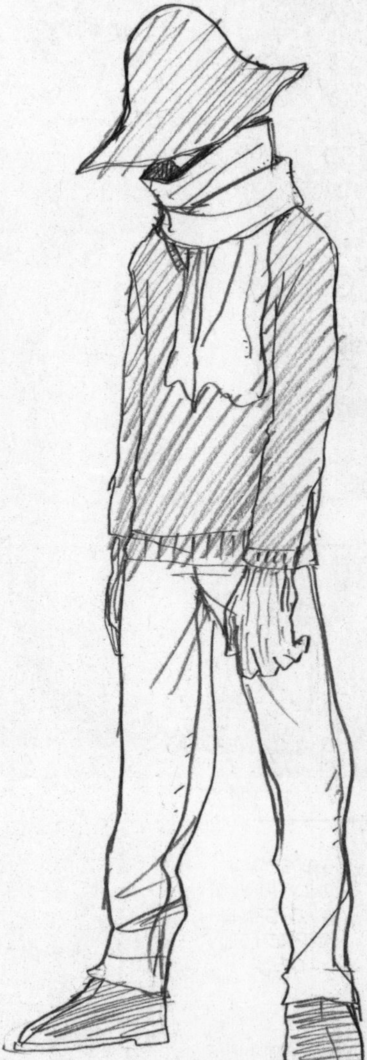

Birthday: 5/20
Height: 168 cm
Favorite Thing: Peaceful walks through the woods

THE SUPPLEMENT
His talents and popularity have sent his stock soaring as a hero.

The backstory of his early childhood is a grand and compelling one. He exploded in popularity when his story was made into a documentary.

Some claim that he will be the one to create the next generation of heroes.

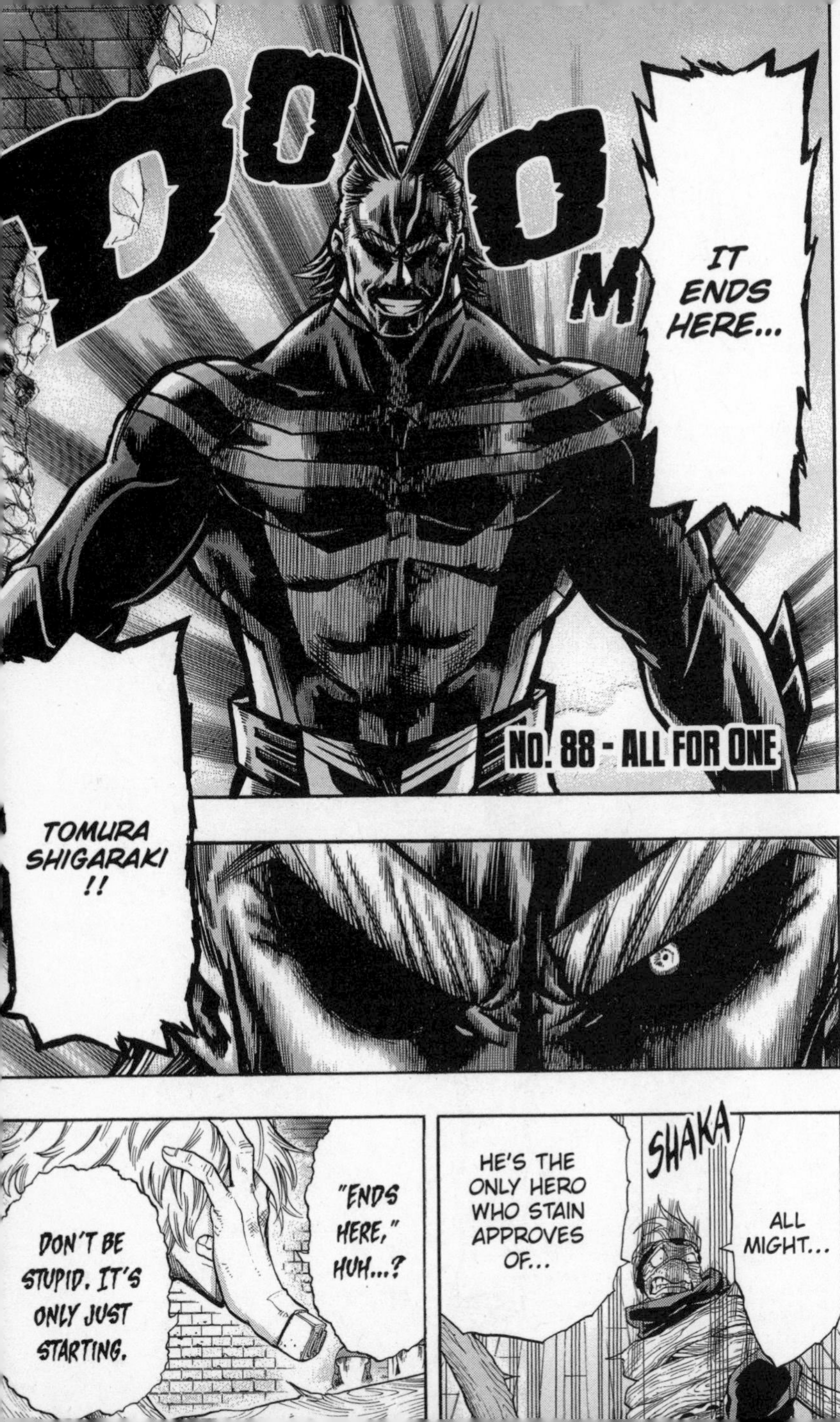
DOOOM
IT ENDS HERE...
No. 88 - ALL FOR ONE
TOMURA SHIGARAKI !!
SHAKA
ALL MIGHT...
HE'S THE ONLY HERO WHO STAIN APPROVES OF...
"ENDS HERE," HUH...?
DON'T BE STUPID. IT'S ONLY JUST STARTING.

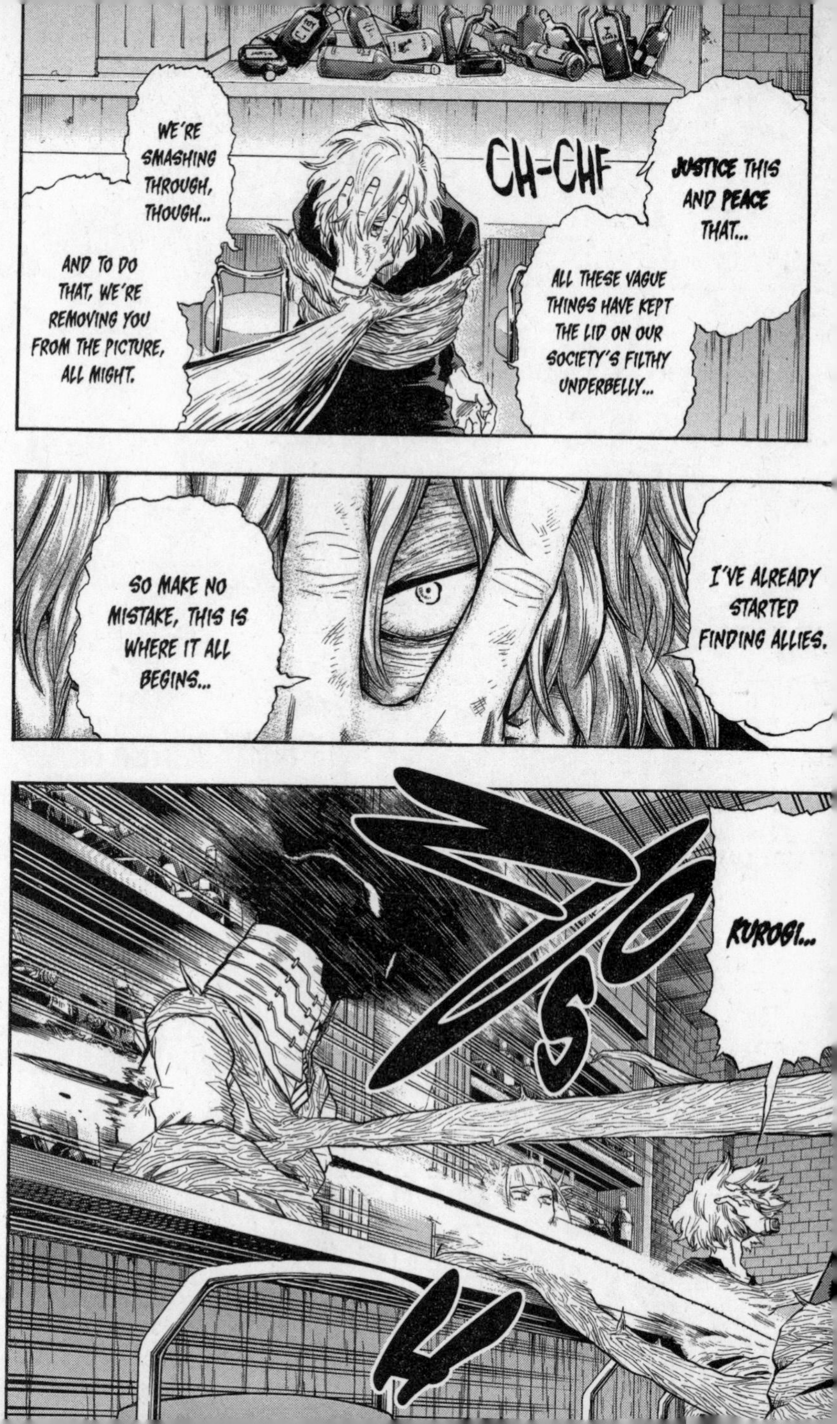
JUSTICE THIS AND PEACE THAT...
ALL THESE VAGUE THINGS HAVE KEPT THE LID ON OUR SOCIETY'S FILTHY UNDERBELLY...
CH-CHF
WE'RE SMASHING THROUGH, THOUGH...
AND TO DO THAT, WE'RE REMOVING YOU FROM THE PICTURE, ALL MIGHT.
I'VE ALREADY STARTED FINDING ALLIES.
SO MAKE NO MISTAKE, THIS IS WHERE IT ALL BEGINS...
KUROGI...

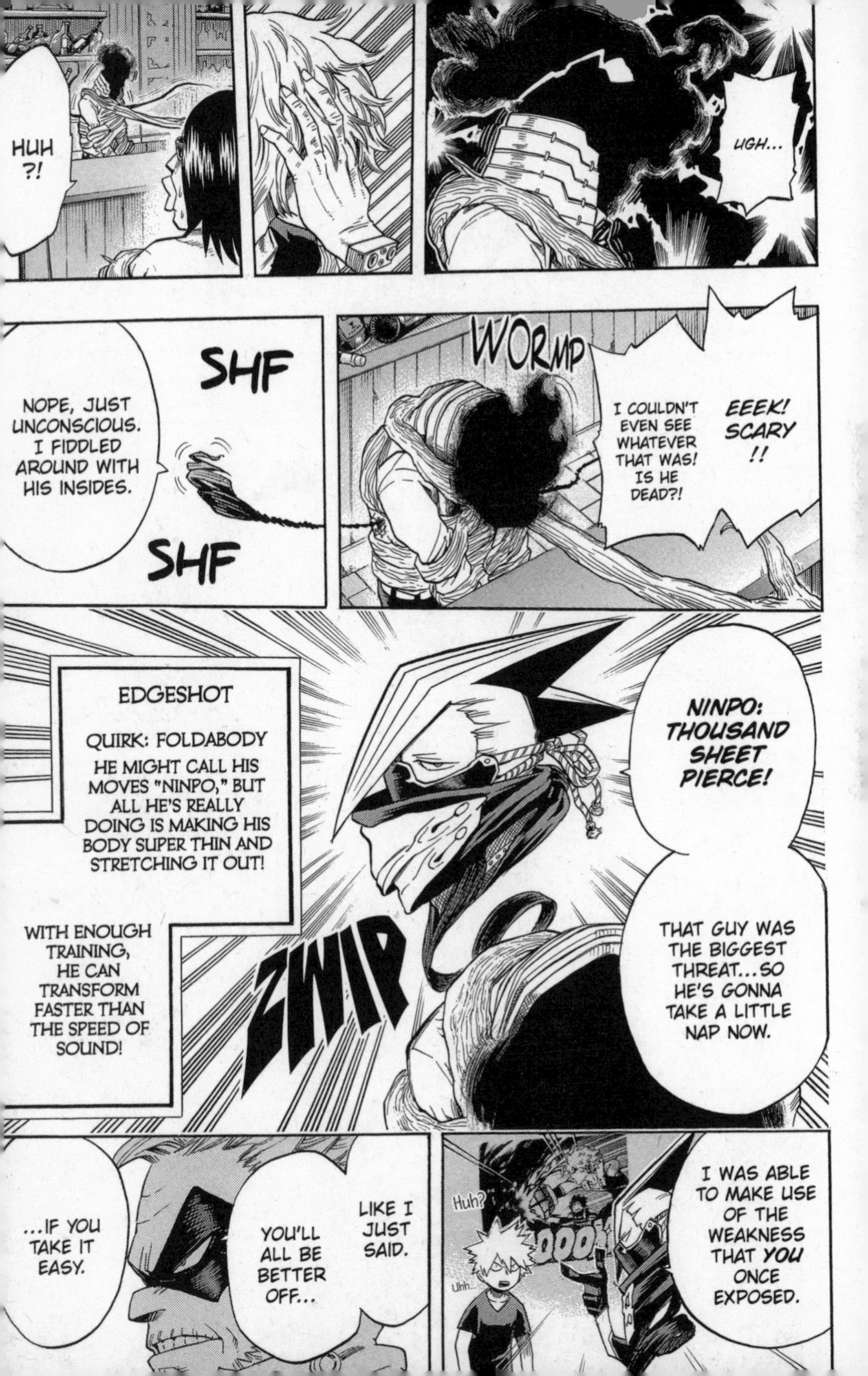
UGH...
HUH ?!
WORMP
EEEK! SCARY !!
I COULDN'T EVEN SEE WHATEVER THAT WAS! IS HE DEAD?!
SHF
NOPE, JUST UNCONSCIOUS. I FIDDLED AROUND WITH HIS INSIDES.
SHF
NINPO: THOUSAND SHEET PIERCE!
THAT GUY WAS THE BIGGEST THREAT...SO HE'S GONNA TAKE A LITTLE NAP NOW.
ZWIP
EDGESHOT
QUIRK: FOLDABODY
HE MIGHT CALL HIS MOVES "NINPO," BUT ALL HE'S REALLY DOING IS MAKING HIS BODY SUPER THIN AND STRETCHING IT OUT!
WITH ENOUGH TRAINING, HE CAN TRANSFORM FASTER THAN THE SPEED OF SOUND!
I WAS ABLE TO MAKE USE OF THE WEAKNESS THAT YOU ONCE EXPOSED.
Huh?
Uhh...
LIKE I JUST SAID.
YOU'LL ALL BE BETTER OFF...
...IF YOU TAKE IT EASY.

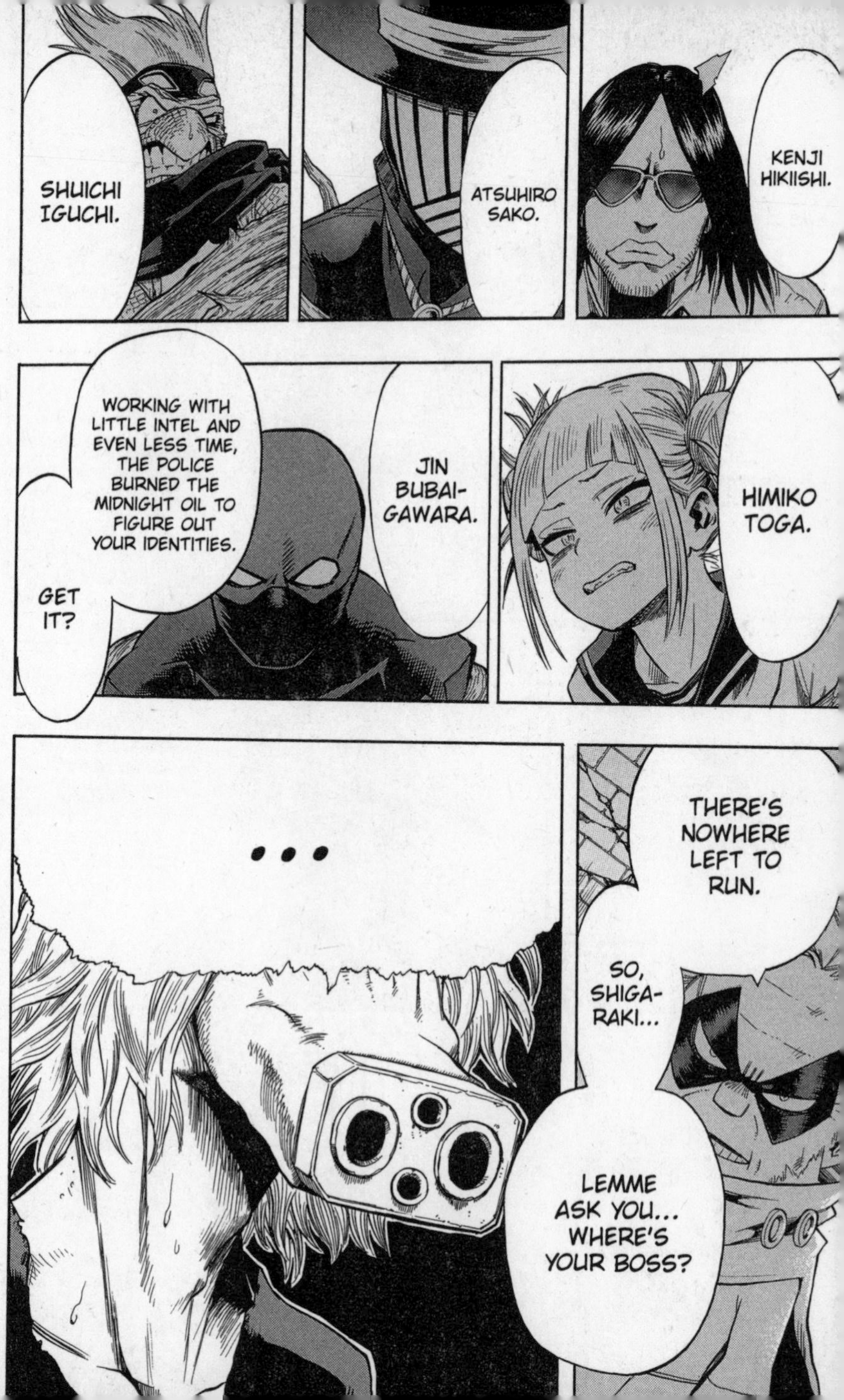
KENJI HIKIISHI.
ATSUHIRO SAKO.
SHUICHI IGUCHI.
HIMIKO TOGA.
JIN BUBAI-GAWARA.
WORKING WITH LITTLE INTEL AND EVEN LESS TIME, THE POLICE BURNED THE MIDNIGHT OIL TO FIGURE OUT YOUR IDENTITIES.
GET IT?
THERE'S NOWHERE LEFT TO RUN.
SO, SHIGA-RAKI...
LEMME ASK YOU... WHERE'S YOUR BOSS?
...

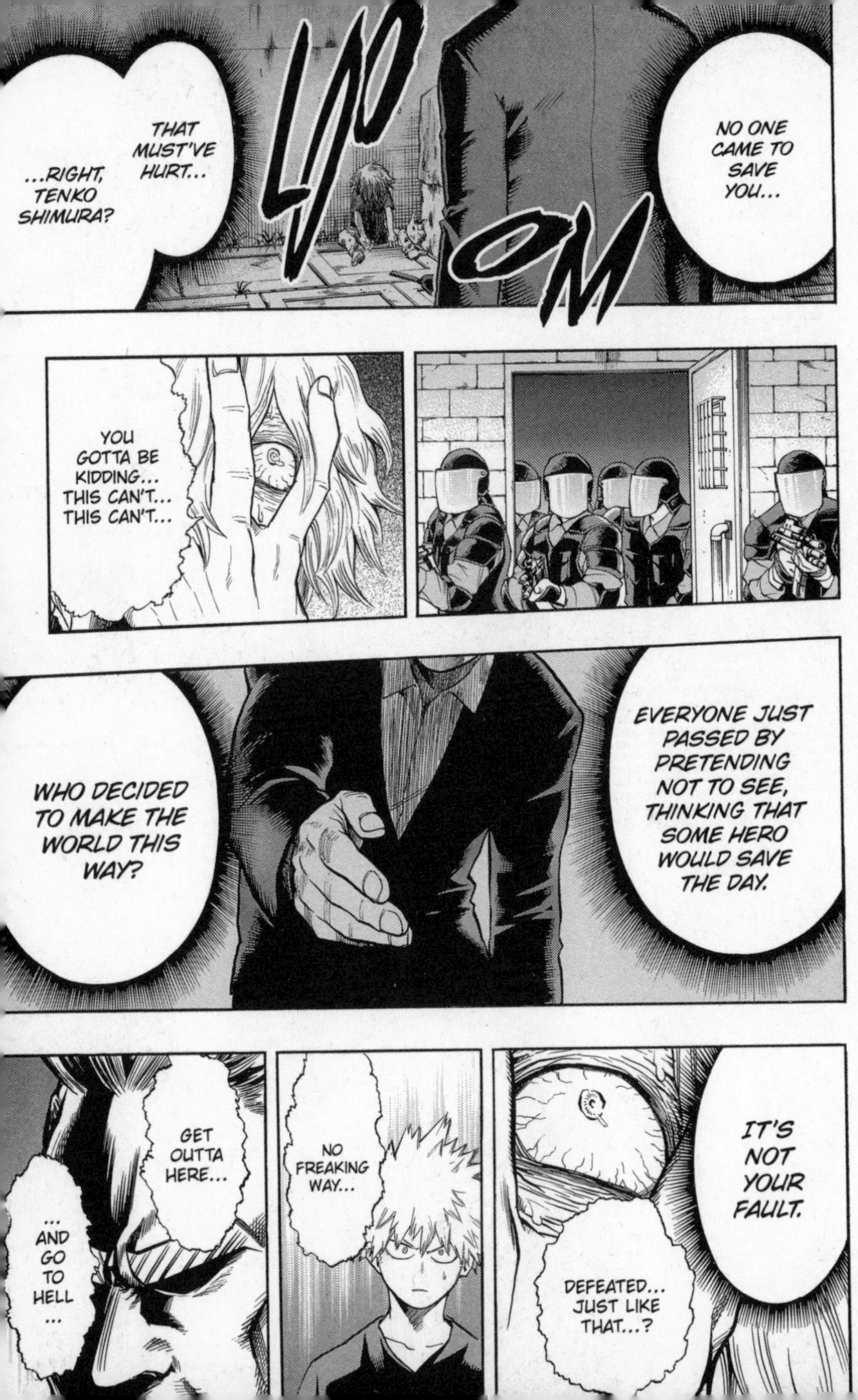
NO ONE CAME TO SAVE YOU...
THAT MUST'VE HURT...
...RIGHT, TENKO SHIMURA?
YOU GOTTA BE KIDDING... THIS CAN'T... THIS CAN'T...
EVERYONE JUST PASSED BY PRETENDING NOT TO SEE, THINKING THAT SOME HERO WOULD SAVE THE DAY.
WHO DECIDED TO MAKE THE WORLD THIS WAY?
IT'S NOT YOUR FAULT.
DEFEATED... JUST LIKE THAT...?
NO FREAKING WAY...
GET OUTTA HERE...
...AND GO TO HELL...

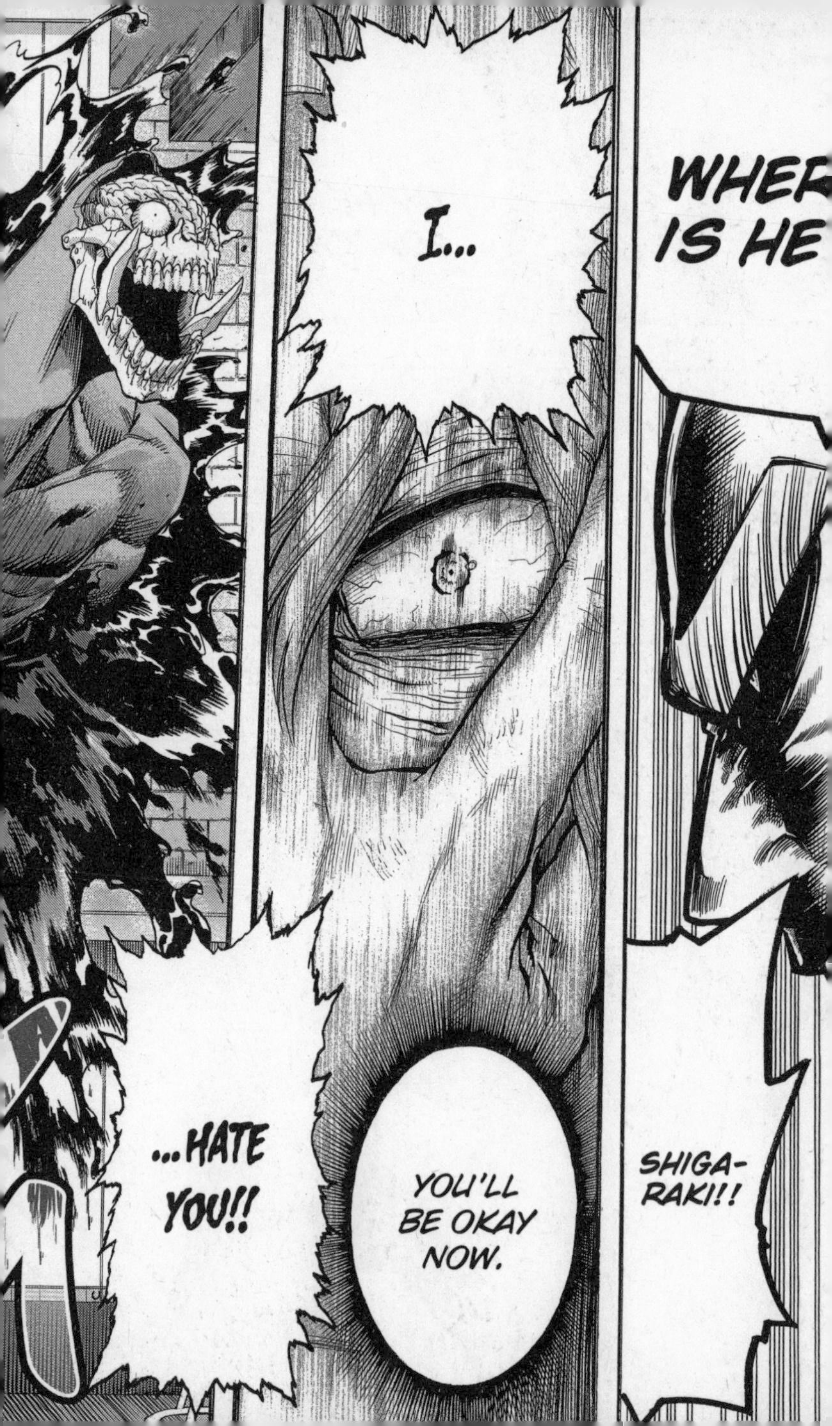
WHER
IS HE
SHIGA-RAKI!!
I...
YOU'LL BE OKAY NOW.
...HATE YOU!!

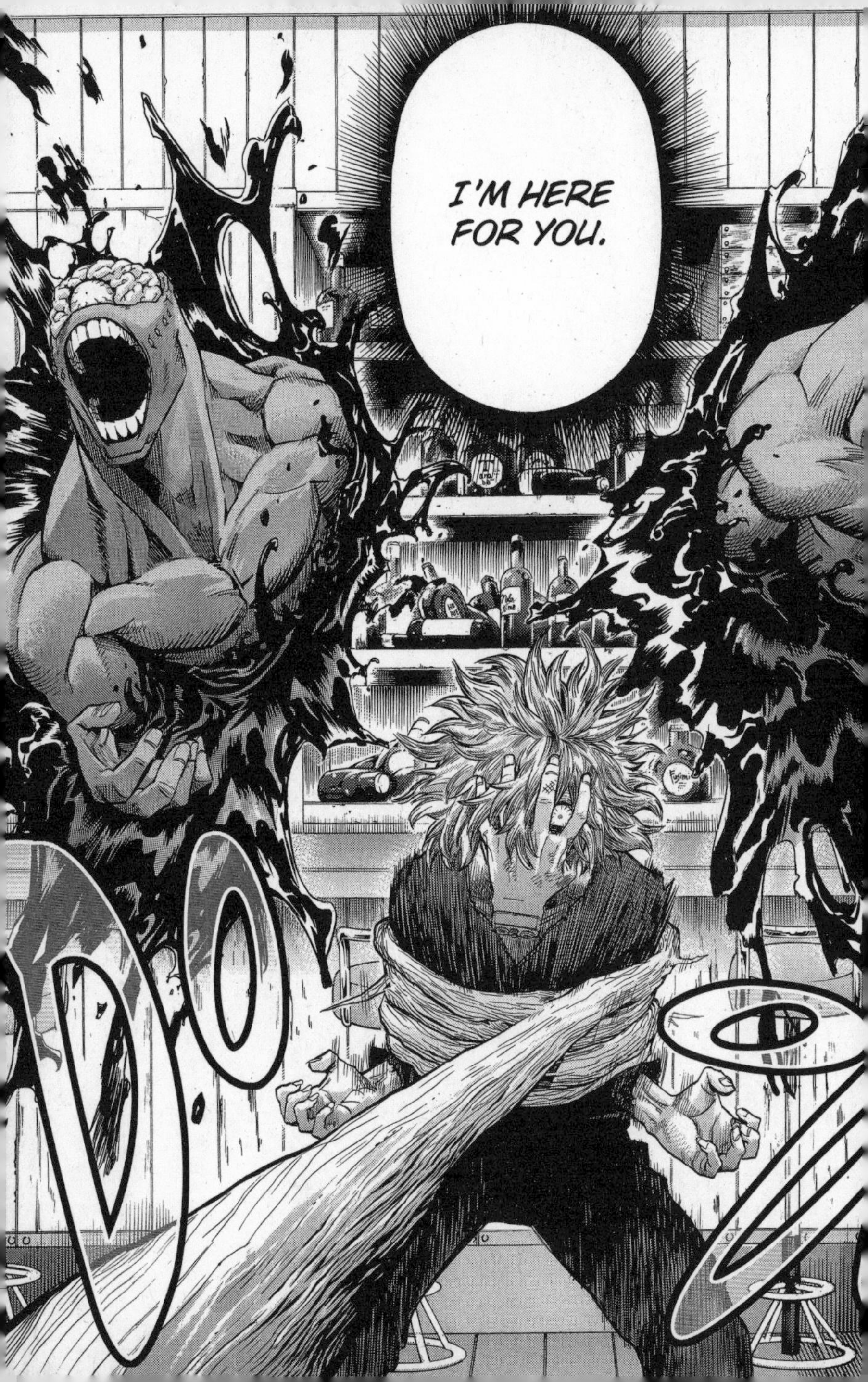
I'M HERE FOR YOU.

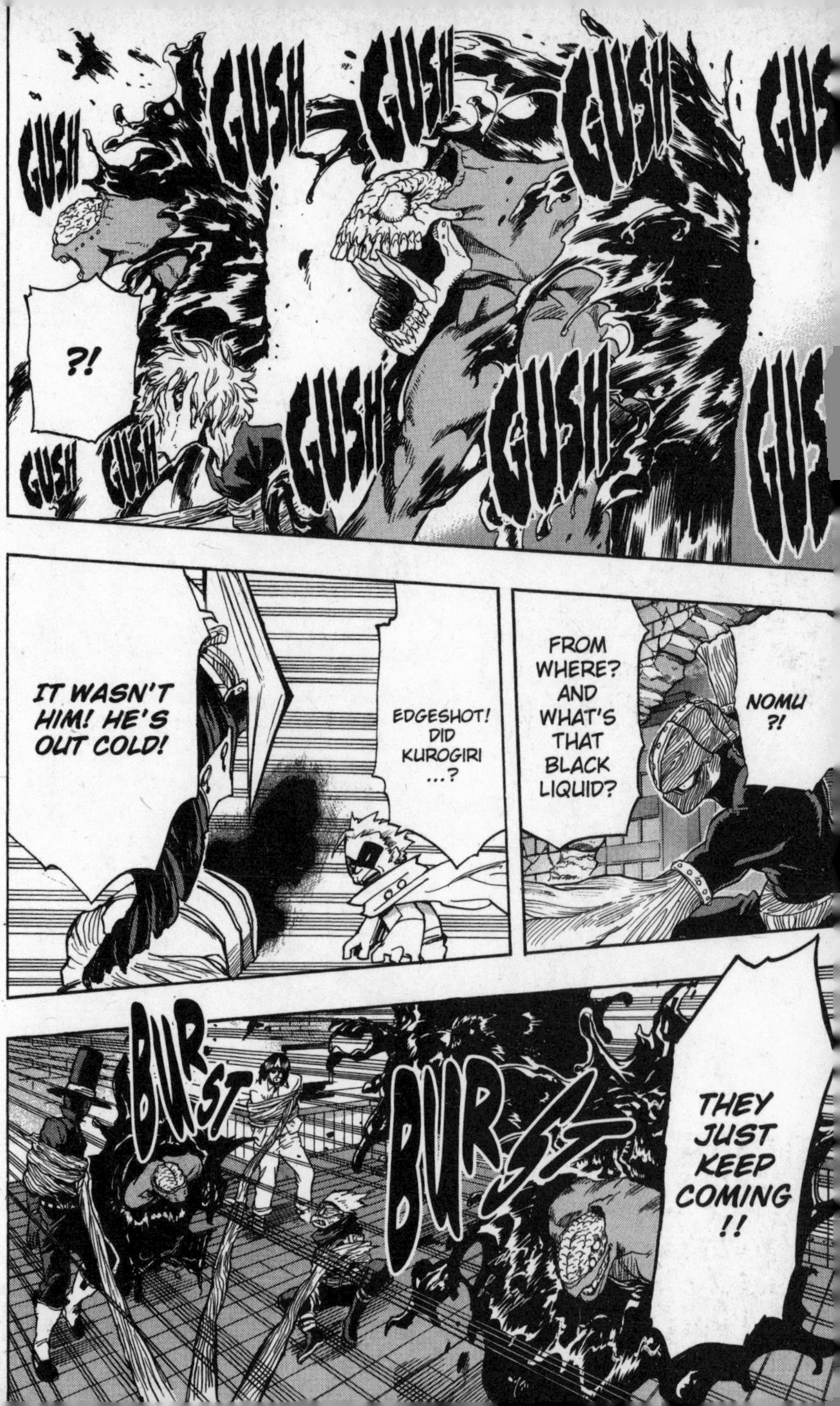
GUSH
GUSH
GUSH
GUSH
GUSH
GUSH
?!
GUSH
GUSH
NOMU ?!
FROM WHERE? AND WHAT'S THAT BLACK LIQUID?
EDGESHOT! DID KUROGIRI ...?
IT WASN'T HIM! HE'S OUT COLD!
THEY JUST KEEP COMING !!
BURST

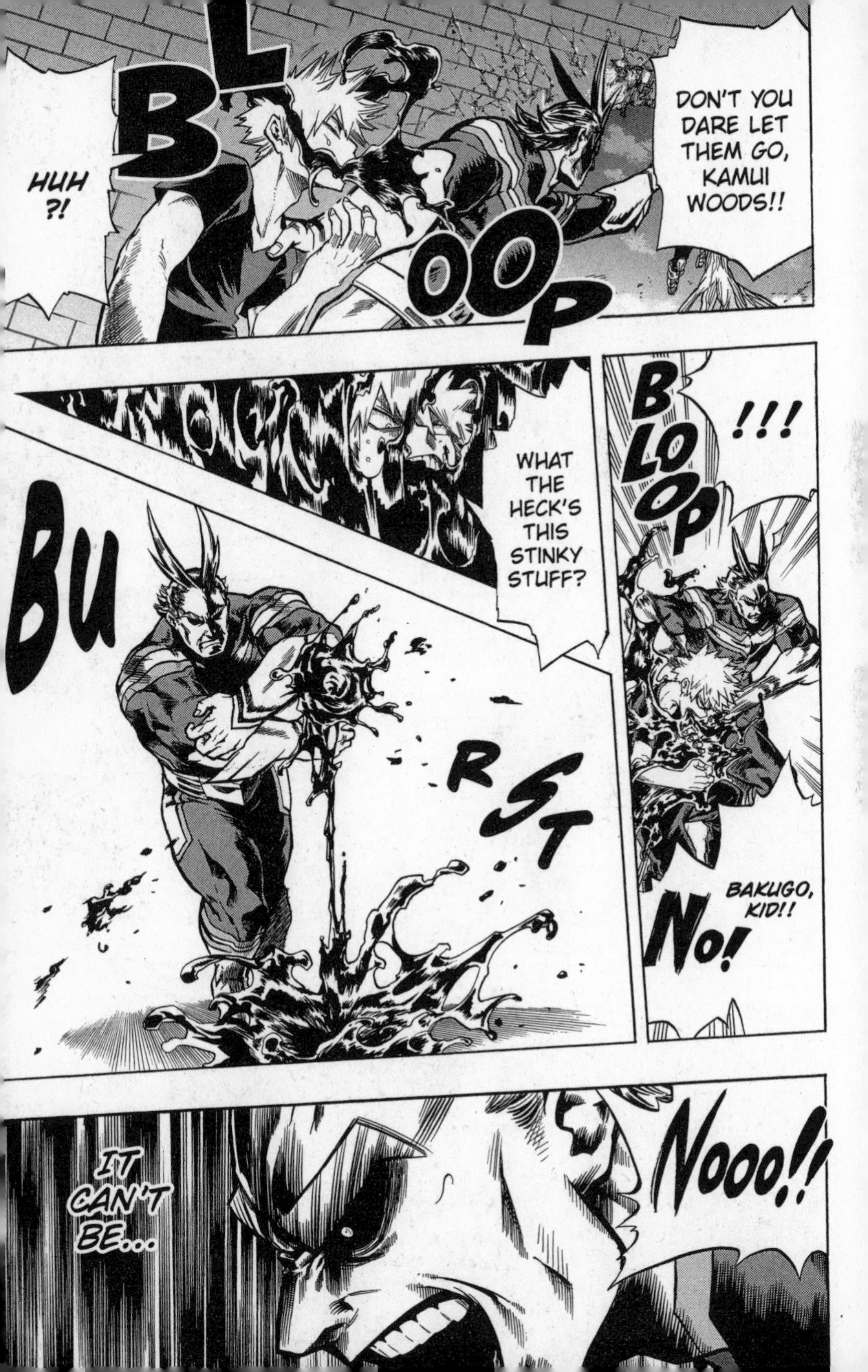

DON'T YOU DARE LET THEM GO, KAMUI WOODS!!
BLOOP
HUH ?!
BLOOP
!!!
BAKUGO, KID!!
No!
WHAT THE HECK'S THIS STINKY STUFF?
Bu
RST
Nooo!!
IT CAN'T BE...

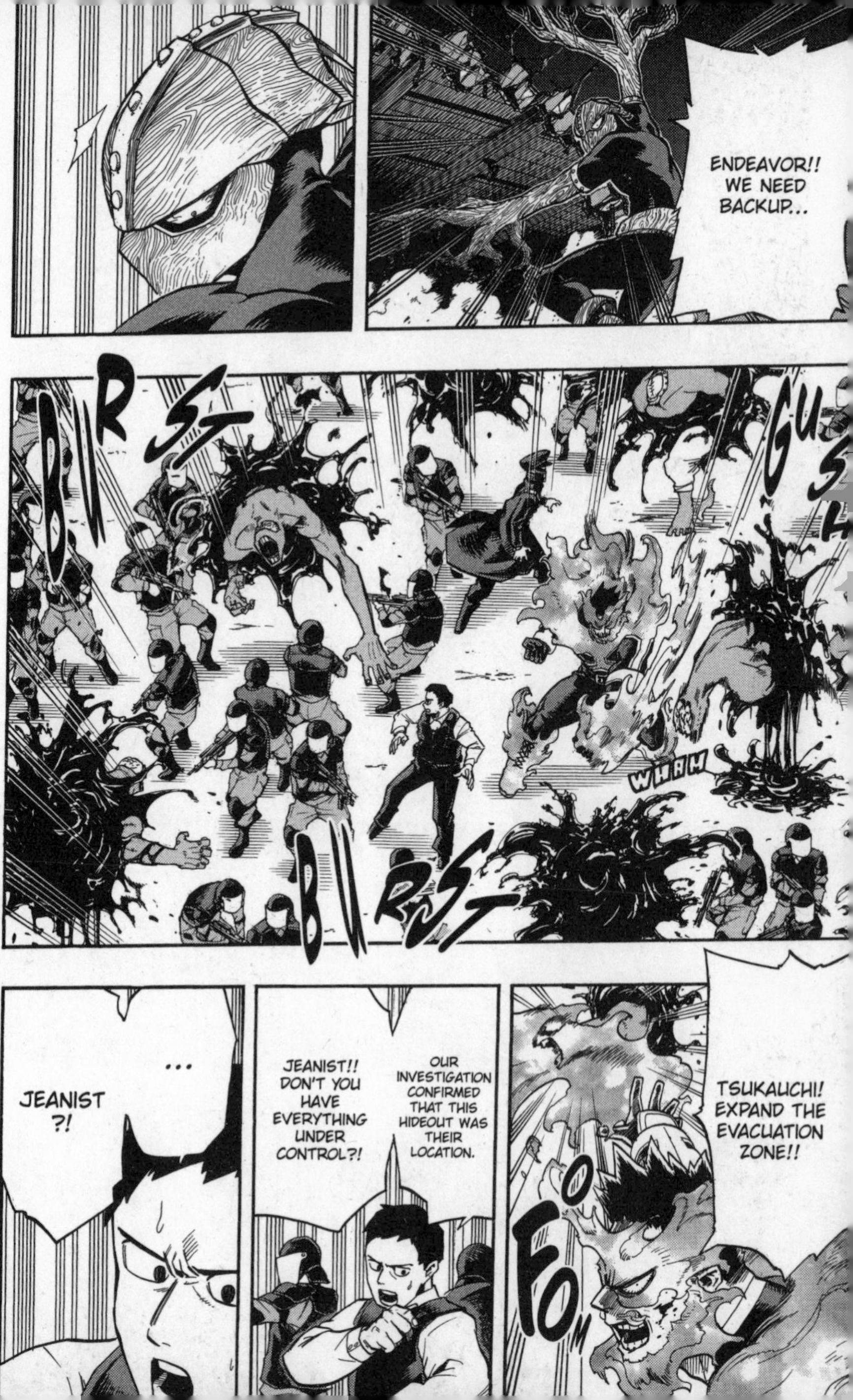
ENDEAVOR!! WE NEED BACKUP...
GUSH
BURST
WHAM
BURST
TSUKAUCHI! EXPAND THE EVACUATION ZONE!!
FOOM
OUR INVESTIGATION CONFIRMED THAT THIS HIDEOUT WAS THEIR LOCATION.
JEANIST!! DON'T YOU HAVE EVERYTHING UNDER CONTROL?!
...
JEANIST ?!

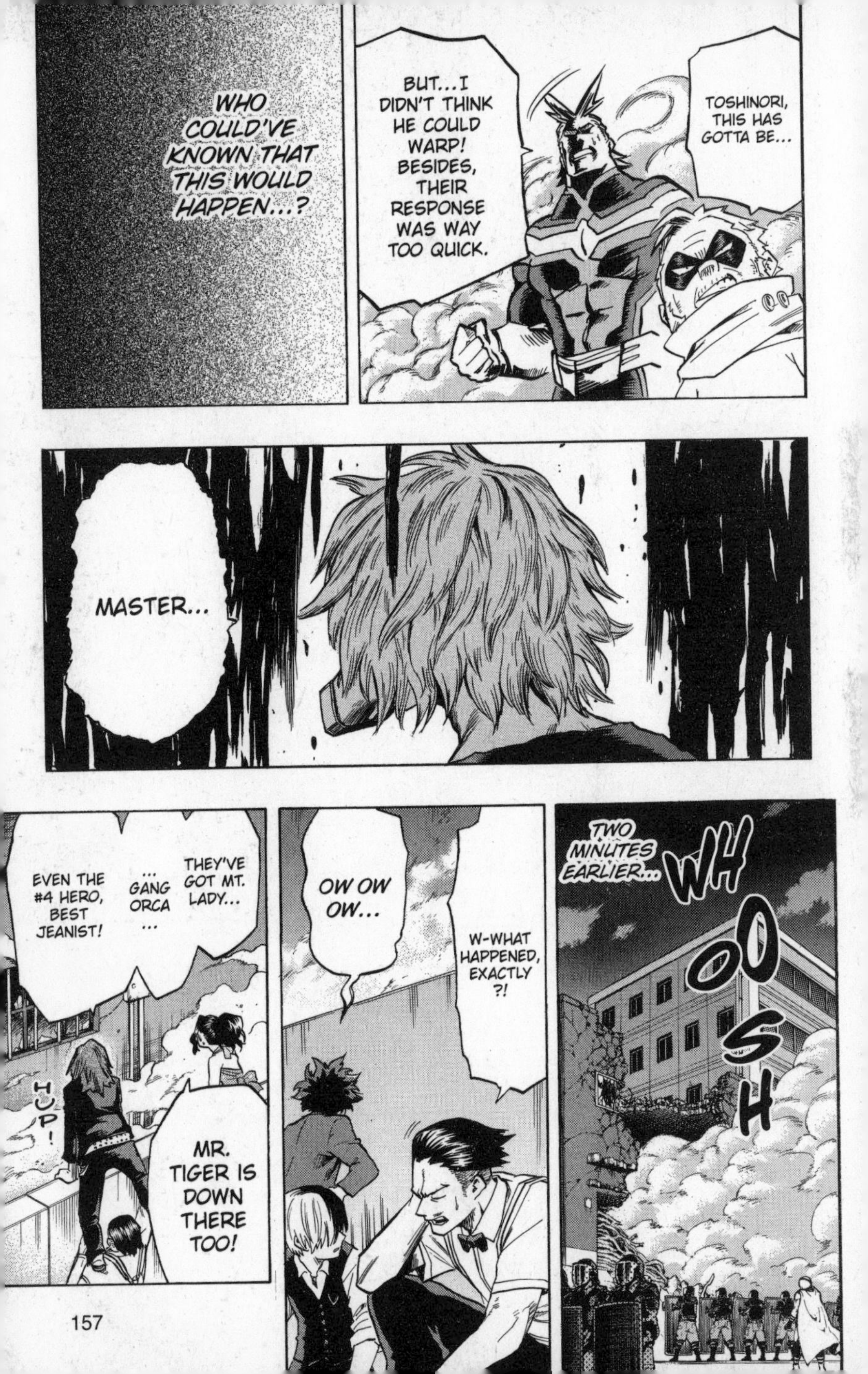
TOSHINORI, THIS HAS GOTTA BE...
BUT...I DIDN'T THINK HE COULD WARP! BESIDES, THEIR RESPONSE WAS WAY TOO QUICK.
WHO COULD'VE KNOWN THAT THIS WOULD HAPPEN...?
MASTER...
TWO MINUTES EARLIER...
WHOOOSH
OW OW OW...
W-WHAT HAPPENED, EXACTLY ?!
THEY'VE GOT MT. LADY...
...GANG ORCA...
EVEN THE #4 HERO, BEST JEANIST!
HUP!
MR. TIGER IS DOWN THERE TOO!

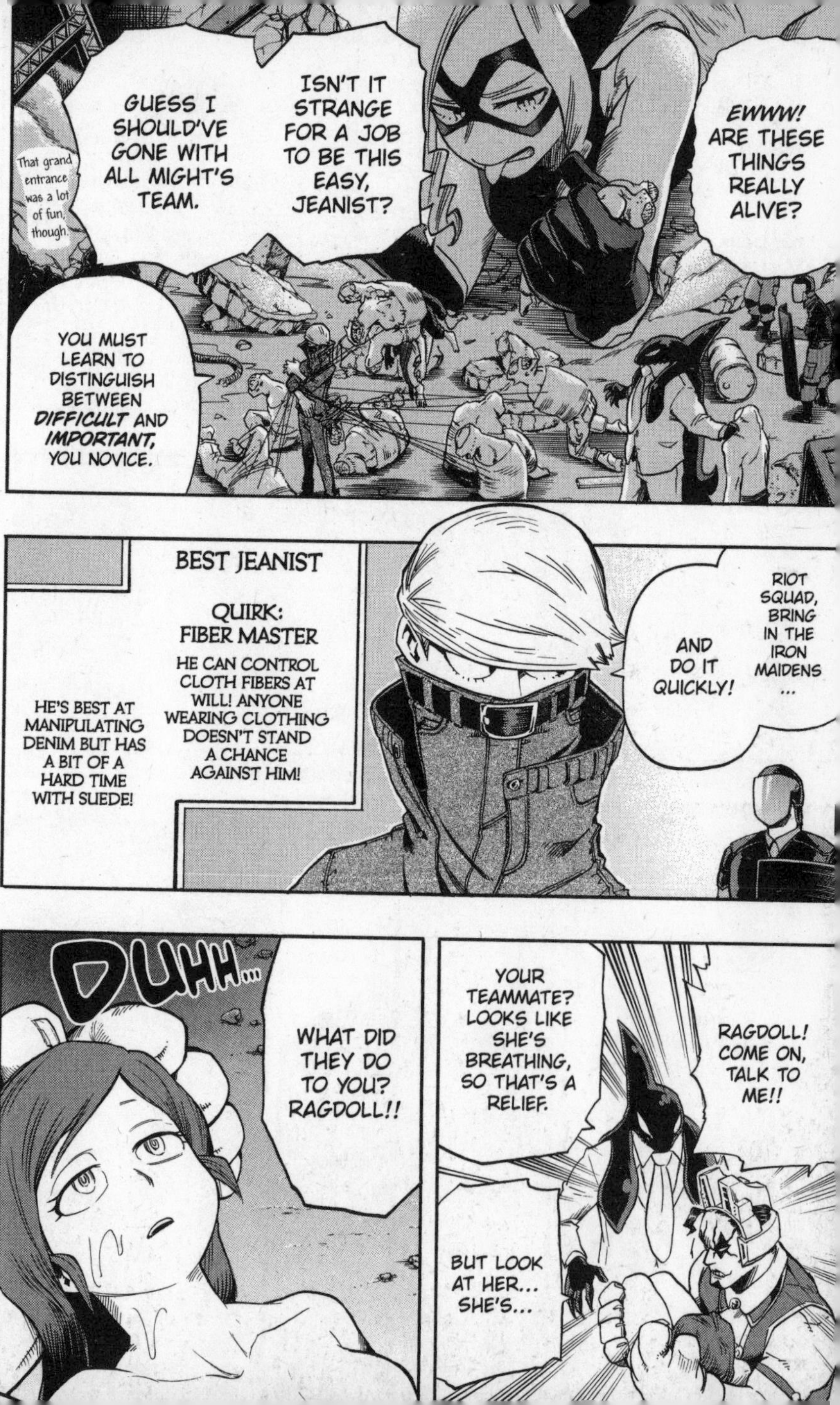

EWWW! ARE THESE THINGS REALLY ALIVE?
ISN'T IT STRANGE FOR A JOB TO BE THIS EASY, JEANIST?
GUESS I SHOULD'VE GONE WITH ALL MIGHT'S TEAM.
That grand entrance was a lot of fun, though.
YOU MUST LEARN TO DISTINGUISH BETWEEN *DIFFICULT* AND *IMPORTANT,* YOU NOVICE.
RIOT SQUAD, BRING IN THE IRON MAIDENS ...
AND DO IT QUICKLY!
BEST JEANIST
QUIRK: FIBER MASTER
HE CAN CONTROL CLOTH FIBERS AT WILL! ANYONE WEARING CLOTHING DOESN'T STAND A CHANCE AGAINST HIM!
HE'S BEST AT MANIPULATING DENIM BUT HAS A BIT OF A HARD TIME WITH SUEDE!
RAGDOLL! COME ON, TALK TO ME!!
YOUR TEAMMATE? LOOKS LIKE SHE'S BREATHING, SO THAT'S A RELIEF.
BUT LOOK AT HER... SHE'S...
DUHH...
WHAT DID THEY DO TO YOU? RAGDOLL!!

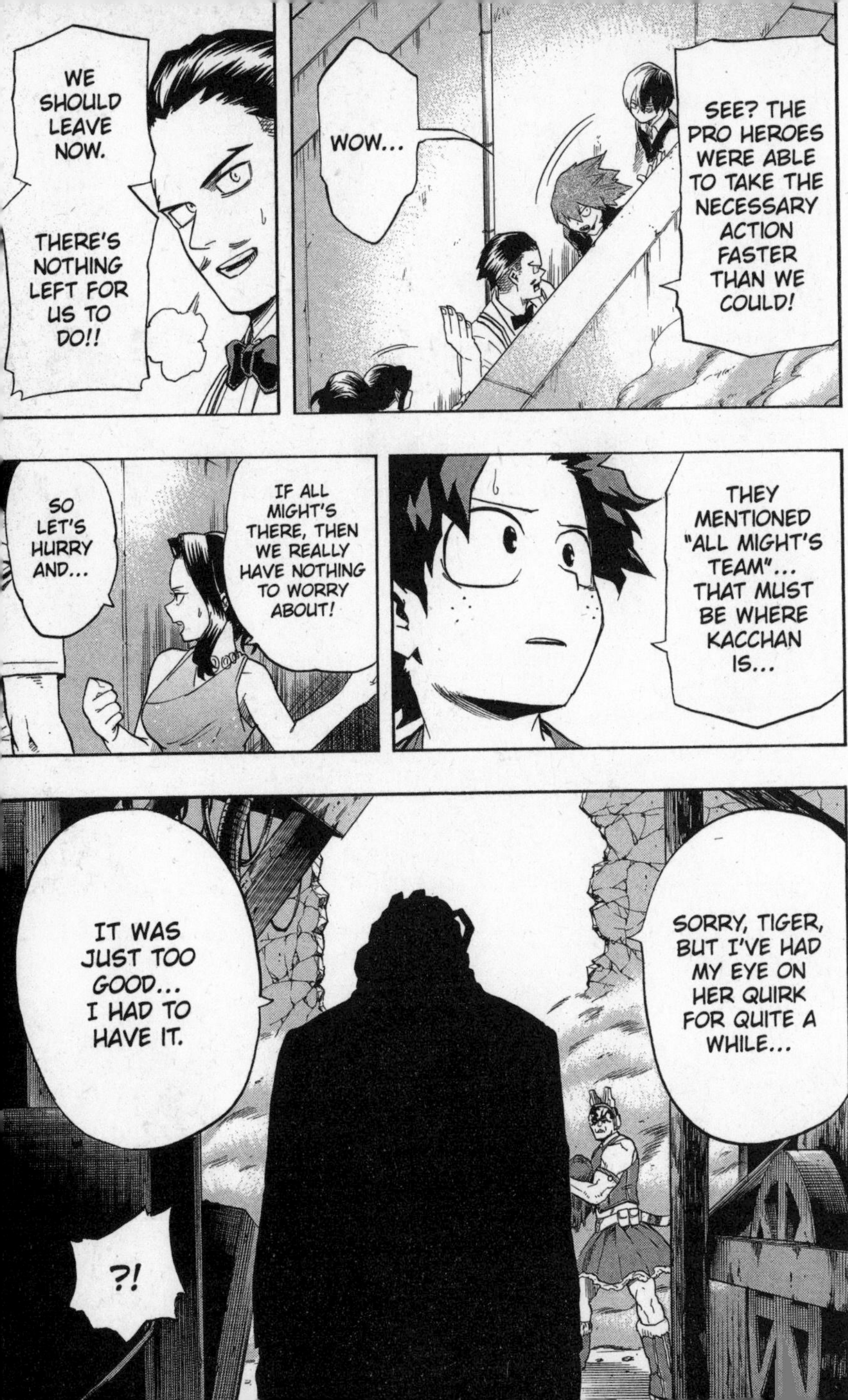
SEE? THE PRO HEROES WERE ABLE TO TAKE THE NECESSARY ACTION FASTER THAN WE COULD!
WOW...
WE SHOULD LEAVE NOW.
THERE'S NOTHING LEFT FOR US TO DO!!
THEY MENTIONED "ALL MIGHT'S TEAM"... THAT MUST BE WHERE KACCHAN IS...
IF ALL MIGHT'S THERE, THEN WE REALLY HAVE NOTHING TO WORRY ABOUT!
SO LET'S HURRY AND...
SORRY, TIGER, BUT I'VE HAD MY EYE ON HER QUIRK FOR QUITE A WHILE...
IT WAS JUST TOO GOOD... I HAD TO HAVE IT.
?!

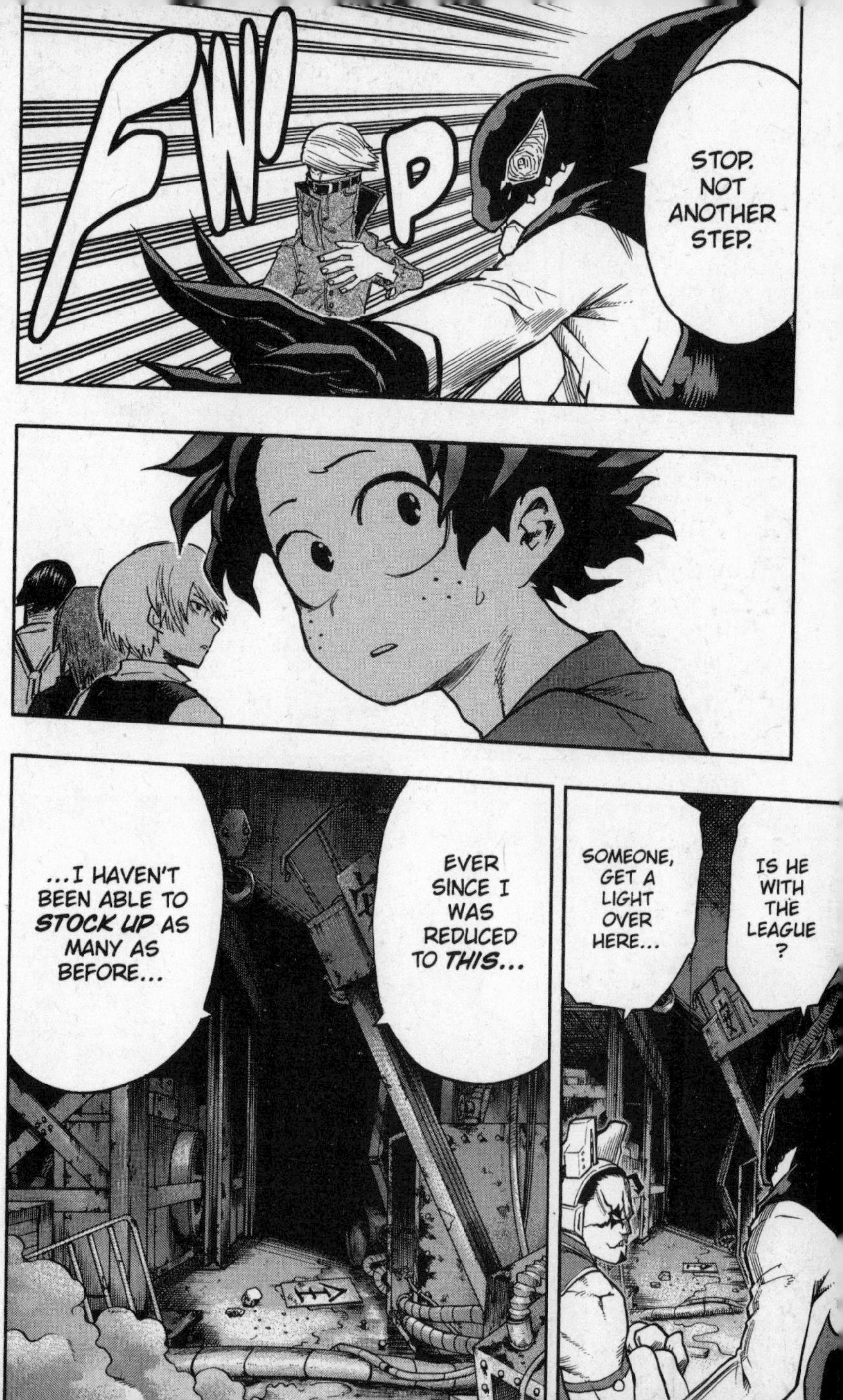
STOP. NOT ANOTHER STEP.
FWIP
IS HE WITH THE LEAGUE?
SOMEONE, GET A LIGHT OVER HERE...
EVER SINCE I WAS REDUCED TO **THIS**...
...I HAVEN'T BEEN ABLE TO **STOCK UP** AS MANY AS BEFORE...

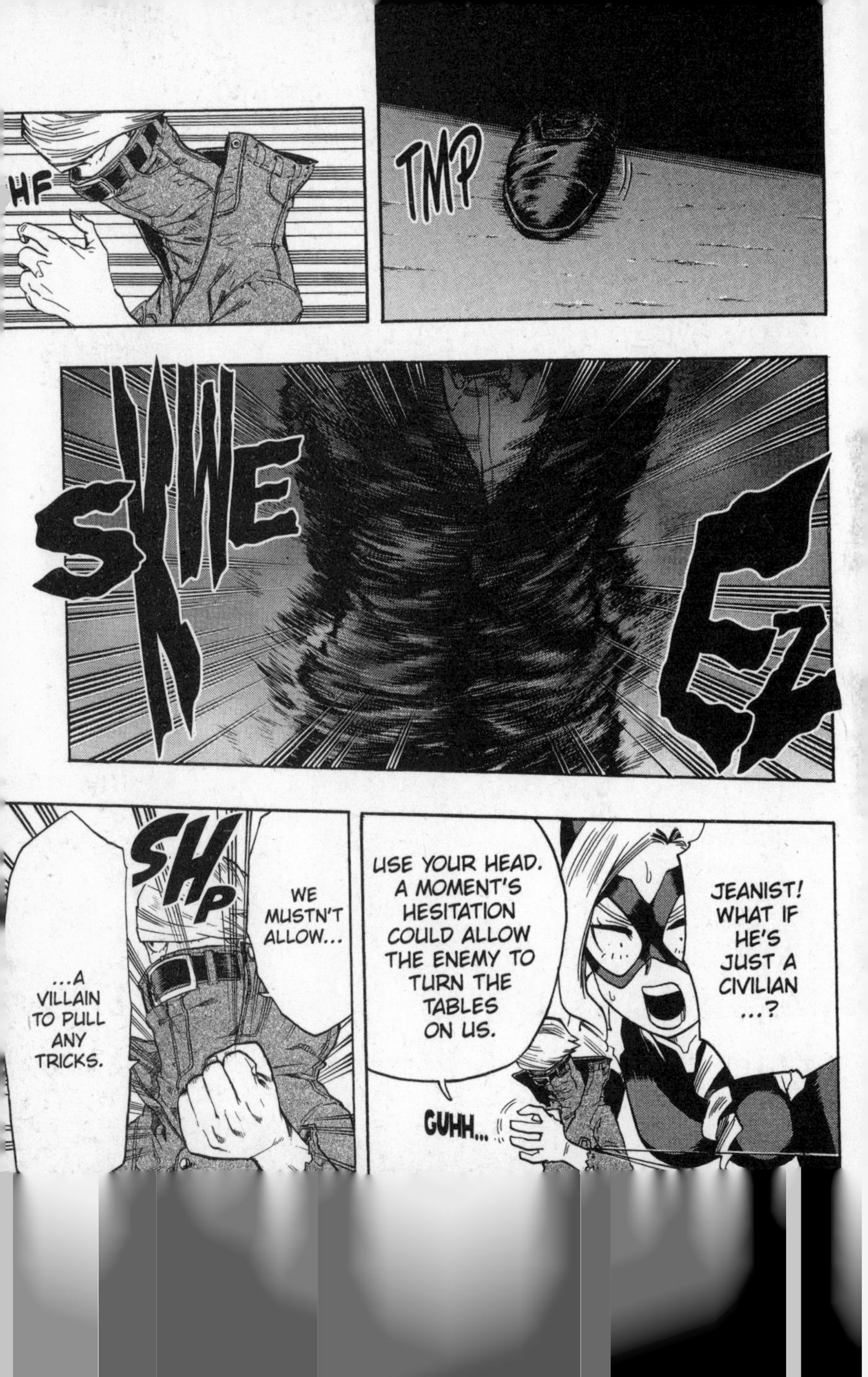
TMP
HF
SKWEEZ
JEANIST! WHAT IF HE'S JUST A CIVILIAN ...?
USE YOUR HEAD. A MOMENT'S HESITATION COULD ALLOW THE ENEMY TO TURN THE TABLES ON US.
GUHH...
SHP
WE MUSTN'T ALLOW...
...A VILLAIN TO PULL ANY TRICKS.

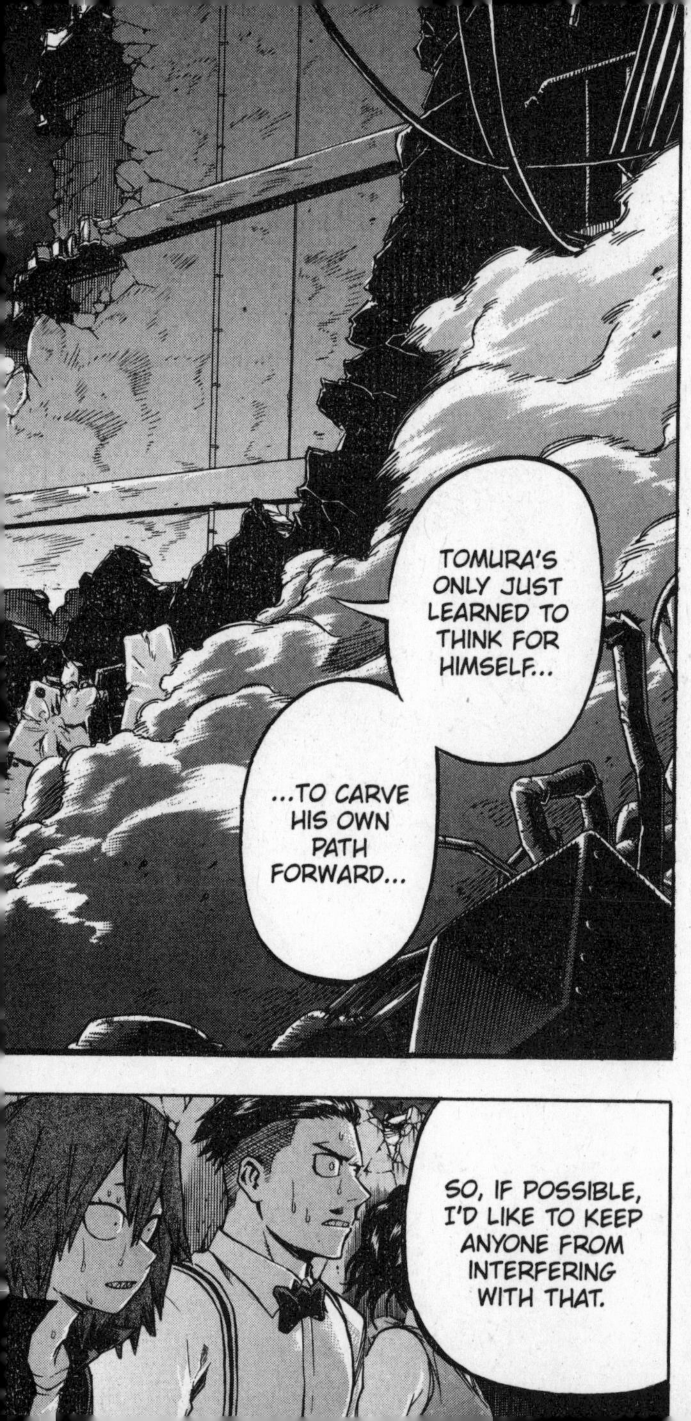
TOMURA'S ONLY JUST LEARNED TO THINK FOR HIMSELF...
...TO CARVE HIS OWN PATH FORWARD...
SO, IF POSSIBLE, I'D LIKE TO KEEP ANYONE FROM INTERFERING WITH THAT.

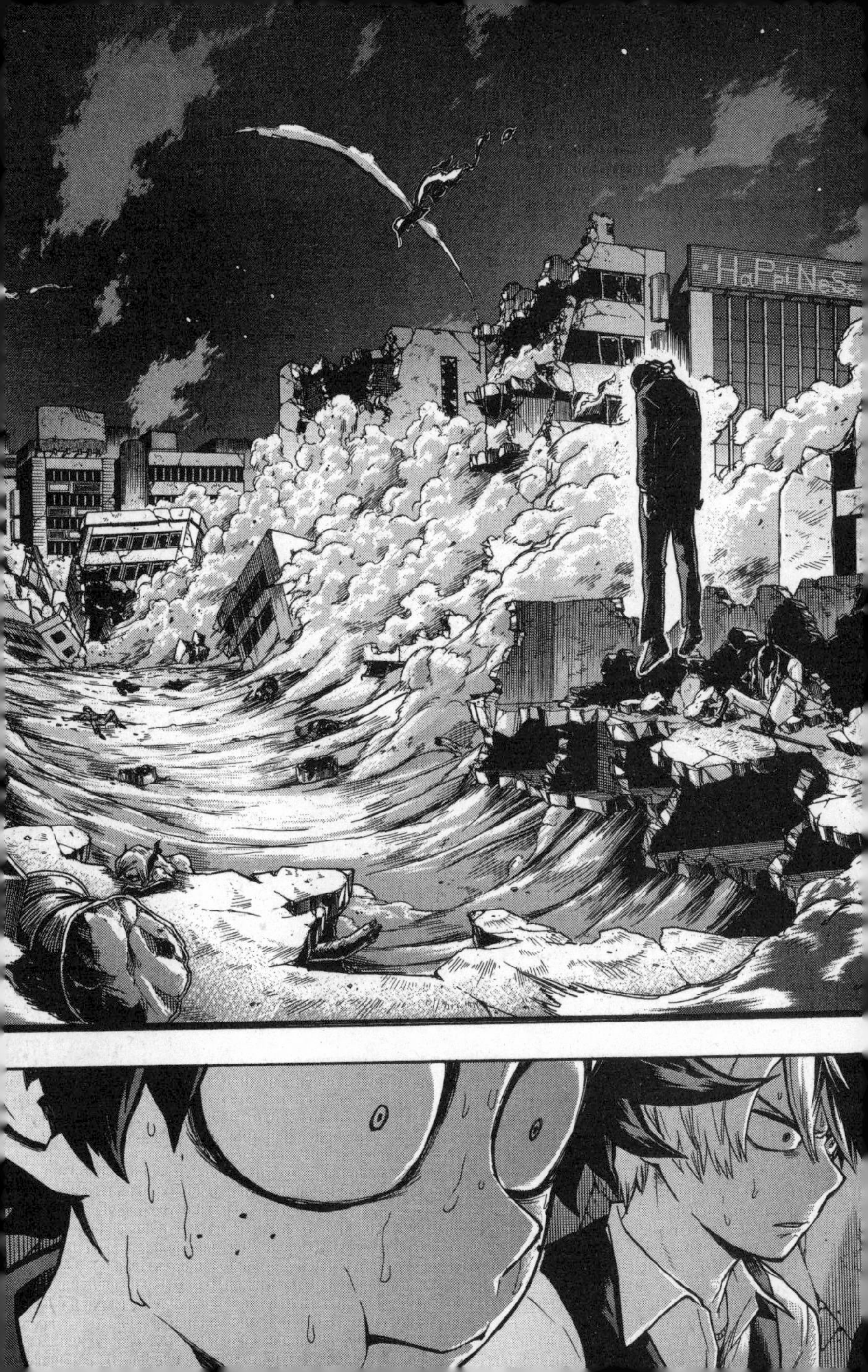

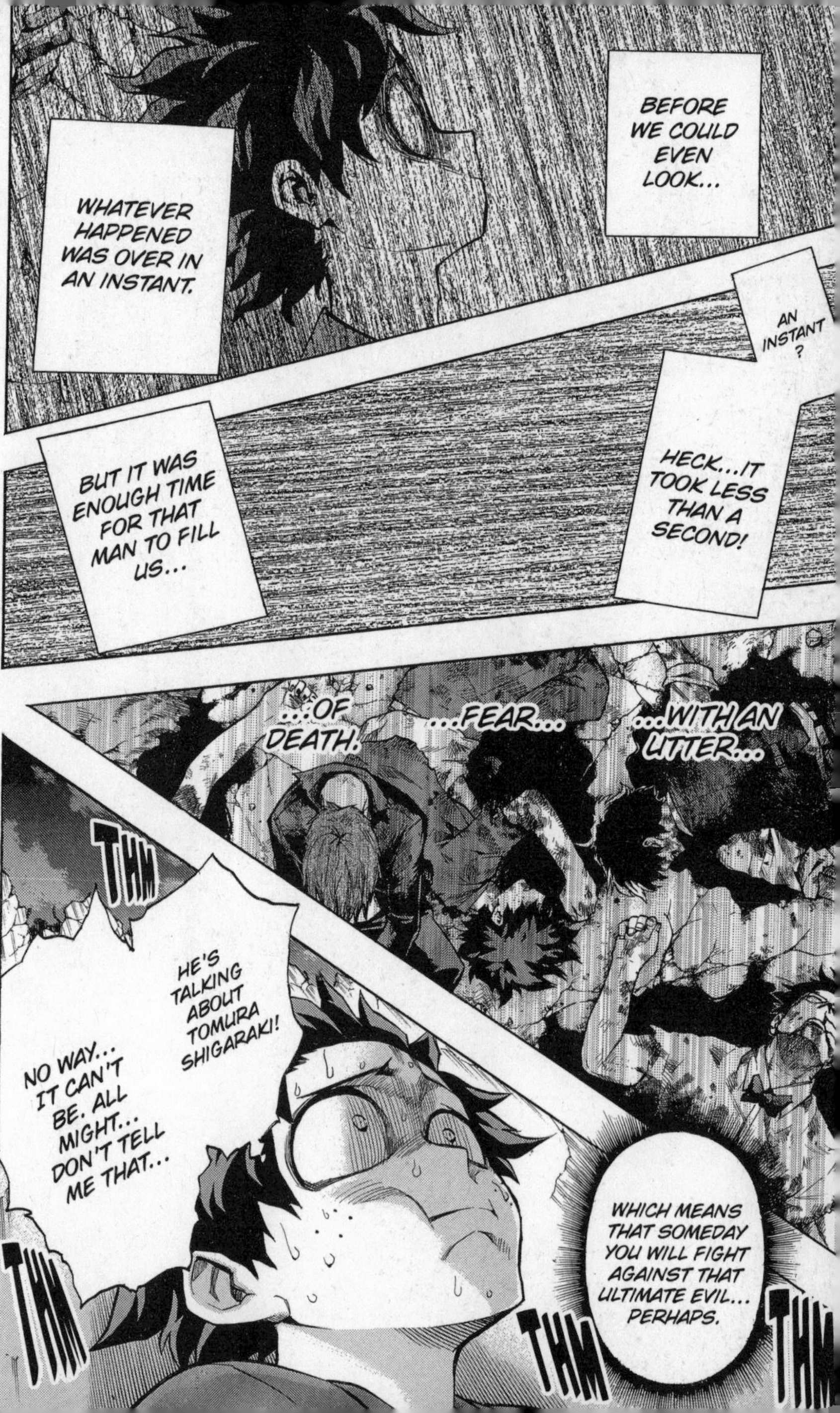
BEFORE WE COULD EVEN LOOK...
WHATEVER HAPPENED WAS OVER IN AN INSTANT.
AN INSTANT?
HECK...IT TOOK LESS THAN A SECOND!
BUT IT WAS ENOUGH TIME FOR THAT MAN TO FILL US...
...WITH AN UTTER...
...FEAR...
...OF DEATH.
THM
THM
WHICH MEANS THAT SOMEDAY YOU WILL FIGHT AGAINST THAT ULTIMATE EVIL... PERHAPS.
THM
HE'S TALKING ABOUT TOMURA SHIGARAKI!
NO WAY... IT CAN'T BE. ALL MIGHT... DON'T TELL ME THAT...
THM

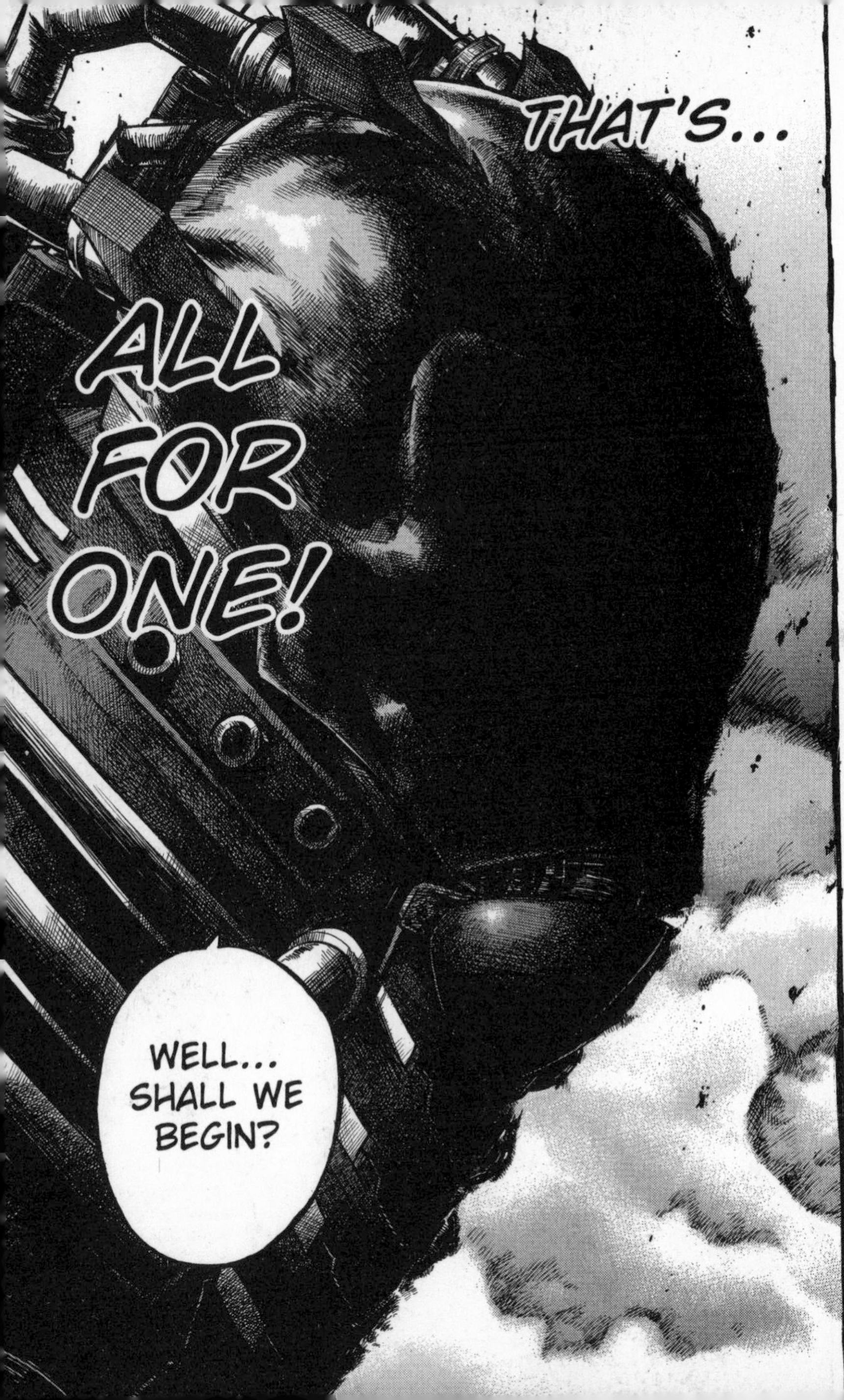
THAT'S...
ALL FOR ONE!
WELL... SHALL WE BEGIN?

HERO

EDGESHOT [33] [SHINYA KAMIHARA]

CIVILIAN CLOTHES

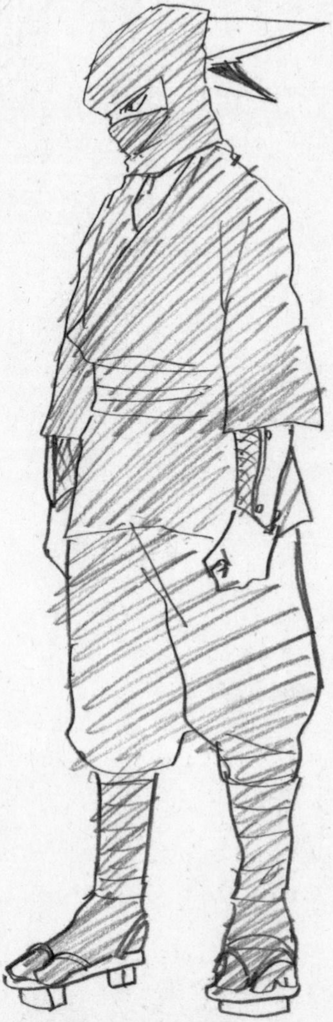

Birthday: 2/22
Height: 170 cm
Favorite Things: Ninja, rice balls

THE SUPPLEMENT

Everyone loves ninja.

This guy is a super-popular hero.

His personal life is shrouded in mystery, and he never makes public appearances except while on the job.

There are two factions among his fans. Some want to discover everything there is to know about him, while others think the mystery adds to his charm. The two groups do not get along.

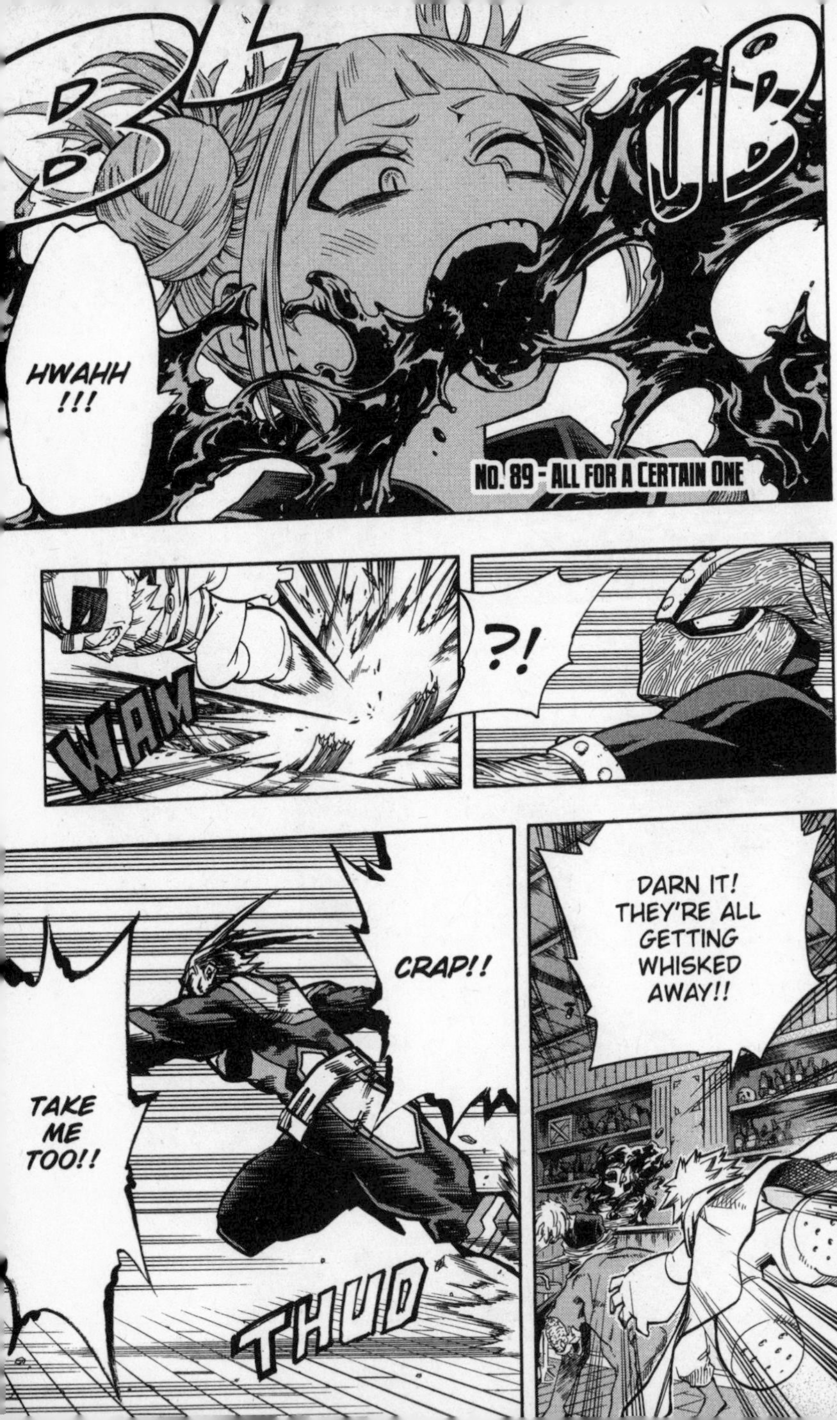
HWAHH !!!
No. 89 - All for a Certain One
?!
WAM
DARN IT! THEY'RE ALL GETTING WHISKED AWAY!!
CRAP!!
TAKE ME TOO!!
THUD

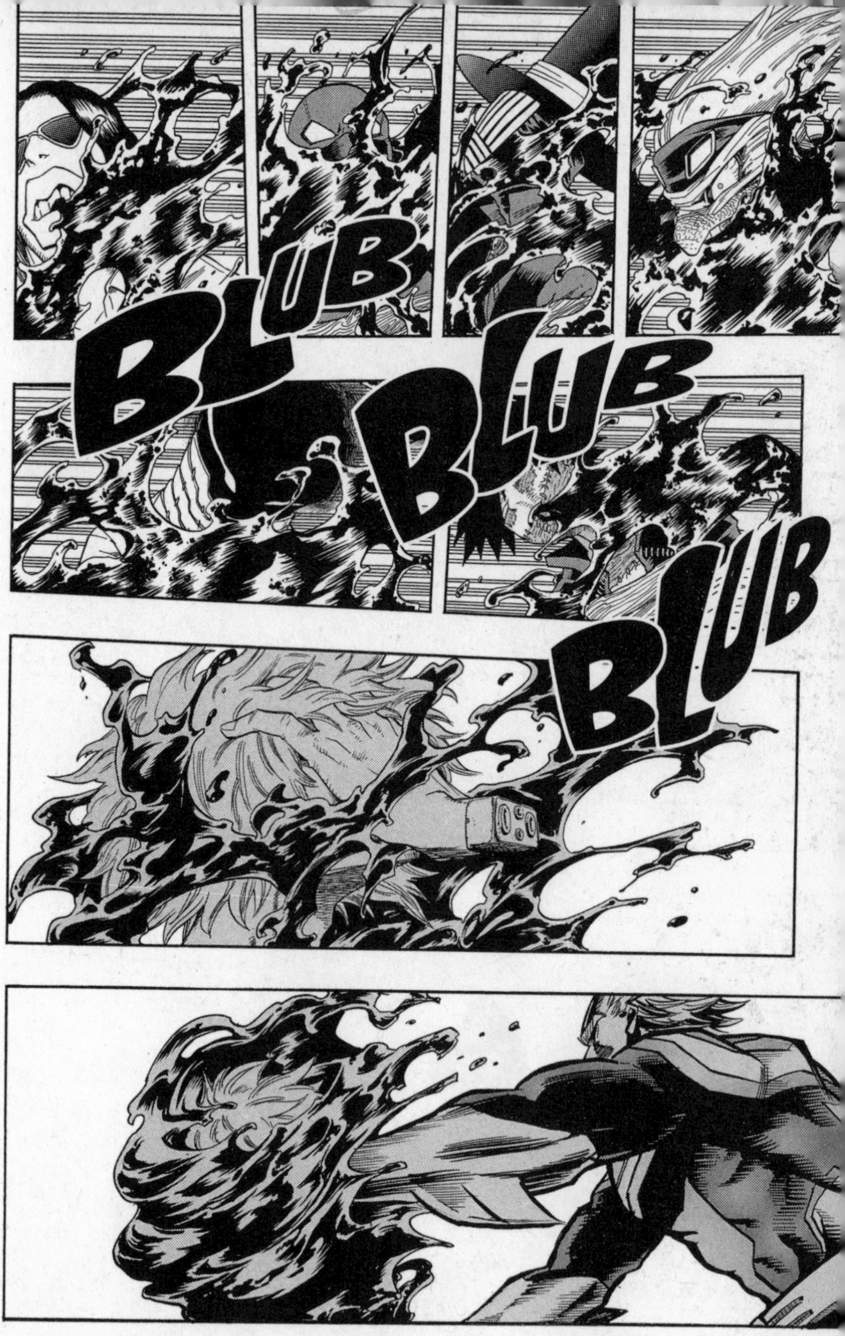
BLUB
BLUB
BLUB

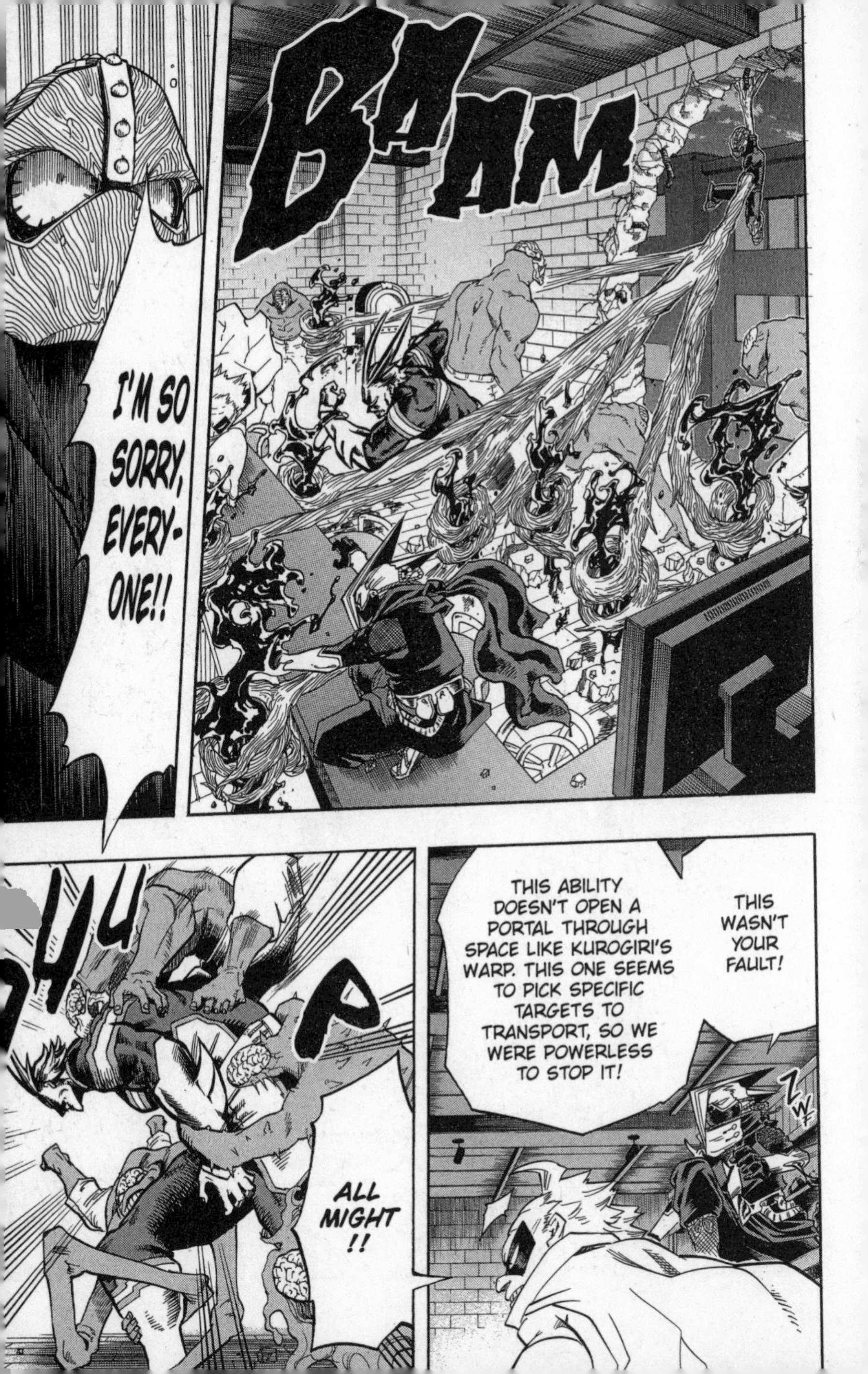
BAAM
I'M SO SORRY, EVERY-ONE!!
THIS WASN'T YOUR FAULT!
THIS ABILITY DOESN'T OPEN A PORTAL THROUGH SPACE LIKE KUROGIRI'S WARP. THIS ONE SEEMS TO PICK SPECIFIC TARGETS TO TRANSPORT, SO WE WERE POWERLESS TO STOP IT!
ALL MIGHT !!

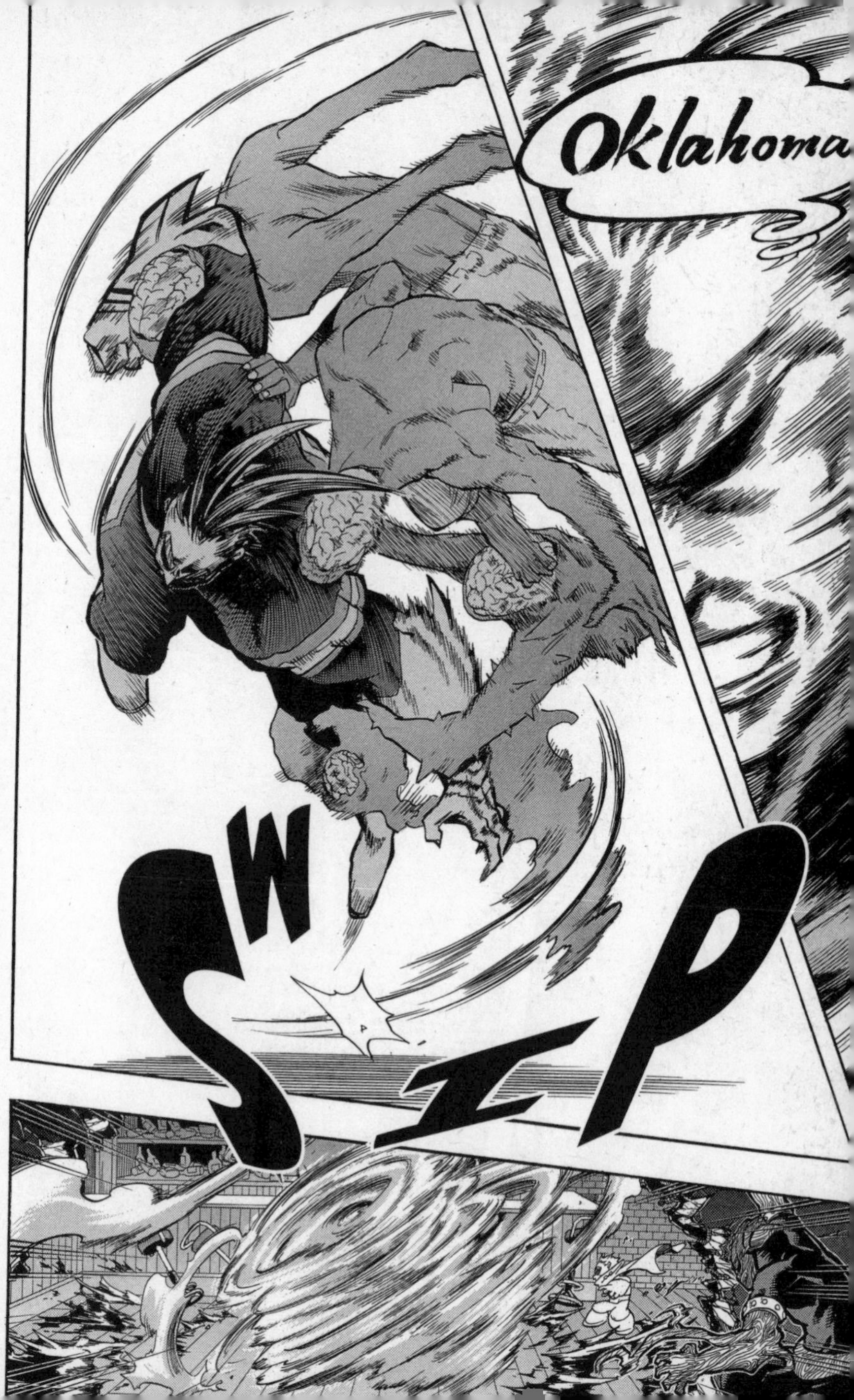
Oklahoma
SWIP

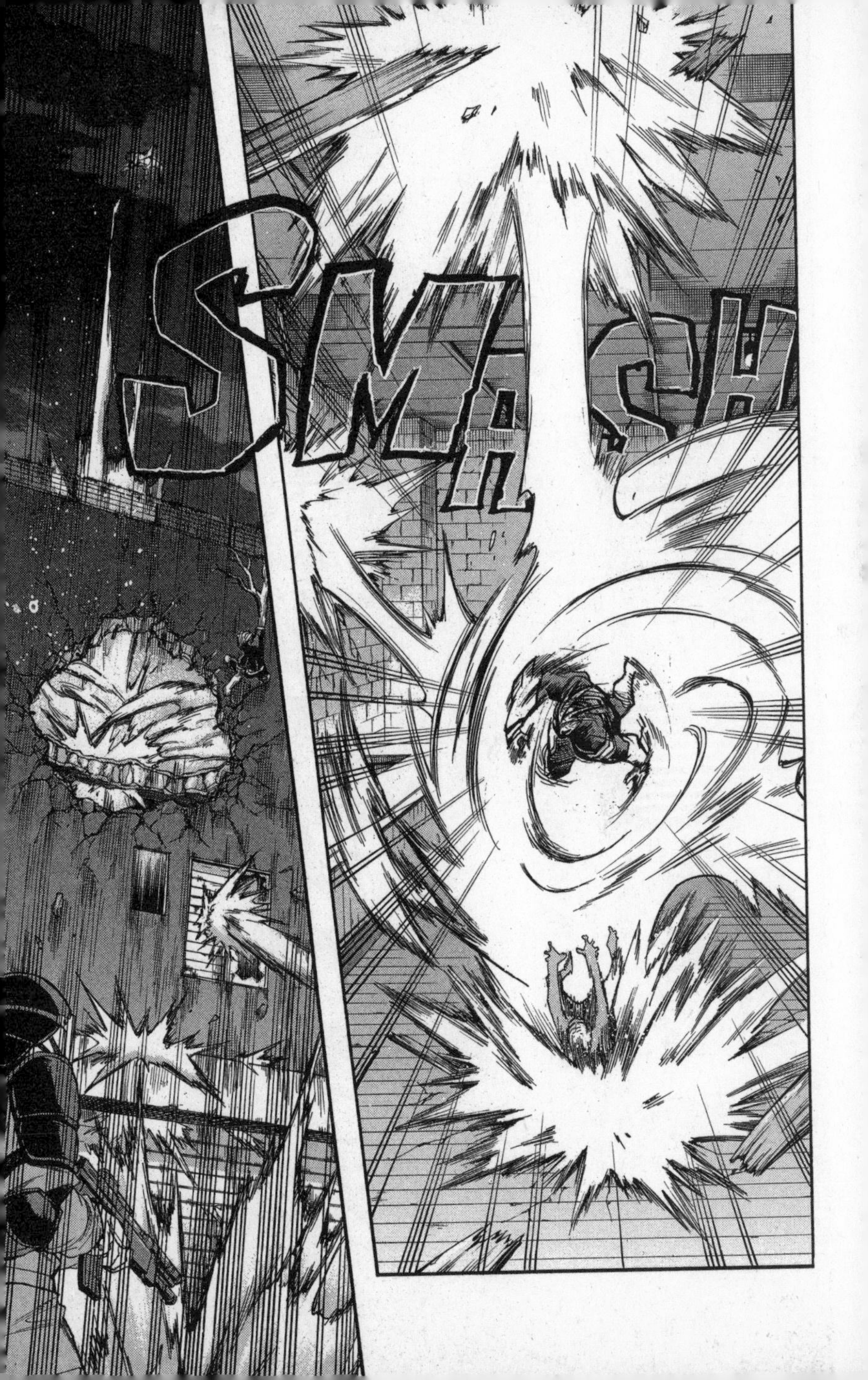
SMASH

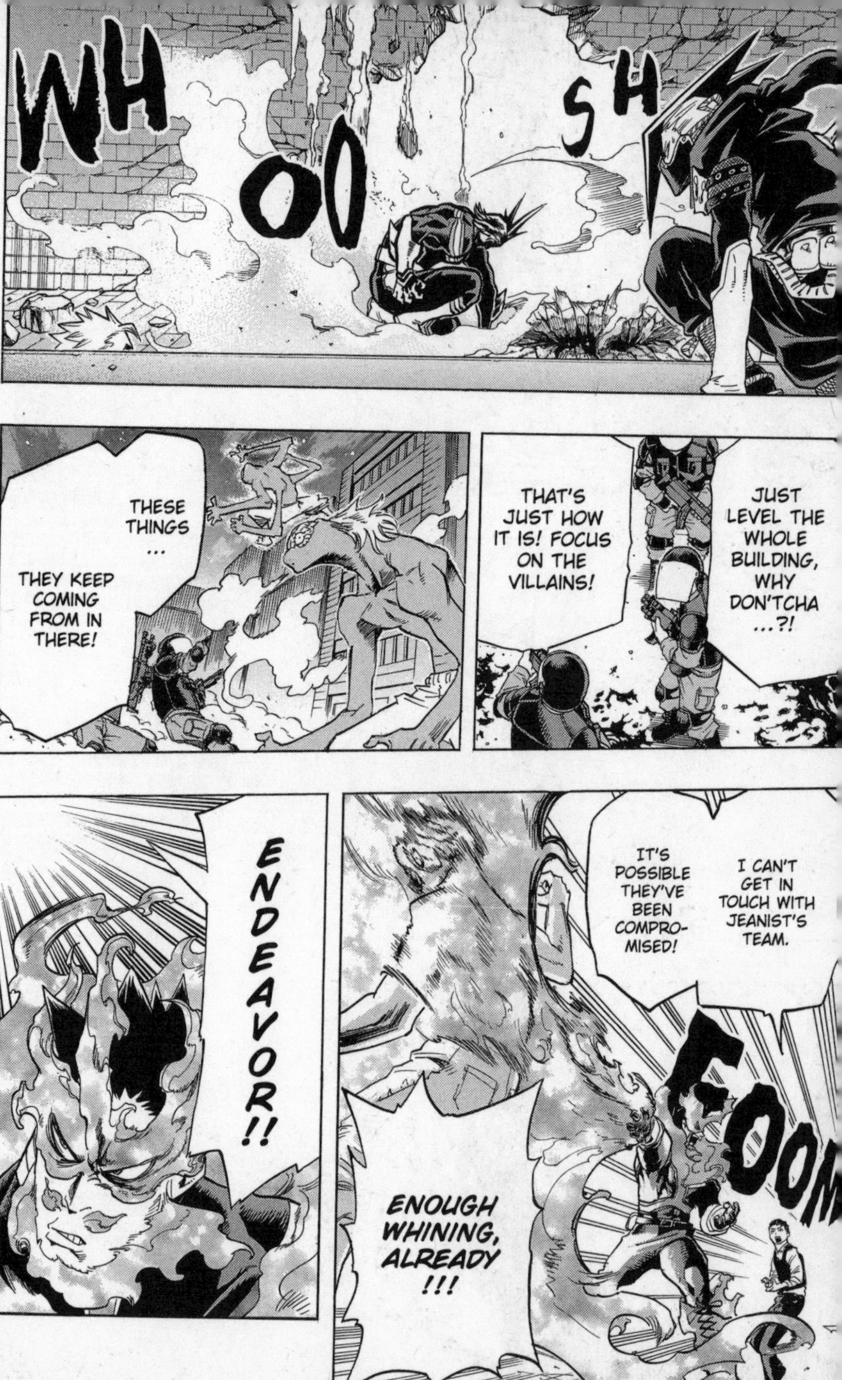
WHOOSH
JUST LEVEL THE WHOLE BUILDING, WHY DON'TCHA ...?!
THAT'S JUST HOW IT IS! FOCUS ON THE VILLAINS!
THESE THINGS ...
THEY KEEP COMING FROM IN THERE!
I CAN'T GET IN TOUCH WITH JEANIST'S TEAM.
IT'S POSSIBLE THEY'VE BEEN COMPRO-MISED!
FOOOM
ENOUGH WHINING, ALREADY!!!
ENDEAVOR!!

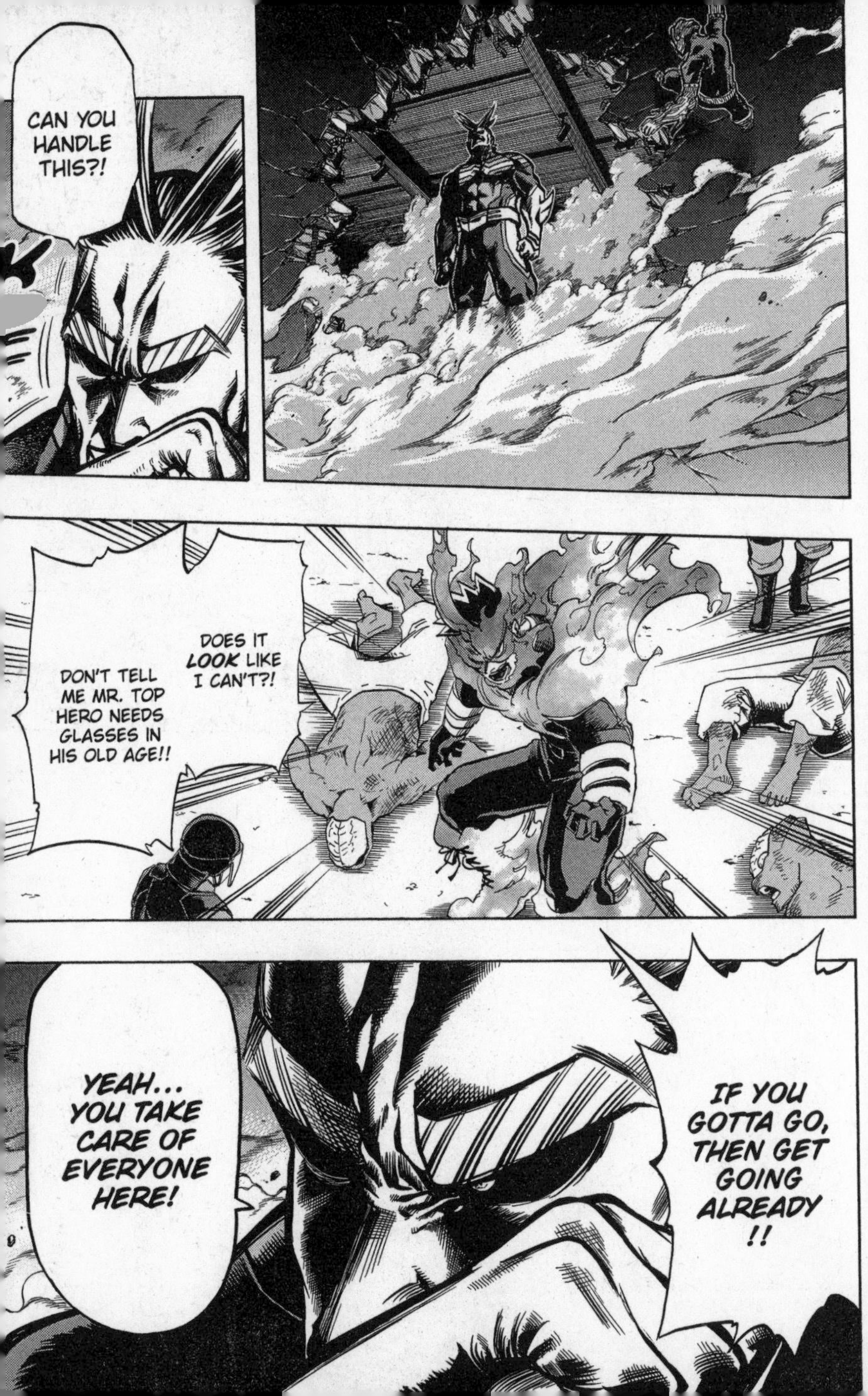
CAN YOU HANDLE THIS?!
DOES IT LOOK LIKE I CAN'T?!
DON'T TELL ME MR. TOP HERO NEEDS GLASSES IN HIS OLD AGE!!
IF YOU GOTTA GO, THEN GET GOING ALREADY!!
YEAH... YOU TAKE CARE OF EVERYONE HERE!

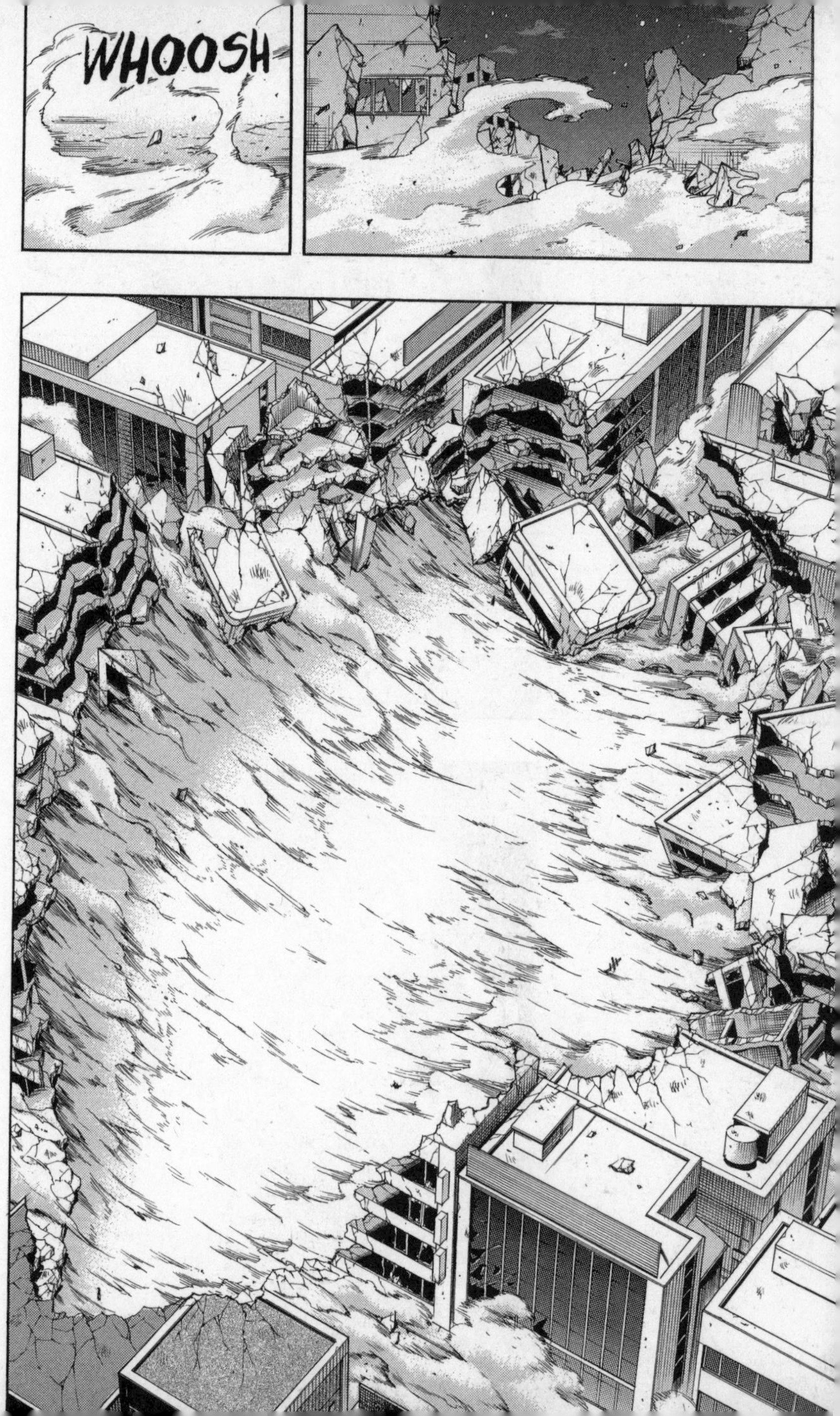
WHOOSH

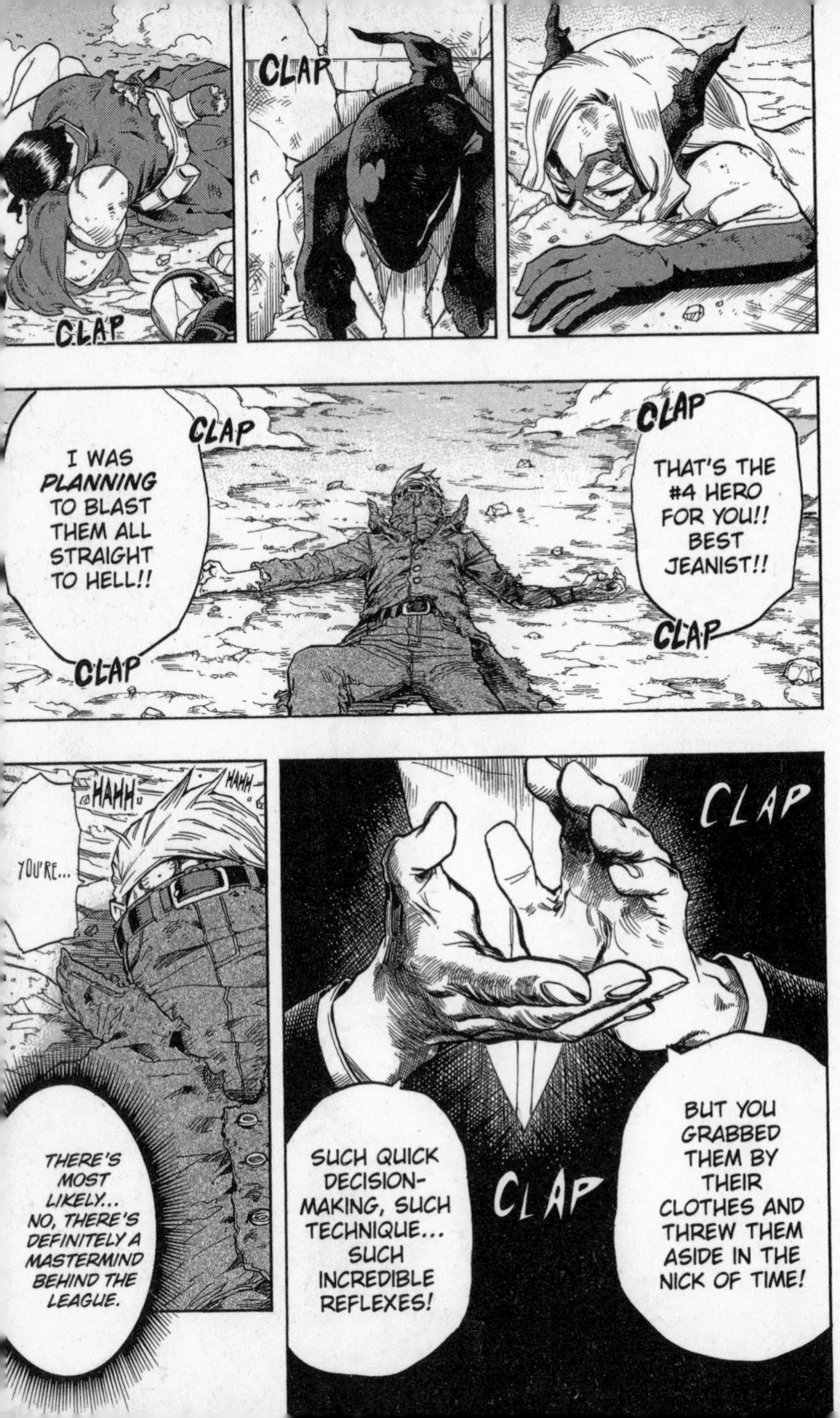
CLAP
CLAP
CLAP
THAT'S THE #4 HERO FOR YOU!! BEST JEANIST!!
CLAP
CLAP
I WAS *PLANNING* TO BLAST THEM ALL STRAIGHT TO HELL!!
CLAP
CLAP
BUT YOU GRABBED THEM BY THEIR CLOTHES AND THREW THEM ASIDE IN THE NICK OF TIME!
CLAP
SUCH QUICK DECISION-MAKING, SUCH TECHNIQUE... SUCH INCREDIBLE REFLEXES!
HAHH
HAHH
YOU'RE...
THERE'S MOST LIKELY... NO, THERE'S DEFINITELY A MASTERMIND BEHIND THE LEAGUE.

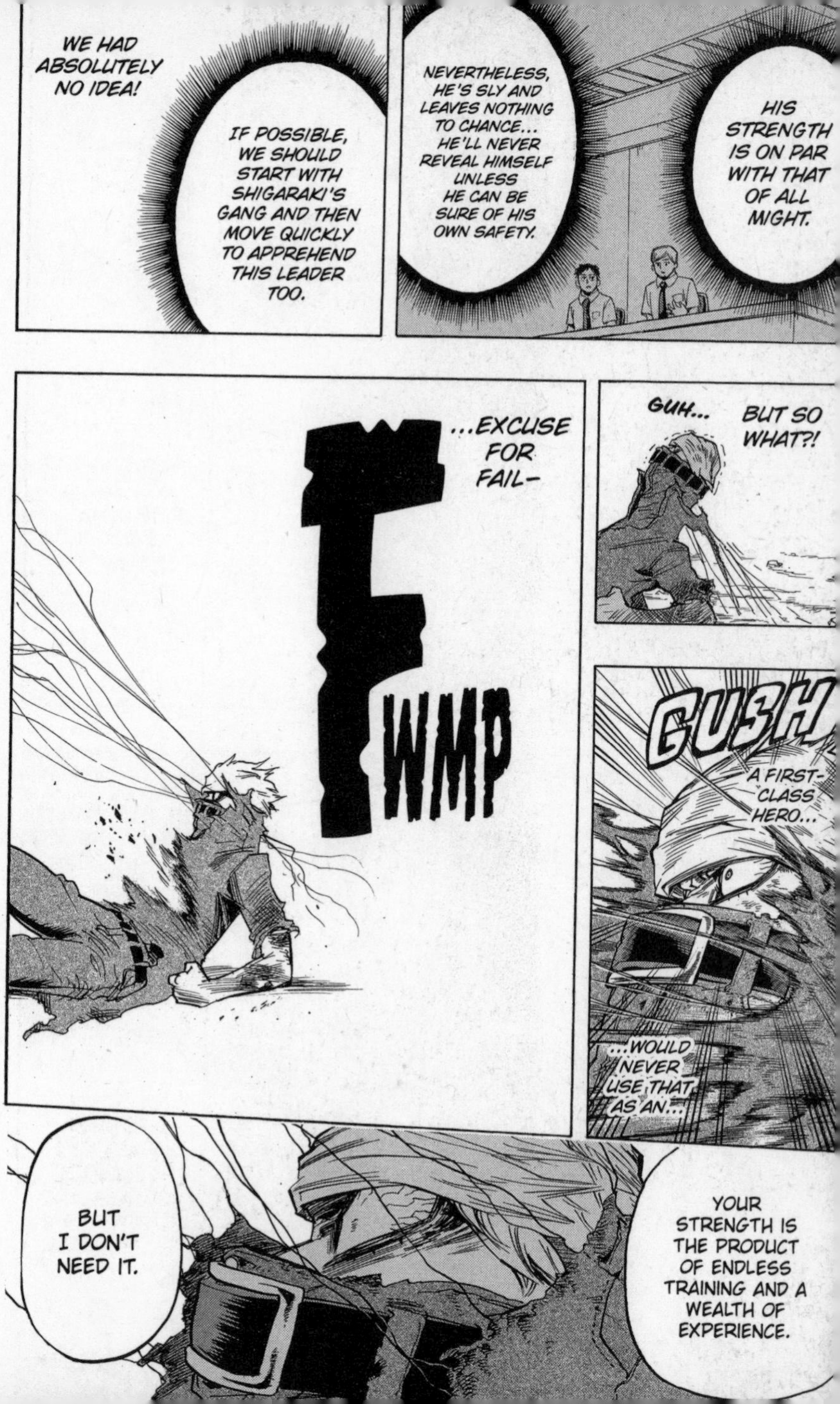
HIS STRENGTH IS ON PAR WITH THAT OF ALL MIGHT.
NEVERTHELESS, HE'S SLY AND LEAVES NOTHING TO CHANCE... HE'LL NEVER REVEAL HIMSELF UNLESS HE CAN BE SURE OF HIS OWN SAFETY.
IF POSSIBLE, WE SHOULD START WITH SHIGARAKI'S GANG AND THEN MOVE QUICKLY TO APPREHEND THIS LEADER TOO.
WE HAD ABSOLUTELY NO IDEA!
BUT SO WHAT?!
GUH...
GUSH
A FIRST-CLASS HERO...
...WOULD NEVER USE THAT AS AN...
WMP
...EXCUSE FOR FAIL-
YOUR STRENGTH IS THE PRODUCT OF ENDLESS TRAINING AND A WEALTH OF EXPERIENCE.
BUT I DON'T NEED IT.

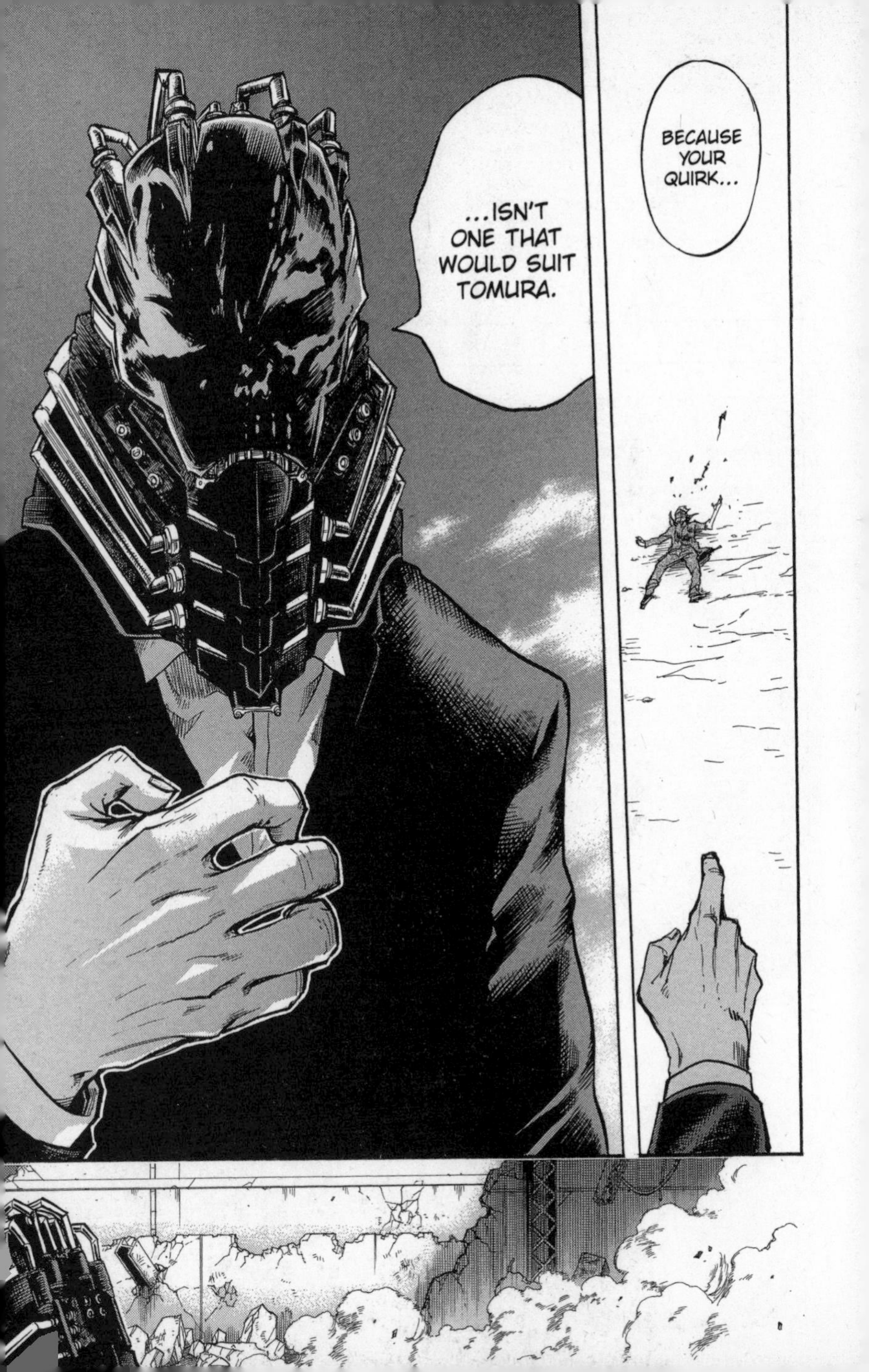
BECAUSE YOUR QUIRK...
...ISN'T ONE THAT WOULD SUIT TOMURA.

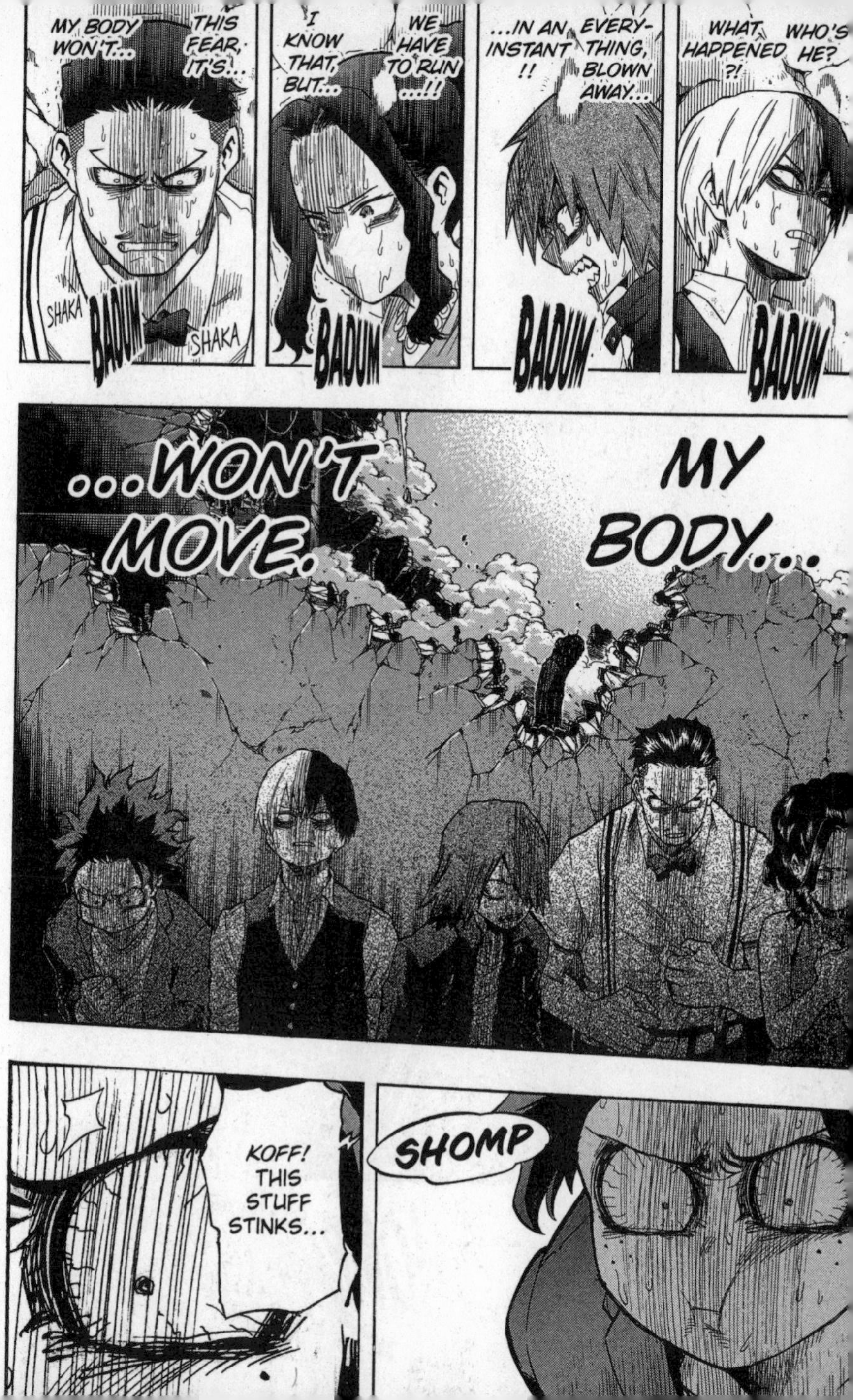
WHO'S HE?
WHAT HAPPENED ?!
BADUM
EVERY-THING, BLOWN AWAY...
...IN AN INSTANT !!
BADUM
WE HAVE TO RUN ...!!
I KNOW THAT, BUT...
BADUM
THIS FEAR, IT'S...
MY BODY WON'T...
SHAKA
BADUM
SHAKA
MY BODY...
...WON'T MOVE.
SHOMP
KOFF! THIS STUFF STINKS...

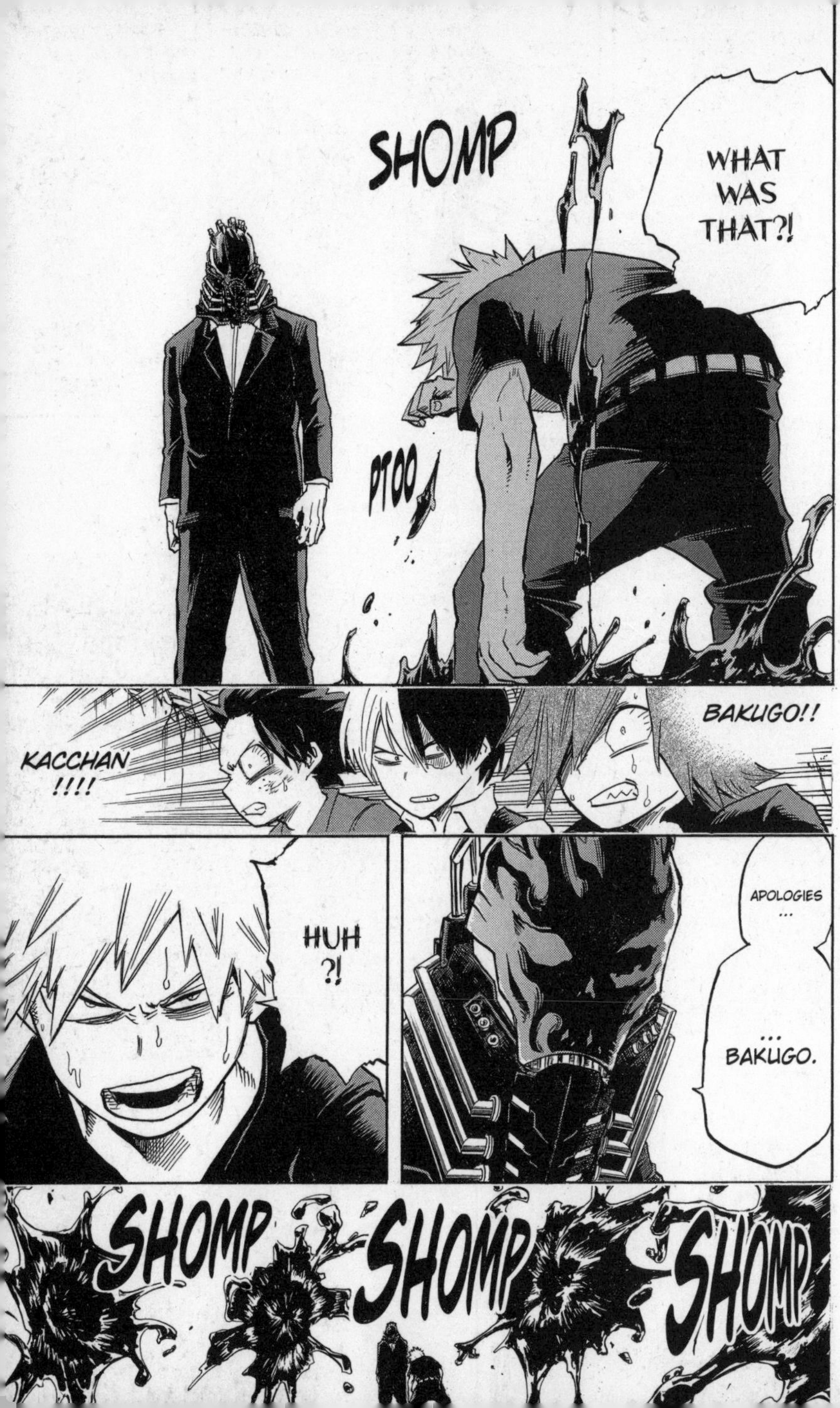
WHAT WAS THAT?!
SHOMP
PTOO
BAKUGO!!
KACCHAN !!!!
APOLOGIES ...
... BAKUGO.
HUH ?!
SHOMP
SHOMP
SHOMP

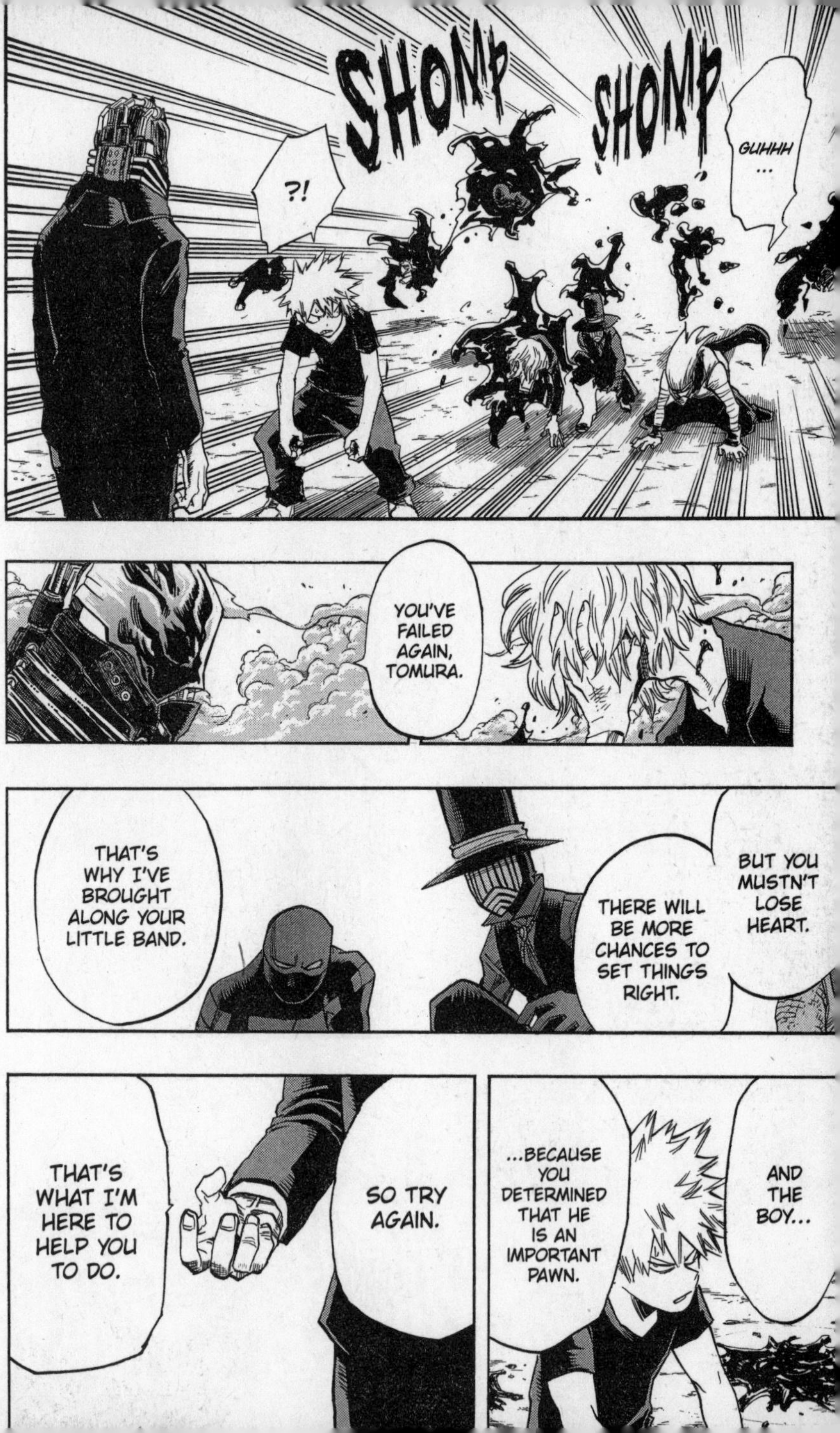
GUHHH...
SHOMP
SHOMP
?!
YOU'VE FAILED AGAIN, TOMURA.
BUT YOU MUSTN'T LOSE HEART.
THERE WILL BE MORE CHANCES TO SET THINGS RIGHT.
THAT'S WHY I'VE BROUGHT ALONG YOUR LITTLE BAND.
AND THE BOY...
...BECAUSE YOU DETERMINED THAT HE IS AN IMPORTANT PAWN.
SO TRY AGAIN.
THAT'S WHAT I'M HERE TO HELP YOU TO DO.

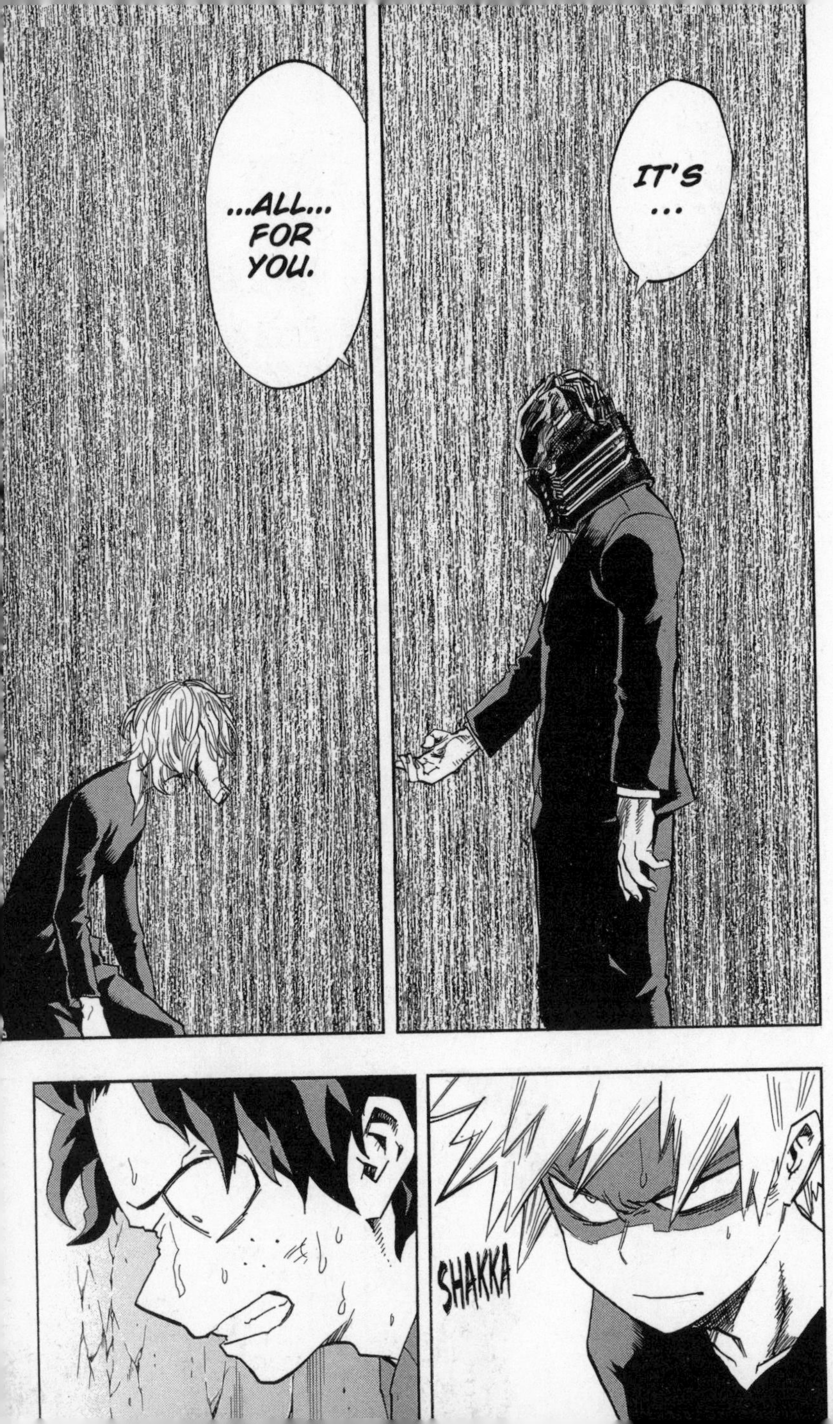
IT'S ...
...ALL... FOR YOU.
SHAKKA

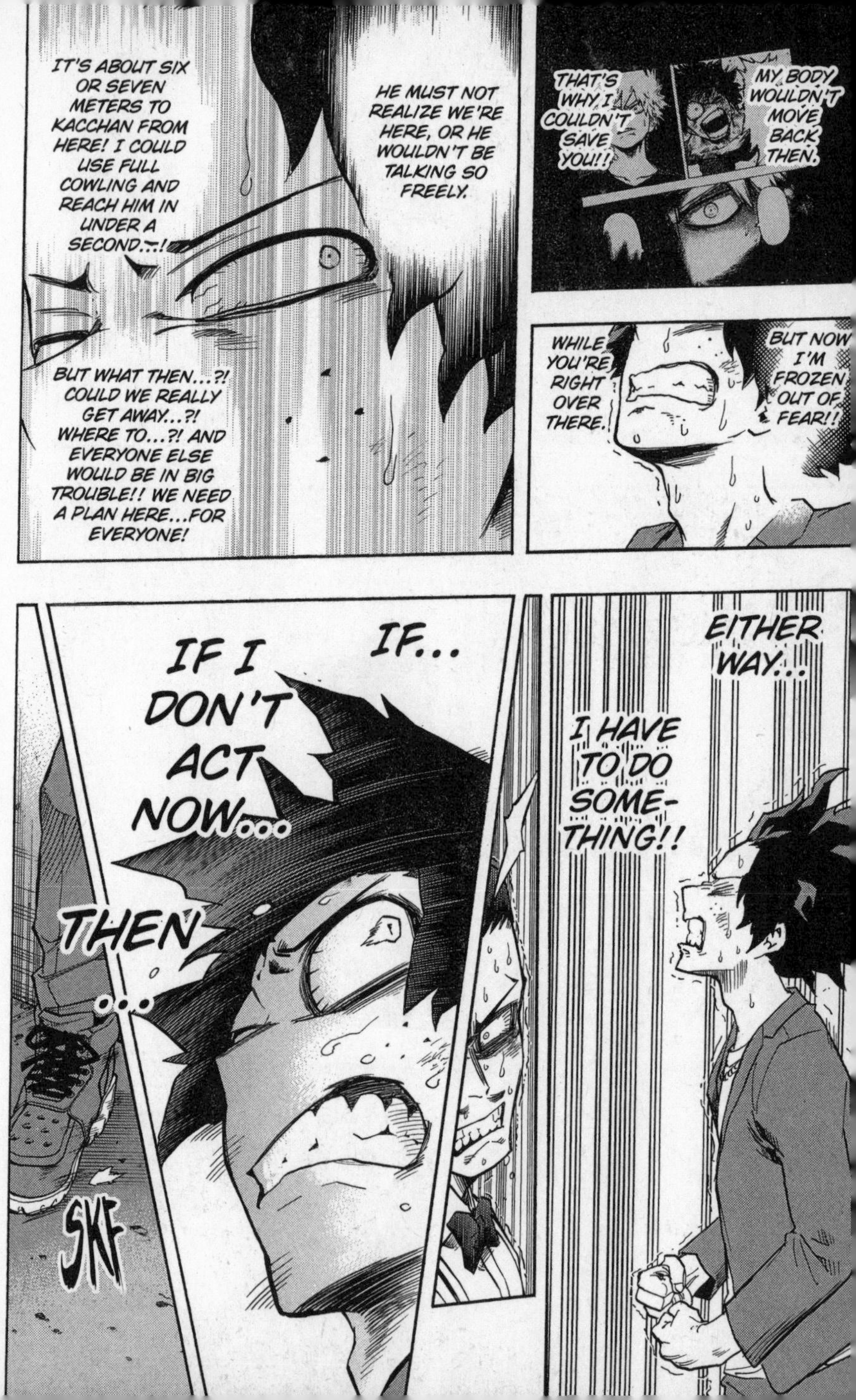
MY BODY WOULDN'T MOVE BACK THEN.
THAT'S WHY I COULDN'T SAVE YOU!!
BUT NOW I'M FROZEN OUT OF FEAR!!
WHILE YOU'RE RIGHT OVER THERE.
HE MUST NOT REALIZE WE'RE HERE, OR HE WOULDN'T BE TALKING SO FREELY.
IT'S ABOUT SIX OR SEVEN METERS TO KACCHAN FROM HERE! I COULD USE FULL COWLING AND REACH HIM IN UNDER A SECOND...!
BUT WHAT THEN...?! COULD WE REALLY GET AWAY...?! WHERE TO...?! AND EVERYONE ELSE WOULD BE IN BIG TROUBLE!! WE NEED A PLAN HERE...FOR EVERYONE!
EITHER WAY...
I HAVE TO DO SOME-THING!!
IF...
IF I DON'T ACT NOW...
THEN...
SKF

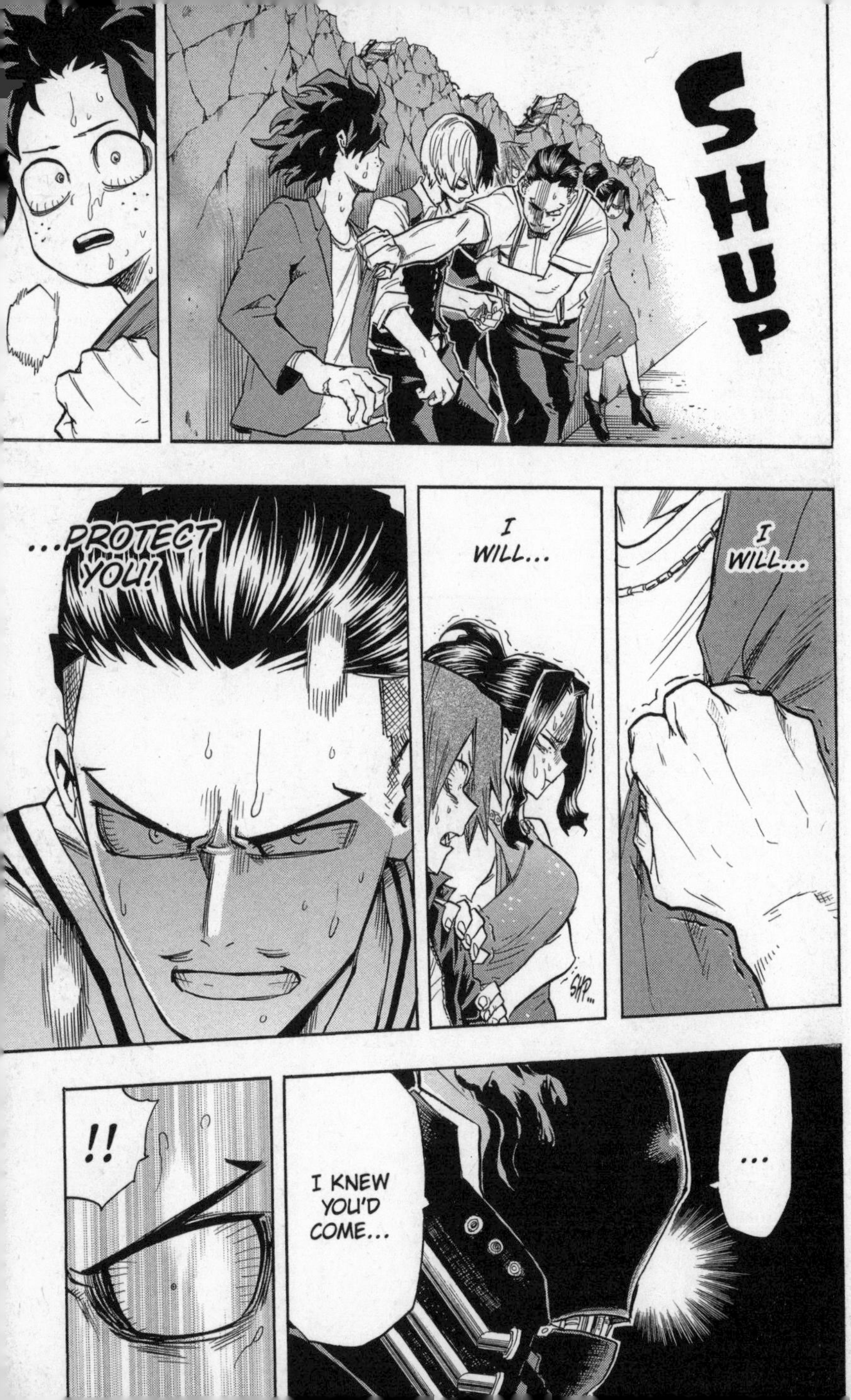
SHUP
I WILL...
I WILL...
SHP...
...PROTECT YOU!
...
I KNEW YOU'D COME...
!!

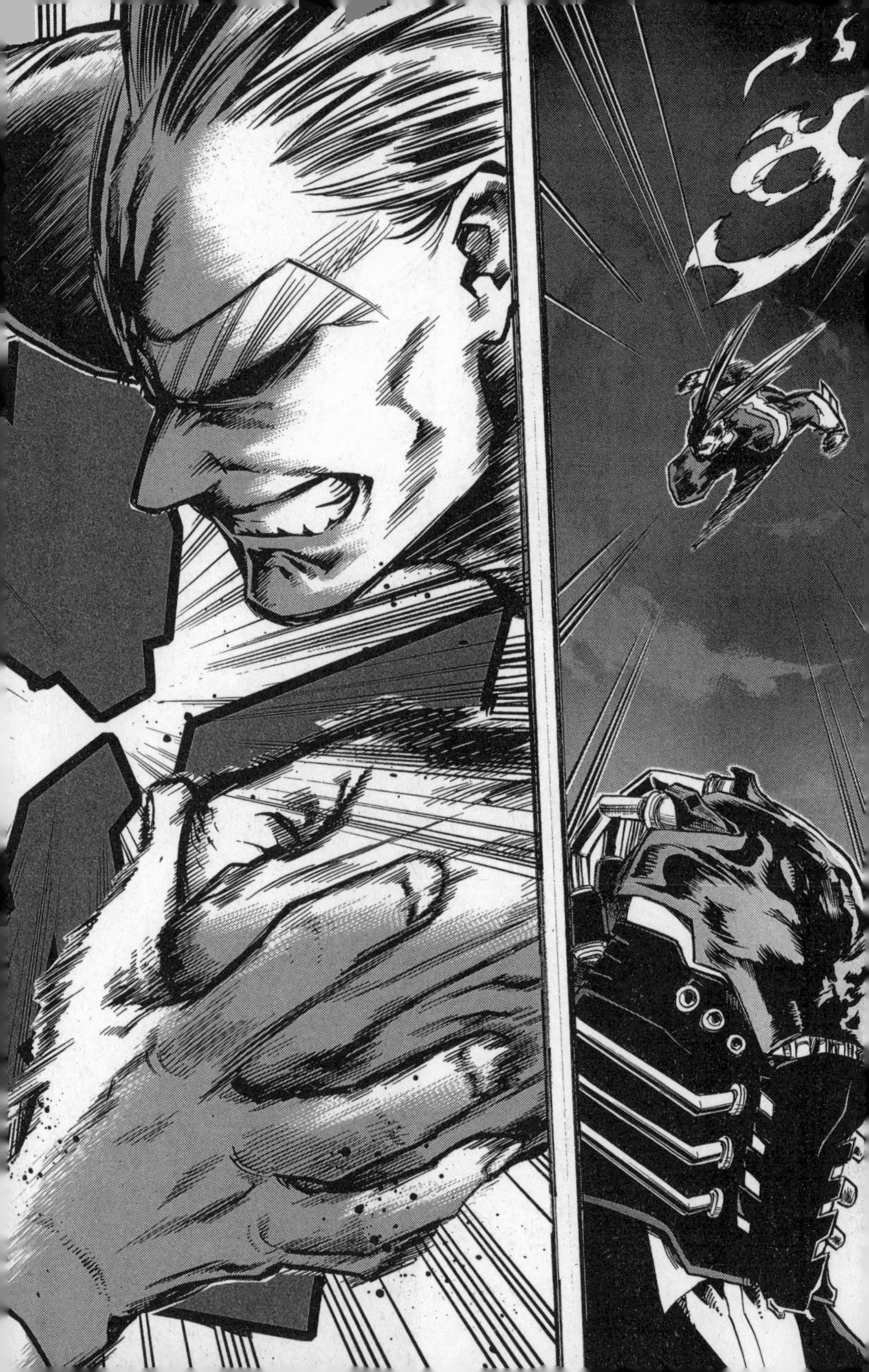

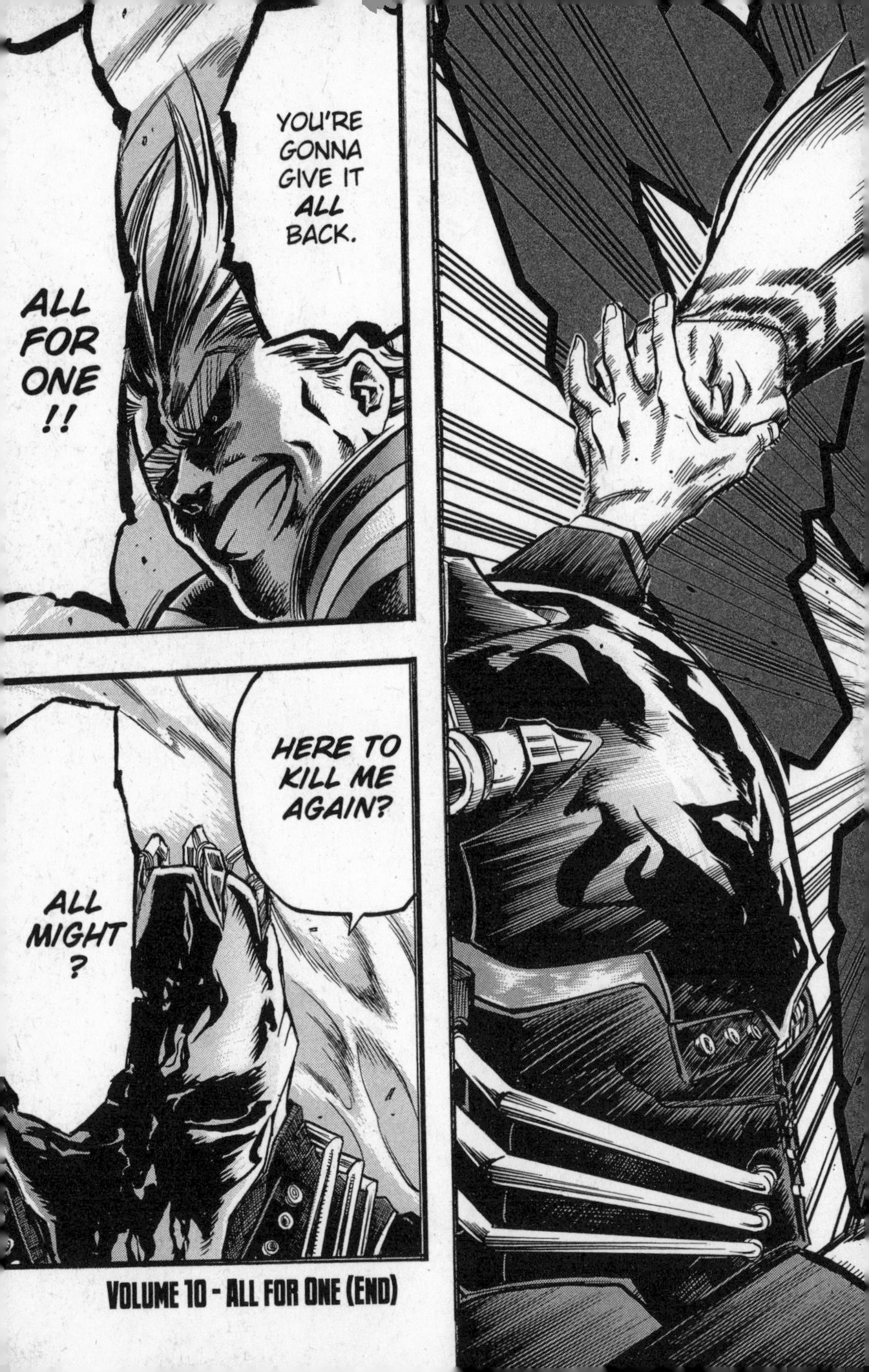
YOU'RE GONNA GIVE IT ALL BACK.
ALL FOR ONE!!
HERE TO KILL ME AGAIN?
ALL MIGHT?

VOLUME 10 - ALL FOR ONE (END)

SIDE STORY
TSUYU'S RIBBITY DIARY

The following five-page story was originally published in *SHONEN JUMP* magazine (in Japan).

The main story was experiencing some dark developments at the time, so this little episode seemed like a good way to relieve some tension and leave people feeling refreshed.

I'd love to do more like this if I get the chance.

INCLUDING MY SIDE STORY MEANT CUTTING OUT ONE OF THE CHARACTER-INTRODUCTION PAGES. THAT'S JUST HOW IT IS.

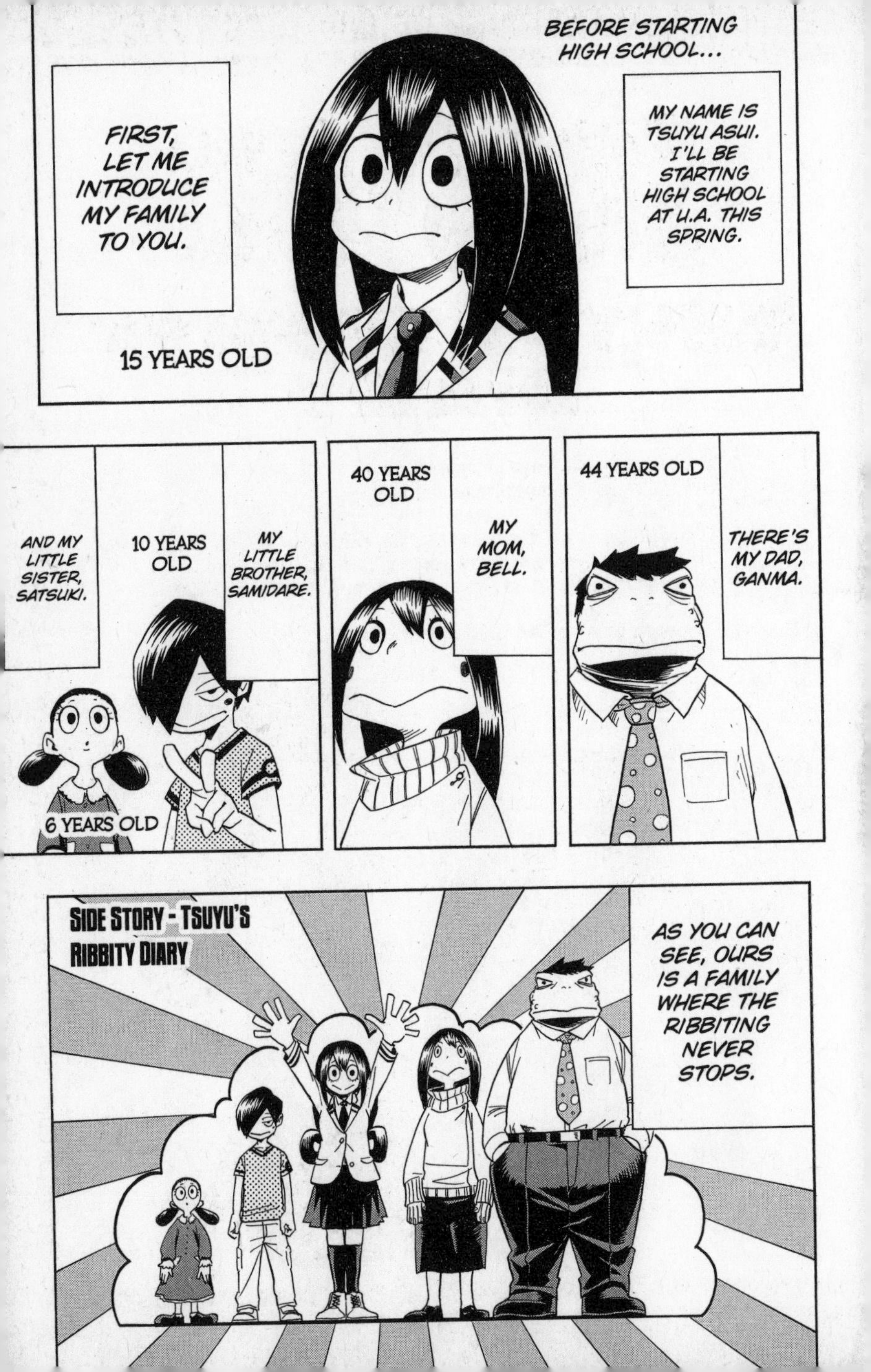
BEFORE STARTING HIGH SCHOOL...
MY NAME IS TSUYU ASUI. I'LL BE STARTING HIGH SCHOOL AT U.A. THIS SPRING.
FIRST, LET ME INTRODUCE MY FAMILY TO YOU.
15 YEARS OLD
THERE'S MY DAD, GANMA.
44 YEARS OLD
MY MOM, BELL.
40 YEARS OLD
MY LITTLE BROTHER, SAMIDARE.
10 YEARS OLD
AND MY LITTLE SISTER, SATSUKI.
6 YEARS OLD
AS YOU CAN SEE, OURS IS A FAMILY WHERE THE RIBBITING NEVER STOPS.
SIDE STORY - TSUYU'S RIBBITY DIARY

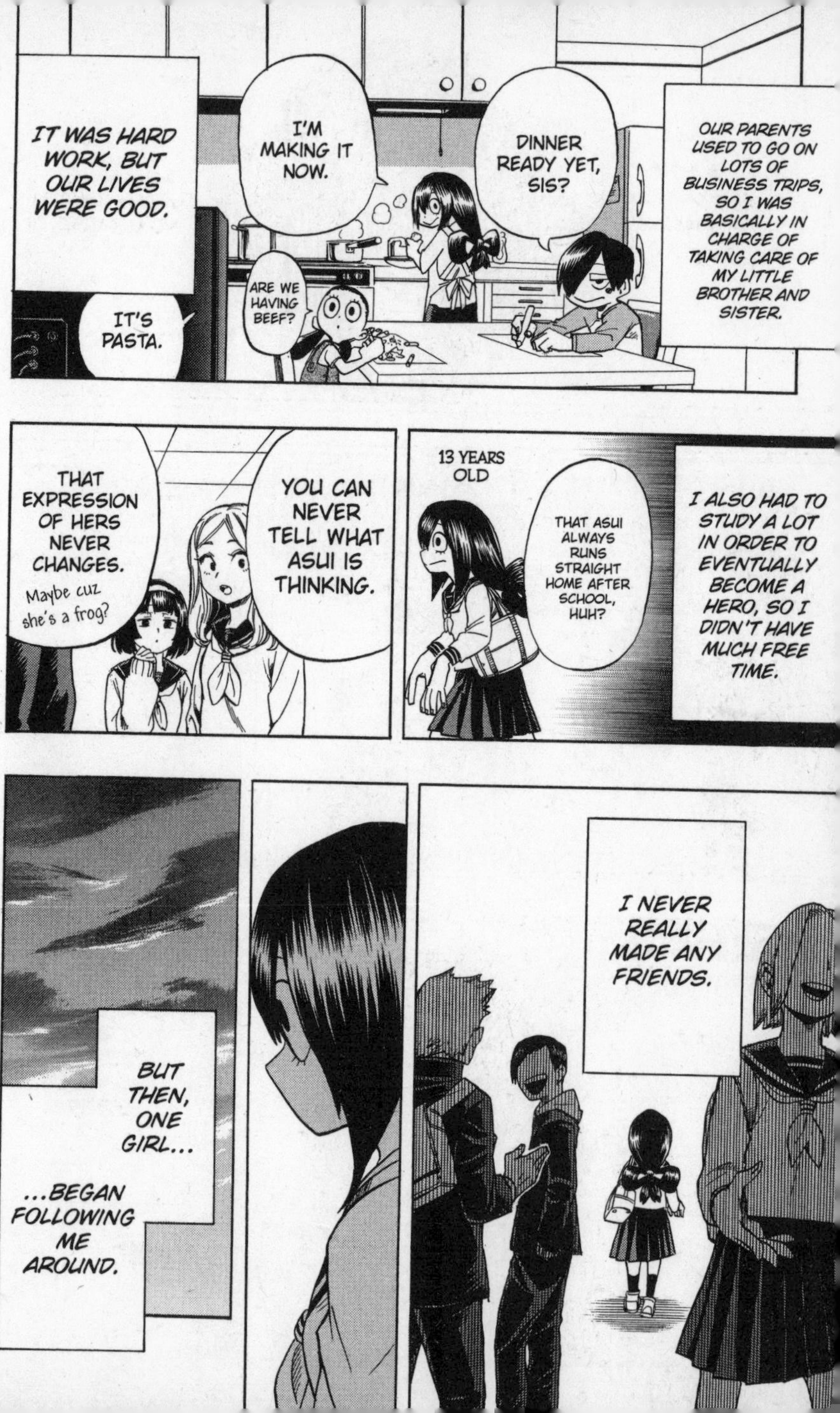
OUR PARENTS USED TO GO ON LOTS OF BUSINESS TRIPS, SO I WAS BASICALLY IN CHARGE OF TAKING CARE OF MY LITTLE BROTHER AND SISTER.
DINNER READY YET, SIS?
I'M MAKING IT NOW.
IT WAS HARD WORK, BUT OUR LIVES WERE GOOD.
ARE WE HAVING BEEF?
IT'S PASTA.
I ALSO HAD TO STUDY A LOT IN ORDER TO EVENTUALLY BECOME A HERO, SO I DIDN'T HAVE MUCH FREE TIME.
13 YEARS OLD
THAT ASUI ALWAYS RUNS STRAIGHT HOME AFTER SCHOOL, HUH?
YOU CAN NEVER TELL WHAT ASUI IS THINKING.
THAT EXPRESSION OF HERS NEVER CHANGES.
Maybe cuz she's a frog?
I NEVER REALLY MADE ANY FRIENDS.
BUT THEN, ONE GIRL...
...BEGAN FOLLOWING ME AROUND.

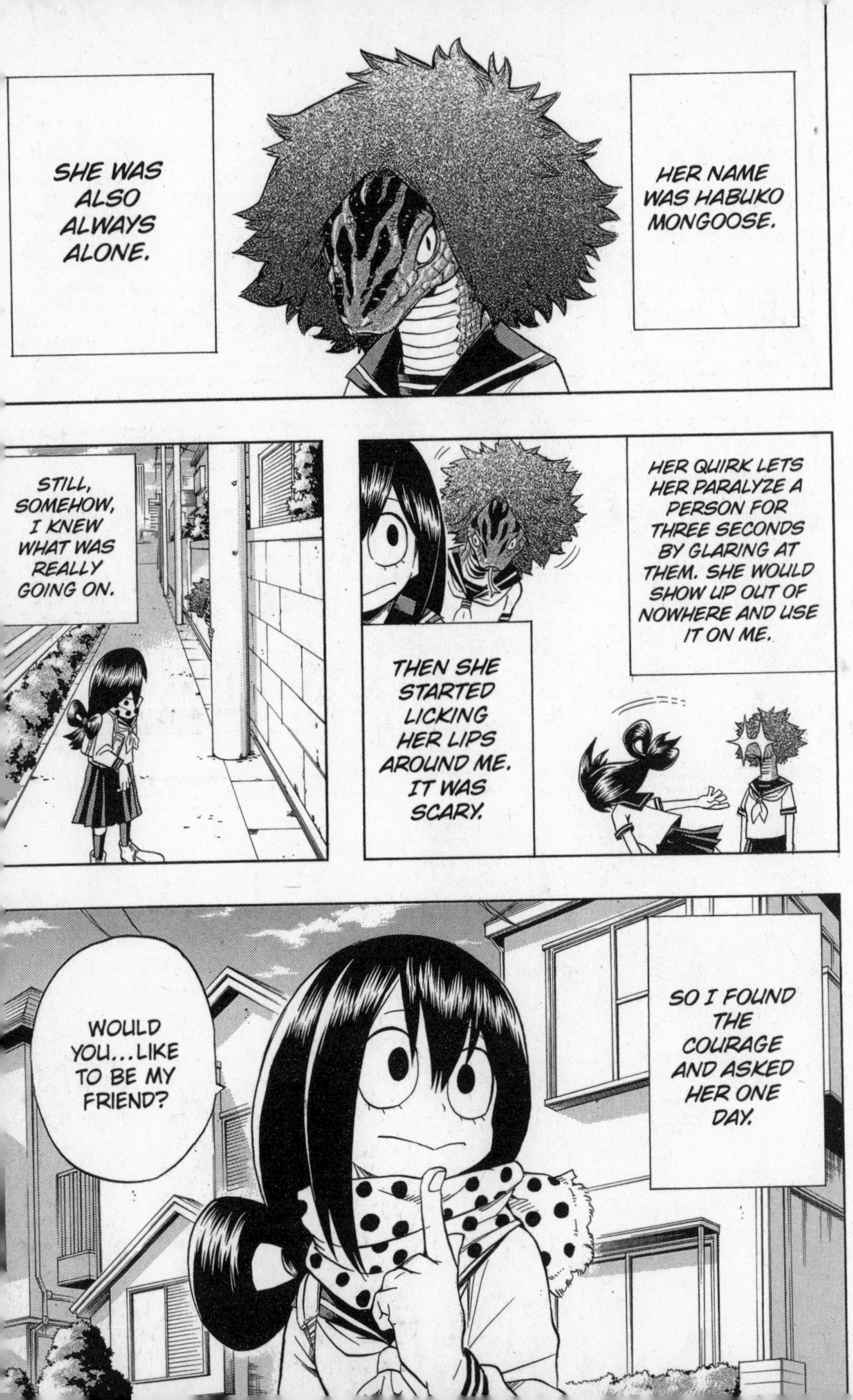
HER NAME WAS HABUKO MONGOOSE.
SHE WAS ALSO ALWAYS ALONE.
HER QUIRK LETS HER PARALYZE A PERSON FOR THREE SECONDS BY GLARING AT THEM. SHE WOULD SHOW UP OUT OF NOWHERE AND USE IT ON ME.
THEN SHE STARTED LICKING HER LIPS AROUND ME. IT WAS SCARY.
STILL, SOMEHOW, I KNEW WHAT WAS REALLY GOING ON.
SO I FOUND THE COURAGE AND ASKED HER ONE DAY.
WOULD YOU...LIKE TO BE MY FRIEND?

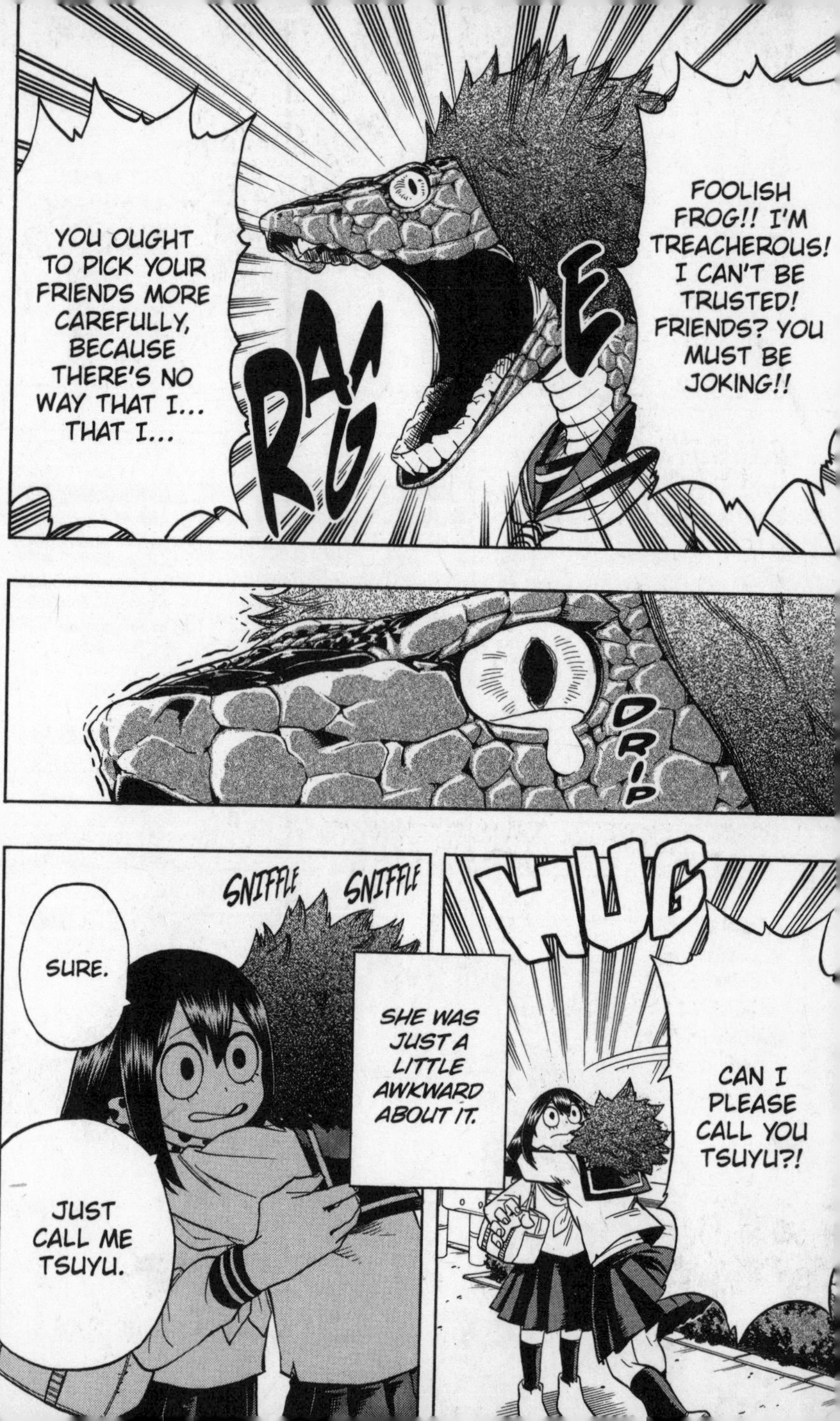
FOOLISH FROG!! I'M TREACHEROUS! I CAN'T BE TRUSTED! FRIENDS? YOU MUST BE JOKING!!
RAGE
YOU OUGHT TO PICK YOUR FRIENDS MORE CAREFULLY, BECAUSE THERE'S NO WAY THAT I... THAT I...
DRIP
HUG
CAN I PLEASE CALL YOU TSUYU?!
SHE WAS JUST A LITTLE AWKWARD ABOUT IT.
SNIFFLE SNIFFLE
SURE.
JUST CALL ME TSUYU.

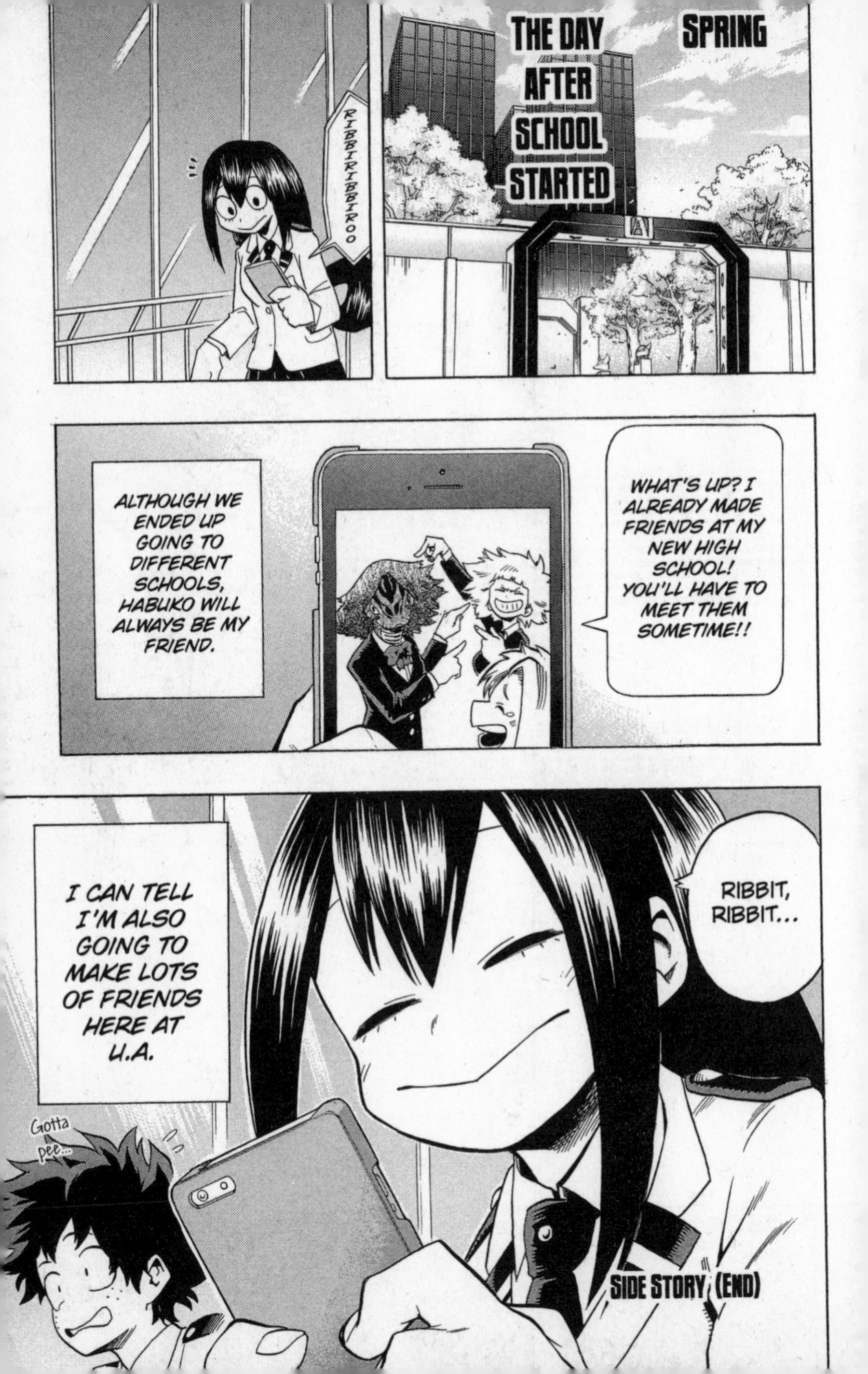
SPRING
THE DAY AFTER SCHOOL STARTED
RIBBIRIBBIROO
WHAT'S UP? I ALREADY MADE FRIENDS AT MY NEW HIGH SCHOOL! YOU'LL HAVE TO MEET THEM SOMETIME!!
ALTHOUGH WE ENDED UP GOING TO DIFFERENT SCHOOLS, HABUKO WILL ALWAYS BE MY FRIEND.
RIBBIT, RIBBIT...
I CAN TELL I'M ALSO GOING TO MAKE LOTS OF FRIENDS HERE AT U.A.
Gotta pee...
SIDE STORY (END)

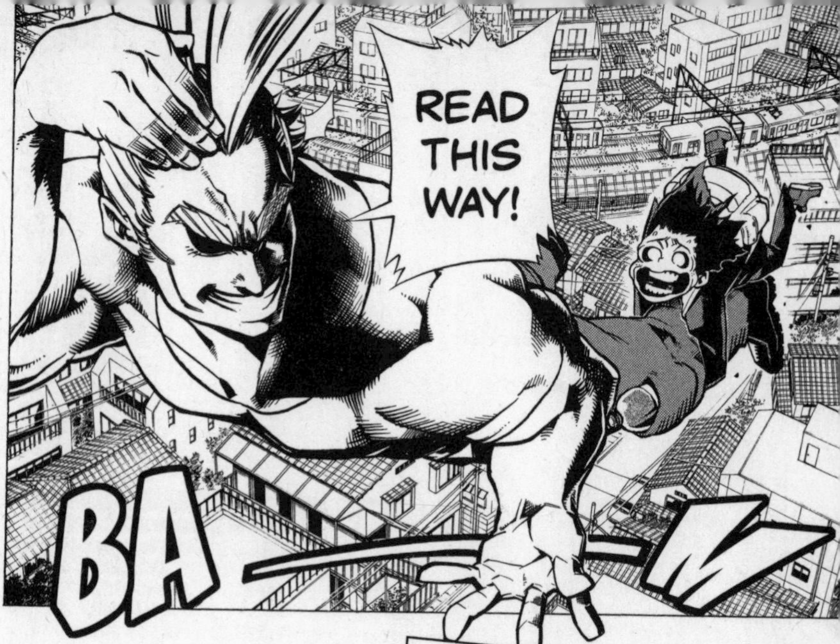
READ THIS WAY!
BA—M

MY HERO ACADEMIA

reads from right to left, starting in the upper-right corner. Japanese is read from right to left, meaning that action, sound effects and word-balloon order are completely reversed from English order.

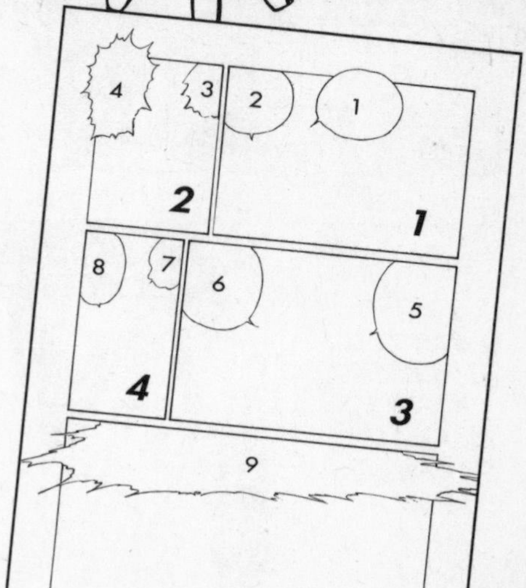
1
2
3
4
5
6
7
8
9
1
2
3
4
5
142